The European Court of Human Rights in the Post-Cold War Era
Universality in Transition
James A. Sweeney

The United Nations Human Rights Council
A Critique and Early Assessment
Rosa Freedman

Children and International Human Rights Law
The Right of the Child to be Heard
Aisling Parkes

Litigating Transnational Human Rights Obligations
Alternative Judgements
Mark Gibney and Wouter Vandenhole

Reproductive Freedom, Torture and International Human Rights
Challenging the Masculinisation of Torture
Ronli Sifris

Applying an International Human Rights Framework to State Budget Allocations
Rights and Resources
Rory O'Connell, Aoife Nolan, Colin Harvey, Mira Dutschke and Eoin Rooney

Human Rights Law in Europe
The Influence, Overlaps and Contradictions of the EU and the ECHR
Kanstantsin Dzehtsiarou, Tobias Lock, Theodore Konstadinides and Noreen O'Meara

Nomadic Peoples and Human Rights
Jérémie Gilbert

Children's Lives in an Era of Children's Rights
The Progress of the Convention on the Rights of the Child in Africa
Afua Twum-Danso Imoh and Nicola Ansell

China's Human Rights Lawyers
Advocacy and Resistance
Eva Pils

The Right to Equality in European Human Rights Law
The Quest for Substance in the Jurisprudence of the European Courts
Charilaos Nikolaidis

Business and Human Rights in Southeast Asia
Risk and Regulatory Turn
Mahdev Mohan and Cynthia Morel

Indigenous Peoples, Title to Territory, Rights and Resources
The Transformative Role of Free Prior and Informed Consent
Cathal M. Doyle

Challenging Territoriality in Human Rights Law
Building Blocks for a Plural and Diverse Duty-Bearer Regime
Wouter Vandenhole

Comparative Executive Clemency
The Constitutional Pardon Power and the Prerogative of Mercy in the Global Perspective
Andrew Novak

Shifting Centres of Gravity in Human Rights Protection
Rethinking Relations between ECHR, EU, and National Legal Orders
Edited by Oddný Mjöll Arnardóttir and Antoine Buyse

Forthcoming titles in this series include:

Jurisdiction, Immunity and Transnational Human Rights Litigation
Xiaodong Yang

Extraterritoriality and International Human Rights Law
The Spatial Reach of African Human Rights Treaties
Takele Soboka Bulto

Human Rights Law and Personal Identity
Jill Marshall

Human Rights and the Politics of Knowledge
Joanne Coysh

The Law and Practice of the European Social Committee
Francesco Seatzu and Amaya Ubeda de Torres

Reconciling Cultural Diversity and International Human Rights Obligations
The Compatibility Approach in the Practice of International Human Rights Institutions
Michael K. Addo

Social and Economic Rights in Theory and Practice
A Critical Assessment
Helena Alviar Garcia, Karl Klare and Lucy A. Williams

The Human Rights Approach to Disability
Cases and Materials
Andreas Dimopoulos

Capturing Caste in Law
The Legal Regulation of Caste Discrimination
Annapurna Waughray

Care, Migration and Human Rights
Law and Practice
Siobhán Mullally

The Protection of Vulnerable Groups under International Human Rights Law
Ingrid Nifosi-Sutton

Human Dignity and Degrading Treatment in the European Convention on Human Rights
The Ends of Article 3 of the European Convention on Human Rights
Elaine Webster

The Istanbul Convention, Domestic Violence and Human Rights
Ronagh McQuigg

The Right to Truth in International Law
Victims' Rights in Human Rights and International Criminal Law
Edited by Melanie Klinkner and Howard Davis

Children's Rights Law in the Global Human Rights Landscape
Isolation, Inspiration, Integration?
Edited by Eva Brems, Ellen Desmet and Wouter Vandenhole

The Democratic Foundations of the European Convention on Human Rights
Sovereignty, Equality, Agency
Alain Zysset

Human Rights in the Media
Representation, Rhetoric, Reality
Edited by Michelle Farrell, Edel Hughes and Eleanor Drywood

Developing the Right to Social Security – A Gender Perspective

The right to social security, found in international law and in the constitutions of many nations, contributes to the alleviation of poverty globally. Social security and its articulation as a human right have received increased attention in recent years both in response to austerity cuts to welfare in developed countries and as a means of lifting millions out of poverty in developing countries. Women, disproportionately affected by poverty in all parts of the world, stand to gain from a right to social security that takes cognisance of gender discrimination and disadvantage.

This book interprets and redefines the right to social security from a gender perspective. Drawing on feminist theory, the book formulates a conceptual approach and a set of principles for a substantively equal, gendered right to social security. In so doing, it challenges the relationship between the right to social security and traditional conceptions of work that exclude women's labour including their caring roles. It argues that the right must have application at the transnational level if it is to address the changing nature of women's work due to globalisation.

The book applies the framework and principles it develops to a study of international law focusing on the work of key United Nations human rights bodies. It also demonstrates the value of this framework in its analysis of three countries' social security programmes – South Africa, Australia and India. In combining feminist thought on the nature of work and care with equality theories in developing the right to social security from a gender perspective, this book expands the capacity of the right to advance gender equality and address gendered poverty.

Beth Goldblatt is an Associate Professor in the Faculty of Law at the University of Technology Sydney. She is a Visiting Fellow of the Australian Human Rights Centre in the Faculty of Law at the University of New South Wales and an Honorary Senior Fellow of the Faculty of Law at the University of the Witwatersrand.

Routledge Research in Human Rights Law

Available titles in this series include:

Socio-Economic Rights in Emerging Free Markets
Comparative Insights from India and China
Surya Deva

The Right to Development in International Law
The Case of Pakistan
Khurshid Iqbal

Global Health and Human Rights
Legal and Philosophical Perspectives
John Harrington and Maria Stuttaford

The Right to Religious Freedom in International Law
Between Group Rights and Individual Rights
Anat Scolnicov

Emerging Areas of Human Rights in the 21st Century
The Role of the Universal Declaration of Human Rights
Marco Odello and Sofia Cavandoli

The Human Right to Water and its Application in the Occupied Palestinian Territories
Amanda Cahill

International Human Rights Law and Domestic Violence
The Effectiveness of International Human Rights Law
Ronagh McQuigg

Human Rights in the Asia-Pacific Region
Towards Institution Building
Hitoshi Nasu and Ben Saul

Human Rights Monitoring Mechanisms of the Council of Europe
Gauthier de Beco

The Positive Obligations of the State under the European Convention of Human Rights
Dimitris Xenos

Vindicating Socio-Economic Rights
International Standards and Comparative Experiences
Paul O'Connell

The EU as a 'Global Player' in Human Rights?
Jan Wetzel

Regulating Corporate Human Rights Violations
Humanizing Business
Surya Deva

The UN Committee on Economic, Social and Cultural Rights
The Law, Process and Practice
Marco Odello and Francesco Seatzu

State Security Regimes and the Right to Freedom of Religion and Belief
Changes in Europe Since 2001
Karen Murphy

Developing the Right to Social Security – A Gender Perspective

Beth Goldblatt

Routledge
Taylor & Francis Group
LONDON AND NEW YORK

First published 2016
by Routledge
2 Park Square, Milton Park, Abingdon, Oxon OX14 4RN

and by Routledge
711 Third Avenue, New York, NY 10017

First issued in paperback 2017

Routledge is an imprint of the Taylor & Francis Group, an informa business

British Library Cataloguing in Publication Data
A catalogue record for this book is available from the British Library

Library of Congress Cataloging in Publication Data
Names: Goldblatt, Beth, author.
Title: Developing the right to social security : a gender perspective / Beth Goldblatt.
Description: Abingdon, Oxon; New York, NY : Routledge, 2016. | Series: Routledge research in human rights law | Includes bibliographical references and index.
Identifiers: LCCN 2015047641| ISBN 9781138120112 (hbk) | ISBN 9781315651880 (ebk)
Subjects: LCSH: Social security--Law and legislation. | Social security--Law and legislation--India. | Social security--Law and legislation--South Africa. | Social security--Law and legislation--Australia. | Sex discrimination against women--Law and legislation. | Sex discrimination against women--Law and legislation--India. | Sex discrimination against women--Law and legislation--South Africa. | Sex discrimination against women--Law and legislation--Australia.
Classification: LCC K1900 .G65 2016 | DDC 344.03/2--dc23
LC record available at http://lccn.loc.gov/2015047641

ISBN 13: 978-0-8153-5459-8 (pbk)
ISBN 13: 978-1-138-12011-2 (hbk)

Typeset in ITC Galliard by
Servis Filmsetting Ltd, Stockport, Cheshire

Contents

Acknowledgements

I am indebted to many people for their advice and support in the writing of this book. My particular thanks go to Andrew Byrnes and Christine Forster for their rigorous and generous assistance. Many other colleagues provided helpful comments on various versions or chapters of the manuscript. These include: Hilary Charlesworth, Julian Disney, Rosalind Dixon, Judy Fudge, Lucie Lamarche, Christopher Michaelsen, Frances Raday and Rosemary Rayfuse. I also appreciate the valuable suggestions of Lucy Williams and Natasa Mavronicola. Further thanks are owed to the following people for their advice on social security rights in India: Priti Darooka, Colin Gonsalves, Elizabeth Hill and Jayna Kothari. I am grateful to the following people for their friendship and intellectual support over many years that have contributed to the evolution of the ideas in this book: Cathi Albertyn, Andrea Durbach, Sandra Fredman, Reg Graycar, Shireen Hassim and Sandra Liebenberg. Thanks also to the editorial team at Routledge and to Heather Edelstein and Sarah Dobinson for their skilful editing. Last but not least I thank my partner, Paul, my children, Gabriel and Rachel, and my parents, Lewis and Maureen, for their unwavering support, love and care.

Some material in this book has appeared in a different form in the following publications and is reprinted with the publishers' permission:

Beth Goldblatt, 'Testing Women's Right to Social Security in Australia: A Poor Score' in Beth Goldblatt and Lucie Lamarche (eds), *Women's Rights to Social Security and Social Protection* (Hart Publishing, 2014), pp. 263–85, used by permission of Bloomsbury Publishing Plc.

Beth Goldblatt, 'Social Security in South Africa – A Gender and Human Rights Analysis' (2014) 47(1) *Verfassung und Recht in Übersee*, pp. 22–42, reprinted with permission of Nomos Verlagsgesellschaft.

Beth Goldblatt, 'Gender, Poverty and the Development of the Right to Social Security' (2014) 10(4) *International Journal of Law in Context*, pp. 460–77, reproduced with permission from Cambridge University Press who hold the copyright.

Abbreviations

ACOSS	Australian Council of Social Service
BIG	Basic Income Grant
CCT	Conditional Cash Transfer
CEACR	Committee of Experts on the Application of Conventions and Recommendations
CEDAW	Convention on the Elimination of All Forms of Discrimination Against Women
CESCR	Committee on Economic, Social and Cultural Rights
CSG	Child Support Grant
DG	Disability Grant
GDP	Gross Domestic Product
ICCPR	International Covenant on Civil and Political Rights
ICESCR	International Covenant on Economic, Social and Cultural Rights
ILC	International Labour Conference
ILO	International Labour Organisation
JSY	Janani Suraksha Yojana
MDG	Millennium Development Goal
NMBS	National Maternity Benefit Scheme
NREGA	National Rural Employment Guarantee Act
NSAP	National Social Assistance Programme
NTER	Northern Territory Emergency Response
OAP	Old Age Pension
OECD	Organisation for Economic Co-operation and Development
OPG	Older Persons Grant
SEAM	School Enrolment and Attendance through Welfare Reform Measure
SEWA	Self Employed Women's Association
SPF	Social Protection Floor
UDHR	Universal Declaration of Human Rights
UN	United Nations
US	United States
UWSSA	Unorganised Workers Social Security Act

1 Introduction

Gender, poverty, social security and rights

Overcoming poverty and gender inequality are urgent, globally acknowledged priorities as evidenced by their inclusion within the recently adopted Sustainable Development Goals (goals 1 and 5 respectively). Social security, provided as a right that takes full account of gender, is one of the important means of achieving these goals. This book develops an interpretive approach to the right to social security from a gender perspective that enables the right to be used to address gender inequality and poverty while contributing to the broader project of the transformation of gender relations in society. To this end, the book does the following: first, it sets out the context of gender-related poverty, the important role of social security in responding to this context, and the need for social security programmes to be located within a rights framework that has been developed to address this context. Second, it engages with feminist theory to formulate the conceptual basis for the gender perspective used in this book and proposes a set of principles for a substantively equal, gendered right to social security. Third, it surveys and critically examines the international right to social security using this conceptual approach and principles to establish how the right has been understood and applied by key interpretive bodies within the UN system. This analysis highlights the positive gendered approaches taken by these groups as well as the gaps and deficiencies in their bodies of work. Fourth, it uses the conceptual approach and principles developed in the book to examine social security law and policy in three different country contexts (South Africa, Australia and India), using selected examples in each country. The book concludes with a comparative analysis of the country studies and a reconsideration of the major themes.

This introductory chapter will now examine the context of women's poverty globally and discuss the way in which such poverty is shaped by gender discrimination (at 1.1). Addressing this challenging context is a central motivation for the development of the right to social security from a gender perspective. The chapter will examine the origins, prevalence and purpose of social security, the definition of the right to social security and the principal concepts and terms used in the field of social security (at 1.2). It will then discuss the gender dimensions of social security, drawing on literature dealing with the developing and the developed world (at 1.3). Thereafter it will argue that human rights have a role in ensuring that social security is responsive to both poverty and gender inequality (at 1.4). Lastly, the chapter will explain the research approach, research choices and methodology used in the book (1.5) and will provide an outline of the remaining chapters (1.6).

1.1 Gender, poverty and discrimination

1.1.1 Women's poverty in global context

Women throughout the world, in developed and developing countries alike, face disproportionate poverty, un- or underemployment, poorer working conditions and greater responsibilities for the care of others. Recent decades have seen positive changes in certain development indicators relating to women and girls in many parts of the world including in educational enrolment and labour force participation.[1] However, despite their increased access to work and income opportunities, women predominate in the informal sector, in work in family enterprises, small-scale farming and other low-profit business such as street-vending and waste-collecting, and in the lowest paid jobs.[2] Because of this, women in all countries generally earn less than men.[3] While employment of women has increased, less than half of the world's women have income-producing work, as opposed to nearly four-fifths of the world's men.[4]

Global economic changes have led to growing inequality, insecurity and loss of workplace rights for workers.[5] Unemployment, underemployment and low-earning self-employment and subsistence work is a reality for most workers in developing countries and many in the developed world.[6] In fact, the model worker around whom social security standards were designed (the formally employed, full-time, male breadwinner)[7] is rapidly becoming a rarity in global terms. Women are particularly vulnerable to these forms of precarious work.[8] As a result of the negative impact of neo-liberal economic policies on women in the developing world,[9] the majority of women are located in precarious informal

1 World Bank, 'World Development Report 2012: Gender Equality and Development' (2011), at 8–10. For a critical analysis of this report see Shahra Razavi, '*World Development Report 2012: Gender Equality and Development* An Opportunity Both Welcome and Missed (An Extended Commentary)' (United Nations Research Institute for Social Development (UNRISD), 2011).

2 UNRISD, 'Combating Poverty and Inequality: Structural Change, Social Policy and Politics' (2010), at 111–19.

3 World Bank (2011), above n 1, at 16–17.

4 World Bank, 'World Development Report 2013: Jobs' (2012), at 6.

5 Guy Standing, *The Precariat: The New Dangerous Class* (Bloomsbury Academic, 2011), at 14.

6 World Bank (2012), above n 4.

7 Lucie Lamarche, 'Le *Pacte international relatif aux droits économiques, sociaux et culturels*, les femmes et le droit à la sécurité sociale: des considérations et des propositions pour un droit "universel" à la securité sociale' (2002) 14(1) *Canadian Journal of Women and the Law* 53.

8 Shahra Razavi et al., 'Gendered Impacts of Globalization – Employment and Social Protection' (UNRISD, 2012), at xxii.

9 Diane Elson, 'Gender Justice, Human Rights, and Neo-Liberal Economic Policies' in Maxine Molyneux and Shahra Razavi (eds), *Gender Justice, Development, and Rights* (Oxford University Press, 2002) 78.

work, including in migrant labour, which is inadequately protected.[10] There has been a 'feminisation' of work in terms of its gender composition alongside a 'feminisation' of working conditions characterised by deregulation, discrimination and reduced protection.[11] This growing feminisation of labour means that women take the bulk of casual and seasonal jobs and work in export processing zones without any expectation of an adequate wage or benefits.[12] Women also engage in home work for multinationals and face harsh working conditions on the bottom rungs of the labour markets of their own countries. The increasing casualisation and informalisation of work ensures flexibility for employers and reduced social responsibility for corporations and states.[13] A further impact of globalisation occurs where land is sold to multinationals, affecting women's subsistence livelihoods.[14]

Globalisation has resulted in growing international migration flows that are increasingly feminised as women migrate to provide care and other labour elsewhere in the world or within states.[15] This work is often exploitative, dangerous and precarious. Women migrant workers are particularly vulnerable. Many take on domestic work in the unprotected confines of private homes, or engage in the sex trade and are trafficked.[16] Women migrate to richer countries to perform care work in part to meet 'care deficits' caused by the increasing entry into the labour market of women in the developed world.[17] The migration of these women workers is in turn causing 'care deficits' in their home countries where they have left children and other dependents.[18]

The increasing number of women in the labour market has not seen a reduction in their caring responsibilities nor an adequate social response to this unequal burden.[19] In fact, increased life expectancy has meant that women are

10 Naila Kabeer, *Mainstreaming Gender in Social Protection for the Informal Economy* (Commonwealth Secretariat, 2008), at 32–3; Standing, above n 5, at 60–3.

11 Rachel Sabates-Wheeler and Naila Kabeer, 'Gender Equality and the Extension of Social Protection' (16, ILO, 2003).

12 Standing, above n 5, at 60.

13 Razavi et al., above n 8, at xxii.

14 UN Women, 'Realizing Women's Rights to Land and Other Productive Resources' (2013), at 3–4.

15 Judy Fudge, 'Precarious Migrant Status and Precarious Employment: The Paradox of International Rights for Migrant Workers' (2012) 34(1) *Comparative Labor Law and Policy Journal* 95.

16 Barbara Ehrenreich and Arlie Russell Hochschild (eds), *Global Woman: Nannies, Maids, and Sex Workers in the New Economy* (Metropolitan/Holt, 2002). According to Equality Now, at least 20.9 million adults and children are trafficked each year, a majority of whom are trafficked for sexual exploitation. The vast majority (98 per cent) of those trafficked for sexual exploitation are women and girls. Equality Now, *Global Sex Trafficking Fact Sheet* www.equalitynow.org/node/1010.

17 Judy Fudge, 'Global care chains, employment agencies and the conundrum of jurisdiction: decent work for domestic workers in Canada' (2011) 23 *Canadian Journal of Women and the Law* 235.

18 Shireen Hassim, 'Global constraints on gender equality in care work' (2008) 36(3) *Politics and Society* 388.

19 Shahra Razavi and Shireen Hassim (eds), *Gender and Social Policy in a Global Context: Uncovering the Gendered Structure of 'the Social'* (Palgrave Macmillan, 2006), at 7.

now caring for both children and elderly relatives while also needing to earn an income – a 'triple burden'.[20] The global financial crisis since 2008 has added to the struggles of poor women. Higher food prices, job losses, austerity measures and cuts to development aid have deepened vulnerability in rich and poor countries.[21]

1.1.2 Gender discrimination underlying poverty

In every country of the world, women are overrepresented among the poor due to a range of inequalities – social, cultural, political and economic – that serve to exclude them from full and equal participation in society. Feminist legal theorists have exposed the way in which different roles are allocated to men and women, through the law, within the public and private spheres.[22] The division of labour in the family restricts women's access to the labour market.[23] This means that women are generally poorer than men and have less power, status and influence both in the home and in society. The 'feminisation of poverty', a term coined to describe the growing number of women who comprise the poor, has been used since to record this phenomenon at both the micro-level of home and family and at the macro-level within nations and globally.[24] Women are primarily responsible for caring in society, an activity which is undervalued, usually unremunerated or poorly paid, and which restricts women's entry into other parts of the labour market.[25] Subsistence work is also women-dominated and, along with care-giving work, is usually poorly paid or unpaid. Feminists working in development and economics have pointed to the significant unpaid and invisible contribution that women make to the economy through such work.[26]

In addition to general disadvantage experienced by women as a result of their gender, specific groups of women face heightened inequality as a result of further

20 Standing, above n 5, at 61. AIDS and other illnesses also place a significant time burden on women who are expected to provide care.

21 Isabel Ortiz and Matthew Cummins (eds), *A Recovery for All: Rethinking Socio-Economic Policies for Children and Poor Households* (UNICEF, 2012), at 4–7.

22 For example, Frances Olsen, 'The family and the market: a study of ideology and legal reform' (1983) 96 *Harvard Law Review* 1497; Katherine O'Donovan, *Sexual Divisions in Law* (Weidenfeld and Nicolson, 1985); Susan Boyd (ed.), *Challenging the Public/Private Divide: Feminism, Law, and Public Policy* (University of Toronto Press, 1997). This is also discussed in Chapter 3.

23 Martha Albertson Fineman, *The Neutered Mother, the Sexual Family and Other Twentieth Cenury Tragedies* (Routledge, 1995); Martha Albertson Fineman, *The Autonomy Myth: A Theory of Dependency* (The New Press, 2004).

24 For a discussion of the history of the term and a valuable critique of its use, see Sylvia Chant, 'Re-thinking the "Feminization of Poverty" in relation to aggregate gender indices' (2006) 7(2) *Journal of Human Development* 201.

25 Joan Williams, *Unbending Gender: Why Family and Work Conflict and What to Do About It* (Oxford University Press, 2000).

26 For example, Marilyn Waring, *Counting For Nothing: What Men Value and What Women Are Worth* (University of Toronto Press, 1999); Nancy Folbre, *The Invisible Heart: Economics and Family Values* (The New Press, 2001). Also see the discussion of this literature in Kabeer, above n 10, at 28–9.

forms of discrimination based on factors such as race, disability, age, religion or geographic location. This discrimination often translates into economic disadvantage affecting vulnerable groups of women's access to resources, resulting in greater poverty. Violence against women, prevalent worldwide,[27] is sometimes used to control women's access to property and often contributes to impoverishment that follows when women leave abusers. Legal, cultural and religious barriers prevent women in many parts of the world from owning land and other property. It is estimated that just 1 per cent of the world's women own land.[28] Even where women do own resources or bring in income, they may not be able to fully access or control these in patriarchal settings where men are designated household heads.[29] Women also encounter stigma and stereotyping in a range of contexts that have bearing on their economic access.[30] For example, women applying to rent property or for bank loans may be turned away because they are seen as incapable of managing money. Women also face exclusion from political representation, decision-making and full participation in many parts of the world that has an impact on their life chances and material position.[31] The many facets of discrimination against women, discussed here in brief, contribute to gendered poverty across the globe.[32]

Multiple responses are required to address gendered poverty including structural economic reforms at the global and domestic level alongside political, social and cultural transformations. The provision of social security is one component of the response to this situation. However, simply providing social security without consideration of the gender dimensions of poverty may ignore and even reinforce underlying inequalities facing women. This book argues that the international human right to social security, developed from a gender perspective, can assist in ensuring that social security better responds to women's poverty and disadvantage. The chapter now discusses the meaning of social security by considering its origins, prevalence and purpose; the definition of the right to social security; and some of the concepts and terms used in the field of social security.

27 World Health Organisation, *Violence Against Women: Intimate Partner and Sexual Violence Against Women*, www.who.int/mediacentre/factsheets/fs239/en/.

28 UN Women (2013), above n 14, at 3.

29 Ibid., at 7.

30 Rebecca J. Cook and Simone Cusack, *Gender Stereotyping: Transnational Legal Perspectives* (University of Pennsylvania Press, 2010), at 22.

31 Working Group on the issue of discrimination against women in law and in practice, *Report of the Working Group on the issue of discrimination against women in law and in practice (political representation and participation)*', A/HRC/23/50 (Human Rights Council (23rd Session), 2013).

32 For an elaboration of the multiple dimensions of gender inequality, see Sandra Fredman, 'Engendering Social and Economic Rights' in Beth Goldblatt and Kirsty McLean (eds), *Women's Social and Economic Rights: Developments in South Africa* (Juta, 2011) 4. Also see Working Group on the issue of discrimination against women in law and in practice, 'Thematic Report (eliminating discrimination against women in economic and social life with a focus on economic crisis)', A/HRC/26/39 (Human Rights Council (26th session), 2014), at 4–23.

1.2 Objectives and definitions of social security

1.2.1 The origins, prevalence, nature and purpose of social security

The nation-state has a central role in addressing the economic needs of its people. One mechanism for achieving this is through social provision, a key component of which is social security. Social security is a central feature of the modern welfare state that emerged from late-nineteenth-century Europe in response to the social problems of industrial capitalism.[33] The combination of democratisation with capitalism enabled the strong working class to demand that the state use its growing resources to address social risk.[34] Every country in the world has some form of social security but for those in the working-age population and their families, the International Labour Organisation (ILO) estimates that 73 per cent do not have comprehensive social security[35] (covering all areas such as old age, unemployment and health care).[36] While high-income countries spend as much as 19 per cent of Gross Domestic Product (GDP) on social security, low-income countries typically spend less than 5 per cent of GDP.[37]

Social security can be provided from a range of sources, sometimes in combination with each other, including the State, employers, employee and individual contributions, communities, families and non-governmental agencies.[38] Social security schemes are sometimes privately funded and managed and may even include community-based schemes. International companies, organisations and institutions may also play a role in the provision and regulation of social security.[39] There are a range of different welfare state forms and approaches to welfare in the developed and developing world.[40] These different systems result in a wide variety of social security policies and programmes. The particular configuration of social security systems is determined by a country's history along with ideological and practical considerations that change over time.

There are many purposes of social security articulated by a range of individuals and groups, often related to their different ideological starting-points. These correspond to contested ideas about the causes of and responses to poverty and

33 Peter Townsend, 'Social Security and Human Rights' in Peter Townsend (ed.), *Building Decent Societies: Rethinking the Role of Social Security in Development* (Palgrave Macmillan, 2009) 29, at 52.

34 Ibid., at 52.

35 ILO, 'World Social Protection Report 2014/15: Building Economic Recovery, Inclusive Development and Social Justice' (ILO, 2014), at 2.

36 International Labour Office, 'World Social Security Report 2010/11: Providing Coverage in Times of Crisis and Beyond' (ILO, 2010), at 1.

37 Ibid., at 3.

38 ILO, 'Social security for social justice and a fair globalization' (VI, International Labour Office, 2011a), at 10.

39 Townsend, above n 33, at 38.

40 See, for example, Gøsta Esping-Andersen, *The Three Worlds of Welfare Capitalism* (Polity Press, 1990); Armando Barrientos, *Social Assistance in Developing Countries* (Cambridge University Press, 2013).

inequality, and about the role of the State in a market economy.[41] Extreme libertarians see economic inequality as an appropriate outcome in a capitalist economy and share their reservations towards social security with left-wing radicals who see it as a mechanism used to mitigate the worst impacts of capitalism while avoiding restructuring the economic system entirely.[42] Between these extremes are a range of ideological and strategic positions that value social security in some form. Some advocates focus on moral, ethical or principled arguments based on social justice, rights or citizenship entitlements while others articulate the benefits of social security in more utilitarian terms such as fiscal affordability and sustainability,[43] the maintenance of a productive and stable workforce, social cohesion and even 'consumption smoothing', a term used by the World Bank.[44] While some see social security providing a residualist function in times of crisis, others see it having a broader role in addressing economic disadvantage in society.[45]

This book views social security as providing a safety net for individuals in times of need, throughout the life cycle, while also playing a broader redistributive role in ensuring that wealth is shared in society, based on principles of equality and dignity.[46] As with social policy more broadly, social security can be designed and used to mitigate inequalities and contribute towards shaping progressive and even transformative social outcomes. From a human rights perspective, social security should be understood as a rights-based entitlement rather than a concessionary benefit. The right to social security as defined in international law is briefly considered so as to begin the book with a working definition. A fuller discussion of the right follows in Chapter 2 where the gender perspective developed in the book leads to a proposed redefinition of the right; and in Chapter 3 where interpretations of the right to social security within international law are examined and critiqued.

41 Terry Carney, *Social Security Law and Policy* (The Federation Press, 2006), Chapter 1.

42 Ibid.

43 ILO (2011a), above n 38, at 8.

44 Emmanuel Reynaud, 'The Right to Social Security – Current Challenges in International Perspective' in Eibe Reidel (ed.), *Social Security as a Human Right* (Springer, 2007) 1, at 4. 'Consumption smoothing' means that contingencies affecting income lead to the use of savings and insurance to keep individual or household consumption stable over the life course: Harold Alderman and Christina H. Paxson, 'Do the Poor Insure? A Synthesis of the Literature on Risk and Consumption in Developing Countries' (Policy Research Working Paper Series No 1008, World Bank, 1992).

45 Reynaud, ibid., at 4–5.

46 How much of the wealth should be shared and, more specifically, what amount of social security is sufficient are complex questions. The reference to an 'adequate standard of living' found in Article 11(1) of the *International Covenant on Economic, Social and Cultural Rights* (1966) begs this question. The principles as well as the human rights to equality and dignity offer a value-based approach to determining sufficiency but these do not in themselves lead to clear or measurable answers.

1.2.2 Concepts and terms

Social security takes a range of forms and can be provided in cash or in some other way (such as goods or social services).[47] Social security in most public systems has three main components – social insurance, universal benefit schemes and social assistance:[48] social insurance is a form of social security generated from contributions by the individual earner, the employer and sometimes also by the State, generally paid out for a period of time to meet certain contingencies. It involves a 'contractual exchange for benefits as of right for those insured and their dependents'.[49] It is prevalent in developed countries, particularly in Europe, and is also available in some developing countries for the small proportion of formal sector workers. These schemes may be universal or specific to certain employee groups. They may involve the collection of flat-rate or percentage contributions of income.[50]

Social security may also be non-contributory and financed through the tax system. Universal schemes may be available to all residents or to all members of certain groups such as the elderly. Social assistance is a form of social security for qualifying groups facing poverty or life-cycle circumstances requiring support. It may be available to groups facing contingencies or risks such as the elderly or people with disabilities and illnesses, the unemployed and children in need. The levels or amounts of payments may vary. It is generally targeted at specific groups, usually by way of means-testing. It may take the form of tax-financed transfers or grants but may also take the form of tax credits. In recent years, social assistance in the form of cash transfers has gained importance in many low- and middle-income developing countries with prominent examples being Brazil, Mexico and South Africa.[51] Cash transfers may be conditional (for example, applicants must show that their children are attending school), described as Conditional Cash Transfers (CCTs), or unconditional.[52]

The term 'social security' is often used interchangeably with the term 'social protection'.[53] However, the latter term has additional meanings. Social protection is sometimes used to refer to the results of the provision of social security, since social security protects people facing a range of difficult circumstances.[54] 'Social protection' can be understood very broadly to include all anti-poverty and development measures,[55] and it can also be used more narrowly than 'social

47 ILO (2011a), above n 38, at 9.
48 Townsend, above n 33, at 36; ILO (2011a), ibid., at 9–10.
49 Townsend, ibid.
50 Ibid.
51 UNDP, 'Sharing Innovative Experiences: Successful Social Protection Floor Experiences' (UNDP, 2011).
52 ILO (2011a), above n 38, at 9.
53 ILO (2010), above n 36, at 13.
54 Armando Barrientos and Miguel Niño-Zarazúa, 'Effects of non-contributory social transfers in developing countries. A compendium' (International Labour Office Social Security Department, 2010), at 38.
55 See Sabates-Wheeler and Kabeer, above n 11.

security' to refer to measures to address the most vulnerable groups facing poverty.[56] Social protection is also seen as including employment protection and promotion (alongside social assistance and social insurance).[57] It has gained prominence in the recent ILO Recommendation for Social Protection Floors (SPFs)[58] that encourages the development of basic levels of social security for countries that do not yet have minimum levels while extending existing social security provision at higher levels to a wider number of people. SPFs are aimed at ensuring access to basic services such as education that extend their reach beyond traditional social security rights.[59]

It is important to note that the terminology set out here and followed in the rest of the book is not always used or understood in the same ways universally. In some countries social security is synonymous with social insurance while in others, where social insurance is limited or absent, social security might mean social assistance or the terms 'welfare', 'benefits' or 'pensions' might be in widest use.

1.2.3 Defining the right to social security

As a matter of international law the right to social security is embodied in the *Universal Declaration of Human Rights* (1948) and the *International Covenant on Economic, Social and Cultural Rights* (1966). It also appears in a number of the major human rights conventions, in the human rights instruments of many regional bodies and in the constitutions and legislation of many States. The International Labour Organisation (ILO) has played a major role in setting standards for social security for almost a century. In 2008 the United Nations (UN) Committee on Economic, Social and Cultural Rights (CESCR) defined the right to social security, in Article 9 of the *International Covenant on Economic, Social and Cultural Rights*, as follows:[60]

> The right to social security encompasses the right to access and maintain benefits, whether in cash or in kind, without discrimination in order to secure protection, inter alia, from
> (a) lack of work-related income caused by sickness, disability, maternity, employment injury, unemployment, old age, or death of a family member;
> (b) unaffordable access to health care;
> (c) insufficient family support, particularly for children and adult dependents.

56 Barrientos and Niño-Zarazúa, above n 54, at 25–6.

57 Armando Barrientos, 'Social Protection for Poverty Reduction: Approaches, effectiveness and challenges' in Katja Bender, Markus Kaltenborn and Christian Pfleiderer (eds), *Social Protection in Developing Countries: Reforming Systems* (Routledge, 2013) 24, at 25–6.

58 ILO, *Recommendation Concerning National Floors of Social Protection*, 2012 (No. 202).

59 The ILO's social protection floors recommendation is discussed in greater detail in Chapter 3.

60 Committee on Economic, Social and Cultural Rights (CESCR) *General Comment No. 19: The Right to Social Security (Art. 9)* (2008) 39th Session 2007, E/C.12/GC/19.

This definition followed the ILO's *Social Security (Minimum Standards) Convention*, 1952, (No. 102) in linking income support to work interruptions based on the listed contingencies. The dual components of income security (a) and (c) and access to health care (b) have their roots in the *Declaration of Philadelphia*, the ILO's fundamental statement of principles.[61] While the CESCR's General Comment recognised that social security plays a role in poverty alleviation,[62] it failed to move from the traditional work-related formulation of social security to a broader inclusion of causes of poverty such as lack of housing, food, natural disasters and emergencies.[63] Recently, however, the ILO has itself begun to define the right to social security more broadly by including a fourth category in the above definition – 'general poverty and social exclusion'.[64] This is significant since the earlier definition may not have covered situations where people earn incomes that are inadequate or where they are excluded from the formal labour market due to discrimination or structural features of the economy. As will be discussed in this book, forms of work such as unpaid household and subsistence labour and care, predominantly performed by women, are generally not treated as work for the purpose of social security. The right to social security, based on the ILO's recent definition, entails protection both for workers facing work interruptions on the basis of various contingencies and for all people facing poverty and need.

The chapter now considers the gender issues that arise in relation to social security design and provision in developed and developing countries through a brief survey of literature in this area.

1.3 Gender and social security

Social security plays a key role in addressing poverty, including gendered poverty. The absence of adequate or appropriate social security adds to the poverty burden faced by women.[65] However, gender-neutral social security programmes that assume the unencumbered male worker or citizen is the norm may discriminate against women. Thus, contribution-based pension schemes tend to favour men, who have fewer work interruptions during their lifetimes than women, who often stop working to have children and care for them. Programmes specifically

61 *Declaration concerning the aims and purposes of the International Labour Organisation (Declaration of Philadelphia)*, 1944 at III(f) which refers to 'the extension of social security measures to provide a basic income to all in need of such protection and comprehensive medical care'. Some definitions of social security also include the provision of social services: Eibe Reidel, 'The Human Right to Social Security: Some Challenges' in Eibe Reidel (ed.), *Social Security as a Human Right* (Springer, 2007) 17, at 21.

62 CESCR, above n 60, at para 3.

63 Malcolm Langford and Jeff A. King, 'Committee on Economic, Social and Cultural Rights: Past, Present and Future' in Malcolm Langford (ed.), *Social Rights Jurisprudence: Emerging Trends in International and Comparative Law* (Cambridge University Press, 2008) 447, at 505.

64 ILO (2010), above n 36, at 13.

65 See Magdalena Sepúlveda and Carly Nyst, *The Human Rights Approach to Social Protection* (Ministry for Foreign Affairs Finland, 2012).

targeted at women that expect them to fulfil socially allocated roles and responsibilities may similarly have discriminatory outcomes for women. Social security can discriminate directly against women but more usually does so indirectly.[66] Direct discrimination may occur where women are deliberately excluded from participating in a scheme. Indirect discrimination may occur where, for example, social assistance payments are provided to household heads. Since these are usually men because of patriarchal assumptions in families and the wider society, such an approach may have a discriminatory impact. Men are less likely than women to use the income for the benefit of the whole household.[67] Access to social security is in some cases more difficult for women who face the danger of violence when collecting payments or within households from men who wish to confiscate their welfare income.[68] Women's caring responsibilities for children, the elderly and sick are often unremunerated or unacknowledged in social security provision. There are limited examples of the use of social security measures to challenge the lack of involvement of men in the care and support of families.[69]

Feminist efforts to understand women's poverty in developed countries and the structures that produce it have led to a critique of the modern welfare state and some of the premises of liberal theory underlying it.[70] A number of feminist theorists have explored the way in which social policy is gendered.[71] They have pointed to the historical premise of the welfare state of a male breadwinner model that casts women, with children, as dependents. Even when women are in the workforce, they often work part-time, are poorly paid, have smaller social security entitlements and therefore still rely on men for support. Welfare states in the developed world and under state socialism have proved generally deficient (to varying degrees) in addressing gender discrimination both in relation to pay and the status of women's work and benefits; and in relation to their reproductive and caring functions in those societies.[72] Comparisons between different welfare

66 A more detailed discussion of equality law and the concepts relating to discrimination can be found in Chapter 2.

67 Sarah Bradshaw, 'From structural adjustment to social adjustment: a gendered analysis of conditional cash transfer programmes in Mexico and Nicaragua' (2008) 8(2) *Global Social Policy* 188, at 191.

68 Beth Goldblatt, 'Gender and social assistance in the first decade of democracy: a case study of South Africa's Child Support Grant' (2005) 32(2) *Politikon* 239, at 249.

69 Shahra Razavi, 'Rethinking care in a development context: an introduction' (2011) 42(4) *Development and Change* 873.

70 See, for example, Nicola Lacey, 'Theories of justice and the welfare state' (1992) 1 *Social and Legal Studies* 323; Carole Pateman, 'The Patriarchal Welfare State' in Carole Pateman (ed.), *The Disorder of Women* (Polity Press, 1989) 179.

71 For example, Diane Sainsbury (ed.), *Gendering Welfare States* (Sage, 1994); Ann Orloff, 'Gender and the social rights of citizenship: the comparative analysis of gender relations and welfare states' (1993) 58(3) *American Sociological Review* 303; Linda Gordon (ed.), *Women, the State, and Welfare* (University of Wisconsin Press, 1990).

72 Razavi and Hassim, above n 19, at 7; also see Nancy Fraser, 'Women, Welfare, and the Politics of Need Interpretation' in *Unruly Practices: Power, Discourse and Gender in Contemporary Social Theory* (Polity Press, 1989) 144, for a discussion of the material and ideological challenges to women welfare recipients in the US in the 1980s; and her vision of a post-industrial welfare state

regimes have shown variations in the position of women that often correspond to their workforce participation and extent of childcare provision.

Even the best welfare models that have moved from male breadwinner to dual breadwinner and even to 'parent-worker-citizen' models (as in Sweden) are still failing to adequately overcome gender inequalities.[73] While some European countries have tried to address the impact of the gender wage gap and work interruptions faced by women assuming caring functions, many countries perpetuate gender inequalities through gender 'neutrality' or indirectly target women through cutbacks to existing programmes.[74] In some countries, welfare provision has become increasingly punitive, especially for sole mothers, with recipients stigmatised, stereotyped and burdened with conditions.[75] Welfare restructuring and cutbacks since the 1980s have been accompanied by a corrosive discourse that casts women recipients of welfare as irresponsible, immoral and lazy and that sees dependency as deviant.[76] Recent austerity measures since the global financial crisis of 2008, often involving reductions to sole-parent payments,[77] have also been accompanied by negative discourse.

More recently, writers in the developing world have conducted analyses of their own countries as well as international trends in the development of gendered social policy.[78] The lack of adequate welfare safety nets in developing

in Nancy Fraser, 'After the family wage: gender equity and the welfare state' (1994) 22(4) *Political Theory* 591.

73 Barbara Hobson, 'The Evolution of the Women-friendly State: Opportunities and Constraints in the Swedish Welfare State' in Shahra Razavi and Shireen Hassim (eds), *Gender and Social Policy in a Global Context: Uncovering the Gendered Structure of 'The Social'* (Palgrave Macmillan 2006) 151; Ann Orloff, 'Should Feminists Aim for Gender Symmetry? Why a Dual-Earner/Dual-Caregiver Society Is Not Every Feminist's Utopia' in Janet C. Gornick and Marcia K. Meyers (eds), *Gender Equality: Transforming Family Divisions of Labor* (Verso, 2009) 129; Ruth Lister, 'A Nordic nirvana? Gender, citizenship, and social justice in the Nordic welfare states' (2009) 16(2) (June 20, 2009) *Social Politics: International Studies in Gender, State and Society* 242.

74 Linda Luckhaus, 'Equal treatment, social protection and income security for women' (2000) 139(2) *International Labour Review* 149, 168–9; Julia Sohrab, *Sexing the Benefit: Women, Social Security, and Financial Independence in EC Sex Equality Law* (Dartmouth, 1996).

75 This trend has been noted in the USA for a number of decades. See, for example, Nancy Fraser and Linda Gordon, 'A genealogy of dependency: tracing a keyword of the U.S. welfare state' (1994) 19(2) *Signs* 309; Lucy Williams, 'Race, rat bites and unfit mothers: how media discourse informs welfare legislation debate' (1994) 22(4) *Fordham Urban Law Journal* 1159.

76 Fineman (1995), above n 23. This discourse has not been limited to developed countries. For a discussion of the South African context, see Beth Goldblatt, 'Teen pregancy and abuse of the child support grant: addressing the myths and stereotypes' (2003) 17(56) *Agenda: Empowering Women for Gender Equity* 79.

77 For examples from Canada, Ireland, Australia, and the USA, see chapters in Beth Goldblatt and Lucie Lamarche (eds), *Women's Rights to Social Security and Social Protection* (Hart, 2014).

78 Kabeer, above n 10; Deborah Kasente, 'Gender and social security reform in Africa' (2000) 53(3) *International Social Security Review* 27; Razavi and Hassim, above n 19; Maxine Molyneux, 'Mothers at the service of the new poverty agenda: Progresa/Oportunidades, Mexico's conditional transfer programme' (2006) 40(4) *Social Policy and Administration* 425; Rebecca Holmes and Nicola Jones, *Gender and Social Protection in the Developing World* (Zed, 2013); Marilyn Waring et al., *Anticipatory Social Protection – Claiming Dignity and Rights* (Commonwealth Secretariat, 2013); Gita Sen, 'Engendering Social Security and Protection: The Case of Asia'

countries has a significant impact on women's poverty.[79] In the past decade some developing countries have introduced social assistance programmes that have had marked impacts on human development.[80] While traditional social security systems were often designed around male-dominated formal employment, some recent programmes in developing countries have responded to this imbalance by specifically targeting women (as citizens rather than as workers). Social assistance programmes targeted at women in some developing countries have had positive results but many gaps in provision remain and certain problems have emerged.

The development literature illustrates how policies based on patriarchal assumptions about work, family and the economy can reinforce existing gender inequalities.[81] Some of the programmes targeted at women have the effect of perpetuating gender divisions by making women responsible for care. This is despite the fact that addressing women's disproportionate responsibility for care in these societies has been highlighted as a critical consideration for social protection policy.[82] Conditions that are attached to such assistance often impose additional burdens on women.[83] There is broad consensus amongst feminist writers in this field that social protection programmes that are rights-based and universal have advantages for women but these are most effective when they are alive to the needs and specificities of gender relations and other dynamics in different country contexts. In addition, social assistance without efforts to bring women into work or to formalise informal work with attendant benefits is insufficient.[84]

At the global or transnational level, women worker migration results in a range of challenges around social security provision and rights[85] – the social insurance and other rights of the migrant workers and the complexities of claiming rights

(2011) *International Policy Analysis* 1, http://library.fes.de/pdf-files/iez/08436.pdf; Shahra Razavi, 'Engendering social security and protection: challenges for making social security and protection gender equitable' (2011) *Dialogue on Globalization (Friedrich Ebert Stiftung)* 1; Sabates-Wheeler and Kabeer, above n 11.

79 UNRISD, above n 2, at Section 1, Chapter 4 ('Gender Inequalities at Home and in the Market') and Section 2, Chapter 7 ('Care and Well-Being in a Development Context').

80 UNDP, above n 51.

81 Sylvia Chant, 'The "Feminisation of Poverty" and the "Feminisation" of anti-poverty programmes: room for revision?' (2008) 44(2) *Journal of Development Studies* 165; Bradshaw, above n 67.

82 UNRISD, above n 2, at Section 2, Chapter 7. For a general discussion of social security in development, see Peter Townsend (ed.), *Building Decent Societies: Rethinking the Role of Social Security in Development* (Palgrave Macmillian, 2009); for a discussion of care policy, see Fiona Wiliams, 'Claiming and Framing in the Making of Care Policies: The Recognition and Redistribution of Care' (United Nations Research Institute for Social Development, 2010); and, Razavi, above n 69.

83 Maxine Molyneux, 'Conditional Cash Transfers: A "Pathway to Women's Empowerment"?' (Institute of Development Studies, 2008); Francie Lund et al., 'Is there a rationale for conditional cash transfers for children in South Africa?' (2009) 70 *Transformation* 70; Sandra Fredman, 'Engendering Social Welfare Rights' in Beth Goldblatt and Lucie Lamarche (eds), *Women's Rights to Social Security and Social Protection* (Hart, 2014) 19. The issue of conditionality is considered in more detail in Chapter 4.

84 James Heintz and Francie Lund, 'Welfare Regimes and Social Policy: A Review of the Role of Labour and Employment' (UNRISD, 2012).

85 Ruth Lister et al., *Gendering Citizenship in Western Europe: New Challenges for Citizenship Research in a Cross-National Context* (Policy Press, 2007).

as non-citizens (and as women)[86]; the adequacy of the social security systems in developed countries generally in meeting the rights of women workers, their dependents and society's care needs; and the rights of women and their dependents in the developing countries from which they come.

This brief review highlights some of the gender issues that arise in social security systems and programmes in both developed and developing countries. Feminists working within the social policy and development fields have proposed a variety of approaches to ensure that social security addresses women's poverty while also promoting gender equality. Framed in terms of these objectives, social security can play a larger role in contributing to the transformation of gender relations in society by redefining the way in which work, family, the economy and the State operate and are understood. Many of these writers place value on a human rights approach to underpin their proposals.[87] The next section examines the potential role of human rights in ensuring that the right to social security addresses poverty and gender inequality and contributes to social transformation.

1.4 The role of human rights

Human rights have an important role in supporting the objectives of social security which include the prevention of poverty and inequality, ensuring solidarity and inclusion, and creating economically and socially fairer societies. They offer a normative basis and, in some countries, a legal imperative for requiring that States realise the right to social security for their people. The international right also requires that richer countries assist poorer countries in meeting their social security obligations. While social security is often understood as a matter for unfettered government policy-making, a number of social policy commentators have called for the use of an 'ethical lens of the human rights standards that all governments have agreed upon' as the principled foundation for social security.[88] Human rights allow for an evaluation of policy compliance, inform policy and legislative development, provide individuals and groups with an elucidation of their rights and provide the basis for legal and other challenges where rights are violated. A human rights approach also requires that men and women have equal rights and opposes discrimination of all kinds, including on the basis of gender.

There has been a growing focus on social security as a human right in the twenty-first century. As stated above, the CESCR produced General Comment 19 on the Right to Social Security in 2008.[89] This is the most comprehensive elaboration of the right by a UN human rights treaty body. Since 2001 the ILO

86 See Fudge, above n 15.

87 In particular, see Sabates-Wheeler and Kabeer, above n 11; Razavi, above n 78; Holmes and Jones, above n 78; Sen, above n 78.

88 Radhika Balakrishnan and Diane Elson (eds), *Economic Policy and Human Rights: Holding Governments to Account* (Zed Books, 2011), at 1. Also see Townsend, above n 33; Sen, above n 78; Ann Neville, *Human Rights and Social Policy* (Edward Elgar, 2010).

89 Above n 60.

has consciously framed its social security work in terms of human rights[90] and, as noted, produced a Recommendation on Social Protection Floors in 2012.[91] The increasing acknowledgment of the right to social security in a variety of country contexts at different stages of development means that it has an important role to play in requiring the provision of social security where it is lacking and its extension and reform where this is needed.

The history of human rights and their current role should not however be understood uncritically. A number of scholars challenge the dominant and possibly co-opting narrative of human rights as linear, inherently progressive and capable of contributing to fundamental social and political change.[92] There are also many valuable feminist challenges to the roles and framing of human rights.[93] Feminist legal theorists have developed a sophisticated critique of international law that draws on many of the foundational feminist concepts such as the public/private divide, the dichotomies and hierarchies that law creates and perpetuates, and the assumption that the subject of law is male.[94] Otto, for example, highlights the way in which international human rights laws represent women as needing protection, requiring comparison with men to be entitled to rights, and as victims.[95] MacKinnon, in another example, points to the limits of an anti-discrimination approach in international law in tackling issues of violence against women where the real concern is power and subordination rather than

90 ILO (2011a), above n 38, at 12.

91 Above n 58.

92 See, for example David Kennedy, 'The international human rights movement: part of the problem?' (2002) 15 *Harvard Human Rights Journal* 101; Wendy Brown, 'The most we can hope for …: human rights and the politics of fatalism' (2004) 103 *South Atlantic Quarterly* 451. Some of the critics of human rights propose a rethinking of human rights rather than a complete rejection: Ben Golder 'Beyond redemption? Problematizing the critique of human rights in contemporary international legal thought' (2014) 2(1) *London Review of International Law* 77.

93 For example: Dianne Otto, 'Disconcerting "Masculinities": Reinventing the Gendered Subject(s) of International Human Rights Law' in Doris Buss and Ambreena Manji (eds), *International Law: Modern Feminist Approaches* (Hart, 2005) 105; Ratna Kapur, 'The tragedy of victimisation rhetoric: resurrecting the "native" subject in international/postcolonial feminist legal politics' (2002) 15 *Harvard Human Rights Law Journal* 1; Karen Engle, 'International Human Rights and Feminisms: When Discourses Keep Meeting' in Doris Buss and Ambreena Manji (eds), *International Law: Modern Feminist Approaches* (Hart Publishing, 2005) 47.

94 For example: Hilary Charlesworth, Christine Chinkin and Shelley Wright, 'Feminist approaches to international law' (1991) 85(4) *The American Journal of International Law* 613; Hilary Charlesworth and Christine Chinkin, *The Boundaries of International Law: A Feminist Analysis* (Manchester University Press, 2000); Christine Chinkin, Shelley Wright and Hilary Charlesworth, 'Feminist Approaches to International Law: Reflections from Another Century' in Doris Buss and Ambreena Manji (eds), *International Law: Modern Feminist Approaches* (Hart, 2005) 17; Catharine A. MacKinnon, *Are Women Human? And Other International Dialogues* (Harvard University Press, 2006); Sari Kouvo and Zoe Pearson (eds), *Feminist Perspectives on Contemporary International Law: Between Resistance and Compliance?* (Hart, 2011).

95 Otto (2005), above n 90; Dianne Otto, 'Women's Rights' in Daniel Moeckli, Sangeeta Shah and Sandesh Sivakumaran (eds), *International Human Rights Law* (Oxford University Press, 2010) 345.

comparative advantage.[96] Many feminist human rights scholars, as in broader feminist legal scholarship, emphasise the need for a critical awareness of and response to diversity and intersectional disadvantage within international law. Scholars from developing countries have also challenged the essentialist, divisive and sometimes imperialist approaches of western feminism to international human rights.[97]

The critiques of international human rights create challenges for feminist scholars who accept these but continue to see value in engaging in efforts to reimagine and reshape this terrain. Charlesworth notes that:[98]

> The tension between critical approaches to international law, which are concerned with identifying the politics of international law, and feminist approaches, which analyse the law to improve the position of women, is often acute.

She considers the views of Janet Halley[99] who challenges feminism to rethink itself and what it has become, in relation to feminist work in international law. Charlesworth finds value in many of Halley's critiques of feminism in this terrain but remains convinced that feminism has value in the international terrain in 'bringing women's lives onto the agenda, but that feminist messages without feminist methods are unlikely to bring change'.[100] Such methods involve 'being explicit about our own historical and cultural background, trying to understand how other women might see us, and recognising the complexities of the lives of other women'.[101]

This self-reflective method is one important aspect of the response to the critique of human rights and feminist engagement within it. It is also important to link the project of developing alternative visions of human rights with broader transformative projects. In addition, alliances with other interest groups such as migrant workers, Indigenous peoples and communities opposing environmental destruction, in the transnational space, open the feminist movement to new ways of thinking and new strategies for challenging dominant power structures and institutions.[102] These new ideas infuse feminist scholarship through reflexive praxis.

96 MacKinnon, above n 94.

97 J. Oloka-Onyango and Sylvia Tamale, '"The personal is political", or why women's rights are indeed human rights: an African perspective on international feminism' (1995) 17 *Human Rights Quarterly* 691; Kapur, above n 93.

98 Hilary Charlesworth 'Talking to Ourselves? Feminist Scholarship in International Law' in Sari Kouvo and Zoe Pearson (eds), *Feminist Perspectives on Contemporary International Law: Between Resistance and Compliance?* (Hart, 2011) 17, at 20.

99 Janet Halley *Split Decisions: How and Why to Take a Break from Feminism* (Princeton University Press, 2006).

100 Charlesworth, above n 98, at 24.

101 Ibid., at 32.

102 See the discussion of new transnational feminist directions in Nancy Fraser, *Scales of Justice – Reimagining Political Space in a Globalizing World* (Polity Press, 2008), at Chapter 6.

This book is premised on a critical understanding of the social/cultural, political and economic forces that generate the deepening poverty and inequality that define our global situation. In proposing a new formulation of the right to social security it aims to contribute to the project of redefining the key social institutions of work and reproduction/care, a long-standing project of critical feminist scholarship. Pursuing this project within the space of human rights contains dangers that face any feminist engagement within the law or other institutions of governance. Awareness of these dangers and ongoing evaluation of the impact of this engagement in light of these dangers is a methodological necessity.

Nicola Lacey notes the strong link between theory and practice in feminist legal scholarship that informs its methodological approach.[103] She argues that while some legal theory aims to rationalise and explain law from within and other theory critiques law from outside of it, much of feminist legal theory adopts a third position that she describes as 'interpretive'. This approach 'aspire(s) to produce a critical interpretation of legal practices: an account which at once takes seriously the legal point of view yet which subjects that point of view to critical scrutiny on the basis of both its professed values and a range of other ethical and political commitments'.[104] The book situates itself within this tradition of feminist legal theory in engaging critically with human rights from within, while being mindful of their shortcomings and limits, in pursuit of tangible and practical benefits that might result from their reinterpretation.

1.5 Research approach and decisions

This section sets out the overall approach that informs the research in this book and discusses the research methodology chosen for the book. It then explains and outlines the specific research choices made in relation to the international law chapter and the three country studies. Lastly, it notes the research cut-off date.

1.5.1 Research approach

The research approach of the book is informed by writing on feminist legal method.[105] This body of theory emphasises the need to locate laws (including rights) within their gendered social context and encourages a critical evaluation of the impact of the laws through the lens of women's lived experience. Feminist legal method draws on broader feminist research approaches. Ackerly and True suggest that a 'feminist research ethic' is attentive to (1) the power of epistemology; (2) boundaries (including intersections and silences); (3) relationships and

103 Nicola Lacey, 'Feminist Legal Theory and the Rights of Women' in Karen Knop (ed.), *Gender and Human Rights* (Oxford University Press, 2004) 13, at 17.

104 Ibid., at 16–17.

105 Regina Graycar and Jenny Morgan, *The Hidden Gender of Law* (The Federation Press, 2nd edn, 2002), at Chapter 4; Karin van Marle and Elsje Bonthuys, 'Feminist Theories and Concepts' in Elsje Bonthuys and Catherine Albertyn (eds), *Gender, Law and Justice* (Juta, 2007) 15, at 46–9.

power differences; and (4) the situation of the researcher.[106] I will briefly discuss each of these as they relate to the research approach for this book.

(1) With regard to epistemology, feminists have criticised 'naturalized identities, social categories and hierarchies' to expose 'structures of oppression'.[107] Feminists have challenged dichotomous thinking and key concepts such as sex and gender.[108] In examining, critiquing and reinterpreting the right to social security from a gender perspective, the book draws on this feminist epistemological approach and unpacks, exposes and rethinks ideas of work and care prevalent within dominant conceptions of the right

(2) In engaging in research, feminists have challenged disciplinary and conceptual boundaries to demonstrate how women's voices are silenced or certain groups of women are marginalised within the research process.[109] Women are not a homogeneous group and particular groups of women such as older women, Indigenous women, girls, women with disabilities, sole mothers and many others may have very different gendered experiences of social security shaped by a range of factors related to their identity and location. The theoretical framework for the book incorporates an understanding of multiple and intersecting discrimination so as to encompass the complex issues entailed in the examination of social security from a gender perspective. This framework aims to ensure methodological attention to the different groups of women affected by various social security schemes. Three case studies consider different groups of women within three countries.[110]

In each country the social security rights and laws are studied in light of the situation of women in that country and the way in which such rights and laws impact on their lives. This approach questions the silences in social security systems and laws where women's circumstances are often ignored. It also points to the way in which such laws and systems define the boundaries of men and women's access to social security through definitions of, for example, work and care, inherent in these systems/laws.

(3) Since the book does not involve primary research into the experiences of the law by women on the ground, secondary sources examining women's circumstances in these countries have been used, where possible, to ensure that the overall feminist methodological approach of attention to the context and circumstances of women is followed. The research approach has been informed by an awareness of the relationship between the researcher and subject within

106 Brooke Ackerly and Jacqui True, *Doing Feminist Research in Political and Social Science* (Palgrave Macmillan, 2010), at 22–39. Also see Carole Smart, 'Shifting horizons: reflections on qualitative methods' (2009) 10(3) *Feminist Theory* 295, for a discussion of feminist research methods and how these must be built on with reference to new innovations in qualitative research.

107 Ackerly and True, ibid., at 26.

108 This debate in feminism is discussed in Chapter 2, section 2.2.

109 Ackerly and True, above n 106, at 29–31.

110 However, the book is limited to the development of the right in broad terms, leaving further exploration of how the developed right might be applied to specific groups for future research and examination.

a feminist research ethic, particularly with regard to gathering information for the Indian country study which involved observations and collaboration with academics and advocates.

(4) Awareness of one's situation as researcher within a feminist research ethic requires ongoing self-reflection of one's location and assumptions.[111] The focus on the right to social security in international law within the book has required an awareness of global political and social issues. The research within three countries has required an awareness of my own research location as a relatively new resident of Australia, my previous residence in South Africa as a member of a privileged group, and my limited knowledge of India as an interested outsider. This awareness has shaped my ethical approach and has encouraged me to re-evaluate my judgments and views regarding the countries studied.

1.5.2 *Research methods*

The book uses desk-based methods that draw on scholarly literature across the disciplines of law, human rights, social policy, sociology, economics, politics, development studies and gender studies. It makes use of case law, national legislation and related regulations, international treaties, international law decisions and reports, parliamentary reports, policy literature, media reports and non-governmental organisational materials. For the purpose of understanding the Indian country context, I worked with a women's rights non-governmental organisation and attended their conference on women's rights to social security in May 2013.[112] While this field trip did not involve formal interviews, observation of the conference and discussions with participants were valuable in informing the writing of the India country study.[113] The South African and Australian country studies have been informed by my own involvement in advocacy (in both countries) and litigation (in South Africa only) on women's social security rights while residing in each of these countries.

1.5.3 *Research choices: international law chapter*

Central to the book is a critical analysis of the international law on the right to social security from a gender perspective. In this regard, Chapter 3 specifically

111 Ackerly and True, above n 106, at 36–7.

112 Programme for Women's Economic, Social and Cultural Rights (PWESCR) organised the conference in collaboration with UN-Women, the Heinrich Böll Foundation, the ILO and the University of New South Wales. The national conference titled 'Women's Social Security and Protection in India' was held on 6–7 May 2013 at the Indian Social Institute, New Delhi. For the conference report, see Anupma Mehta, 'Women's Social Security and Protection in India: A Report: National Conference 6–7 May 2013, New Delhi' (Programme on Women's Economic, Social and Cultural Rights, 2013).

113 Ethics approval was obtained from the University of New South Wales Human Research Ethics Committee for this field trip on 27 March 2013. The reference number for this approval is HREC Ref: # HC13010.

considers the work of four UN bodies: the Committee on the Elimination of Discrimination against Women (the CEDAW Committee); the Committee on Economic, Social and Cultural Rights (the CESCR); the International Labour Organisation (ILO); and the Special Rapporteur on extreme poverty and human rights. The CESCR, ILO and Special Rapporteur have been chosen because they are the UN bodies most centrally concerned with the interpretation of the right to social security. The CEDAW Committee has been chosen because of its specific focus on women in relation to the right to social security. While other treaty committees and special mandate holders have also made important pronouncements on the right to social security, a selective approach limited to these four main bodies has been chosen for this study.

The specific choice of material produced by the different international bodies under examination is detailed in Chapter 3.

1.5.4 Research choices: country studies

The book uses three country studies (Chapters 4, 5 and 6) as a means of illustrating that the development of the right to social security from a gender perspective has utility, relevance and significance across national contexts. The countries selected for study are Australia, India and South Africa. They have been chosen for the following reasons:

First and most importantly, they represent countries at different stages of economic development.[114] Australia is a developed, high-income economy; South Africa and India are both developing countries, with South Africa classified as an upper-middle-income economy and India classified as a lower-middle-income economy. The three countries represent a broad spectrum of economic and social provision and need. Understanding the different conditions in these countries helps to ensure that development of the right to social security from a gender perspective is sensitive to a variety of social, economic, political and cultural circumstances while also having universal application and value.

Second, and related to this, the three countries represent different approaches to welfare provision arising from their particular history and context. Australia has an advanced welfare system; South Africa has a sizeable but non-comprehensive welfare system; and India has a more limited but growing welfare system. Each country has dealt differently with gender in its social security system. Any framework for approaching a right to social security from a gender perspective will need to take account of the varieties in State provision of welfare, in both form and reach, in order to have universal application. At the same time, there are certain commonalities in the systems of the three countries chosen that emerge from the historical influence of colonial Britain on all three Commonwealth

114 The classifications are based on the World Bank measure of gross national income per capita, http://data.worldbank.org/about/country-classifications.

countries.[115] These commonalities make understanding, studying and comparing the different systems both easier and more effective.

A third and more practical methodological reason for choosing the three countries relates to the languages used and the resulting ease of access to legislation, case law and literature. English is one of the languages spoken in each country and official documents are widely available in English.

Fourth, and related to this, because they are all common law countries historically influenced by the English legal system,[116] the legal systems and processes of the three countries are similar in some respects and therefore comparable. As well as similarities, there are important differences between the three countries that allow for useful contrast in analysis. For example, each of the three countries takes a different approach to rights. At one end of the spectrum, South Africa's constitution contains a justiciable right to social security. The Indian constitution contains directive principles which refer to aspects of the right to social security. These principles, although not directly enforceable as rights, place a duty on the State to apply them in making laws. Australia has no Bill of Rights or federal human rights legislation so the courts have a limited role to play in considering human rights in welfare adjudication. All three countries are party to a number of international human rights treaties that guarantee the right to social security.

A fifth reason is that feminists, human rights lawyers and women's rights advocates play a significant role in each country in using rights arguments, along with other strategies, to address issues of social security for women. This has led to the emergence of a valuable body of writing that offers insights into the issues facing women in relation to social security in each country.

The country studies contain the following common features:

- An outline of the country's social security system;
- An analysis of gender within the social security system;
- The human rights and legal framework for social security in that country;
- A consideration and evaluation of key issues in the social security systems of each country from the gender perspective developed in the book.

The country studies do not comprehensively evaluate all aspects of the social security system, but instead identify key social security programmes and measures with an observable impact (both positive and negative) on women in those countries for close examination.[117]

The country studies, together with literature from elsewhere in the world, provide a picture of the variety of issues entailed in the development of a universally applicable right to social security that incorporates a gender perspective.

115 See James Midgley and David Pichaud, *Colonialism and Welfare: Social Policy and the British Imperial Legacy* (Edward Elgar, 2011).

116 Note that South Africa's legal system contains a mix of English common law, Roman-Dutch law and some African customary law.

117 The explanation for the choice of programmes is provided in each of the country chapters.

The country studies represent only a small part of the international terrain. They do not include civil law jurisdictions, exemplar regions such as Scandinavia (advanced, gender-sensitive social democracies) or Latin American countries such as Mexico and Brazil (with interesting recent developments around gender and social assistance). Some of the lessons from these other jurisdictions are considered in examining the international feminist and social policy literature; however, the scope of the book is limited to manageable proportions. The three countries chosen provide insight into three very different contexts and each contributes to the development of the international right to social security from a gender perspective.

1.5.5 *Research cut-off date*

The cut-off date for the research conducted in this book is 30 June 2014. The cut-off date for the survey of Concluding Observations and Recommendations by the CEDAW Committee and the CESCR is 31 December 2013.[118] There has been considerable change over the period in which the research for this book was conducted (2012–2014) and since then, at the level of international law and within the countries studied. In all three countries, national elections were held during the period of the research, leading to a change of government in two of these countries (India and Australia). Where appropriate, the likely impact of such political changes is mentioned in relation to the laws and policies being discussed in each country study, but given the pace of change in the area of social policy, some of these may now be different.

1.6 Chapter outline

The following is an outline of the remaining chapters:

Chapter 2 constructs the conceptual approach of the book, drawing on feminist theories from a range of disciplines. In so doing it explores and reinterprets the meaning of 'work' within the right to social security; it examines and applies a transformative substantive equality approach to the development of the right to social security; and it develops principles for a substantively equal, gendered social security right.

Chapter 3 surveys the international law on the right to social security and analyses it in light of the discussion in Chapter 2. It focuses on the work of the CEDAW Committee; the CESCR; the ILO, with specific emphasis on the recent Social Protection Floors Recommendation;[119] and the Special Rapporteur on extreme poverty and human rights.

Chapter 4 is the South African country study. It concentrates on the Child Support Grant and recent moves to add conditions to this previously unconditional

118 The period of study for this aspect of the research is further detailed within Chapter 3.

119 ILO, *Recommendation Concerning National Floors of Social Protection*, 2012 (No. 202).

social assistance payment. It provides a more general consideration of the issue of conditionality in social security programmes.

Chapter 5 is the Australian country study. It considers two developments in the area of social security: 'income management' affecting Indigenous communities in the Northern Territory and further areas elsewhere in the country; and cutbacks to sole parent benefits.

Chapter 6 is the Indian country study. It focuses on the National Social Assistance Programme and the *Mahatma Gandhi National Rural Employment Guarantee Act* that establishes a public works scheme.

Chapter 7, the conclusion, discusses the main findings of the book. It draws out the themes and lessons of the three country studies and the survey of international law in light of the conceptual framework and the set of principles for a substantively equal, gendered social security right developed in this book, and makes certain recommendations.

2 A gender perspective

Conceptual approach and principles

2.1 Introduction

This chapter develops a conceptual framework for approaching the reinterpretation and development of the right to social security from a gender perspective, drawing on feminist theory, feminist legal theory, as well as writing from other disciplines. The project of reinterpretation and development of the right to social security is undertaken in this chapter through the synthesis of two approaches.[1] The first approach closely engages with the content of the right, challenging existing interpretations and developing more fully the gender dimensions of the right.[2] In particular, this approach rethinks fundamental issues relating to gender and work that underpin the right. It also suggests that the right must have application beyond the level of the nation state and at the sub-national level if it is to reach women in need of social security in a globalised workforce. The second approach uses gender equality, a human rights principle and a self-standing right, to ensure the full realisation of the right to social security.[3] In particular, it applies

1 Different approaches to the interpretation of the right to social security are discussed in Beth Goldblatt and Lucie Lamarche, 'Introduction: Interpreting and Advancing Women's Rights to Social Security and Social Protection' in Beth Goldblatt and Lucie Lamarche (eds), *Women's Rights to Social Security and Social Protection* (Hart, 2014) 1.

2 The book is part of a broader feminist project to give gender content to social and economic rights. See Dianne Otto, 'Gender comment: why does the UN Committee on Economic, Social and Cultural Rights need a general comment on women?' (2002) 14(1) *Canadian Journal of Women and the Law* 1, at 50; 'Montreal principles on women's economic, social and cultural rights' (2004) 26 *Human Rights Quarterly* 760.

3 A third approach chooses to 'mainstream' gender into the discussion of social protection and human rights by ensuring that gender issues are central to the understanding of the set of rights required to address poverty. This last approach is the one adopted by the former Special Rapporteur on extreme poverty and human rights, Magdalena Sepúlveda Carmona, in her various reports to the Human Rights Council in pursuance of her mandate. See the website of the Special Rapporteur on extreme poverty and human rights, www.ohchr.org/EN/ISSUES/POVERTY/Pages/SRExtremePovertyIndex.aspx and see Magdalena Sepúlveda and Carly Nyst, *The Human Rights Approach to Social Protection* (Ministry for Foreign Affairs Finland, 2012). Her focus is broader than the social security right as it concerns many aspects of social protection in the wider sense; however, she makes a number of useful observations and recommendations regarding women's social security rights. (These are discussed in Chapter 3.) This approach, while extremely

a transformative substantive equality approach to the redevelopment of the right to embed gender equality within the right to social security, taking account of the diversity of women. The chapter then draws on the reinterpretation and development of the right to propose a set of principles for a substantively equal, gendered right to social security.

The chapter begins (in 2.2) by discussing what is meant by a gender perspective in the book. This perspective emerges from feminist theory and more specifically, from feminist legal theory as it applies to law and rights. It then examines (in 2.3) the concept of 'work' within the right to social security and critiques the way in which traditional conceptions of work have excluded women from social security rights. It proposes a reformulation of what is meant by work as a central concept within the right to social security. The chapter also draws (in 2.4) on the idea of 'scale' in framing an approach to the right to social security from a gender perspective that ensures that the right has the fullest breadth and depth in reaching those who should properly be entitled to it. The chapter then engages (in 2.5) with principles of non-discrimination and equality and, drawing on Sandra Fredman's four-dimensional approach to equality, proposes a transformative substantive equality approach to the right to social security. Addressing multiple and intersecting forms of discrimination against different groups of women is integral to the approach taken in this book. The chapter qualifies (in 2.6) the centrality of equality by emphasising the interdependence of rights. The right to social security, together with the right to equality and other rights, is part of a human rights package that, as a whole, contributes towards addressing (and redressing) women's poverty and disadvantage. Lastly, the chapter identifies (in 2.7) principles for a substantively equal, gendered social security right. The conceptual approach developed in this chapter and the set of principles with which it concludes are used in the remainder of the book to inform the evaluation of international law and domestic social security programmes in the three country studies.

2.2 A gender perspective

A focus on gender as the central category of analysis is the defining feature of feminism. Feminism is both a political movement and a body of thought that challenges the subordination of women in society. Feminist theory encompasses a significant diversity of views containing major categories such as liberal, radical, socialist, cultural, postcolonial and postmodern feminisms and many related or additional approaches. Feminist theory has three central features: first, its focus on the role of gender in shaping oppression of women in society (its 'women-centeredness');[4] second, its efforts to engage with and draw on a wide range of

valuable for the development of a human rights framework for social protection, does not entail a specific reinterpretation of the right to social security from a gender perspective.

4 Joanne Conaghan, 'Reassessing the feminist theoretical project in law' (2000) 27(3) *Journal of Law and Society* 351, at 363.

disciplines using a gender analysis; and third, its normative goal of changing society to address women's disadvantage.[5]

Feminist legal theory contains all of these features of feminist theory. In particular it directs its attention to the role of law in shaping the subordination of women and uses law to address this subordination. Lacey sees feminist legal theory as engaging in critique of the law, in its reform and in its normative reconstruction (utopianism).[6] Feminist legal theory is concerned, amongst other things, with the gendered legal subject,[7] the nature of legal language and reasoning,[8] the way in which law operates through its explicit pronouncements and in its neutrality to oppress women and discriminate against them,[9] and the implementation of law as it impacts on women.[10] Feminist lawyers have drawn on the powerful role of law in society in using it to advance their (varied) goals.[11]

Feminist legal theorists have produced key insights into the ways in which the law structures and reinforces gender inequalities within the home, workplace and society. They have illustrated the centrality of the law to liberalism's ideological separation of the public and private spheres that serve to designate (and undervalue) work in the home as women's work and to advantage men in the workforce and society more generally.[12] Private sphere ideology has also allowed violence against women in the home to continue, often unchallenged, on the basis that this is a realm of non-intervention by the State and other actors. In relation to the family, writers have shown how dependency is primarily located within the private sphere and care is inadequately supported through law by the State and the market.[13] An example of law's role in the family can be found in its handling of relationship breakdown, which often leaves women (and the children for whom they care) in a worse financial position than they were before and as compared

5 This analysis of the features of feminism is explored in Conaghan, ibid., and is discussed in Martha Albertson Fineman, 'Gender and law: feminist legal theory's role in the new legal realism' (2005) 2005 *Wisconsin Law Review* 405, at 406–7.

6 Nicola Lacey, 'Feminist Legal Theory and the Rights of Women' in Karen Knop (ed.), *Gender and Human Rights* (Oxford University Press, 2004) 13, at 42–3. Also see Rosalind Dixon, 'Feminist disagreement (comparatively) recast' (2008) 31 *Harvard Journal of Law and Gender* 277 for a categorisation of different feminist legal theories in terms of their capacity to be disruptive, ameliorative and transformative.

7 See, for example, Ngaire Naffine, 'Sexing the Subject (of Law)' in Margaret Thornton (ed.), *Public and Private: Feminist Legal Debates* (Oxford University Press, 1995) 18.

8 See, for example, Lucinda M. Finley, 'Breaking women's silence in law: the dilemma of the gendered nature of legal reasoning' (1989) 64 *Notre Dame Law Review* 886.

9 For one overview, see Regina Graycar and Jenny Morgan, *The Hidden Gender of Law* (The Federation Press, 2nd edn, 2002).

10 Lacey, above n 6, at 30.

11 Conaghan, above n 4, at 362.

12 Katherine O'Donovan, *Sexual Divisions in Law* (Weidenfeld and Nicolson, 1985); Frances Olsen, 'The family and the market: a study of ideology and legal reform' (1983) 96 *Harvard Law Review* 1497; Susan Boyd (ed.), *Challenging the Public/Private Divide: Feminism, Law, and Public Policy* (University of Toronto Press, 1997).

13 Martha Albertson Fineman, 'Contract and care' (2001) 76 *Chicago-Kent Law Review* 1403.

with men.[14] Within the workplace, women tend to hold the least protected and least valued jobs as well as the lowest paid jobs.[15] This is, in part, structured by law, which generally protects the interests of powerful economic actors. For example, informal sector work, in which women predominate, is inadequately recognised in law as work for the purposes of employment and social insurance benefits, to the advantage of employers.[16] Another example is the persistence of lower pay for women. Gender-based salary differentials exist worldwide because the work categories in which women are located are less valued by the economy. Courts are often unable or unwilling to tackle this underlying inequality. With globalisation, women migrant workers experience new forms of legal exclusion and denial of their rights.[17]

Feminist legal theorists have critiqued, reinterpreted and developed human rights law.[18] Human rights, within national and international law, are potentially powerful instruments for far-reaching change. However, like other laws, they may be used in a manner that fails to challenge (and even reinforces) existing gender oppression and inequality. Many foundational human rights have been reconceived by feminist scholars to ensure their responsiveness to gender inequality. Robin West, in the United States (US) context, has argued for a reconstruction of liberal rights as positive and relational rights that protect and guarantee fundamental capabilities.[19] Specifically, she has proposed that a liberal state 'structured by rights, but committed to securing the minimal preconditions of capabilities as well as autonomy, would explicitly recognize additional fundamental rights, including welfare rights and rights to work'.[20] She has suggested it would also recognise two other core rights: a right to security against private violence and a right to care.[21] Her argument that rights are 'relational' and must recognise our 'inescapable dependence on each other' is echoed in the writings of Canadian constitutional theorist Jennifer Nedelsky who has reframed ideas of autonomy in law and as rights.[22] Along similar lines, Martha Fineman offers a fruitful perspective on welfare and rights. She focuses on the US commitment to equality of opportunity and access to argue for a more active and responsive

14 Martha Albertson Fineman, *The Illusion of Equality: The Rhetoric and Reality of Divorce Reform* (1991); Martha Albertson Fineman, *The Neutered Mother, the Sexual Family and Other Twentieth Cenury Tragedies* (Routledge, 1995).

15 These issues are also canvassed in Chapter 1.

16 See Lucy Williams, 'The legal construction of poverty: gender, "work" and the "social contract"' (2011) 2011(3) *Stelllenbosch Law Review* 463, who argues that neo-liberal social contract theory relies on legal rules that construct social understandings of poverty to legitimise gender subordination.

17 Judy Fudge, 'Precarious migrant status and precarious employment: the paradox of international rights for migrant workers' (2012) 34(1) *Comparative Labor Law and Policy Journal* 95.

18 This is discussed in Chapter 1.

19 Robin West, 'Rights, capabilities and the good society' (2001) 69 *Fordham Law Review* 1901.

20 Ibid.

21 Ibid.

22 Jennifer Nedelsky, *Law's Relations: A Relational Theory of Self, Autonomy, and Law* (Oxford University Press, 2011).

state.[23] She argues that the principle of equality has been undermined by the principle of autonomy when, instead, autonomy should be informed by 'a lens of equality' to 'carry social and reciprocal duties to others'.[24]

This book is part of a feminist legal project to critically examine human rights and reinterpret them to ensure that they reflect women's experiences and contribute to transforming gender relations. The gender perspective adopted in this book draws on many of the foundational insights of feminism and feminist legal scholarship set out briefly above. As with feminism, there are different understandings of what a gender perspective might entail based on a range of views as to the meaning of gender. Generally, discussions of gender distinguish between 'sex', the biological differences between men and women, and 'gender', the social construction of men and women as different. This approach has found its way into international law. The CEDAW Committee has adopted the following definition:[25]

> Gender is defined as the social meanings given to biological sex differences. It is an ideological and cultural construct, but is also reproduced within the realm of material practices; in turn it influences the outcomes of such practices. It affects the distribution of resources, wealth, work, decision-making and political power, and enjoyment of rights and entitlements within the family as well as public life. Despite variations across cultures and over time, gender relations throughout the world entail asymmetry of power between men and women as a pervasive trait. Thus, gender is a social stratifier, and in this sense it is similar to other stratifiers such as race, class, ethnicity, sexuality, and age. It helps us understand the social construction of gender identities and the unequal structure of power that underlies the relationship between the sexes.

This characterisation of sex/biology and gender/culture has proved important for feminism since it has enabled the argument that while sex may be immutable social constructions can be changed.[26] As Margaret Davies has put it:[27]

> Detaching what is natural – body parts – from what is cultural, has given feminists the freedom to analyse critically the social consequences of being biologically female or male.

23 Martha Albertson Fineman, 'The vulnerable subject and the responsive state' (2010) 60 *Emory Law Journal* 251; also, see Martha Albertson Fineman, *The Autonomy Myth: A Theory of Dependency* (The New Press, 2004).

24 Fineman (2010), ibid., at 261.

25 CEDAW, '*General recommendation No. 25, on Article 4, Paragraph 1, of the Convention on the Elimination of All Forms of Discrimination against Women, on temporary special measures*' (2004) 30th Session, UN Doc A/59/38, annex I, at footnote 2 citing the 1999 World Survey on the Role of Women in Development, United Nations, New York, 1999, page ix.

26 Karin van Marle and Elsje Bonthuys, 'Feminist Theories and Concepts' in Catherine Albertyn and Elsje Bonthuys (eds), *Gender, Law and Justice* (Juta, 2007) 15, at 22.

27 Margaret Davies, 'Taking the Inside out – Sex and Gender in the Legal Subject' in Ngaire Naffine and Rosemary J. Owens (eds), *Sexing the Subject of Law* (Sweet and Maxwell, 1997) 25, at 29.

However, this approach has led to criticism within feminism with the realisation that sex differences are also socially constructed and require challenge and reimagining.[28] The ideas of feminist philosopher Judith Butler are influential in this respect. Butler has challenged the binary of sex and gender and explores how identity is constituted through what she terms 'performativity'.[29] Butler understands gender as an unstable identity 'instituted through a *stylized repetition of acts*' and through the body – what she calls 'a performative accomplishment compelled by social sanction and taboo'.[30] Importantly, because gender is not a given, different forms of repeating or performing can lead to subverting such acts with the possibility of gender transformation. Politically, Butler suggests, it remains important to represent women but this must be done 'in a way that does not distort and reify the very collectivity the theory is supposed to emancipate'.[31]

Feminist legal theorists have drawn on these ideas to critique the way that law participates in the construction of sex and gender even while trying to challenge discrimination. Katherine Franke has argued that anti-discrimination law is incorrectly premised on the idea that sex, seen as biological difference, is:[32]

> prior to, less normative than, and more real than gender.... By accepting these biological differences, equality jurisprudence reifies as foundational *fact* that which is really an *effect* of normative gender ideology.

While Butler retains the term 'gender' (as does Franke), Davies prefers the term 'sex'[33] and Otto argues for the term 'sex/gender'[34] as language best able to challenge the earlier conceptions of the terms. This book uses the term 'gender' shaped by an understanding of this debate. The gender perspective used in this book recognises that conceptions of masculinity and femininity and sex and gender are socially produced and regulated, requiring interrogation, disruption and transformation. Gender should be conceived, in Davies' words, as 'a process which is relational and dynamic: gender cannot be reduced to a fixed set of traits, but as something contextual, historical and interactive with other major categories of social identity such as race, culture and class'.[35] Gender inequality

28 Ibid. For some of the objections to this definition of gender, see Raewyn Connell, *Gender in World Perspective* (Polity, 2nd edn 2009), at 10–11.

29 Judith Butler, *Gender Trouble: Feminism and the Subversion of Identity* (Routledge, 1990); and see Gill Jagger, *Judith Butler: Sexual Politics, Social Change and the Power of the Performative* (Routledge, 2008).

30 Judith Butler, 'Performative acts and gender constitution: an essay in phenomenology and feminist theory' (1988) 40(4) *Theatre Journal* 519, 519–20.

31 Ibid., at 530.

32 Katherine M. Franke, 'The central mistake of sex discrimination law: the disaggregation of sex from gender' (1995) 144(1) *University of Pennsylvania Law Review* 1, at 2.

33 Davies, above n 27.

34 Dianne Otto 'International Human Rights Law: Towards Rethinking Sex/Gender Dualism' in Margaret Davies and Vanessa E. Munroe (eds), *The Ashgate Research Companion to Feminist Legal Theory* (Ashgate, 2013) 197.

35 Davies, above n 27, at 38.

is causally linked to economic structures that produce disadvantage but also arises in complex interrelation with additional factors such as culture, religion and imbalances of power.[36] Attention must thus be paid to underlying and systemic disadvantage based on gender (along with other forms of disadvantage). Understood in this way, 'gender' is a useful analytical device that allows for a contextual examination of the different circumstances of men and women as well as the impact of laws, policies, systems and practices on their lives.

Flowing from this is the recognition that both men and women suffer harm as a result of the way in which society and the law constructs sex and gender. Because disadvantage is disproportionately skewed against women, their experiences are the major focus of this book. But this does not preclude an awareness of the ways in which social institutions must be reshaped to include men and redefine masculinity.[37] The gender perspective used in this book recognises that while men may experience relative advantage over women in many areas of life, this comes with some costs to their own identity formation and quality of life. Thus, for example, public/private divisions may prevent men from fully experiencing the positive aspects of caring for others. Addressing the way in which society currently structures gender relations requires challenging male and female gender stereotypes and expectations and envisioning new ways of being human. Given the material and cultural underpinnings of gender inequality, this requires a systemic transformation of society.[38] While the book focuses on women as the group primarily experiencing gender disadvantage, this transformative understanding informs both the critical analysis of the law and proposals for its development advanced in this book.

The book considers the ways in which the right to social security has been defined on the premise that the right-holder is male (and employed). Its aim, in developing the right from a gender perspective, is to question this assumption and imagine a right that can accommodate a variety of forms of activity that both men and women undertake. In so doing, a redeveloped right might challenge the

36 See Sandra Fredman, *Discrimination Law* (Oxford University Press, 2nd edn, 2011).

37 Otto, above n 34, at 208, commends the definition in CESCR '*General Comment No 16: Article 3: the equal right of men and women to the enjoyment of all economic, social and cultural rights*' (2005) 34th Session 2005, E/C 12/2005/4, para 14, for disavowing an assymetrical approach that focuses only on women and considering the gender constructions that harm men while recognising that inequality operates primarily to disadvantage women. The definition reads as follows: 'Gender refers to cultural expectations and assumptions about the behaviour, attitudes, personality traits, and physical and intellectual capacities of men and women, based solely on their identity as men or women. Gender-based assumptions and expectations generally place women at a disadvantage with respect to substantive enjoyment of rights, such as freedom to act and to be recognized as autonomous, fully capable adults, to participate fully in economic, social and political development, and to make decisions concerning their circumstances and conditions. Gender-based assumptions about economic, social and cultural roles preclude the sharing of responsibility between men and women in all spheres that is necessary to equality.'

38 See Nancy Fraser, 'After the family wage: gender equity and the welfare state' (1994) 22(4) *Political Theory* 591, who argues, at 594, that 'with respect to social welfare, at least, the deconstruction of gender difference is a necessary condition for gender equity; and, at 600, that the principle of anti-androcentrism entails changing men and women.

exclusion of both women and men from activity that is socially defined as male or female, such as reproductive labour and care work, and in so doing, contribute to transforming gendered social relations.

It is important to note that any examination of the situation of women should not treat this group as undifferentiated. In exploring gender inequality in society and its articulation in law, close attention must be paid to context – the lived experience of individuals and groups of women. This involves an awareness of multiple differences among women along axes of race, class, sexuality, ethnicity, age, disability, and many others. It also requires an appreciation of different national and regional contexts. The way in which gender and other categories intersect to create additional forms of disadvantage is central to the gender perspective used in this book.[39]

2.3 The relationship between the right to social security and 'work'

As discussed in Chapter 1, this book engages with the current meaning of social security in international human rights law. The 2008 definition provided by the Committee on Economic, Social and Cultural Rights (CESCR)[40] views the right to social security as protecting against lack of work-related income caused by seven contingencies (sickness, disability, maternity, employment injury, unemployment, old age, or death of a family member) as well as 'unaffordable access to health care' and 'insufficient family support, particularly for children and adult dependents'. This definition accords with the International Labour Organisation's (ILO) traditional formulation of social security for the purpose of setting standards for workers, employers and the State.[41] An additional contingency, 'general poverty and social exclusion', has been included in recent ILO documents,[42] reflecting a growing recognition that traditional work-related rights will not reach all people who need and are entitled to social security.

While the ILO's Social Protection Floor Recommendation[43] and wider international use of the term 'social protection' is drawing poverty into understandings of the scope of social security, the CESCR's narrower, worker-oriented definition of social security still has prominence in some areas of human rights law.[44] 'Work' is central to the meaning of social security in this definition since it

39 This is discussed further in 2.5.4 below.

40 Committee on Economic, Social and Cultural Rights (CESCR) '*General Comment No 19: The Right to Social Security (Art. 9)*' (2008) 39th Session 2007, E/C.12/GC/19, at para 2.

41 ILO, *Social Security (Minimum Standards) Convention*, 1952, (No. 102).

42 ILO, 'World Social Security Report 2010/11: Providing coverage in times of crisis and beyond' (ILO, 2010), at 13; Armando Barrientos and Miguel Niño-Zarazúa, 'Effects of non-contributory social transfers in developing countries. a compendium' (International Labour Office Social Security Department, 2010).

43 ILO, *Recommendation concerning National Floors of Social Protection*, 2012 (No. 202).

44 Priti Darooka (speaking on a webinar for the International Initiative to Promote Women's Rights to Social Security and Protection, on 26 April 2012, www.cdp-hrc.uottawa.ca/?p=4575) argued that the CESCR's General Comment 19 takes a workers' rights perspective rather than a human

is the absence of 'work-related income' that prompts the operation of the right. Thus, it is essential to deconstruct the meaning of 'work' as it is used in human rights law, to consider what work means for the world's women, and to redefine this core concept to better reflect these realities. This is important for two reasons: first, it means that where social security is linked to work, greater numbers of women workers should be given access to social insurance benefits by being brought within the definition of worker; and second, it suggests the concurrent need to ensure that social security, delinked from work, is also available to all who need it (often women) as a citizenship entitlement (in the forms of universal schemes and social assistance).

2.3.1 Changing nature of work

The worker around whom social security standards were designed (the formally employed, full-time, male breadwinner) is rapidly becoming a rarity in global terms. A small minority in most developing countries, this 'model' worker is disappearing even in developed economies where the nature of work is undergoing major changes with casualisation and other forms of labour market 'flexibility'. These changes, accompanied by globalisation, have resulted in growing inequality, insecurity and loss of workplace rights for people within the workforce.[45] Unemployment, under-employment and low-earning self-employment and subsistence work is a reality for most workers in developing countries and many in the developed world.[46]

2.3.2 Women and work

Social security benefits and rights typically attach primarily to formal labour and paid work. Accordingly, many forms of work in which women predominate do not create the necessary conditions for the operation of the right. As noted in Chapter 1, the majority of the world's women are excluded from the paid labour market.[47] Rapid urbanisation and globalisation is, however, seeing larger numbers of women enter the labour force, although they continue to be paid less than men.[48] Feminists have noted that the 'feminisation' of the labour force, a result

rights perspective in requiring a loss of work to access social security benefits. In commenting on an earlier version of this chapter, Diane Elson noted that women only exist as subjects of social security rights if they constitute an economic risk – otherwise they are invisible.

45 Guy Standing, *The Precariat: The New Dangerous Class* (Bloomsbury Academic, 2011) who describes this group of precarious workers as the 'denizenry' rather than the citizenry since their access to the full range of rights is circumscribed (at 14).

46 World Bank, 'World Development Report 2013: Jobs' (2012), at 48–50.

47 Ibid., at 6.

48 Shahra Razavi et al., 'Gendered Impacts of Globalization – Employment and Social Protection' (UNRISD, 2012), at xxi. Christine L. Williams, Chandra Muller and Kristine Kilanski, 'Gendered organizations in the new economy' (2012) 26 *Gender and Society*, 549, at 551, note, drawing on the work of Joan Acker, that gender is 'embedded in the organizational logic of the new economy'.

of globalisation's demand for cheap labour, has led to informalisation of work which is less remunerative and offers workers less social protection.[49] Precarious work deepens women's vulnerability and social exclusion as part of the global poor.[50] Women engaging in migrant work, much of it to provide care for people in richer countries, is on the rise, providing particular challenges for women's social security rights as non-citizens.[51]

2.3.3 Rethinking 'work'

Social security is generally linked to formal work, which is just one of the categories of work within which women are located. Even then, not all of the benefits attaching to formal work always extend to forms of formal work such as part-time or casual work in which women predominate. The small formal sector in the developing world and the shrinking formal sector in the developed world results in limited social security arising from work in most countries of the world. The past decade has seen important growth in social assistance in Latin America, Asia and Africa, often directed at women. While social assistance is usually the major form of income support where it exists, it is often minimalist in developing countries[52] and facing attrition in many developed countries. In addition, social assistance, without efforts to recognise women's existing contribution through unpaid work, to bring women into work, or to formalise informal work with attendant benefits,[53] is not enough. As Molyneux has noted, 'women want the means to escape poverty, not just the means to manage it'.[54]

Many of the types of work that women engage in, whether paid or unpaid, do not attract any form of social security.[55] In order to ensure that the right to social security accommodates all forms of labour in which women participate, 'work' requires reimagining from a gender perspective.[56] It is important to delink

49 Ibid., at xxii. Also see Rachel Sabates-Wheeler and Naila Kabeer, 'Gender equality and the extension of social protection' (16, ILO, 2003).

50 This is a reality for many women in the developed world. For a discussion of the erosion of the standard employment contract in one developed economy context and its implications for working class women, see Lucy A. Williams, 'Rethinking Social Protection Beyond Waged Work: A United States Perspective' in Beth Goldblatt and Lucie Lamarche (eds), *Women's Rights to Social Security and Social Protection*, (Hart, 2014) 145.

51 Fudge, above n 17.

52 The lack of adequate welfare safety nets in the developing world has a significant impact on women's poverty (UNRISD, 'Combating Poverty and Inequality: Structural Change, Social Policy and Politics' (2010), Section 1, Chapter 4: 'Gender Inequalities at Home and in the Market' and Section 2, Chapter 7: 'Care and Well-Being in a Development Context').

53 James Heintz and Francie Lund, 'Welfare Regimes and Social Policy: A Review of the Role of Labour and Employment' (UNRISD, 2012).

54 Maxine Molyneux, 'Cash transfers do not address the underlying causes of women's poverty', 2012, www.theguardian.com/global-development/poverty-matters/2012/mar/07/cash-transfers-not-addressing-women-poverty.

55 Even in developed countries, women perform the bulk of the unpaid caring and reproductive labour and are more exposed to precarious employment that is less likely to be regulated.

56 There is a long-standing consideration within feminist theory of the nature of women's work

Table 2.1 Categories representing women's labour and other activity

Form of labour/activity	*Paid*	*Unpaid*
Reproductive	✓ (examples: domestic and caring work outside the home, surrogacy) Note: this can be *formal* or *informal* depending on the availability of protections/benefits	✓ (examples: giving birth, caring, housework)
Productive – formal	✓ (examples: office work, factory work, professional work with protections/benefits)	✓ (examples: volunteering, unpaid interning)
Productive – informal	✓ (examples: farm work, self-employment such as hawking, piece work without protections/benefits)	✓ (examples: subsistence labour, work in family enterprises, volunteering)
Non-productive		✓ (examples: life activities such as eating, talking, resting, thinking, leisure)

notions of work from formal employment. Further, work should be understood as an activity that may not lead to payment of income. In addition, many forms of activity may not be counted as work but should still entitle those who perform them to social security rights. The right to social security should be available, as a citizenship entitlement, in those situations where people participate in society but do not necessarily have access to 'work-related income'.[57] In order to appreciate the different dimensions of women's labour and other activity, the following categories are represented in Table 2.1 and discussed below: reproductive work (unpaid and paid); productive work (formal and informal that is paid and unpaid); and non-productive activity.

Reproductive work is both unpaid work in the home and paid domestic, caring and other reproductive work such as surrogacy.[58] It can be formalised or informal. Because unpaid reproductive work (household labour and care activities) is located in the home it is deemed private and is not recognised as work. It is seen as the 'natural' responsibility of women and separate from the public world of work where labour requires remuneration and (sometimes) social security.

Productive work can be formal work that is paid[59] (recognising that this in itself is gender defined, i.e. certain jobs are reserved for women at lower status and

and its role in the production of commodities and the reproduction of labour. See, for example, Michelle Barrett, *Women's Oppression Today: Problems in Marxist Feminist Analysis* (Verso, 1981); Sylvia Walby, *Patriarchy at Work* (Polity Press, 1986).

57 For a similar argument, see Dianne Otto, 'Gendering the Right to Social Security in the Era of Crisis Governance: The Need for Transformative Strategies' in Beth Goldblatt and Lucie Lamarche (eds), *Women's Rights to Social Security and Social Protection* (Hart, 2014) 215.

58 For a discussion of reproductive labour and how it has been understood by different feminist legal scholars, see Prabha Kotiswaran, 'Abject labors, informal markets: revisiting the law's (re)production boundary', (2014) 18(1) *Employee Rights and Employment Law Journal* 353.

59 Unpaid formal work can take the form of volunteering and interning. Voluntary work in communities is most often provided by women.

pay) and informal work that is paid but unregulated. It can also include work that is unpaid such as subsistence work or work in family enterprises where women receive no income for their labour. As with unpaid reproductive work, this type of labour is 'privatised' and seen as falling outside of the market economy or the employment contract.

Note that some of these categories may be concurrent – for example, unpaid reproductive and unpaid or paid productive labour. Women may perform different types of work simultaneously – for example, by looking after children while engaging in homework for income and also undertaking unpaid subsistence work such as collecting water or looking after livestock. Paid care work is both reproductive and productive work. In fact, care work highlights the blurring of the boundaries between different categories of work that are used to justify hierarchies of reward.

Non-productive activity must also be acknowledged as a dimension of human experience. Not every person is able to engage in reproductive or productive labour due to their age, disability or illness. In addition, structural unemployment means that there are millions of men and women who are capable of work but are not in a position to do so. The added dimension of gender discrimination means that women in particular are frequently excluded, directly or indirectly, from the labour market. Yet such people are part of society and have equal entitlement to the fundamental preconditions to a dignified life.[60] In some countries a person will have to have been engaged in paid productive labour before their subsequent inability to work entitles them to social security. Non-productive activity requires recognition in the conceptualisation of social security as a social good that meets the needs of all people, regardless of their capacity or opportunity to produce.

This reformulation of the concept of 'work' within the right to social security requires the following: first, the work that women already do (reproductive and productive) should be recognised as work attracting rights to social security, including social insurance. This should occur alongside the generation of additional opportunities for work and livelihood for women,[61] and the reconception of society's approach to employment and care-giving work.[62] Second, and at the same time, social security should be understood as an entitlement, not linked to an individual's location within the labour market, provided through universal schemes or as social assistance, in a manner that promotes gender equality.

The redefinition of work within the right to social security can co-exist, without contradiction, with the delinking of work and social security. Social insurance can be an important component of social security[63] and is dependent on

60 Martha Nussbaum, *Frontiers of Justice: Disability, Nationality, Species Membership* (Harvard University Press, 2006); Martha Albertson Fineman, 'The vulnerable subject and the responsive state' (2010) 60 *Emory Law Journal* 252.

61 The right to social security is closely related to the right to livelihood and the right to work. For a discussion of the interdependence of rights, see section 2.6.

62 See Fraser, above n 38, at 612–13.

63 Social insurance is included in Article 9 of the *International Covenant on Economic, Social and Cultural Rights* as follows: 'The States Parties to the present Covenant recognize the right of everyone to social security, including social insurance.'

a definition of work. Thus, it becomes critical to redefine the notion of work, from a gender perspective, leading to a much broader reach of the work-related aspects of the right to social security. Where such redefinition and extension of work-related social security has not yet occurred or where people are not engaged in work, universal programmes and social assistance schemes become essential. These must also be expanded and redefined from a gender perspective.[64]

2.4 The right to social security at different levels

Women's work in its multiple forms is crossing borders in a range of new ways with profound implications for their working conditions, family responsibilities and entitlements. Globalisation means that a woman from country A might be employed by a company located in country B in a workplace in country C with her family remaining in country A or accompanying her to country C. The issues of transnational commerce, global work flows and multiple levels of labour regulation (or lack thereof) require a right to social security that has the flexibility to accommodate work (and its absence) across national boundaries.

Writers in the field of legal geography have employed the geographic concept of 'scale' used in mapping to focus on the impact of law and justice at different levels of spatial and legal experience.[65] Nancy Fraser has drawn on this geographic idea of scale in combination with the metaphor of justice as the balancing of scales to think about ways of applying her theory of justice in a 'post-Westphalian' world.[66] Fraser has noted an historical focus on the territorial state as the site of citizenship entitlements and a growing contemporary awareness that social and economic issues 'routinely overflow national borders'.[67] She argues that political space has been 'misframed' to exclude certain groups such as the global poor (what she terms the 'transnational precariat') from justice claims.[68] Ideas of

64 In a market economy, social insurance and other forms of retirement saving, particularly for highly paid jobs, may generate significantly larger pensions than state-provided schemes. Where women remain outside of the workforce or continue to face job interruptions due to reproductive and caring responsibilities, their material benefits on retirement are likely to be significantly smaller than other retirees who have better work-related benefits. This raises the issue of what is required for the minimum fulfilment of the right to social security in social insurance, universal and social assistance schemes to address this inequality and the financial gap it generates. Social security must be adequate to meet the needs of a dignified life. This is undoubtedly a very open and, possibly, relative idea. Defining adequacy must be related to the achievement of substantive equality, discussed in section 2.5. Also see Chapter 1, at footnote 46.

65 For a discussion of this literature, see Lisa Pruitt, 'Gender, geography and rural justice' (2008) 23 *Berkeley Journal of Gender, Law and Justice* 338. In her own approach, Pruitt combines concepts developed by legal geographers together with those of feminist geographers to understand how women's physical location contributes to their experience of law and justice, at 383.

66 Nancy Fraser, *Scales of Justice: Reimagining Political Space in a Globalizing World* (Polity Press, 2008). A 'Westphalian state' is a state committed to its territorial integrity. This term originated from the 1648 Peace of Westphalia, which is arguably the source of the modern system of international relations.

67 Fraser, ibid., at 13.

68 Nancy Fraser, 'Injustice at intersecting scales: on "social exclusion" and the "global poor"' (2010)

justice are often framed as citizenship entitlements that are restricted to members of nation states without addressing what she terms 'transborder injustices'.[69] Her concern is with the question of *who* 'counts as a bona fide subject of justice'[70] and *how* justice can be achieved rather than just *what* the idea of justice contains. She points to a growing transformative politics that reframes justice struggles at multiple levels in multiple dimensions.[71] For Fraser, 'scale' is a conceptual device or lens to ensure that justice (in all its dimensions) takes account of transnational realities in this 'politics of framing'.

Fraser's notion of 'scale' within her political theory of justice has value in developing a right to social security that has relevance and application to multinationals with workers in many countries, migrants who are often denied rights in destination countries, international bodies, arrangements between states, and so on.[72] It encourages the examination of not only the content of the right and what it promises but also the contextual realities of the subjects of the right and the agents that hold the power to realise or frustrate it.[73] These are important insights in using the right to social security to address global poverty at a range of levels and not to look only to states to accommodate the needs of their own workers and local poor. International human rights law recognises that richer countries will need to assist poorer countries through international assistance and co-operation.[74] Recent thinking and activism around transnational or extraterritorial obligations indicate that rights may have a potentially wider purview in global distributions,[75] including in relation to non-state actors.[76] Ensuring that these obligations include a clear conceptualisation of the gender dimensions of human rights is essential.

13(3) *European Journal of Social Theory* 363; Nancy Fraser, 'Social exclusion, global poverty, and scales of (in)justice: rethinking law and poverty in a globalizing world' (2011) 3 *Stellenbosch Law Review* 452.

69 Fraser, above n 66, at 2.

70 Ibid., at 5.

71 Ibid., at 22.

72 Like Thomas Pogge, she supports challenging transnational institutions but also highlights the role of social movements that struggle across boundaries in reframing global issues of justice and social exclusion. For work by Pogge on this issue, see Thomas Pogge, 'Are We Violating the Human Rights of the World's Poor?' (2011) 14(2) *Yale Human Rights and Development Law Journal* 1; Thomas Pogge (ed.), *Freedom from Poverty as a Human Right: Who Owes What to the Very Poor?* (Oxford University Press, 2007), particularly Thomas Pogge, 'Severe Poverty as a Human Rights Violation', 11–53.

73 It also requires consideration of the 'how' of rights – the politics of realising rights in a complex global context, although this is not considered in this book. (This gap is also noted in Chapter 7.)

74 The *International Covenant on Economic, Social and Cultural Rights*, Article 2; CESCR General Comment 19, above n 40, at paras 52–8, sets out international obligations with respect to the right to social security.

75 See, for example, Olivier De Schutter et al., 'Commentary to the Maastricht principles on extraterritorial obligations of states in the area of economic, social and cultural rights' (2012) 34 *Human Rights Quarterly* 1084.

76 'Maastricht principles on extraterritorial obligations of states in the area of economic, social and cultural rights', ibid., at para 12.

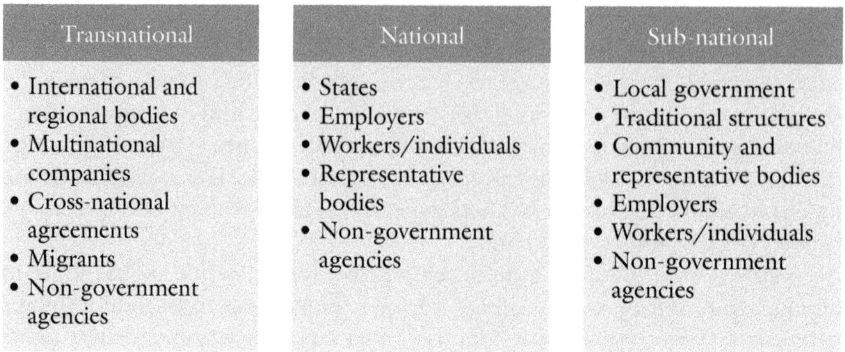

Figure 2.1 Social security actors at different levels

Susan Williams has suggested that Fraser's concept of scale can also be extended to the local or sub-national level.[77] Using the example of customary law and gender equality in South Sudan, Williams looks at Fraser's theory of justice[78] in relation to each of the three scales or levels (international, national and sub-national). Williams's additional level also has relevance for the development of the right to social security. If the right is to have value across contexts, it should be able to operate at the village or community level where women are subject to (often male) traditional leaders, local authorities and customary rules. These bodies play a role in allocating benefits and work and defining social entitlements. Private provision of social security through burial and loan societies, micro-insurance, trade union and worker association funds and so on should also be covered fully by the right. In addition, internal migration, affecting large numbers of workers in countries such as China,[79] should not lead to reduced social security rights for women.

The graphic above (Figure 1) illustrates the diversity of actors operating at the transnational, national and sub-national levels that participate in the allocation and receipt of social security benefits.

These levels overlap and intersect with each other. Thus, for example, a migrant worker should be recognised as a rights bearer by her employer, by the country in which she works, by the country from which she has migrated, and by the trade unions in both countries. Her needs and those of her family should also be covered by national and local service providers in both countries. If her employer is a multinational company originating in a third country, it should be

77 Susan H. Williams, 'Customary Law, Constitutional Law, and Women's Equality' in Kim Rubenstein and Katherine Young (eds), *The Public Law of Gender: From the Local to the Global* (Cambridge University Press, 2016) forthcoming.

78 In brief, Fraser's theory of justice entails participatory parity within the dimensions of recognition, redistribution and representation, above n 66, and see below at footnotes 107 and 108.

79 Mankui Li, 'Social Protection in China: Is There a Gender Equality Problem?' in Beth Goldblatt and Lucie Lamarche (eds), *Women's Rights to Social Security and Social Protection* (Hart, 2014) 89.

bound by laws that ensure her rights. Trade unions in the third country might have some role to play. Agreements between countries and international and regional standards also need to ensure that her rights are protected and met.[80] Social security rights need to reach women not just through state provision and regulation at the national level but also across transnational and within sub-national boundaries through the co-ordinated efforts of a range of role-players. Fraser's reframing of justice across 'scales', with Williams's modification, is a valuable lens through which to develop the right to social security as a contextually responsive and effective right.

2.5 Using equality to develop the right to social security

The chapter has engaged with the content of the right to social security from a gender perspective by redefining the meaning of work and its relationship to the right to social security. The discussion of scale has developed this further by including the multiple levels at which the right must operate to ensure its full realisation for women. This section now examines how the right to social security can be reinterpreted and developed with reference to equality as a human rights principle and a self-standing right.

2.5.1 Equality as a human right

Before examining equality within human rights usage, it should be noted that equality has been a central principle informing feminist efforts to rethink the role of the welfare state[81] and, more recently, in approaching social protection in a development context.[82] Drawing on broader feminist thinking on equality, human rights and feminist legal theorists have used the promise of the rights to equality and non-discrimination to address women's issues.[83] At the international level human rights law has consistently required equal enjoyment by men and

80 At the international law level, the *International Convention on the Protection of the Rights of All Migrant Workers and Members of Their Families*, at Article 27, requires bilateral or multilateral agreements to provide contributory social security schemes for migrants. The ILO provides for migrant workers' social security rights in *Migrant Workers (Supplementary Provisions) Convention*, 1975 (No. 143) and *Migration for Employment Convention (Revised)*, 1949 (No. 97). For a discussion of recent developments concerning the social security rights of migrant workers, see Pablo Arellano Ortiz et al. (eds) *Social Security and Migrant Workers: Selected Studies of Cross-Border Social Security Mechanisms* (Kluwer Law International, 2013).

81 See, for example, the classic article by Fraser, above n 38.

82 See, for example, Rebecca Holmes and Nicola Jones, *Gender and Social Protection in the Developing World* (Zed, 2013) who draw strongly on Nancy Fraser's ideas regarding gender equality and welfare.

83 For a discussion of this history and the nature of women's rights in international law, see Dianne Otto, 'Women's Rights' in Daniel Moeckli, Sangeeta Shah and Sandesh Sivakumaran (eds), *International Human Rights Law* (Oxford University Press, 2010) 345; for a critique of the equality approach to the interpretation of the right to social security, see Otto, above n 57.

women of all rights without discrimination on the basis of sex.[84] Feminists have both shaped and engaged with the *Convention on the Elimination of All Forms of Discrimination Against Women* (CEDAW) which is explicitly framed as an anti-discrimination document. The Committee on the Elimination of Discrimination against Women, in interpreting the Convention, has given detailed definition to the concept of substantive equality (the achievement of equality in fact, discussed more fully below).[85]

In the context of the International Covenant on Economic, Social and Cultural Rights the CESCR has also articulated an understanding of substantive equality. Its General Comment 16 on the equal rights of men and women to the enjoyment of all economic, social and cultural rights refers to 'substantive equality' that ensures the alleviation of existing inequalities and that goes beyond formal or gender-neutral responses.[86] Similarly, the Committee's General Comment 20 on non-discrimination refers to substantive discrimination and equality.[87]

In many international, regional and domestic jurisdictions and forums, equality/non-discrimination is a central paradigm for feminist legal engagement. Claims relating to both status and distributive issues in the family, the workplace, the economy and to sharing of social goods have been brought under equality guarantees. Even violence, reproduction, pornography and other traditional 'private sphere' issues have increasingly been framed in equality terms.[88] Legal scholars attempting to use international human rights, constitutional equality guarantees and anti-discrimination laws to address gender disadvantage have engaged in complex debates over the contested meaning of equality.[89] Important insights have emerged in recent years from Canadian scholars and lawyers who put energy into developing a progressive equality jurisprudence under their Charter of Rights and Freedoms.[90] Similar engagement has occurred in South

84 See the *International Covenant on Civil and Political Rights*, Article 3; the *International Covenant on Economic, Social and Cultural Rights*, Article 3; the *Convention on the Rights of Persons with Disabilities*, Article 3(g); the *Convention on the Rights of the Child*, Article 2.

85 CEDAW, *General recommendation No. 25, on Article 4, Paragraph 1, of the Convention on the Elimination of All Forms of Discrimination against Women, on temporary special measures* (2004) 30th Session, UN Doc A/59/38, annex I.

86 CESCR, *General Comment No. 16, Article 3: the equal right of men and women to the enjoyment of all economic, social and cultural rights* (2005) 34th Session 2005, E/C.12/2005/3, paras 7 and 8.

87 CESCR, *General Comment No. 20, Non-discrimination in economic, social and cultural rights (art. 2, para. 2, of the* International Covenant on Economic, Social and Cultural Rights) (2009) 42nd Session 2009, E/C.12/GC/20, paras 8 and 9.

88 As discussed by Catharine A. MacKinnon, *Are Women Human? And Other International Dialogues* (Harvard University Press, 2006), at 105–11, who praises Canadian feminist lawyers for successfully influencing the jurisprudence of the Supreme Court of Canada to extend equality principles to issues such as sexual harassment and pornography.

89 Some of the US scholars include: Martha Minow, *Making All the Difference* (Harvard University Press, 1990); Catharine A. MacKinnon, *Feminism Unmodified: Discourses on Life and Law* (Harvard University Press, 1987); Deborah L. Rhode, *Justice and Gender: Sex Discrimination and the Law* (Harvard University Press, 1989).

90 See, for example, Fay Faraday, Margaret Denike and M. Kate Stephenson, *Making Equality Rights Real: Securing Substantive Equality Under the Charter* (Irwin Law, 2009).

Africa following the enactment of the post-Apartheid constitutions with strong equality guarantees.[91] Many important contributions have emerged from elsewhere in the world.[92] Substantive equality, which is central to this body of work, is now discussed.

2.5.2 *Substantive equality*

Formal approaches to equality that require the same treatment for women as for men, while essential, have proved inadequate to address the underlying inequalities that privilege men in society. Formal equality treats everyone alike without regard to their actual circumstances. This abstract and supposedly neutral approach has been criticised for failing to acknowledge the existing patterns of group-based inequalities in society. For example, allowing women to stand for political office will not necessarily lead to equal numbers of men and women in parliament if the culture in political parties is patriarchal and women fail to get onto party lists. Without deeper, structural change, the patterns of gender-based disadvantage will continue and women will simply be assimilated into a male social and legal order without significant improvement to their position.[93]

This has led to claims for 'substantive equality' whereby underlying inequalities are addressed either through similar or differential treatment, depending on the circumstances. This approach to equality requires an analysis of the context in which the discrimination occurred and pays attention to systemic inequality and the impact of the harmful act or measures to address it.[94] Substantive equality sees affirmative action, special measures or positive measures to address inequality as part of equality rather than as exceptions to it.[95] Substantive equality can

91 See, for example, Catherine Albertyn and Beth Goldblatt, 'Facing the challenge of transformation: difficulties in the development of an indigenous jurisprudence of equality' (1998) 14 *South African Journal on Human Rights* 248; Catherine Albertyn and Elsje Bonthuys, *Gender, Law and Justice* (Juta, 2007), at 82–119.

92 See examples cited in Sandra Fredman, 'Comparative study of anti-discrimination and equality laws of the US, Canada, South Africa and India' (European Commission, 2012).

93 Sandra Fredman, 'Beyond the Dichotomy of Formal and Substantive Equality: Towards a New Definition of Equal Rights' in Ineke Boerefijn et al. (eds), *Temporary Special Measures: Accelerating de facto Equality of Women under Article 4(1) UN Convention on the Elimination of All Forms of Discrimination Against Women* (Intersentia, 2003) 111, who also discusses other critiques of formal equality including that: 1) it is a relative concept – thus men and women can be treated equally badly or well; 2) benefits can be removed from a relatively privileged group to equalise (levelling down); and, 3) specific measures to advantage previously disadvantaged groups can be seen as discrimination (at 112–13).

94 Nedelsky, above n 22, at 160–2 and 186–9, argues for the recognition of equal moral worth as the starting point of any equality pursuit followed by detailed contextual enquiries to 'know what it would take to give effect to equal moral worth, to actually treat every person as inherently equal', at 162.

95 These three terms all concern measures to promote people from disadvantaged groups. For a discussion of these terms, see Fredman, above n 36. Other terms commonly found in discrimination law are direct and indirect discrimination: direct gender discrimination occurs when a law, policy

itself have a range of meanings and purposes.[96] It can be used to achieve 'equality of opportunity' by ensuring that everyone shares the same starting point; or it can go further in requiring 'equality of results' where the outcomes of equality measures are judged to see whether they have resulted in change.

However, even this substantive equality approach has been criticised for not being sufficiently far-reaching.[97] Thus, the proportion of women in a particular job type might increase due to affirmative policies but this may be a result of women paying large portions of their income on childcare because the broader structural issues of care have not been addressed. It may also not be long-lasting as it may lead to a devaluing of that type of job over time.[98]

Some feminist anti-discrimination scholars have argued for a substantive equality leading to 'transformation' that entails a fundamental restructuring of society to address gender inequality.[99] Fredman describes 'equality as transformation' as:[100]

> a restructuring (of) society so that it is no longer male-defined. Transformation requires a redistribution of power and resources and a change in the institutional structures which perpetuate women's oppression. It requires a dismantling of the public-private divide, and a reconstruction of the public world so that child-care and parenting are seen as valued common responsibilities of both parents and the community. It aims to facilitate the full expression of women's capabilities and choices, and the full participation of women in society.

The CEDAW Committee has also stressed the link between substantive equality and transformation. It noted, in General Recommendation 25, that:[101]

or practice overtly discriminates against women. Indirect gender discrimination occurs when a law, policy or practice appears to be gender-neutral but impacts most severely on women. For example, where a law privileges tall and strong people for a particular job it may have the effect of precluding most women from successfully applying for the job.

96 Albertyn distinguishes between a liberal egalitarian model of substantive equality and a more radical or critical idea of substantive equality, Catherine Albertyn, 'Gendered transformation in South African jurisprudence: poor women and the constitutional court' (2011) 3 *Stellenbosch Law Review* 591, at 605–7.

97 Fredman, above n 93, at 115.

98 Ibid., at 114–15.

99 See, for example, Catherine Albertyn, 'Substantive equality and transformation in South Africa' (2007) 23(2) *South African Journal on Human Rights* 253. Albertyn and Goldblatt, above n 91, at 249, argue for: 'a complete reconstruction of the state and society, including a redistribution of power and resources along egalitarian lines. The challenge of achieving equality within this transformation project involves the eradication of systemic forms of domination and material disadvantage based on race, gender, class and other grounds of inequality. It also entails the development of opportunities which allow people to realise their full human potential within positive social relationships.'

100 Fredman, above n 36, at 115.

101 CEDAW, *General recommendation No. 25, on Article 4, Paragraph 1, of the Convention on the Elimination of All Forms of Discrimination against Women, on temporary special measures* (2004) 30th Session, UN Doc A/59/38, annex I, para 10.

> The position of women will not be improved as long as the underlying causes of discrimination against women, and of their inequality, are not effectively addressed. The lives of women and men must be considered in a contextual way, and measures adopted towards a real transformation of opportunities, institutions and systems so that they are no longer grounded in historically determined male paradigms of power and life patterns.

2.5.3 *Transformative substantive equality*

The transformative understanding of substantive equality offers a valuable means of developing the right to social security in a way that fundamentally challenges existing structures of subordination and disadvantage. Sandra Fredman's 'multi-dimensional concept of substantive equality pursuing four overlapping aims'[102] is used here to further develop the right to social security from a gender perspective:

> First, it aims to break the cycle of disadvantage associated with status or out-groups. This reflects the redistributive dimension of equality. Secondly, it aims to promote respect for dignity and worth, thereby redressing stigma, stereotyping, humiliation, and violence because of membership of an identity group. This reflects a recognition dimension. Thirdly, it should not exact conformity as a price of equality. Instead, it should accommodate difference and aim to achieve structural change. This captures the transformative dimension. Finally, substantive equality should facilitate full participation in society, both socially and politically. This is the participative dimension.[103]

In formulating this concept of equality, Fredman draws on the work of Amartya Sen and Martha Nussbaum whose capabilities approach requires attention to the constraints on people's capacities to exercise choice. The capabilities approach, formulated for use in development theory, has a strong gender dimension.[104] It requires a distribution of those resources in society that provide the liberties and opportunities for individuals to function fully as humans with dignity.[105]

102 Fredman, above n 36, at Chapter 1.

103 Sandra Fredman, 'The potential and limits of an equal rights paradigm in addressing poverty' (2011) 3 *Stellenbosch Law Review* 566, at 577; for a general discussion of Fredman's approach to equality as a positive right, see Sandra Fredman, *Human Rights Transformed: Positive Rights and Positive Duties* (Oxford University Press, 2008), at 175–203.

104 Amartya Sen, *Development as Freedom* (Oxford University Press, 1999); Martha Nussbaum, *Women and Human Development: The Capabilities Approach* (Cambridge University Press, 2000). Both writers have explored the implications of their approach as it relates to human rights (with some differences about the value of a human rights approach). See Martha Nussbaum, 'Capabilities and human rights' (1997) 66(2) *Fordham Law Review* 273; Martha Nussbaum, 'Women's Capabilities and Social Justice' in Maxine Molyneux and Shahra Razavi (eds), *Gender Justice, Development, and Rights* (Oxford University Press, 2002) 45; Amartya Sen, 'Elements of a theory of human rights' (2004) 32(4) *Philosophy and Public Affairs* 315; Amartya Sen, 'Human rights and capabilities' (2005) 6(2) *Journal of Human Development* 151.

105 However, Fredman notes her concerns with the capabilities approach. She argues that, while it is

Fredman also draws on the work of Nancy Fraser and Iris Marion Young in examining distributive and status-based disadvantage and emphasising the importance of participation in ensuring equal citizenship.[106] Fraser's conception of justice is of 'parity of participation' which requires social arrangements that allow 'all members of society to interact with one another as peers'.[107] This requires material distribution, a status order ensuring equal respect, and equal political voice (redistribution, recognition and representation).[108]

Fredman's articulation of the features of substantive equality makes it a valuable theoretical and practical tool. It offers both a normative understanding of equality as a central feature of justice and an interpretive approach to equality as a right or legal principle. In this latter respect, equality can be operationalised in relation to the interpretation of other human rights.

The substantive equality framework assists in understanding the multi-dimensional nature of inequality as it affects women's experience of social security. Thus, for example, obtaining a smaller pension on retirement because of child-rearing responsibilities and lower income over a lifetime denies women their equal rights to social security. They face economic disadvantage, lower social status and less control over their life choices. The underlying conditions that create this disadvantage are not being addressed and their voices and views are not shaping new responses to these circumstances.[109] A social security right that is interpreted in terms of this approach to substantive equality must be a right that addresses the material dimensions of women's unequal status in the economy that result in women earning less and consequently suffering disadvantage in relation to social security (redistribution). It must also take account of factors such as stereotyping that prevent women from accessing certain forms of work or controlling social security payments within households (recognition). It must be a right that does not simply extend existing male-oriented social security

valuable, it is minimalistic and also individualistic with regard to social relationships and issues of care: Sandra Fredman, 'Engendering Social and Economic Rights' in Beth Goldblatt and Kirsty McLean (eds), *Women's Social and Economic Rights: Developments in South Africa* (Juta, 2011) 4.

106 Fredman (2011), above n 103, at 577–8; Fredman, ibid., at 17–18. Participation has been considered a human rights principle in relation to issues of gender and social security: Special Rapporteur on extreme poverty and human rights, Report to Human Rights Council, 23rd Session, A/HRC/23/36; Hester Lessard, 'Participatory Inclusion and Women's Rights to Social Security' in Beth Goldblatt and Lucie Lamarche (eds), *Women's Rights to Social Security and Social Protection* (Hart, 2014) 41. It has been considered more generally by the Working Group on the issue of discrimination against women in law and in practice, '*Report of the Working Group on the issue of discrimination against women in law and in practice (political representation and participation)*', (Human Rights Council (23rd Session), 2013) A/HRC/23/50.

107 Fraser (2011), above n 68, at 455; Nancy Fraser, 'Social Justice in the Age of Identity Politics' in Nancy Fraser and Axel Honneth (eds), *Redistribution or Recognition? A Political-Philosophical Exchange* (Verso, 2003) 7.

108 Fraser explains that remedying injustice that is transformative involves 'correcting inequitable outcomes … by restructuring the underlying generative framework' in Nancy Fraser, *Adding Insult to Injury: Nancy Fraser Debates Her Critics* (Verso, 2008), at 28.

109 Further applications of Fredman's substantive equality approach are found in the country studies in Chapters 4, 5 and 6 below.

models to women but requires a fundamental restructuring of such systems (transformation). Lastly, it must be a right that requires the involvement of women in the design and management of appropriate forms of social security and encourages their inclusion in society (participation).

Before examining how this substantive equality approach might inform the development of principles for the interpretation of the right to social security in the concluding section of this chapter, a further feature of equality, multiple and intersectional discrimination, is briefly discussed.

2.5.4 *Multiple and intersectional discrimination*

Gender discrimination cannot be understood with reference to the experience of one group of women alone. It occurs alongside many other forms of discrimination such as race, age and disability. Forms of gender discrimination may affect women of one economic class differently from another and may take very different forms in different cultural contexts.

This recognition emerges from a history of engagement within feminism about representation of different groups of women. The Black feminist movement in the US, as well as postmodern and post-colonial feminists, have suggested that white, developed world feminists have used a white, middle-class, heterosexual standard for the 'woman' that feminism is trying to liberate (essentialism) and, in so doing, have ignored the differences between women.[110] Some writers have criticised western feminism for its gender and cultural essentialism in treating women in developing countries as 'victim subjects' without agency and devoid of differences.[111] These criticisms have been important in shifting debates within feminism to recognise differences amongst women.[112]

Intersectionality is a response to and an extension of the anti-essentialist argument. Crenshaw, its originator, has explained that the intersection of multiple differences such as race and gender create new forms of disadvantage that anti-discrimination law has been unable to address.[113] Her response (both political and legal) is to place those most marginalised at the centre as the most effective way to address a variety of disadvantages. Intersectionality is being increasingly incorporated into international human rights law.[114] Sandra Fredman has considered its relationship to her four dimensional substantive equality approach by

110 See, for example, Angela Harris, 'Race and Essentialism in Feminist Legal Theory' (1989–90) 42 *Stanford Law Review* 581; Marlee Klein, 'Race, Racism, and Feminist Legal Theory' (1989) 12 *Harvard Women's Law Journal* 115.

111 Ratna Kapur, 'The tragedy of victimisation rhetoric: resurrecting the "native" subject in international/postcolonial feminist legal politics' (2002) 15 *Harvard Human Rights Law Journal* 1.

112 Nancy Fraser, 'Equality, Difference and Democracy: Recent Feminist Debates in the United States' in Jodi Dean (ed.), *Feminism and the New Democracy* (Sage, 1997) 98.

113 Kimberle Crenshaw, 'Demarginalizing the intersection of race and sex: a black feminist critique of antidiscrimination doctrine, feminist theory and antiracist politics' (1989) *University of Chicago Legal Forum* 139.

114 Beth Goldblatt, 'Intersectionality in international anti-discrimination law – addressing poverty in its complexity' (2015) 21(1) *Australian Journal of Human Rights* 47.

mapping intersectionality onto each of these dimensions.[115] She argues that this leads to a 'closer relationship between aims (of equality) and group demarcation (which) makes it possible to identify those groups who should be the focus of attention in positive duties and how their claims should rank in the order of priorities'.[116]

Intersectionality has, however, come under recent criticism within feminism by writers who suggest that a focus on increasing numbers of disadvantaged groups renders anti-discrimination law inoperable; that the problem with reducing identity to categories such as race and gender is perpetuated through intersectional analysis; and that the focus on representation means that the deeper structural foundations of inequality are not unearthed.[117]

The understanding of discrimination against women used in this book is informed by an awareness of multiple and intersectional discrimination. This understanding takes account of the concerns with intersectionality but remains convinced that the concept has value if incorporated into a substantive equality approach that is transformative. The development of the social security right, informed by this transformative substantive equality approach, requires careful attention to the particular context in which women are located. The right must be equally effective for an elderly widow living in a rural area in India facing caste discrimination as it is for a lesbian sole mother employed in part-time work in Portugal or a married migrant from the Philippines employed as a domestic worker in Saudi Arabia.[118] Close attention to diversity, vulnerability, the structural nature of inequality and the complexity of discrimination must underpin a gendered interpretation of the right to social security.

2.6 Interdependence – a role for other rights

The right to equality has been given a central position in the development of women's social and economic rights, as it has in the development of the right to social security in this book. This close relationship is supported by the principle of international human rights law that human rights are universal, indivisible, interrelated and interdependent.[119] Understanding the nature of gender and other status-based disadvantage assists in understanding the complex nature of socio-economic deprivation. At the same time, inequality faced by women cannot be properly explained without exploring material disadvantage. Thus, although

115 Sandra Fredman, 'Positive Rights and Duties: Addressing Intersectionality' in Dagmar Schiek and Victoria Chege (eds), *European Union Non-Discrimination Law: Comparative Perspectives on Multidimensional Equality Law* (Routledge-Cavendish, 2008), 73.

116 Ibid., at 84.

117 See, for example, the chapters in Emily Grabham, Davina Cooper, J. Krishnadas and Didi Herman (eds), *Intersectionality and Beyond: Law, Power and the Politics of Location* (Routledge, 2009).

118 Recognition of a plurality of family forms within and between different societies is essential in developing appropriate rights frameworks. See Holmes and Jones, above n 82, at 30 and 35–61.

119 *Vienna Declaration and Programme of Action* (1993) adopted by the World Conference on Human Rights, 25 June 1993, A/CONF.157/23, Part 1, at para 5.

the right to equality may be understood as a civil or political right relating to women's status in society, it is closely related to the social and economic rights that affect women's material position. Developing appropriate interpretations of rights requires an awareness of this close relationship.[120]

Additionally, other rights have relevance in interpreting the right to social security.[121] Social and economic rights such as the right to an adequate standard of living, the right to work and the right to health have a close association with the right to social security. Others such as the right to education and the right to housing also relate to social security and its provision. Civil and political rights such as the right to security of person are important in ensuring that women are able to benefit from social security free from violence. Dignity, a value underlying many civil and political rights, also has special relevance for the enjoyment of social and economic rights.[122] Attention to dignity requires an appreciation of the ways in which poverty undermines women's humanity and worth. Social security measures should be designed to ensure both a material impact and an impact on the way in which women recipients are accorded respect. Acknowledgment of the interdependence of human rights will assist in ensuring the fullest application of the right to social security for women.

2.7 Developing the right to social security from a gender perspective

As discussed,[123] feminists have identified a range of concerns with the way in which the economy, the State and society are structured to the disadvantage of women and the consequent negative impact on their rights to social security. Some of these concerns include: the failure to recognise care as work; the under-valuing of women's work; the linking of benefits to formal employment; the erosion of formal employment and of the welfare state with particular impacts on poor women and sole mothers; the inadequacy of women's pensions; the sometimes onerous conditions attached to social assistance; the failure to provide

120 Sandra Liebenberg and Beth Goldblatt, 'The interrelationship between equality and socio-economic rights in South Africa's transformative constitution' (2007) 23 *South African Journal on Human Rights* 335. Also see Gwen Brodsky and Shelagh Day, 'Beyond the social and economic rights debate: substantive equality speaks to poverty' (2002) 14(1) *Canadian Journal of Women and the Law* 185; Dianne Otto, 'Defending Women's Economic and Social Rights: Some Thoughts on Indivisibility and a New Standard of Equality' in Isfahan Merali and Valerie Oosterveld (eds), *Giving Meaning to Economic, Social and Cultural Rights* (University of Pennsylvania Press, 2001) 52.

121 See CESCR, above n 40, at para 28.

122 The 'inherent dignity' of humans is referred to in the Preamble and in Article 10 of the *International Covenant on Civil and Political Rights*. Also see, Sandra Liebenberg, 'Value of human dignity in interpreting socio-economic rights' (2005) 21(1) *South African Journal on Human Rights* 1; Barbara Y. Phillips, 'Dignity and Human Rights: A Missing Dialogue?' (PWESCR, 2011); Marilyn Waring et al., *Anticipatory Social Protection: Claiming dignity and rights* (Commonwealth Secretariat, 2013).

123 Above, in section 2.2, and in Chapter 1.

social protection to the poor in the context of the feminisation of poverty; the failure to accommodate the circumstances and wishes of women in the design and implementation of social security programmes; and the failure to use social security, as one component of social policy, to challenge problematic gender roles and relationships in society.

This chapter has considered ways of redefining and developing the right to social security to enhance its capacity to address these concerns. It has followed two different routes to achieve this. First, it has developed the content of the right by reconceiving the idea of work that underlies the traditional definition of social security. It has suggested that work, understood from a gender perspective, should include a range of activities involving reproductive and productive labour that is currently unpaid, paid, informal and formal. It has also argued that the right to social security is a human entitlement regardless of an individual's capacity to participate in productive/reproductive labour. In addition, it has noted that the right to social security should have effect transnationally and at all levels within countries so that women may benefit wherever they are located. Fraser's ideas of 'scale' and Williams's modification of this concept are useful lenses for ensuring that the right to social security is able to address the challenges of globalisation.

Second, the chapter has developed the right to social security with reference to the right to equality using a transformative substantive equality approach best articulated by Fredman. Equality has been given a major role in the development of the right to social security from a gender perspective because of the centrality of this foundational value in feminism and because of the important principle of non-discrimination against women in international law.[124] Fredman's four-dimensional approach to substantive equality, used to address gender discrimination, encompasses the following: equality in the *redistribution* of resources to meet the needs of women facing disadvantage; *recognition* of women's dignity, integrity and worth; full *representation* and inclusion of women; and *transformation* of unequal gendered structures of society. Ensuring substantive gender equality also involves recognition of women's differences and the multiple and intersecting forms of discrimination that different groups of women face. Applying this to the interpretation of the right to social security requires a careful consideration of each of the four dimensions as they relate to women's experiences of social security.

The following section now combines the equality framework with the reconceived content of the right (based on the proposed ideas about work) to set out seven principles for a redeveloped right to social security from a gender perspective. It should be added that the CESCR's General Comment 19, in addition to requiring that social security be provided to address a list of contingencies,

124 However, it has also been argued above at 2.6 that the right to social security should be complemented by the full range of human rights based on the principle of the interdependence of rights.

also requires that a social security system is available, adequate and accessible.[125] These elements are built into some of the principles developed below.

2.7.1 Principles for a substantively equal, gendered right to social security

The principles for a substantively equal, gendered right to social security serve a dual purpose. First, they provide a normative basis against which to test the current realisation of the right to social security as it affects men and women. Second, they provide a principled, rights-based framework for ensuring improved design and implementation of social security policies and programmes that advance gender equality.

1. *Women's* ***reproductive*** *labour and care work* (of children, the sick, elderly and disabled) *must be recognised and supported and care must be understood as a responsibility of the whole society.* This fundamental feminist principle has important implications for the right to social security. Providing the right in a substantively equal way requires ensuring that social security measures do not discriminate against women due to their reproductive and caring functions. Framed positively, this means that social security systems must overcome substantive inequalities in the distribution of care. The right can play a redistributive role in allocating resources to care work. It can also address the negative value attached to this work and therefore fulfil the recognition dimension of substantive equality. It should bring men into care (ensuring transformation of gender relations) and challenge fixed notions of family (rather than State) responsibility for care. The participation dimension requires considering the views of carers as well as those in their care in designing improved social responses to care that enable women's greater participation in society. Attention to the transnational dimensions of care will make the right more responsive to migrant labour and other features of the 'global care chain'.
2. *Women's other* ***unpaid work*** *such as in subsistence production and family industries must be recognised and supported for the purpose of social security.* The recognition, redistribution, participation and transformation dimensions of substantive equality are very apparent as they apply to this issue: women as a disadvantaged group require material and social acknowledgement of their labour and a voice in decisions relating to this work and the social security entitlements that attach to it. The cultural, religious and other barriers that render women's work invisible require transformative responses to which a right to social security can contribute.
3. *Women's work in the* ***informal*** *sector, in the many forms this takes, requires an accompanying right to social security.* This entails the recognition and protection of work that is often hidden from view (such as home-based work) or

125 Above n 40, at paras 10–27.

is purposefully unregulated (such as in free trade zones). Precarious work within and across borders requires a right that is responsive on a global scale.

4. *Women's work must be valued and attract sufficient and equal social security.* Even within **formal** employment, where social security exists, there are gender inequalities. Equal pay, a long-standing demand of the women's movement, has not yet been achieved. Low pay for women reflects the value ascribed to the types of work that women perform – work that is related to caring is associated with unpaid caring work and is often the domain of women workers who receive poor remuneration and have low status. In addition, work interruptions and part-time work necessitated by caring responsibilities lead to smaller accrued benefits for women who, as a result, may have insufficient resources to support a decent standard of living in their retirement. A right to social security that fails to acknowledge these problems will perpetuate this structural inequality.
5. *Social security must be provided to all women who* ***need*** *it, regardless of their relationship to work.*[126] Gendered understandings of dependency across the life cycle and the nature of human vulnerability and need should inform the right to social security. This has important recognition and redistribution dimensions and requires a transformative approach to supporting those in need of care and those providing care. The participation of vulnerable groups is central to the development of appropriate social security.
6. *The* ***design*** *of social security systems must promote gender equality.*[127] The issue of transnational work should also be addressed in this design as should provision at the sub-national level. Participation of women affected is central to ensuring that gender issues are addressed. A right that is responsive to the needs of different groups of women is critical.[128] The transformation dimension of substantive equality requires the reform and creation of social security systems that challenge gender inequality in society. Such systems must operate to advance gender equality at national and sub-national levels and interact with regional and national bodies to protect women migrants.
7. *Women must have full and equal* ***access*** *to social security.*[129] Issues of illiteracy, violence, culture and other factors that affect women's ability to access the right are important. The recognition dimension of substantive equality is central to access, but redistribution will also be needed to address many of the barriers women face. Access also relates to issues of dignity, choice and agency in providing appropriate services that take account of women's (diverse) needs and views. Transforming the unequal power relations that

126 This relates to the 'availability' dimension of the right.

127 This is articulated elegantly in *Report on the question of human rights and extreme poverty submitted by Magdalena Sepúlveda Carmona, independent expert on the question of human rights and extreme poverty* (2010) GA 65th Session, A/65/259, at 21–2. Also see Sepúlveda and Nyst, above n 3, at 34–7.

128 This relates to the 'adequacy' dimension of the right.

129 This relates to the 'accessibility' dimension of the right.

limit women's access is essential if the right is to have meaning for all men and women.

2.8 Conclusion

This chapter has developed a conceptual framework and a set of principles for the interpretation and development of the right to social security from a gender perspective. These draw on feminist theory and feminist legal theory in unseating dominant conceptions of work that underlie the right to social security. As Joanne Conaghan puts it:[130]

> There is clearly an interconnection between how we understand gender roles, attributions, and relations and how we approach the allocation of socially necessary tasks. This is manifest not only in the material realities of people's lives in which men and women must learn to navigate the structural and relational constraints imposed by deeply gendered working arrangements but also in the realm of socio-cultural and/or symbolic expression where gender and labour often coalesce in processes of value and meaning conferral, making labour a signifier of gender and vice-versa. Thus understood, gender and labour interact symbiotically to mutually constitute and reinforce one another.

Understanding the relationship between labour and gender is a long-standing preoccupation of feminists and continues to engage feminist legal scholars concerned with labour law and related fields including social security law. This chapter has participated in the process of re-examining the key concepts of gender and work as they give meaning to the human right to social security. This re-examination has potential significance for the restructuring of social security systems but also has implications for broader questions of social, political and economic organisation.

The framework and the principles for a substantively equal, gendered right to social security are concretely applied in the remainder of the book through a critical analysis of the way in which certain of the human rights treaty bodies understand, approach and interpret the right to social security; and through an assessment of the extent to which the right is being realised for women in three different countries. This application of the framework to the international law and the country studies demonstrates its usefulness as both an evaluative tool and a guide to inform change within countries and internationally.

130 Joanne Conaghan, 'Gender and the Idea of Labour Law' (2014) 4(1) *feminists@law* 1, at 2.

3 The right to social security in international law

A gendered consideration

3.1 Introduction

This chapter sets out the history and sources of the right to social security in international law (in 3.2). It gives particular attention to the way gender is understood in relation to the right by the United Nations (UN) Committees responsible for the *Convention on the Elimination of All Forms of Discrimination against Women* (CEDAW) (in 3.3) and the *International Covenant on Economic, Social and Cultural Rights* (ICESCR) (in 3.4). It also considers the work of the International Labour Organisation (ILO) (in 3.5) and the UN Special Rapporteur on extreme poverty and human rights (in 3.6) as they relate to the right to social security from a gender perspective.

The ILO, the Special Rapporteur and the Committee on Economic, Social and Cultural Rights (CESCR) have been selected for special consideration because they are the UN bodies most centrally concerned with the interpretation of the right to social security. The CEDAW Committee has been chosen because of its focus on women in relation to the right to social security. While other treaty bodies and mandate holders under the special procedures of the Human Rights Council have considered the right to social security from a gender perspective, complementing the broad normative approach of the four main bodies to be examined, this chapter does not attempt to provide a comprehensive survey of all international law on this topic.

The chapter draws on the gender perspective developed in Chapter 2 in its examination of the international law considered here. It analyses this law in light of the conceptual framework and principles for a substantively equal, gendered right to social security set out in that chapter.

3.2 History and sources of the right

The term 'social security' originated in the United States' *Social Security Act* 1934.[1] Although both the term and the idea of a right to social security were

1 Jef Van Langendonck, 'The Meaning of the Right to Social Security' in Jef Van Langendonck (ed.), *The Right to Social Security* (Intersentia, 2007) 3, 4.

new, social protection measures had existed in a number of countries for many decades, originating in 1880s Germany when Bismarck set up a social security system to 'pacify public unrest'.[2] The measures in this system were primarily aimed at supporting unemployed, sick, disabled and aged workers.

Reference to social security appeared in international law in the *Declaration of Philadelphia* 1944, adopted by the International Labour Conference, which listed as one of the obligations of the International Labour Organisation (ILO) at III(f):

> the extension of social security measures to provide a basic income to all in need of such protection and comprehensive medical care.

The use of the words 'all in need' is significant in denoting that social security should be available to everyone regardless of their status as a worker or a non-worker. The obligation to provide a basic income suggests that anyone who cannot obtain employment or income sufficient for an adequate standard of living is entitled to state assistance. This puts the obligation on states rather than individuals to accommodate the deficiencies of the market and other structural contributors that result in poverty.

3.2.1 The Universal Declaration of Human Rights

The recognition of a right to social security first appeared in 1948 in Article 22 of the *Universal Declaration of Human Rights* (UDHR) as follows:

> Everyone, as a member of society, has the right to social security and is entitled to realisation, through national effort and international co-operation and in accordance with the organisation and resources of each State, of the economic, social and cultural rights indispensable for his dignity and the free development of his personality.

Interestingly, despite their application of the right to social security in practice, the Communist countries abstained from the vote on social and economic rights within the UDHR as they were seen as inadequate,[3] while developing countries failed to participate in the debate about Article 22, probably because it seemed for them, unachievable.[4]

Article 25 of the UDHR is closely related to Article 22:

2 Eibe Reidel, 'The Human Right to Social Security: Some Challenges' in Eibe Reidel (ed.), *Social Security as a Human Right* (Springer, 2007) 17, 19.

3 Henry J. Steiner and Philip Alston, *International Human Rights in Context: Law, Politics, Morals* (Oxford University Press, 3rd edn, 2008), at 264.

4 Van Langendonck, above n 1, at 5. For a full discussion of the drafting history of Articles 22 and 25, see Johannes Morsink, *The Universal Declaration of Human Rights: Origins, Drafting and Intent* (University of Pennsylvania Press, 1999), 191–238.

> (1) Everyone has the right to a standard of living adequate for the health and well-being of himself and of his family, including food, clothing, housing and medical care and necessary social services, and the right to security in the event of unemployment, sickness, disability, widowhood, old age or other lack of livelihood in circumstances beyond his control.
> (2) Motherhood and childhood are entitled to special care and assistance. All children, whether born in or out of wedlock, shall enjoy the same social protection.

Article 22 provides the right to social security to 'everyone, as a member of society', whereas Article 25 is more qualified in extending the right only in situations of contingency such as unemployment and disability. Article 25 does however refer to 'other lack of livelihood', implying that poverty and structural factors that make an adequate standard of living impossible are included in the meaning of 'circumstances beyond his control'. The broader objectives of the right to social security in Article 22 (along with other economic, social and cultural rights) to achieve dignity and free development of personality suggest that the purpose of the right goes beyond a narrow economic one. The reference to 'health and well-being' in Article 25 similarly implies that social security should meet more than just the survival needs of rights holders. As will be seen in the discussion below,[5] the CESCR, in interpreting the right to social security in the ICESCR, has taken a narrower, worker-based approach than is implied by the wording of the UDHR. The male language in both Articles and the sexist assumption in Article 25(1) that the right attaches specifically to men for themselves and their families are notable. Article 25(2), in referring to motherhood, uses gender-specific and protective language rather than promising parental rights for men and women. (While pregnancy requires specific rights, other aspects of parenting that are not premised on biology also require recognition and protection.)

3.2.2 The International Covenant on Economic, Social and Cultural Rights

It took from 1948 until 1966 for the social and economic rights in the UDHR to be included in a binding treaty of general application.[6] The *International Covenant on Economic, Social and Cultural Rights* (ICESCR) was adopted by the General Assembly on 16 December 1966 and entered into force on 3 January 1976.[7] Article 9 of the ICESCR sets out the right to social security as follows:

5 And as discussed in Chapter 2.

6 Social and economic rights had, however, been included in international instruments by the ILO since it began its work in 1919.

7 ICESCR (1966) 993 UNTS 3. It was only in 1987 that an expert body, the Committee on Economic, Social and Cultural Rights (CESCR), was established to consider compliance with the Covenant by states parties. (This was preceded by a Working Group of Government Experts established in 1982). On 10 December 2008, the General Assembly adopted an Optional Protocol

> The States Parties to the present Covenant recognize the right of everyone to social security, including social insurance.

The inclusion of social insurance in the right to social security followed debates about whether to keep the right general and open or to specify its meaning in more detail.[8] While social insurance was widely seen as implicit in the meaning of social security, there was agreement to explicitly include it.[9] The right to social insurance, likened to a 'property right' that 'cannot be subject to discretionary administration', was included to secure the entitlements of contributing members to benefits.[10] Aside from this addition, the text is sparse and the Covenant, unlike the UDHR, does not contain an elaboration of the right. The existence of the ILO, which had been established in 1919 as an independent organisation and became a specialised agency of the United Nations after the Second World War with a specific mandate to establish labour standards that included social security,[11] may explain this omission. The drafters were of the view that Article 9 was to be understood with reference to ILO *Social Security (Minimum Standards) Convention*, 1952, (No. 102) (as discussed below).[12] The ILO was regarded as the international agency responsible for the 'implementation and promotion of the right to social security'.[13]

3.2.3 Other sources of the right

ILO *Social Security (Minimum Standards) Convention*, 1952, (No. 102) is described as the 'flagship' convention on social security as it is the most comprehensive of the conventions and deals with all nine branches of social security.[14] These are: medical care; sickness benefit; unemployment benefit; old-age benefit; employment injury benefit; family benefit; maternity benefit; invalidity benefit; and survivors' benefit.

The Convention recognises a minimum level of social security that all states must ensure but acknowledges differences between states and the need for

to the ICESCR, (2009) 869 UNTS 34, allowing for individual complaints to the Committee. This came into force on 10 May 2013.

8 For a discussion of the drafting history of Article 9, see Ben Saul, David Kinley and Jacqueline Mowbray, *The International Covenant on Economic, Social and Cultural Rights: Commentary, Cases and Materials* (Oxford University Press, 2014), at 612–17.

9 Reidel, above n 2, at 21.

10 Van Langendonck, above n 1, at 6.

11 Ibid., at 6–7.

12 Reidel, above n 2, at 21. See Lucie Lamarche, 'The Right to Social Security in the International Covenenant on Economic, Social and Culural Rights' in Audrey Chapman and Sage Russell (eds), *Core Obligations: Building a Framework for Economic, Social and Cultural Rights* (Intersentia, 2002) 87, for a discussion of the relationship between the ICESCR and the ILO conventions.

13 Lamarche, ibid., at 89.

14 Ursula Kulke, Michael Cichon and Karuna Pal, 'Changing Tides: A Revival of a Rights-Based Approach to Social Security' in Jef Van Langendonck (ed.), *The Right to Social Security* (Intersentia, 2007) 13, at 15.

flexibility in implementation of the Convention.[15] The Convention, together with other ILO conventions and recommendations, sets out standards aimed at achieving social protection, including the levels of benefits and the classes of people to be protected. They also set out the requirements for an acceptable national social security system.[16]

In addition to ILO conventions and the ICESCR, there are further UN human rights conventions that refer to the right to social security.

These include:

- *Convention on the Elimination of All Forms of Discrimination against Women*;[17]
- *Convention on the Rights of the Child*;[18]
- *International Convention on the Elimination of All Forms of Racial Discrimination*;[19]
- *International Convention on the Protection of the Rights of All Migrant Workers and Their Families*;[20]
- *Convention on the Rights of Persons with Disabilities*.[21]

The committees with supervisory responsibility for these conventions have interpreted and elaborated on the meaning of the right to social security in response to country reports, individual communications and in general comments, recommendations and statements. This body of 'soft law' provides important guidance to states, individuals and groups participating in the human rights treaty system.[22]

The Human Rights Committee, the treaty body established by the *International Covenant on Civil and Political Rights* (ICCPR), has considered gender equality issues in relation to social security on a number of occasions.[23] While the ICCPR does not require states parties to provide social security, the right to non-discrimination in Article 26 has been used by the Committee to address discrimination in relation to social security.[24]

15 Emmanuel Reynaud, 'The Right to Social Security – Current Challenges in International Perspective' in Eibe Reidel (ed.), *Social Security as a Human Right* (Springer, 2007) 1, at 1.
16 Lamarche, above n 12, at 91–5. For further discussion on the ILO, see below at 3.5.
17 (1979) 1249 UNTS 13, Articles 11, 12, 13 and 14(2).
18 (1989) 1577 UNTS 3, Articles 18, 23, 26 and 27.
19 (1965) 660 UNTS 195, Articles 2(2) and 5(e).
20 (1990) 2220 UNTS 3, Articles 27, 28 and 54.
21 (2006) UN Doc A/61/106, Articles 25, 27, and 28.
22 Discussed in Linda Jansen van Rensburg and Lucie Lamarche, 'The Right to Social Security and Assistance' in Danie Brand and Christof Heyns (eds), *Socio-Economic Rights in South Africa* (PULP, 2005) 209, at 230–1.
23 ICCPR (1966) 999 UNTS 171. For example, in *Zwaan-de Vries v the Netherlands* (Communication No. 182/1984), views of 9 April 1987, and *Broeks v the Netherlands* (Communication No.172/1984), Views of 9 April 1987 dealing with discrimination against married women in relation to unemployment benefits; *Vos v The Netherlands* Communication No. 786/1997), Views of 26 July 1999, and *Pauger v Austria* (Communication No. 716/1996), Views of 30 April 1999 dealing with discrimination against men regarding pension benefits.
24 See Martin Scheinin, 'Human Rights Committee – Not Only a Committee on Civil and Political

The UN Human Rights Council has appointed various mandate holders under its thematic special procedures, some of whose reports concern issues related to gender and social security and social protection. The work of the Special Rapporteur on extreme poverty and human rights,[25] covering these issues extensively, will be discussed in 3.6 below.

In addition to the above sources of the right to social security in international law, other non-binding documents that are relevant to the development of the right to social security include: the Limburg Principles (1987)[26] that deal with the implementation of the ICESCR and the Maastricht Guidelines (1997)[27] that deal with violations of the ICESCR. These were interpretations of the law formulated by groups of experts independently of the UN[28] and relate to the nature of states parties' obligations under the ICESCR. Similarly, the Montreal Principles on Women's Economic, Social and Cultural Rights (2002)[29] offer assistance in the development of the right to social security from a gender perspective. A more recent expert document of relevance to social and economic rights is the Maastricht Principles on Extraterritorial Obligations of States in the Area of Economic, Social and Cultural Rights (2012).[30] Although not official in character, these documents (particularly the earlier ones) have frequently been invoked by treaty bodies, advocates and others as useful guidance for the interpretation of treaties.

There are also regional instruments providing a right to social security including:

- *The European Social Charter*;[31]
- *The Charter of Fundamental Rights of the European Union*;[32]

Rights' in Malcolm Langford (ed.), *Social Rights Jurisprudence* (Cambridge University Press, 2008) 540, at 542; Saul et al., above n 8, at 654–8.

25 See the website of the Special Rapporteur on extreme poverty and human rights: www.ohchr.org/EN/Issues/Poverty/Pages/PovertyExpertIndex.aspx.

26 'Limburg Principles on the implementation of the International Covenant on Economic, Social and Cultural Rights' (1987) 9 *Human Rights Quarterly* 122. The principles have been acknowledged by the UN and published as a UN document: E/CN.4/1987/17.

27 'Maastricht guidelines on violations of economic, social and cultural rights' (1998) 20 *Human Rights Quarterly* 691. These guidelines have been acknowledged by the UN and published as a UN Document: E/C.12/2000/13.

28 Although some of the experts are members of UN treaty body committees or mandate holders in terms of the special procedures of the UN's Human Rights Council.

29 'Montreal principles on women's economic, social and cultural rights' (2004) 26 *Human Rights Quarterly* 760. For an analysis of these principles, see Dianne Otto, 'Gendering the Right to Social Security in the Era of Crisis Governance: The Need for Transformative Strategies' in Beth Goldblatt and Lucie Lamarche (eds), *Women's Rights to Social Security and Social Protection* (Hart, 2014) 215.

30 Olivier De Schutter et al., 'Commentary to the Maastricht principles on extraterritorial obligations of states in the area of economic, social and cultural rights' (2012) 34 *Human Rights Quarterly* 1084.

31 Adopted by the Council of Europe, 1961 (CETS No. 35); *Revised European Social Charter*, adopted by the Council of Europe, 1996 (CETS No. 163), Part I 12, Articles 8 (1), 12, 13.

32 2000/C 364/01, Article 34.

- *The American Declaration of the Rights and Duties of Man*;[33]
- *The Additional Protocol to the American Convention on Human Rights in the Area of Economic, Social and Cultural Rights* ('Protocol of San Salvador');[34]
- *The Protocol to the African Charter on Human and Peoples' Rights on the Rights of Women in Africa* (1995).[35]

The legislation, rights framework and jurisprudence of Europe deserve special mention given its long-standing and developed consideration of issues of social security.[36] Within the framework of the 47-member Council of Europe, the European Court of Human Rights has considered a number of cases concerning social security under the *European Convention on Human Rights* despite the lack of any express right to social security in that Convention.[37] There is also a *European Code of Social Security* (1964) and a *Protocol to the European Code of Social Security* (1964) which sets standards for countries within the Council of Europe.[38] The Code is monitored in co-operation with the ILO but the ILO conventions are still the 'main standard setting instruments in the area of social security'.[39] The European Committee of Social Rights has played an active role in

33 (1948) Article XV.

34 Adopted at San Salvador, El Salvador, on 17 November 1988, at the eighteenth regular session of the General Assembly, Article 9.

35 Endorsed by resolution AHG/Res.240 (XXXI). It makes specific reference to social protection and insurance for women in the informal sector (Art 13(f)) and calls for the economic recognition of women's unpaid work (Article 13(h)). *The African Charter on Human and People's Rights* does not make specific reference to a right to social security but this may be inferred from the wording of Article 18. *The African Charter on the Rights and Welfare of the Child*, (1990) OAU Doc CAB/LEG/24.9/49 (1990), contains a range of circumstances where protection of children requires social security.

36 Lisa Conant, 'Regional Legal Frameworks for Human Rights and Social Policy in Europe' in Ann Neville (ed.), *Human Rights and Social Policy: A Comparative Analysis of Values and Citizenship in OECD Countries* (Edward Elgar, 2010) 47; Matti Mikkola, 'Common Denominators of European Social Security' in Jef van Langendonck (ed.), *The Right to Social Security* (Intersentia, 2007) 225.

37 See Luke Clements and Alan Simmons, 'European Court of Human Rights – Sympathetic Unease' in Malcolm Langford (ed.), *Social Rights Jurisprudence: Emerging Trends in International and Comparative Law* (Cambridge University Press, 2008) 409, at 420–4. Most of these cases concern a right to a fair hearing in Article 6(1) and some concern welfare benefits of non-nationals as property rights under Article 1 of Protocol 1. It is less certain whether more substantive claims under Article 3 concerning inhuman and degrading treatment would apply to cases where social security is lacking. Also see Ana Gómez Heredero, *Social Security as a Human Right: The Protection Afforded by the European Convention on Human Rights* (Council of Europe Publishing, 2007); Ana Gómez Heredero, *Social Security: Protection at the International Level and Developments in Europe* (Council of Europe Publishing, 2009); Wouter van Ginneken, *Sustaining European Social Security Systems in a Globalised Economy* (Council of Europe Publishing, 2011).

38 *European Code of Social Security*, adopted by the Council of Europe, 1964 (CETS No. 48); *Protocol to the European Code of Social Security*, adopted by the Council of Europe, 1964 (CETS No. 48A). There is also a *Revised European Code of Social Security*, adopted by the Council of Europe, 1990 (CETS No. 139) but it has not yet entered into force.

39 Frans Pennings (ed.), *Between Soft and Hard Law: The Impact of Social Security Standards on National Social Security Law*, Studies in Employment and Social Policy (Kluwer Law International,

interpreting social security rights under the *European Social Charter*,[40] including on gender issues.[41] Within the 28-member European Union the European Court of Justice has decided a number of cases concerning health benefits under social security systems in its determination of European Community treaties.[42]

Many countries have given constitutional recognition and protection to the right to social security.[43] In some countries the courts have developed detailed jurisprudence on the right.[44]

Having briefly sketched the history and sources of the right to social security in international law, this chapter now provides a more detailed discussion of four key sources of international law on social security and gender: CEDAW as interpreted by the Committee on the Elimination of Discrimination against Women; the ICESCR as interpreted by the CESCR; the ILO; and the UN Special Rapporteur on extreme poverty and human rights

3.3 The Convention on the Elimination of All Forms of Discrimination Against Women

This section first examines the provisions of CEDAW as they relate to the right to social security for women. It then looks at the interpretive work of the Committee on the Elimination of Discrimination Against Women ('the CEDAW Committee') in its General Recommendations and its Concluding Observations

2006). Also see Frans Pennings, *European Social Security Law* (Intersentia, 5th edn, 2010). Since 2012 issues falling under the European Social Charter and the European Code of Social Security have been considered together.

40 See Urfan Khaliq and Robin Churchill, 'The European Committee of Social Rights – Putting Flesh on the Bare Bones of the European Social Charter' in Malcolm Langford (ed.), *Social Rights Jurisprudence: Emerging Trends in International and Comparative Law* (Cambridge University Press, 2008) 428, at 437–40. Also see Martin Scheinin, 'The Right to Social Security' in Asbjorn Eide, Catarina Krause and Allan Rosas (eds), *Economic, Social and Cultural Rights: A Textbook* (Martinus Nijhoff Publishers, Revised 2nd edn, 2001) 211; Holly Cullen, 'The collective complaints system of the European social charter: interpretative methods of the European Committee of Social Rights' (2009) 9(1) *Human Rights Law Review* 61.

41 Karin Lukas, *The Scope and Boundaries of an Effective Right to Social Security: The Experience of the European Committee of Social Rights*, University of Ottawa, www.cdp-hrc.uottawa.ca/?p=4776.

42 Philippa Watson, 'European Court of Justice – Creative Responses in Uncharted Territory' in Malcolm Langford (ed.), *Social Rights Jurisprudence: Emerging Trends in International and Comparative Law* (Cambridge University Press, 2008) 453, at 461–3. Also see Linda Luckhaus, 'Equal treatment, social protection and income security for women' (2000) 139(2) *International Labour Review* 149 for a discussion of gender equality and social security, particularly in Europe and regarding decisions of the European Court of Justice. For further discussion of social security in the European Union, see Vicki Paskalia, *Free Movement, Social Security and Gender in the EU* (Hart, 2007); Eleanor Spaventa and Michael Dougan (eds), *Social Welfare and EU Law* (Hart, 2005).

43 ILO (2011b), 'Social Security and the Rule of Law: General Survey concerning social security instruments in light of the 2008 Declaration on Social Justice for a Fair Globalization' (2011), at 99–111.

44 Ibid., at 111–19. Also see various chapters on national systems in Jef Van Langendonck (ed.), *The Right to Social Security* (Intersentia, 2007).

and Recommendations to countries reporting to the Committee. Where appropriate, the Committee's jurisprudence (in the form of communications) relating to individual complaints under the CEDAW Optional Protocol is considered.[45] All of the jurisprudence and General Recommendations are surveyed for the purpose of this research. A selective approach is taken in the survey of Concluding Observations and Recommendations given the large number prepared over the life of the Committee. The Concluding Observations and Recommendations from 2000 up to and including 2013 are considered.[46]

3.3.1 *The Convention*

It is important to evaluate the approach taken in CEDAW to the gender dimensions of the right to social security given the Convention's focus on equality for women. This section examines the text of the Convention while the subsequent section considers the interpretation of the text by the CEDAW Committee.

CEDAW obliges states parties to eliminate discrimination and to guarantee the equal enjoyment of human rights, including civil and political, and economic, social and cultural rights. The Convention contains various references to aspects of the right to social security. The Preamble recognises the disadvantaged economic position of many women 'in situations of poverty (where) women have the least access to food, health, education, training and opportunities for employment and other needs'. It also states:

> Bearing in mind the great contribution of women to the welfare of the family and to the development of society, so far not fully recognized, the social significance of maternity and the role of both parents in the family and in the upbringing of children, and aware that the role of women in procreation should not be a basis for discrimination but that the upbringing of children requires a sharing of responsibility between men and women and society as a whole.

This paragraph is an important recognition of the gendered division of labour in society and the need to address discrimination that occurs in both the public and private spheres of home and work as a result of this division. The reference to the shared responsibility of men, women and 'the society as a whole' suggests the importance of the role of the state in overcoming unfair gendered divisions, particularly as they relate to maternity, childcare, the workplace and work within the household. The provision of social security is clearly one of the mechanisms that

45 (1999) 2131 UNTS 83.

46 Using the Universal Human Rights Index (developed and run by the Office of the United Nations High Commissioner for Human Rights), http://uhri.ohchr.org/. The following search terms were used: 'social security' and 'social protection' as modified by checking the 'right to social security' in the list of rights; the same search terms modified by checking 'the right to an adequate standard of living'; additional searches were undertaken using the following terms: 'poverty alleviation'; 'childcare'; 'welfare'; 'pension'; 'austerity'; and 'insurance'.

can contribute to the achievement of these goals. This paragraph also highlights the substantive equality approach that underscores CEDAW envisaging social transformation through far-reaching change to the way in which care is undertaken by men and women alongside the broader responsibilities of the society.

Before looking at the articles of CEDAW that specifically relate to the right to social security, it is important to identify the principles of equality and non-discrimination that underpin the Convention. Article 1 of CEDAW defines 'discrimination against women' while Article 2 sets out how states parties should eliminate discrimination against women 'in all its forms'. Both Articles reflect the substantive equality approach that is embedded in CEDAW with references to discrimination in law and in practice (Article 2) and to the effect of discrimination on women (Article 1).[47]

Article 11, which relates to discrimination against women in the field of employment, contains the right to non-discrimination in relation to social security. Article 11(1)(e) provides for 'The right to social security, particularly in cases of retirement, unemployment, sickness, invalidity and old age and other incapacity to work, as well as the right to paid leave'.[48] Since this right is located within the article dealing with employment-related discrimination, its reach is limited to workers. As discussed in Chapter 2, social security should attach to everyone as a citizenship entitlement regardless of their relationship to work. This is of special significance to women who are often left outside of employment as it is (narrowly) defined in traditional understandings of the concept. However, the inclusion of references to both 'retirement' and 'old age' suggests that the right to social security in Article 11 might also apply to the period following the end of a working life as well as a period when a person is not able to work due to their age. This seems to imply that social security must be provided equally to men and women whether as a result of their relationship to particular work or as a consequence of their need for state support due to their inability to work in old age and consequent lack of income from employment. This could be interpreted as obligating the State to provide support to certain groups of the elderly both by way of social insurance and (non-contributory) social assistance.

Article 11(2) requires states parties to prevent discrimination against women on the grounds of marriage or maternity and to ensure their effective right to work. It specifically requires the introduction of paid maternity leave (para b); and the provision of childcare and other social services to support working parents (para c). Parental leave and support for parents may form part of a country's social security system. While the latter paragraph (c) recognises the role of male and female parents, the former (b) fails to refer to more inclusive and transformative notions of paternity or parental leave. This may be because

47 For a discussion of the concepts of discrimination and equality in CEDAW, see Andrew Byrnes, 'Article 1' in Marsha A. Freeman, Christine Chinkin and Beate Rudolf (eds), *The UN Convention on the Elimination of All Forms of Discrimination Against Women: A Commentary* (Oxford University Press, 2012) 51.

48 Article 11(1)(c) also concerns social security since it refers to workplace 'benefits and conditions of service'.

(b) is aimed at protecting women's physiological needs related to childbirth while other parental care obligations after the birth are covered in Article 5(b) of CEDAW which refers to the 'responsibility of men and women in the upbringing and development of children'.[49]

The Convention takes a formal equality approach to employment rights in Article 11 where equality is simply an add-on to existing work-related entitlements.[50] The Article represents an 'intensely male model of work' since work is assumed to be 'paid work outside of the home'.[51] However, structural reform of paid work and sharing of responsibility for unpaid work in the home by men and women are necessary to alter women's access to paid work.[52] The social security rights in Article 11(1)(e) will not achieve de facto equality for women unless 'eligibility criteria and contribution requirements are changed to reflect women's interrupted work patterns'.[53] The formal employment context implied by these rights leaves out the millions of women workers in the informal sector, leading one commentator to argue that Article 11 may be interpreted as 'protecting the labour rights of more privileged women over more marginalised women'.[54] Women who engage in unpaid labour in family enterprises, in subsistence activities, and in reproductive and care work in the home and community fall outside the scope of the benefits of this Article.

While acknowledging these concerns, Article 11 highlights important gender issues that were new to international conventions: Article 11(2)(c) was the first international convention to specifically provide for childcare, even before the ILO addressed this.[55] However, the wording of the Article does not obligate states parties to provide childcare but rather to take measures to 'encourage' and 'promote' 'the establishment and development of a network of child-care facilities'.[56] This less forceful statement on states parties, obligations regarding childcare is in contrast to the Preamble which emphasises the sharing of responsibility for families and Article 5(b) which refers to the 'common responsibility of men and women in the upbringing and development of children'. Nevertheless, the identification of states parties' responsibilities to address gendered divisions in the home and workplace is an innovative and valuable inclusion in CEDAW.

49 Frances Raday, 'Article 11' in Freeman et al. (eds), *The UN Convention on the Elimination of All Forms of Discrimination Against Women: A Commentary* (Oxford University Press, 2012) 279, at 301.

50 Sandra Fredman, 'Engendering Social and Economic Rights' in Beth Goldblatt and Kirsty McLean (eds), *Women's Social and Economic Rights: Developments in South Africa* (Juta, 2011) 4, at 29–30.

51 Ibid., at 30.

52 Ibid.

53 Ibid.

54 Leilani Farha, 'Committee on the Elimination of Discrimination Against Women: Women Claiming Economic, Social and Cultural Rights – The CEDAW Potential' in Malcolm Langford (ed.), *Social Rights Jurisprudence: Emerging Trends in International and Comparative Law* (Cambridge University Press, 2008) 553, at 560.

55 Raday, above n 49, at 301. The relevant ILO convention is the *Workers with Family Responsibilities Convention*, 1981 (No. 156).

56 Ibid., at 302.

Articles 12 and 13 of the Convention relate to women's social and economic rights. Article 12 requires states parties to eliminate discrimination against women in the field of health care and to ensure, 'on a basis of equality of men and women, access to health care services' (Article 12(1)). Such services may relate to the health care dimensions of the right to social security. Article 13 relates more generally to the elimination of discrimination against women in 'other areas of economic and social life' and refers specifically to 'the right to family benefits' (Article 13(a)), which would include social security entitlements available to families. This broad framing of social and economic rights and the general silence on social security and other important and related rights such as housing, food and the right to an adequate standard of living makes it important to refer to other international human rights instruments that include such rights.[57] These rights are incorporated into CEDAW through Article 1 which protects the enjoyment or exercise by women of their 'human rights and fundamental freedoms in the political, economic, social, cultural, civil or any other field'.[58]

Article 14 requires states to eliminate discrimination against women in rural areas. In particular, Article 14 specifically refers to 'work in the non-monetized sectors of the economy' or subsistence work. Social security is mentioned directly in Article 14(2)(c) which requires states to ensure rural women the right 'to benefit directly from social security programmes'. The inclusion of this sub-article followed debate as to whether social security should be provided to 'those in formal employment or to all citizens including women engaging in subsistence agriculture'.[59] Its inclusion suggests that CEDAW provides a broad right to non-discrimination in relation to social security that encompasses social assistance for all who need it, and particularly for women facing poverty and barriers to accessing income, whether in the informal economy or in unpaid labour. This is an important recognition of the nature of women's work across the formal, informal and subsistence sectors of the economy. Article 14 provides therefore a right to non-discriminatory access to social security for all rural women; however, 'work in the non-monetized sectors of the economy' is also undertaken by urban women who are not extended the same coverage as their rural counterparts under CEDAW. Article 14 is valuable in linking issues of social security to rural development and to the social and economic rights to adequate living conditions through the provision of housing, electricity, water, sanitation, transport and communications (Article 14(2)(h)). Article 14 represents a commendable example of an interdependent approach to rights for women facing poverty and disadvantage. However, the terminology of 'benefitting directly from social security programmes' suggests an inclusionary approach rather than a transformative one; that is, women are to be brought into existing programmes instead of there

57 Beate Rudolf, 'Article 13' in Freeman et al. (eds), *The UN Convention on the Elimination of All Forms of Discrimination Against Women: A Commentary* (Oxford University Press, 2012), at 339.

58 See Byrnes, above n 47, at 67.

59 Fareda Banda, 'Article 14' in Freeman et al. (eds), *The UN Convention on the Elimination of All Forms of Discrimination Against Women: A Commentary* (Oxford University Press, 2012) 357, at 369.

being an obligation on states parties to establish new, more substantively equal programmes.

There are clearly some limitations in the language of the Convention with regard to women's social security rights, although there are also many far-reaching guarantees that cannot be found in any other international conventions. In addition, many of the gaps or problems with the framing of the social security rights in CEDAW have been addressed through the work of the Committee on the Elimination of Discrimination against Women ('the Committee') which has elaborated and expanded the meaning of the right to social security to ensure that it entails a more substantive approach to equality for women.

3.3.2 The CEDAW Committee

The General Recommendations of the CEDAW Committee, its Concluding Observations concerning the reports of countries under review, and its jurisprudence under the Optional Protocol to CEDAW[60] cover a wide range of issues relating to the right to social security. In the Committee's Concluding Observations from 2000–2013 there are limited instances of direct discrimination between men and women in social security provision as evidenced by the small number of references to such disparities (for example, in Belgium,[61] Surinam[62] and Uganda[63]). Instead, most observations and recommendations concern indirect discrimination in social security provision that results from the unequal location of women within the labour market.[64] The Committee also focuses on, and requires remedies for, the different groups of women requiring access to social security. There is a more limited focus on gendered poverty and its alleviation through social security measures, although the Committee's engagement with social assistance has increased in recent years, as has its concern with reductions in social security provisions following the global financial crisis. The Committee's treatment of the following themes: 1) types of work; 2) affected groups (facing specific, multiple and intersectional discrimination); and 3) poverty, are now discussed.

60 There are two decisions relating to social security: *Dung Thi Thuy Nguyen v The Netherlands*, Communication 3/2004 (2006) CEDAW/C/36/D/3/2004, concerns restricted maternity benefits for women who are both employed and self-employed. The minority found that there may have been indirect discrimination in these circumstances. In *Elisabeth de Blok et al. v The Netherlands*, Communication 36/2012 (2014) CEDAW/C/57/D/36/2012, the Committee found that the state party had violated the rights of self-employed women to maternity leave payments. Also note the inadmissible communication in *B.-J. v. Germany* 1/2003 (2004) CEDAW/31st Session, Excerpt from A/59/38 Annex VIII, concerning a claim that the divorce system, including the equalisation of pensions, unfairly discriminated against older women who worked in the home.

61 CO Belgium CEDAW/C/BEL/CO/6 (CEDAW, 2008), at para 25.

62 CO Surinam CEDAW/C/SUR/CO/3 (CEDAW, 2007), at para 28.

63 CO Uganda A/57/38(SUPP) 27th Session (CEDAW, 2002), at para 143.

64 For example, CO Austria CEDAW/C/AUT/CO/7-8 (CEDAW, 2013), at para 37. Also note the reference to indirect sex discrimination against women arising from pension calculations based on life expectancy in Chile, CO Chile CEDAW/C/CHL/CO/5-6 (CEDAW, 2012), at para 36–7.

Types of work and social security

INFORMAL SECTOR

Generally, there has been a strong emphasis by the Committee on the need for states parties to provide social security to women in the informal sector on the basis that women predominate in this part of the economy and receive no social security. For example, in 2002 the Committee referred to the 'precarious conditions of women working in the informal sector and at part-time work who have … no access to social security' in Peru.[65] In 2007 the Committee recommended that Mozambique 'embrace support for women in the informal sector, including by creating opportunities for training and ensuring access to credit, as well as social security and social protection measures'.[66] And most recently, the Committee has urged a number of countries to 'provide a regulatory framework for the informal sector, with a view to providing women working in this sector with access to social security and other benefits'.[67]

UNPAID WORK

The Committee addressed unpaid work specifically in its early General Recommendation 16 (1991), possibly in response to the gap in the text of the Convention regarding unpaid work that occurs outside of rural areas. In this General Recommendation the Committee referred to the 'high percentage of women in the states parties (who) work without payment, social security and social benefits in enterprises owned usually by a male member of the family'.[68] It recommended that states parties 'take the necessary steps to guarantee payment, social security and social benefits for women who work without such benefits in enterprises owned by a family member'. In recent Concluding Observations building on General Recommendation 16, the Committee has made further references to unpaid work and social security provision. For example, concerned at the low rate of women's employment in Turkey, the Committee referred to the concentration of women in 'agriculture in rural areas as unpaid family workers with no entitlements within the social security system'.[69] In its Concluding Observations on the Bahamas the Committee recommended that the state party ensure that women carrying out unpaid work are eligible for retirement benefits.[70]

65 CO Peru A/57/38(SUPP); 27th Session (CEDAW, 2002), at para 478.

66 CO Mozambique CEDAW/C/MOZ/CO/2 (CEDAW, 2007), at para 35.

67 For example: CO Lesotho CEDAW/C/LSO/CO/1-4 (CEDAW, 2011), at para 31(c); CO Angola CEDAW/C/AGO/CO/6 (CEDAW, 2013), at para 30; CO Togo CEDAW/C/TGO/CO/6-7 (CEDAW, 2012), at para 33(b).

68 *General Recommendation 16 on unpaid women workers in rural and urban family enterprises*, 10th session, 1991, HRI/GEN/1/Rev.9 (vol II).

69 CO Turkey CEDAW/C/TUR/CO/6 (CEDAW, 2010), at paras 32–3.

70 CO Bahamas CEDAW/C/BHS/CO/1-5 (CEDAW, 2012), at para 34(e).

HOUSEHOLD LABOUR[71]

The Committee addressed the lack of reference to domestic work in the home within the Convention in General Recommendation 17 (1991).[72] However, the focus was on measuring and valuing women's unremunerated domestic activities in the national accounts rather than on any mechanisms to address the imbalance between men and women in the household or to remunerate or provide social security to women for such work. While this General Recommendation was a progressive attempt to 'count' women's unpaid work in the home, it did not address the substantive implications of the unpaid work that women provide in a global context and therefore failed to recommend social restructuring that would address this underlying and pervasive global phenomenon.[73] General Recommendation 27 on Older Women (2010), adopted two decades later, identified the financial and emotional costs of unpaid care that older women bear when caring for children, partners, parents and relatives[74] and called on states parties to ensure that older women have access to benefits such as childcare when providing this care.[75]

PRECARIOUS WORK

The Committee has pointed to the many situations in which women workers are subject to unequal treatment and to the impact this has on their social security entitlements.

- Domestic and home-care work: in the Netherlands, for example, several hundred thousand domestic workers in private households and home-care workers financed by public schemes (95 per cent of whom are women) have limited access to unemployment, disability or pension benefits.[76] The Committee has noted with concern the multiple forms of discrimination against women migrant domestic workers in Kuwait, including their lack of access to social security.[77] Recently, the Committee called on states to ratify

71 For a discussion of the CEDAW Committee's approach to the issues of the sharing of responsibilities in families and the male breadwinner model, see Rikki Holtmaat, 'Article 5' in Marsha A. Freeman, Christine Chinkin and Beate Rudolf (eds), *The UN Convention on the Elimination of All Forms of Discrimination Against Women: A Commentary* (Oxford University Press, 2012) 141.

72 *General Recommendation 17 on measurement and quantification of the unremunerated domestic activities of women and their recognition in the GNP*, 10th session, 1991, HRI/GEN/1/Rev.9 (vol II).

73 However, see the Committee's more recent recommendation to France to implement the French President's expressed desire to provide retirement pensions for homemakers who had not worked professionally, CO France CEDAW/C/FRA/CO/6 (CEDAW, 2008), at para 27.

74 *General Recommendation 27 on Older Women*, 47th Session (2010) CEDAW/C/GC/27, at para 17.

75 Ibid., at para 43.

76 CO Netherlands CEDAW/C/NLD/CO/5 (CEDAW, 2010), at para 38.

77 CO Kuwait CEDAW/C/KWT/CO/3-4 (CEDAW, 2011), at para 40.

the new ILO *Domestic Workers Convention*, 2011, (No. 189) that extends rights, including social security rights, to this vulnerable group of workers.[78]

- Export processing zones: women predominate in work in free trade zones where they have limited or no access to social security. The Committee has recommended that this be addressed through improved regulation and enforcement.[79]
- Agricultural work: the Committee has noted the situation of women agricultural workers who are excluded from labour laws and consequently have no access to social security benefits.[80]
- Unskilled and low-wage work: due to occupational segregation and the concentration of women in low-wage and unskilled labour sectors, as well as weak laws and enforcement, women have restricted rights to social security and protection.[81] The Committee has urged states to adopt legislation on home-based work and to ratify the ILO *Home Work Convention*, 1996 (No.177).[82]
- Temporary and part-time work: the Committee has recognised that women dominate part-time and temporary work with negative consequences for their careers, pensions and other social security benefits.[83] In the *Nguyen* communication[84] the dissenters found that maternity benefit laws in the Netherlands may discriminate against workers who are both part-time in salaried employment and self-employed (often in family businesses). They speculated that women predominated in this type of work combination and that there was indirect gender discrimination involved in their treatment.[85] The Committee has expressed concern at the 'increased and ongoing conversion of women's contracts from regular workers to non-regular, part-time or short-term workers' in the Republic of Korea and the negative impact this has on their social security entitlements.[86]

Multiple discrimination against different groups of women relating to social security

The Committee has highlighted the varied and vulnerable types of work that women do and also the intersectional forms of discrimination that different

78 For example, CO Bahamas CEDAW C/BHS/CO/1-5 (CEDAW, 2012), at para 33(e).
79 CO Vietnam CEDAW/C/VNM/CO/6 (CEDAW, 2007), at para 23.
80 CO Lebanon CEDAW/C/LBN/CO/3 (CEDAW, 2008), at para 36.
81 CO Cambodia CEDAW/C/KHM/CO/3 (CEDAW, 2006), at para 27.
82 For example, CO Pakistan CEDAW/C/PAK/CO/4 (CEDAW, 2013), at para 30(c).
83 For example, CO Liechtenstein CEDAW/C/LIE/CO/4 (CEDAW, 2011), at paras 34–7. In this report it is notable that the Committee also recommended that men be provided with part-time and flexible employment to allow them to play a greater role in childcare.
84 Above n 60. The majority found that there had not been any discriminatory treatment or violation of the author's rights under CEDAW. Also see the *de Blok* communication concerning maternity benefits available to self-employed women, above n 60.
85 Ibid., at 14–16. Also see Raday, above n 49, at 291.
86 CO Republic of Korea CEDAW/C/KOR/C/7 (CEDAW, 2011), at para 32.

groups of women face in relation to social security.[87] It has referred to a range of vulnerable groups including migrants, refugees and internally displaced women; Roma and other ethnic minority women; rural and remote women; Indigenous women; women with disabilities; older women; pregnant women; married women; single women; and women with care responsibilities. A number of General Recommendations and Statements of the Committee refer to the social security rights of various groups of women including the following:

OLDER WOMEN

The Committee has raised concerns about lower retirement ages for women than men in some countries and indicated that this may be discriminatory.[88] Raday points to the complexities of this issue – women who retire earlier may get smaller pensions than men but women, who are generally poorer than men and face lower employment prospects as they age, may require earlier pensions to survive.[89] General Recommendation 27 on Older Women recommended the need for an optional retirement age for women.[90] It also called on states parties to ensure there are adequate non-contributory pensions for women who require them.[91]

RURAL WOMEN

As noted above, this group is given special focus in the Convention, including in relation to social security rights. In a General Statement the Committee recommended that states put in place social safety nets for rural women in developing countries facing food insecurity and economic restructuring.[92] This has been reinforced by the Committee in its Concluding Observations, where, for example, it has urged Togo to ensure access to social security for rural women.[93]

87 *General Recommendation 28 on the core obligations of CEDAW*, 47th Session (2010) CEDAW/C/GC/28, at para 18, explains intersectional discrimination as follows: 'The discrimination of women based on sex and gender is inextricably linked with other factors that affect women, such as race, ethnicity, religion or belief, health, status, age, class, caste and sexual orientation, and gender identity. Discrimination on the basis of sex or gender may affect women belonging to such groups to a different degree or in different ways to men.'

88 *General Recommendation 27*, above n 74, at para 17.

89 Above n 49, at 295.

90 Above n 74, at para 20.

91 Ibid., at para 44.

92 *General Statement of the Committee on the Elimination of Discrimination against Women on Rural Women*, Adopted on 19 October 2011 during the 50th session, Results of the 49th and 50th sessions of the Committee on the Elimination of Discrimination against Women, E/CN.6/2012/CRP.1 (Annex v), at 19. The Committee is currently preparing a General Recommendation on Article 14 of CEDAW, see: www.ohchr.org/EN/HRBodies/CEDAW/Pages/RuralWomen.aspx.

93 CO Togo CEDAW/C/TGO/CO/6-7 (CEDAW, 2012), at para 37(b).

WOMEN WITH DISABILITIES

The Committee's General Recommendation 18 on women with disabilities called on states to provide information on measures taken to ensure equal access to social security by this group of women.[94] In its Concluding Observations on Uganda the Committee identified the vulnerable situation of women with disabilities and recommended the introduction of a 'universal non-contributory pension' within the framework of a broader social protection strategy.[95]

WOMEN MIGRANTS AND REFUGEES

General Recommendation 26 on women migrant workers has emphasised the need for such workers to have the same rights as other workers in the country[96] but it does not specifically refer to the social security entitlements of this precarious group. In its Concluding Observations the Committee has noted the lack of access to social security benefits of women with insecure immigration status in the United Kingdom.[97] It has called for Kuwait to consider measures that would require employers to provide a 'minimal level of social protection' to migrant domestic workers.[98] In a stronger response the Committee has urged Canada to 'ensure adequate social security protection' for migrant live-in care-givers.[99] The Committee could, however, consider more forceful recommendations for this extremely vulnerable group of women.[100]

WOMEN IN FAMILIES, MARRIAGE AND FOLLOWING DISSOLUTION

The Committee's recent General Recommendation 29 dealing with the position of women in marriage and other forms of family notes the greater poverty many women face on dissolution of partnerships.[101] This may be exacerbated by social security systems that are meant to assist but instead discriminate against women.[102] The General Recommendation, adopting an apparently formal equality approach, requires states parties to treat men and women equally on dissolution of relationships (following separation or death) for the purpose of social

94 *General Recommendation 18 on women with disabilities*, 10th session, 1991, HRI/GEN/1/Rev.9 (vol II)

95 CO Uganda CEDAW/C/UGA/CO/7(CEDAW, 2010), at para 46.

96 *General Recommendation 26 on women migrant workers*, 42nd Session (2008) CEDAW/C/2009/WP.1/R, at para 26.

97 CO United Kingdom CEDAW/C/UK/CO/6 (CEDAW, 2009), at para 295.

98 CO Kuwait CEDAW/C/KWT/CO/3-4 (CEDAW, 2011), at para 41.

99 CO Canada A/58/38(SUPP) (CEDAW, 2003), at para 366.

100 The recent *General Recommendation 30 on women in conflict prevention, conflict and post-conflict situations*, 56th Session (2013) CEDAW/C/GC/30, is strangely silent on the subject of social security given the poverty and multiple difficulties of women following conflict, often as refugees.

101 *General Recommendation 29 on the economic consequences of marriage, family relations and their dissolution*, 54th Session (2013) CEDAW/C/GC/29.

102 Ibid., at para 5.

security pensions and other benefits.[103] However, unequal contributions to social insurance may be a result of women's caring responsibilities and shorter periods of less remunerative employment and therefore a formally equal approach will disadvantage many women. General Recommendation 29 could have been strengthened by requiring states to develop measures to adjust social insurance and related pay-outs on the basis of women's unpaid contributions to families. The issue of women's ability to control their welfare payments paid to abusive partners following United Kingdom (UK) reforms was raised by the Committee.[104]

Poverty alleviation and social security

Despite the problematic location of the right to social security within the provision of the Convention dealing with employment (Article 11), the Committee has provided clear direction on the need for social assistance, unrelated to employment, as a mechanism to alleviate poverty for vulnerable women. In its Concluding Observations to developed countries such as Austria,[105] Canada[106] and France[107] the Committee has linked the need for adequate pensions to the problem of women's poverty. In recent years it has made reference to the negative impact of austerity measures on women's social and economic rights in Greece[108] and Austria.[109] In developing countries such as China,[110] Uganda[111] and Romania[112] it has identified the need for pensions and other forms of social assistance to address the situation of women in poverty. In relation to Bulgaria it specifically addressed the inadequacy of social security benefits for women and their families, requiring that the level of benefits should guarantee an 'adequate standard of living'.[113] The Committee has also noted the issue of access to social assistance by vulnerable women in relation to location of offices and lack of identity documentation.[114] The Committee has not, however, articulated clear

103 Ibid., at para 51.

104 CO United Kingdom CEDAW/C/GBR/CO/7 (CEDAW, 2013), at para 62–3. The UK reforms consolidated all welfare payments into a single payment paid to one family member. The Committee was concerned that abusive men in receipt of such payments might prevent their women partners from accessing this income.

105 CO Austria CEDAW/C/AUT/CO/6 (CEDAW, 2007), at para 20.

106 CO Canada A/58/38(SUPP) (CEDAW, 2003), at para 378.

107 CO France CEDAW/C/FRA/CO/6 (CEDAW, 2008), at paras 26–7.

108 CO Greece CEDAW/C/GRC/CO/7 (CEDAW, 2013), at para 11(a).

109 CO Austria CEDAW/C/AUT/CO/7-8 (CEDAW, 2013), at para 39. Note Dianne Otto's view that the CESCR has taken a weak approach to the issue of rights violations following austerity measures (above n 29). A similar critique can be levelled at the CEDAW Committee.

110 CO China CEDAW/C/CHN/CO/6 (CEDAW, 2006), at para 32.

111 CO Uganda CEDAW/C/UGA/CO/7 (CEDAW, 2010), at para 46.

112 CO Romania A/55/38(SUPP) (CEDAW, 2000), at para 317.

113 CO Bulgaria CEDAW/C/BLG/CO/4-7 (CEDAW, 2012), at para 40.

114 Banda above n 59, at 369–70; The Committee called on Mozambique to provide free identity cards to guarantee full access to social services and protection: CO Mozambique CEDAW/C/MOZ/CO/2 (CEDAW, 2007), at para 43.

recommendations on the right to social assistance for all groups of women facing economic insecurity.

3.3.3 Assessment of CEDAW

CEDAW's approach to the right to social security has a number of strengths. First, the Convention is women-centred and thus allows for a contextual, grounded understanding of the issues affecting women as they relate to social security in a range of different labour contexts,[115] and in other respects. While the right to social security may be overly linked to formal employment in Article 11 of the Convention, the Committee has attempted to remedy this through its interpretations of CEDAW in a contemporary context. In particular, the critique of unpaid subsistence work and work in family enterprises and the resulting lack of social security are based on both a contextually insightful and sophisticated conceptual understanding of the position of women in the family and in these types of work. Awareness of the context of unequal gender power relations within the home has led the Committee to recognise, for example, that welfare payments may not reach women if abusive partners are given control over them. Second, the Convention's focus on substantive equality means that realising women's social security rights requires fundamental social change to address gender discrimination and the underlying inequalities that produce such discrimination.[116] The Committee's understanding of the various dimensions of substantive equality is evident in its attention to recognition issues of stereotyping and violence, issues of redistribution for women in relation to social security benefits, and transformative approaches that accept that different treatment is sometimes necessary, together with the need to change male roles in society. An example of a substantive equality approach is the Committee's recommendation that childcare services be provided to address the care burden of older women. Third, CEDAW responds to the variety of groups of women affected by inadequate or discriminatory social security and the intersectional discrimination that arises as a result of women's location across a range of vulnerable groups.

A central gap in the text of CEDAW relates to the lack of a clear statement defining women's unpaid household and caring labour as work with attendant rights to social security and protection. The reference in Article 5 to the sharing of responsibility between men and women and the wording of the Preamble regarding the role of society in relation to this work is important. However, the restructuring of work and the provision of childcare is recommended but not required by the Convention. This is an area that has been addressed to some extent through the work of the Committee but stronger recommendations would be valuable. The substantive equality approach adopted by the Committee

115 Farha, above n 54.

116 Farha, above n 54, at 562. But see Dianne Otto, 'Women's Rights' in Daniel Moeckli, Sangeeta Shah and Sandesh Sivakumaran (eds), *International Human Rights Law* (Oxford University Press, 2010) 345 for a critique of the equality paradigm of the Convention.

does not always entail far-reaching, structural solutions or responses that involve greater participation by men in areas of responsibility traditionally occupied by women.[117] A greater elaboration of the role, nature and extent of social assistance in addressing women's poverty for all women in need of income support would also be beneficial. Greater attention could be given to the participatory dimension of substantive equality to ensure that women's views are built into social security measures and that their capacity to participate fully in society is enhanced through social security programmes.

3.4 The International Covenant on Economic, Social and Cultural Rights

This section first examines the text of the *International Covenant on Economic, Social and Cultural Rights* (ICESCR), as it relates to the right to social security, from a gender perspective. It then considers the work of the Committee on Economic, Social and Cultural Rights (CESCR) that is responsible for interpretation and monitoring of the implementation of the International Covenant. This work includes the preparation of Concluding Observations and Recommendations, and the production of General Comments, statements and open letters, on key issues under the ICESCR. The Committee also has the competence to receive communications lodged under the Optional Protocol to ICESCR (which entered into force on 10 May 2013).[118] As of 30 June 2014, there was no reported jurisprudence. The main focus in the analysis, from a gender perspective, of the Committee's work is on General Comment 19 on the right to social security.[119] General Comment 20 on non-discrimination[120] and General Comment 16 on the equal right of men and women to the enjoyment of their economic, social and cultural rights[121] are also considered as they relate to the right to social security. The analysis draws on the theoretical framework and principles for a substantively equal, gendered right to social security set out in Chapter 2.

3.4.1 The International Covenant

Article 9 of the ICESCR sets out the right to social security briefly as follows:

117 Otto, above n 29, argues that this is a failing of the equality paradigm that necessarily requires comparison with men and adjustments that fail to envision entirely new ways of ordering society.

118 Above n 7.

119 CESCR '*General Comment No 19: The Right to Social Security (Art. 9)*' (2008) 39th Session 2007, E/C.12/GC/19 (hereafter 'General Comment 19').

120 CESCR '*General Comment No 20: Non-discrimination in economic, social and cultural rights (art. 2, para. 2, of the* International Covenant on Economic, Social and Cultural Rights)' (2009) 42nd Session 2009, E/C 12/GC/20 (hereafter 'General Comment 20').

121 CESCR '*General Comment No 16: Article 3: the equal right of men and women to the enjoyment of all economic, social and cultural rights*' (2005) 34th Session 2005, E/C 12/2005/4 (hereafter 'General Comment 16').

> The States Parties to the present Covenant recognize the right of everyone to social security, including social insurance.

Article 3 of the ICESCR requires states parties to 'undertake to ensure the equal right of men and women to the enjoyment of all economic, social and cultural rights set forth in the present Covenant', while Article 2(2) requires states to guarantee that all Covenant rights are exercised without discrimination of any kind including on the basis of sex. The word 'enjoyment' implies a substantive notion of equality that is focused on actual outcomes not just equality in form.[122] The substantive equality tone of Articles 2 and 3 is in contrast to the language of the Covenant which in certain articles is male and which in other articles reinforces the stereotype of men as breadwinners.[123] For example, Article 6(1) on the right to work, speaks of 'the opportunity to gain **his** living by work which **he** freely chooses or accepts' (my emphasis). In contrast to this, Article 7(a)(i) provides the right to equal pay and conditions for women. More protective (and paternalistic) language (as opposed to language framed in rights-terms) is used in Article 10(2) which requires that:

> Special protection should be accorded to mothers during a reasonable period before and after childbirth. During such period working mothers should be accorded paid leave or leave with adequate social security benefits.

By approaching women as 'special', the ICESCR constructs their experience as 'non-universal and has the effect of buttressing the masculinity of the universal subject'.[124] The emphasis on 'working mothers' in Article 10(2) implies that women engaged in unpaid labour are not entitled to maternity benefits. However, women who cannot engage in subsistence work or work within family enterprises due to maternity may lose out economically, requiring financial or other support for themselves and their families.

Similarly protective language is used in Article 10(1) with regard to assisting the family which is 'responsible for the care and education of dependent children'. The recognition that the state has a role to play in the care of children is important; however, this should be framed in rights language. In addition, naming the family as 'responsible' detracts from the State's role as a partner in the care of children. The Preamble to CEDAW reflects a clearer approach in referring to the 'sharing of responsibility between men and women and society as a whole'.

122 Otto, above n 116, at 349.

123 For a critical discussion of the ICESCR's utility from a feminist perspective, see Diane Elson and Jasmine Gideon, 'Organising for women's economic and social rights: how useful is the International Covenant on Economic, Social and Cultural Rights?' (2004) 8(1&2) *Journal of Interdisciplinary Gender Studies* 133.

124 Otto, above n 116, at 351 argues that they should be given rights rather than protections. Raday, above n 49 at 302, in discussing a similar provision in CEDAW (Article 11(2)(d)) protecting pregnant women, notes the CEDAW Committee's concern that protective measures be used to assist rather than further discriminate against women.

Article 11, also using male language, guarantees a right to 'an adequate standard of living for **himself** and **his** family, including adequate food, clothing and housing, and to the continuous improvement of living conditions' (my emphasis). This language implies that men are rights holders while women and children are dependent beneficiaries of male rights. However, despite this language and because it has been interpreted more broadly to apply to women, this right is of central importance within the Covenant and is closely related to the right to social security which contributes significantly to ensuring adequate living standards and ongoing improvements to these.

International co-operation and assistance (set out in Article 2(1)), as a means to achieve the rights in the ICESCR for all people in the world, is emphasised throughout the Covenant and has relevance for realising the right to social security for poorer countries.

3.4.2 The CESCR

The CESCR has considered the right to social security from a gender perspective in many of its Concluding Observations and Recommendations and in some of its General Comments, Statements and open letters.[125] The CESCR's responses to country reports on women's social security rights will be discussed and compared with those of the CEDAW Committee before the key General Comments are considered in greater detail.

Concluding Observations and Recommendations[126]

The CESCR, like the CEDAW Committee, has shown an understanding of many of the forms of work in which women are located, the intersectional discrimination experienced by different groups of women in accessing social security, and the need for social assistance to address gendered poverty.

TYPES OF WORK AND SOCIAL SECURITY

In the context of formal employment, the CESCR has called for the removal of sex discrimination in pension schemes, recommending the adoption of the same

125 Farha (above n 54, at 554–5) has noted that certain members of the Committee believe (unofficially) that an examination of women's economic, social and cultural rights is better dealt with by the CEDAW Committee. However, she acknowledges that in many of the Concluding Observations, the CESCR has shown a thorough analysis of women's issues with regards to the rights in the ICESCR.

126 A selective approach was taken in the survey of Concluding Observations and Recommendations given the large number of reports prepared over the life of the Committee. This study surveyed reports of the CESCR in the period 2000–2013 using the Universal Human Rights Index (developed and run by the Office of the United Nations High Commissioner for Human Rights http://uhri.ohchr.org/). The search used the term 'women' and checked the 'right to social security' in the list of rights. The word 'austerity' was also searched.

age of retirement for men and women. It has explained that this discrimination reduces women's pensions and prevents them from accessing senior positions.[127] It has noted the lack of availability of parental and paternity leave (as well as maternity leave), demonstrating a substantive understanding of equality.[128] The Committee has recognised that large numbers of women workers are employed in the informal sector where social security coverage is absent or very limited. It has called on countries to ensure women are included and covered.[129] It has also pointed to the difficulties faced by women who are forced to migrate to find work as domestic workers, often in 'slavery-like conditions'.[130] The CESCR has expressed concern about women who work for low wages in the home (home workers) who have no social protection.[131]

The CESCR has gone further than the CEDAW Committee in its condemnation of the exclusion of women's household labour from social insurance schemes and hence from old-age benefits. It criticised the exclusion of 'homemakers' from provident schemes in Hong Kong[132] and the exclusion of 'housewives' from old-age benefits in Chile as a result of the privatisation of the pension system.[133] The CEDAW Committee, however, has been more responsive than the CESCR to the issue of unpaid subsistence work in agriculture and unpaid work in family enterprises.

MULTIPLE DISCRIMINATION AGAINST DIFFERENT GROUPS OF WOMEN RELATING TO SOCIAL SECURITY

Many of the Committee's Concluding Observations reflect a good understanding of the intersecting forms of discrimination faced by women due to their race, ethnicity, nationality, age and marital status in accessing social security.[134] For example, the CESCR has condemned the gender disparities in social security coverage in Ecuador where Indigenous and Afro-Ecuadoran women are particularly

127 CO Poland E/C.12/POL/CO/5 (CESCR, 2009), at para 21. But note the CEDAW Committee's concern that women should be given a choice as earlier retirement may be in some women's interests, as discussed in Raday above n 49, at 295.

128 CO United Kingdom E/C.12/GBR/CO/5 (CESCR, 2009), at para 19.

129 CO Turkey, E/C.12/TUR/CO/1 (CESCR, 2011), at para 20.

130 CO Sri Lanka, E/C.12/LKA/CO/2-4 (CESCR, 2010), at para 21.

131 CO Australia E/C.12/1/ADD.50 (CESCR, 2000), at para 18.

132 CO China E/C.12/1/ADD.107 (CESCR, 2005), at para 78(e).

133 CO Chile E/C.12/1/ADD.105 (CESCR, 2004), at para 20. The language on this issue is noteworthy. The committee said that '"housewives" and about 40 per cent of working women do not contribute to social security schemes and are consequently not entitled to old-age benefits'. The distinction in the language between 'housewives', itself a gender-loaded term, and 'working women' implies that the former are not actually working. This is because work is defined economically as paid work. Nevertheless, acknowledgement of this group in relation to social security is a significant step by the Committee. Despite these references, the CESCR failed to address the social security needs and rights of unpaid workers performing care work, household reproduction, work in family enterprises or subsistence work in General Comment 19 (see further below).

134 Such as CO France E/C.12/FRA/CO/3 (CESCR, 2008), at para 13.

disadvantaged.[135] Like the CEDAW Committee, the CESCR has identified the difficulties faced by women refugees, migrants and displaced people and has highlighted their lack of identification documents as a barrier to social security benefits and services.[136]

POVERTY ALLEVIATION AND SOCIAL SECURITY

Outside of the workplace, the CESCR has challenged the lack of social assistance provision for women in certain developing countries.[137] It has also condemned the inadequacy of pension entitlements for marginalised groups including women in developed countries such as the United Kingdom[138] and those on widows' pensions in Spain,[139] and has criticised welfare conditionality as having a punitive effect on marginalized women in Australia.[140] It has noted the exclusion of women from contributory pension eligibility and the poverty and disadvantage this has caused in Japan.[141] Recently, the CESCR has commented on the negative impact of austerity measures in Spain on the realisation of the economic and social rights of women.[142] Although these are important and useful contributions, Otto has criticised the Committee's statements as overly general and noted it lacks more 'effective tools to guide implementation of Article 9'.[143] As with the CEDAW Committee there is a lack of clear guidance on what is entailed in the development of a gender-equal social assistance system and how states should respond to economic crises while preserving women's right to social security.

General Comments

The chapter now considers the CESCR's General Comments and some of the statements and open letters produced by the Committee relating to gender and the right to social security.[144] It looks specifically at two General Comments on equality for men and women, and non-discrimination, as they relate to social

135 CO Ecuador E/C.12/ECU/CO/3 (CESCR, 2012), at para 20.
136 CO Cyprus E/C.12/CYP/CO/5 (CESCR, 2009), at para 12.
137 CO Dominican Republic E/C.12/DOM/CO/3 (CESCR, 2010), at para 20.
138 CO United Kingdom E/C.12/GBR/CO/5 (CESCR, 2009), at para 23.
139 CO Spain E/C.12/ESP/CO/5 (CESCR, 2012), at para 20.
140 CO Australia E/C.12/AUS/CO/4 (CESCR, 2009), at para 20.
141 CO Japan E/C.12/JPN/CO/3 (CESCR, 2013), at para 22.
142 CO Spain E/C.12/ESP/CO/5 (CESCR, 2012), at para 8.
143 Otto, above n 29, at 227.
144 Note that the CESCR has also prepared reporting guidelines that specifically refer to social security among the listed rights. These guidelines call on states parties to report on whether there is 'equal enjoyment by men and women of pension rights as regards the age of access, qualifying periods and amounts'. They also require information on the availability of non-contributory social assistance schemes as well as provision for informal workers and non-nationals – all significant from a gender perspective: CESCR 'Guidelines on Treaty-Specific Documents to be Submitted by States Parties Under Articles 16 And 17 of the International Covenant on Economic, Social and Cultural Rights' (2008), E/C.12/2008/2, at 8–9.

security, before undertaking a more detailed gender analysis of the key General Comment on the right to social security, General Comment 19.

The CESCR considered the right to social security briefly in developing some of its earlier General Comments.[145] General Comment 6 on Older Persons[146] is surprisingly gender-neutral in its references to social security; however, General Comment 5 on Persons with Disabilities recognises that carers of people with disabilities, 'who are overwhelmingly female', must be provided with assistance.[147] In a letter addressed to states parties in 2012 on the protection of ICESCR rights in the context of financial crisis, the chairperson of the CESCR set out requirements to be followed in considering a policy change that might affect people's rights under ICESCR.[148] In addition to the policy being temporary, necessary and proportionate, it should 'support social transfers to mitigate inequalities that can grow in times of crisis' and 'ensure that the rights of the disadvantaged and marginalized individuals and groups are not disproportionately affected'. The letter also stated that any policy change should protect the minimum core content of rights or a social protection floor as developed by the ILO. This letter is an important recognition by the CESCR of the relationship between inequality and poverty and the role of economic and social rights, including the right to social security, in protecting marginalised groups from carrying the burden of financial crises.

GENERAL COMMENT 16 (MEN AND WOMEN) AND GENERAL COMMENT 20 (NON-DISCRIMINATION)

Prior to the drafting of General Comment 16 a group of experts prepared the Montreal Principles on Women's Economic, Social and Cultural Rights in 2002.[149] The Principles took a substantive equality approach and stressed the interdependence and indivisibility of rights. The Principles were intended to inform the drafting of General Comment 16 and to encourage the CESCR to take the substantive equality approach already adopted by the CEDAW Committee.[150] While many of the ideas found in the Montreal Principles are reflected in General Comment 16, the General Comment takes a different approach to equality due

145 As listed in Reidel, above n 2, at 18, fn 5. Also listed within CESCR General Comment 19, at fn 7.

146 CESCR, '*General Comment No. 6: The Economic, Social and Cultural Rights of Older Persons*' (1995) 30th Session 1995, E/1996/22.

147 CESCR, '*General Comment No. 5: Persons with Disabilities*' (1994) 11th Session 1994, E/1995/22, at para 28.

148 A.G. Pillay (Chairperson of CESCR), 'Letter dated 16 May 2012 addressed by the Chairperson of the Committee on Economic, Social and Cultural Rights to States parties to the International Covenant on Economic, Social and Cultural Rights' (4 June 2012), http://tbinternet.ohchr.org/_layouts/treatybodyexternal/TBSearch.aspx?Lang=en&TreatyID=9&DocTypeID=68.

149 Above n 29.

150 See Dianne Otto, 'Gender comment: why does the UN Committee on Economic, Social and Cultural Rights need a general comment on women?' (2002) 14(1) *Canadian Journal of Women and the Law* 1.

to its focus on discrimination against women and men, rather than on women alone.[151]

General Comment 16 notes the significance of the inclusion of Article 3 in the ICESCR, relating specifically to men and women, when Article 2(2) already guarantees non-discrimination, including on the ground of sex. It approaches both provisions as mutually reinforcing and states that they must 'be read in conjunction with each specific right' in the Covenant.[152] General Comment 16 recognises that equality carries a 'substantive meaning'[153] and refers to de facto or substantive equality as removing 'inherent disadvantage'[154] and ensuring enjoyment of rights 'in practice'.[155] The General Comment makes specific reference to social security rights and provides some examples of states parties' obligations in this regard.[156] These examples, repeated in General Comment 19 in its consideration of gender equality,[157] are limited in scope as they refer only to pensions and retirement age as well as maternity. They do, however, raise issues of paternity and parental rights, illustrating an understanding of the importance of further involving men in care. General Comment 16 also contains a clear statement on gender-based violence, which is described as a form of discrimination that prevents the equal realisation of other rights.[158] Some of the examples in General Comment 16 (such as those dealing with work) treat equality as an 'add-on', without requiring structural change to ensure women's realisation of their rights.[159] However, the emphasis on issues of joint responsibility for care is more 'hopeful'.[160]

Otto argues that General Comment 16 is an improvement on the Montreal Principles as men are included in the concept of gender rather than treating gender as a synonym for women. In this way, General Comment 16 is effective in 'disrupting gender stereotypes, militating against protective responses to women, and opening possibilities for transformative change in gender relations'.[161] However, an overly symmetrical approach can lead to a failure to appreciate the specific conditions in which women suffer disadvantage. General Comment 16 is responsive to this concern in acknowledging that women's full participation

151 For a discussion of the differences between the Montreal Principles and General Comment 16, see Otto, above n 29.

152 At para 2.

153 At para 6.

154 At para 7.

155 At para 6.

156 At para 26. These include: 'equalizing the compulsory retirement age for both men and women; ensuring that women receive the equal benefit of public and private pension schemes; and guaranteeing adequate maternity leave for women, paternity leave for men, and parental leave for both men and women'.

157 At para 32 of General Comment 19, discussed below.

158 At para 27.

159 Fredman, above n 50, at 25.

160 Ibid.

161 Above n 29, at 224.

in economic and social life is limited due to gendered assumptions, expectations and lower status.[162]

General Comment 20 on non-discrimination expressly recognises historical group-based prejudice, naming this systemic discrimination.[163] It adopts the language of substantive equality and, as with General Comment 16, is alive to the distinction between direct and indirect discrimination.[164] It also allows for differential treatment that is 'reasonable and objective'.[165] It notes, in line with feminist theory, that discrimination frequently occurs in the private spheres of home, work and elsewhere, requiring specific measures to prevent this.[166] General Comment 20 highlights 'sex' as an express ground of discrimination and notes that this includes the 'social construction of gender stereotypes, prejudices and expected roles'.[167] The examples of sex discrimination it uses are drawn from the world of work and include: failing to hire women who might become pregnant; allocating them to lower-level or part-time jobs on the stereotyped assumption that they will not commit as much time to their jobs as men; and refusing to grant paternity leave.[168]

These examples reflect an awareness of the recognition and redistribution dimensions of substantive equality. The acknowledgment of discrimination against men and the need to involve men in care points to an understanding of the transformative dimension of substantive equality. Marital and family status is identified as an additional ground of discrimination, and General Comment 20 recognises that marital status can profoundly impact social security entitlements.[169] Being married, single or widowed can have a significant impact on social security entitlements. In addition, women may be required to obtain their husband's consent in order to access certain benefits. The recognition in General Comment 20 that class-based discrimination occurs against people living in poverty or facing homelessness[170] is significant as this form of discrimination frequently intersects with sex discrimination since women face poverty in disproportionate numbers.

Both General Comments are important in deepening the understanding of non-discrimination and gender equality within the ICESCR. They reflect an understanding of substantive equality in relation to social security, although this is not always illustrated fully in the examples provided. They appreciate the different dimensions of substantive equality discussed in Chapter 2 but are strongest on issues of recognition and redistribution, with some acknowledgement of the

162 At paras 5 and 14.
163 At para 12. Para 39 deals with measures to eliminate systemic discrimination.
164 At para 10.
165 At para 13.
166 At para 11.
167 At para 20.
168 Ibid.
169 At para 31.
170 At para 35.

transformative dimension. There is limited reference in both General Comments to participation by groups affected by discrimination.[171]

GENERAL COMMENT 19: THE RIGHT TO SOCIAL SECURITY

This section first provides some background to General Comment 19. It then discusses the definition and content of the right as set out in the General Comment before considering the specific provisions on gender equality and non-discrimination within the General Comment.

Background Despite the clear statement of the right to social security in international, regional and national law, with the exception of the ILO[172] and the European Committee of Social Rights,[173] until the mid-2000s very little work was done (by UN bodies or academics) on developing the right.[174] In its earlier General Comments the CESCR had elaborated its understanding of other rights in the Covenant, including the rights to education, health, housing, food and water, but had not undertaken similar work on the development of the right to social security. It began, however, to draft a general comment in 2004.[175] In 2005 a conference was held in Brussels and an International Expert Workshop was held in Berlin to consider the right to social security. Both events and the books[176] that followed them informed the development in 2007 by the CESCR of General Comment 19 on the right to social security, the first detailed consideration of the meaning and scope of the right.

The need for the development of the General Comment arose from the context of increased economic globalisation, privatisation of welfare, attacks against the welfare systems of developed countries, the ageing populations of these countries, and the lack of coverage in developing countries facing deepening poverty.[177] Langford listed three reasons for an elaboration of the right to social security in a General Comment that would go beyond the existing ILO framework.[178] First, the right to social security is universal and an examination by the CESCR might avoid the formal employment bias of the ILO, thus bringing in previously excluded groups of workers and categories of people facing discrimination within

171 General Comment 20, at para 36; General Comment 16, at para 37.

172 See below at 3.5.

173 See discussion of the European law in 3.2.2 above.

174 Lamarche, above n 12, at 89, writing in 2002, said that 'social security is a highly technical domain too often neglected by human rights activists. The basic issue of establishing the normative content of the right to social security has not been addressed by the human rights literature.'

175 Malcolm Langford and Jeff A. King, 'Committee on Economic, Social and Cultural Rights: Past, Present and Future' in Malcolm Langford (ed.), *Social Rights Jurisprudence: Emerging Trends in International and Comparative Law* (Cambridge University Press, 2008) 447, at 505.

176 Van Langendonck, above n 1; Eibe Reidel (ed.), *Social Security as a Human Right: Drafting a General Comment on Article 9 ICESCR – Some Challenges* (Springer, 2007).

177 Reynaud, above n 15; Van Langendonck, above n 1; Langford and King, above n 175, at 504.

178 Malcolm Langford, 'The Right to Social Security and Implications for Law, Policy and Practice' in Eibe Reidel (ed.), *Social Security as a Human Right* (Springer, 2007) 29, at 30–2.

and outside of the workforce. Second, human rights instruments have been ratified by many more countries than ILO conventions (approximately a quarter of the countries that have ratified ICESCR have also ratified ILO Convention No. 102).[179] Human rights treaties might assist countries to respond to the pressures of globalisation. Interpretation of the right might assist domestic courts when a right to social security exists in their countries' constitutions. Third, the right to social security, as with the human rights approach in general, requires participation and accountability. States are required to justify their decisions as well as consider the views of the 'beneficiaries of human rights' in meeting their international obligations. Reidel notes that 'the quality of State reporting to the Committee improves greatly after the adoption of a General Comment.'[180]

Lamarche, writing before General Comment 19 was produced, emphasised the need to draw on the work of the ILO to interpret and develop the right.[181] She was, however, critical of some aspects of the ILO approach. She explained that while ILO conventions may find a national scheme acceptable because it includes a protected class of worker, other groups of workers (such as informal sector workers, female atypical workers and the self-employed) might be left out.[182] This potential for discrimination or social exclusion relates to the inbuilt paradox of the right to social security as developed in social security instruments: 'designed eventually to attain universality of coverage, it authorises ratifying states to halt progress at the gate of modern forms of exclusion'.[183] Lamarche noted, however, that ILO conventions offer important benchmarks and are highly influential internationally. She argued that they have a significant role in informing the content of the human right to social security set out in international instruments such as the ICESCR but that the right must be further developed.[184] She also stressed that gender equality issues needed to be addressed within such efforts.[185]

The chapter now analyses the provisions of General Comment 19 from a gender perspective, starting with the definition and content of the right to social security and then examining the explicit provisions on gender equality and non-discrimination.

179 Ibid.

180 Reidel, above n 2, at vii.

181 Lamarche, above n 12.

182 Lamarche, ibid., at 95.

183 Ibid.

184 Ibid. Also see Lucie Lamarche, 'Social Protection is a Matter of Human Rights: Exploring the ICESCR Right to Social Security in the Context of Globalisation' in Koen De Feyter and Felipe Gomez Isa (eds), *Privatisation and Human Rights in the Age of Globalisation* (Intersentia, 2005) 129; Jennifer Tooze, 'The Rights to Social Security and Social Assistance: Towards an Analytical Framework' in Mashood A. Baderin and Robert McCorquodale (eds), *Economic, Social and Cultural Rights in Action* (Oxford University Press, 2007) 331.

185 Lucie Lamarche, 'Le *Pacte international relatif aux droits économiques, sociaux et culturels*, les femmes et le droit à la sécurité sociale: des considérations et des propositions pour un droit "universel" à la sécurité sociale' (2002) 14(1) *Canadian Journal of Women and the Law* 53.

Definition and content of the right to social security General Comment 19 states that social security 'through its redistributive character, plays an important role in poverty reduction and alleviation, preventing social exclusion and promoting social inclusion',[186] and is central to the fulfilment of all other Covenant rights and in guaranteeing human dignity.[187] It also emphasises the interdependence of human rights since social security is represented as closely related to the realisation of other fundamental rights such as the right to a livelihood, health, housing, food and education.[188] The General Comment stresses that social security is a social good and should not be regarded, 'primarily as a mere instrument of economic or financial policy'.[189] This principled focus on the normative content of the right as a citizenship entitlement militates against utilitarian rationales and technocratic approaches to the right.

These are important statements on the purpose of the right and seem to position the General Comment beyond the employment paradigm of the ILO. However, the definition of social security in General Comment 19 has been strongly influenced by the ILO conventions. It defines the right to social security as encompassing:[190]

> (T)he right to access and maintain benefits, whether in cash or in kind, without discrimination in order to secure protection, inter alia, from
> (a) lack of work-related income caused by sickness, disability, maternity, employment injury, unemployment, old age, or death of a family member;
> (b) unaffordable access to health care;
> (c) insufficient family support, particularly for children and adult dependents.

Langford and King note that this formulation, which follows the list of nine contingencies set out in ILO Convention 102 (and in (a) above), was more broadly framed in the Committee's draft of General Comment 19. The draft included other risks such as lack of housing, water, food for specific groups and protection from natural disasters and emergencies;[191] however, this approach was opposed by the ILO representative.[192] The failure to include these risks in the final version of the General Comment is detrimental since the ILO formulation is based on a traditional, formal employment model that does not fully reflect the needs of women. The broader formulation would have included people facing poverty due to their location outside of the formal labour market or paid work. While (b) and (c) in the Committee's definition may not be directly tied to the employment

186 Ibid., para 3.
187 Ibid., para 1.
188 The relationship between the right to social security and other rights is developed further in the General Comment at para 5.
189 At para 10.
190 At para 2.
191 Langford and King, above n 175, at 505.
192 Ibid.

relationship, they do not seem broad enough to cover all non-employment-related risks that require social security protection. An interpretation of the right to social security, delinked from work or inclusive of non-work related contingencies, would have created a fuller sense of the right, in that it would have required states parties to ensure that all people are provided with necessary income support and would have been more inclusive of women.[193]

The General Comment does, however, differ from ILO Convention 102, which allows a state party to choose a certain number of contingencies to which its obligations will apply. This accommodation is not provided for by General Comment 19 in its elaboration of the right – states parties are expected to provide for all of the enumerated risks. This indicates the higher standard demanded by the ICESCR. The ILO Convention also sets targets for state compliance, such as a requirement that a certain percentage of all employees and residents must receive medical benefits.[194] The General Comment does not take this approach but instead requires that all people are provided with their rights on a universal basis.[195]

As with other ICESCR rights, states parties must take steps to progressively realise rights within their maximum available resources.[196] However, the General Comment does require, in its discussion of the core obligations under the right, that states parties must satisfy minimum essential levels of the right.[197] This minimum level is defined as providing 'benefits to all individuals and families that will enable them to acquire at least essential health care, basic shelter and housing, water and sanitation, foodstuffs, and the most basic forms of education'.[198] It is only when a state is unable to provide this minimum level for all contingencies that it should select a 'core group of social risks and contingencies' following a wide process of consultation.[199] What this might include and the criteria that might be used to achieve this are not set out in the General Comment. This omission could lead to the exclusion of women, who are often given low priority when there are competing needs. The process of consultation will only have value if women are adequately and (substantively) equally represented and their concerns are given sufficient weight and acknowledgment.[200] The General Comment

193 Also see the discussion of this definition in Chapter 1 at 1.2.3 and Chapter 2 at 2.3 above. Langford and King, ibid., at footnote 225, refer to Liebenberg's definition of social security as covering 'all those risks that impinge upon a person's ability to generate income and maintain an adequate standard of living'.

194 Article 9 of ILO *Social Security (Minimum Standards) Convention*, 1952, (No. 102).

195 Langford and King, above n 175, at 506.

196 However, certain obligations under ICESCR have immediate effect including ensuring that the right to social security is exercised without discrimination (Article 2, para 2) and equally for men and women (Article 3): General Comment 19, at para 40.

197 At para 59–61.

198 Ibid., at para 59(a). This highlights the role of the right to social security as the facilitator of other Covenant rights and emphasises the interdependency of rights.

199 Ibid.

200 This may require quotas or other mechanisms to ensure the process properly accommodates women.

stresses the 'strong presumption that retrogressive measures taken in relation to the right to social security are prohibited under the Covenant'.[201] This is important with regard to state party cutbacks and the withdrawal of benefits in pursuit of austerity in both developed and developing countries.[202] General Comment 19 sets out criteria for assessing whether a violation of this type has occurred.[203] Discrimination is one of the criteria as is genuine participation of affected groups: women must thus be empowered to actively participate in any consultations.

The normative content of the right includes elements (availability, adequacy and accessibility) found in interpretations of other ICESCR rights with the addition of the element of social risks and contingencies (the nine principal branches of social security as set out in ILO Convention 102).

Availability[204] The General Comment points to the responsibility of each state party for ensuring that a system is in place, is properly administered and is sustainable. Social security can take various forms including social insurance, social assistance and private or community schemes.[205] This is critical for the majority of people in the world, with women amongst the poorest, who currently have no access to social security.[206]

Adequacy[207] General Comment 19 uses criteria that ensure a rights-based approach rather than the incremental approach of the ILO which may not always ensure adequate minimum levels of coverage.[208] The adequacy criteria include

201 At para 42.
202 See Chapter 5 for an evaluation of the removal of benefits for single parents in Australia against these criteria.
203 Ibid. The criteria include whether: (a) there was reasonable justification for the action; (b) alternatives were comprehensively examined; (c) there was genuine participation of affected groups in examining the proposed measures and alternatives; (d) the measures were directly or indirectly discriminatory; (e) the measures will have a sustained impact on the realisation of the right to social security, an unreasonable impact on acquired social security rights or whether an individual or group is deprived of access to the minimum essential level of social security; and (f) whether there was an independent review of the measures at the national level.
204 At para 11.
205 At paras 4–5.
206 Some commentators have suggested that the introduction of an international social security scheme or fund might address the inability of poor countries to establish social security systems without outside assistance: Jef Van Langendonck, 'The Meaning of the Right to Social Security' in Jef Van Langendonck (ed.), *The Right to Social Security* (Intersentia, 2007) 3. Also see the proposal for a global fund for social protection proposed by two UN Special Rapporteurs: Olivier De Schutter and Magdalena Sepúlveda, 'Underwriting the Poor – A Global Fund for Social Protection' (2012), www.srfood.org/images/stories/pdf/otherdocuments/20121009_gfsp_en.pdf. Such suggestions arise from changing ideas of state sovereignty, the notion of universal solidarity, the current expenditure on aid, and the utility of addressing poverty and inequality in the interests of peace and security. In the absence, however, of such a scheme, States parties must put domestic social security systems in place where these do not exist.
207 At para 22.
208 Malcolm Langford, 'The Right to Social Security and Implications for Law, Policy and Practice' in Eibe Reidel (ed.), *Social Security as a Human Right* (Springer, 2007) 29, at 33–4.

the principles of human dignity and non-discrimination in the interpretation of this element of the right 'so as to avoid any adverse effect on the levels of benefits and the form in which they are provided'.[209] This is of importance to women who may not be able to contribute as much as men to contributory schemes due to work interruptions or lack of participation in the formal workforce.

Accessibility[210] This dimension of the right contains the further categories of coverage, eligibility, affordability, participation and information, and physical access. General Comment 19 stresses that non-contributory schemes are necessary to ensure universal *coverage* of marginal and disadvantaged groups. The issue of *eligibility* is important as it relates to requirements such as documentation, means testing, conditionality and other mechanisms that often serve as barriers to accessing social assistance by women and other disadvantaged groups.[211] *Affordability* of contribution-based schemes is very important for low-income earners, many of whom are women. The element of *participation and information* is critical for poor people who are often illiterate and disempowered. Women in particular may have less access to representation and may be less able to assert their rights. Ensuring that this element has meaning for such women may require specific efforts to communicate with women and equip them to voice their needs and concerns about social security administration and provision. This may require training of officials to develop sensitivity and gender awareness. The element of *physical access* is of special importance to women in rural areas and women with disabilities.

While the General Comment refers to situations of armed conflict and disasters, it does not refer to gender-based violence that affects women in accessing social security. In addition, women's care responsibilities may act as barriers to access, for example, when they cannot leave small children or sick relatives to attend appointments at social security offices or pay points.[212] There may also be situations where women are unable or are not permitted to attend at government offices without being accompanied by male relatives that may also act as barriers to access. Appropriate responses to these issues must be addressed if women are to have full and equal rights of access to social security. Ensuring that gender does not prevent access to social security should also require: that benefits are not tied to land or property; that women are entitled to benefits in their own right and not as dependents of others; that a physical address is not required for registration of beneficiaries, as poor women do not always have one; that illiteracy and lack of information should not disadvantage women; and that women should

209 At para 22.

210 At paras 23–7.

211 For a discussion of conditionality, see Chapter 4. For some examples of barriers to access social assistance, see Beth Goldblatt, 'Gender and social assistance in the first decade of democracy: a case study of South Africa's Child Support Grant' (2005) 32(2) *Politikon* 239; Beth Goldblatt, 'Gender, rights and the disability grant in South Africa' (2009) 26(3) *Development Southern Africa* 369.

212 Goldblatt (2005), ibid.; Goldblatt (2009), ibid.

be entitled to representation in decision-making that might affect their access to social security.[213]

Social risks and contingencies[214] The nine social risks and contingencies, all of which have significant gender dimensions, include:

- Health care[215]
- Sickness[216]
- Old age[217]
- Unemployment[218]
- Employment injury[219]

213 Priti Darooka, 'Social Security: A Women's Human Right' (PWESCR, 2008) 1, at 8–10.

214 General Comment 19, at paras 12–21.

215 General Comment 19 does not refer to access to women's specific health needs but these are of obvious importance in any social security system. Medical needs for women and children are, however, referred to in relation to the contingency of maternity.

216 General Comment 19 also fails to refer specifically to women, many of whom will not be able to use sickness benefits due to their location in the informal labour market or unpaid work.

217 General Comment 19 does not refer to gender but emphasis is given to non-contributory social assistance for people who have been unable to contribute adequately or are not entitled to social insurance and have no other source of income. As noted, women in formal, paid work are generally unable to contribute to social insurance in the same amount as men due to work interruptions (related to birth and caring) and because they earn less. They also live longer than men. This means that in a social security system based on contributions women are, in general, likely to retire on smaller amounts than men, which they must use over a longer period. Adequate social assistance is thus critical alongside more far-reaching efforts to address the underlying inequalities in the labour market.

218 General Comment 19 recognises the need for social assistance to protect unemployed people after social insurance benefits run out. The General Comment also refers to the need for coverage of non-traditional workers including 'part-time workers, seasonal workers, the self-employed, (and) those working in atypical forms of work in the informal economy'. This is critically important for the large numbers of women in the informal economy. The consideration of unemployment recognises that benefits must be provided to those who have lost work but also those unable to obtain work. It also covers structural unemployment where the economy is not able to provide sufficient jobs for the working population. It does not, however, refer to underemployment where people are in work but nevertheless do not have sufficient income to live on, a situation that affects marginal workers, many of whom are women. For a discussion of gender-related underemployment in Australia, see Belinda Smith, 'What Would an Engendered Human Rights Approach to Social Security Mean for Sole Parents in Australia?' in Beth Goldblatt and Lucie Lamarche (eds), *Women's Rights to Social Security and Social Protection* (Hart, 2014) 191. Conditional unemployment benefits such as 'workfare' in the US or other programmes that require women (often single mothers) to take on work allocated to them following unemployment (no matter how inappropriate or inconvenient it is for them in their circumstances) are not considered in the General Comment. For a discussion of the system in the US in this regard, see Lucy A. Williams, 'Rethinking Social Protection Beyond Waged Work: A United States Perspective' in Beth Goldblatt and Lucie Lamarche (eds), *Women's Rights to Social Security and Social Protection* (Hart, 2014) 145. However, it is implicit from the approach of the General Comment that social security should not be subject to harsh or discriminatory conditions.

219 This includes loss of support following the injury or death of a breadwinner and should take the form of access to health care and cash benefits. Like other benefits, these are often not available in

- Family and child support[220]
- Maternity[221]
- Disability[222]
- Survivors and orphans.[223]

Having discussed the definition and content of the right to social security in General Comment 19, this section now considers the specific provision in the General Comment relating to gender equality and non-discrimination.

Gender equality and non-discrimination General Comment 19 identifies seven 'special topics of broad application', which include various categories of vulnerability and principled approaches to each of these. The first is ***non-discrimination and equality*** which restates the guarantee in Articles 2 and 3 of ICESCR that

informal work where women are prevalent. General Comment 19 states these benefits must not be linked to the length of employment or contribution which is also of assistance to women who have interrupted working lives and lower earnings.

220 General Comment 19 approaches such benefits as 'crucial' to the realisation of the rights of children and adult dependents (such as the elderly or ill) in Articles 9 and 10 of ICESCR. While these benefits are often crucial for parents (usually mothers) and the only source of social assistance paid to them, the money is directed at meeting the needs of the children or other dependents and not as compensation for the work of the women themselves as carers or for their own use to address their own poverty. See Chapter 4 for a critique of South Africa's Child Support Grant for its failure to include support for the carers of the children being assisted. The failure to compensate women carers is because care, which is both invisible and gendered, is usually not considered work to be remunerated by society. Women are expected to do this as a 'natural' responsibility within the family and society. General Comment 19 does however state that the circumstances and resources of those responsible for the maintenance of children and other dependents should be taken into account by states parties in providing benefits (at para 18).

221 General Comment 19 importantly refers to women in 'atypical' work in the context of maternity. Although some countries provide for longer periods of maternity leave, adequacy is linked to the ILO's standard of 14 weeks' paid maternity leave. The amount of pay is not defined and the implication is that this may be lower than the income the woman was receiving, which is problematic. Giving birth is a social function that societies should properly acknowledge and compensate. There is no mention here of paternity benefits or parental leave although this is referred to later in the General Comment in its discussion of gender equality. The failure to list such benefits here indicates a view that these are not 'principal' branches of social security requiring realisation by States parties.

222 General Comment 19 recognises that support should also cover 'family members and other informal carers'. This is a significant addition as it acknowledges that a person with a disability requires social security as well as those persons providing care to a person with a disability. This is in contrast to the contingency of family and child support benefits where children and other dependent family members in need of social security are seen as worthy recipients of social security but those providing for their care, often women, are not similarly provided for.

223 The General Comment notes that such groups must not be discriminated against in social security schemes but does not specifically refer to the compounding gender discrimination that frequently accompanies discrimination of survivors and orphans. In many countries widows face severe disadvantage and vulnerability as a result of such discrimination. For a discussion of the situation of widows in India, see Robert T. Jensen, 'Caste, Culture, and the Status and Well-Being of Widows in India' in David A. Wise (ed.), *Analyses in the Economics of Aging* (University of Chicago Press, 2005) 357.

the right to social security must be enjoyed without discrimination and equally between men and women.[224] General Comment 19 requires states parties to remove 'de facto discrimination' in access to adequate social security. While it fails to use the language of 'substantive equality' referred to in its General Comment 16 on equality between men and women and General Comment 20 on non-discrimination, the reference to de facto discrimination and discussion of the need for special attention to vulnerable groups implies an awareness of the distinction between formal and substantive equality. The text also distinguishes between discrimination in law and in fact, demonstrating an understanding that goes beyond formal equality. It calls for special attention to traditionally disadvantaged groups, including women, as well as:

> the unemployed, workers inadequately protected by social security, persons working in the informal economy, sick or injured workers, people with disabilities, older persons, children and adult dependents, domestic workers, homeworkers, minority groups, refugees, asylum-seekers, internally displaced persons, returnees, non-nationals, prisoners and detainees.[225]

Women make up large proportions of many of these groups. The General Comment uses the ILO definition of home work to mean 'those who work from home for remuneration for an employer or similar business enterprise or activity'. It is important that this category of work is recognised in international human rights law. However, unpaid work in family enterprises, subsistence work and care/household work is not recognised in the General Comment. This is a significant omission which excludes millions of women.[226]

The second 'special topic of broad application' is *gender equality*.[227] Here, there is a specific cross reference to General Comment 16 which highlights:

> equalization of the compulsory retirement age for both men and women; ensuring that women receive equal benefits in both public and private pension schemes; and guaranteeing adequate maternity leave for women, paternity leave for men, and parental leave for both men and women.

General Comment 19 then adds the following:

> In social security schemes that link benefits with contributions, States parties should take steps to eliminate the factors that prevent women from making equal contributions to such schemes (for example, intermittent participation in the workforce on account of family responsibilities and unequal wage

224 At para 29.
225 At para 31.
226 The scale of women's exclusion from paid work is noted in World Bank, 'World Development Report 2013: Jobs' (2012), at 6.
227 At para 32.

> outcomes) or ensure that schemes take account of such factors in the design of benefit formulas (for example by considering child rearing periods or periods to take care of adult dependents in relation to pension entitlements). Differences in the average life expectancy of men and women can also lead directly or indirectly to discrimination in provision of benefits (particularly in the case of pensions) and thus need to be taken into account in the design of schemes. Non-contributory schemes must also take account of the fact that women are more likely to live in poverty than men and often have sole responsibility for the care of children.

This paragraph raises a number of important issues. It gives further content to General Comment 16 by showing how equality in public and private pension schemes can be achieved. By recommending that states parties remove factors that create unequal wage outcomes or address the impact of family responsibilities, presumably by providing for example, childcare or equal pay laws, the General Comment hints at structural changes to the workplace, economy and society. This substantive and far-reaching approach is necessary if gender inequalities in social security are to be addressed. Similarly, by requiring states to take account of care responsibilities in calculating benefits the General Comment goes considerably further than most countries have to date and renders visible care work that is so often naturalised and ignored. Requiring non-contributory schemes to take account of women's poverty and their responsibility for the care of children is recognition of the gendered division of labour and that women face greater financial hardship than men.

While acknowledging gender poverty and unequal care responsibilities, the General Comment does not expressly state that women are often involved in unpaid subsistence work and work in family enterprises and in household and reproductive labour, with the result that they have no opportunities to access contributory social insurance. As discussed in Chapter 2, their labour in these contexts is not seen as work. In addition, the fact that some members of society have access to higher paid social insurance benefits while others, often women, must settle for more modest social assistance benefits (where these exist at all) is not canvassed. Thus, the structural gender and class inequalities, while acknowledged, are not challenged.[228] The General Comment also fails to acknowledge the impact of violence against women and sexual harassment which operate as social risks or contingencies in many women's lives, requiring them to leave or move jobs or remain unemployed[229] and hindering their access to social security. Addressing gender-based violence, labour market restructuring and the reconfiguration of care are essential if women are to have equal rights to social security.

228 See Otto, above n 29, for a discussion of the role of rights in going beyond minimum requirements by playing a role in redistribution towards economic equality.

229 Ludo McFerran, 'Safe at Home, Safe at Work? National Domestic Violence and the Workplace Survey (2011)' (Australian Domestic and Family Violence Clearinghouse, 2011), www.adfvc.unsw.edu.au/PDF%20files/Domestic_violence_and_work_survey_report_2011.pdf.

In addition to its consideration of gender equality and non-discrimination, the General Comment considers the needs of certain vulnerable groups. These groups are often comprised primarily of women, or represent vulnerabilities that, together with gender discrimination, lead to intersectional discrimination against women in relation to social security. They include: workers inadequately protected by social security (part-time, casual, self-employed and homeworkers;[230] those in the informal economy;[231] Indigenous Peoples and minority groups;[232] non-nationals (including migrant workers, refugees, asylum-seekers and stateless persons)[233] and internally displaced persons and internal migrants.[234]

Assessment of General Comment 19 General Comment 19 on the right to social security is the key interpretive statement on the right within international human rights law. It provides valuable definition and content to the right in the ICESCR. General Comment 19 displays a keen awareness of the principles of

230 At para 33. These categories of work have obvious importance for women, many of whom are required to undertake non-traditional forms of work because of care responsibilities or because full-time, ongoing employment is not available to them. As discussed, these categories do not accommodate unpaid work although the CESCR has noted, in Concluding Observations, the need to recognise unpaid household labour (above at 3.4.2.1).

231 At para 34. Social security coverage for informal sector workers is crucial for women who make up a significant part of this group. General Comment 19 uses the International Labour Conference definition of the informal economy as 'all economic activities by workers and economic units that are – in law or in practice – not covered or insufficiently covered by formal arrangements'. Unpaid work, largely undertaken by women, is not seen as economic activity, despite its essential role in social reproduction. The General Comment, while recognising the importance of social insurance for informal workers, notes that universal pensions and health care are often the solution adopted by states with large informal sectors. Social assistance and the provision of services are essential for women in both developed and developing countries engaged in precarious work or not receiving any pay.

232 At para 35.

233 At paras 36–8.

234 At para 39. Internal migrants and displaced people are frequently denied equal access to social security schemes and benefits in other parts of their countries with specific gender impacts. For a discussion of the hierarchies within the social security system in China and the gender implications of this, see Mankui Li, 'Social Protection in China: Is There a Gender Equality Problem?' in Beth Goldblatt and Lucie Lamarche (eds), *Women's Rights to Social Security and Social Protection* (Hart, 2014) 89. General Comment 19 requires that non-nationals who have contributed to a scheme must be entitled to the benefits but falls short of requiring them to be included in schemes. It does, however, state that non-nationals should be able to access non-contributory schemes for income support, affordable access to health care and family care (with some conditions). This is of critical importance as many countries refuse to extend such benefits to non-nationals. See Ben Saul, David Kinley and Jacqueline Mowbray, *The International Covenant on Economic, Social and Cultural Rights: Commentary, Cases and Materials* (Oxford University Press, 2014), at 667–90. Also see Lucy Williams, 'Issues and challenges in addressing poverty and legal rights: a comparative United States/South Africa analysis' (2005) 21 *South African Journal on Human Rights* 436. General Comment 19 states (at para 38) that there is a similar right for refugees, stateless persons and asylum-seekers to social assistance but fails to specifically mention income support. This distinction appears to reinforce a discriminatory hierarchy in the treatment of different groups of non-nationals.

non-discrimination and gender equality across many of its provisions. It provides important guidance to states parties on the nature and dimensions of the right to social security previously absent in the human rights field. Analysed in terms of the gender perspective developed in Chapter 2, the General Comment is positive on many fronts: it recognises the complex and precarious (gendered) nature of work and the need for social security to reach beyond the formal, traditional definitions of the past; it is aware of the challenges in developing countries where poverty (often gendered) is itself a social risk/contingency and the need to provide social assistance to address this; it is attentive to the different forms of social security and the different levels at which the right requires implementation (including the local and transnational) and the actors that span these levels (such as migrants and international financial agencies); it is alive to the issues of intersectional discrimination; and it is cognisant of the close interdependence between the right to social security and other social and economic rights as well as rights such as equality and dignity. It distinguishes between formal and substantive equality although it does not expressly use this language.

However, General Comment 19 is disappointing in its failure to acknowledge the issues of unpaid work and care that are fundamental to women's experiences globally. It also retains the inappropriate ILO risk and contingency model as the basis for the definition of the right without expanding sufficiently on the issues of poverty, social exclusion and need, and the role of the right to social security as a fundamental citizenship entitlement rather than a work-related right. While it recognises that equality must be substantive, it emphasises some dimensions (redistribution and participation) over other dimensions (recognition and transformation). Thus, it acknowledges women's poverty and the need to ensure women's participation in social security programmes.

It is not, however, as explicit in acknowledging how stigma, stereotyping and violence limit women's access to social security, and it does not propose that social security programmes be used to challenge structural inequalities between men and women, sometimes by treating these groups differently. For example, it recognises that women receive lower pensions due to smaller contributions following work interruptions for childbirth and care and recommends that adjustments be made to pension calculations to ensure that women are not disadvantaged. While this may address pension gaps for women, it does not address the fact that it is still women who undertake these care responsibilities during their working lives. Providing adequate childcare and ensuring that fathers assume greater responsibilities for parenting would ensure more substantively equal outcomes (on the transformation dimension).

3.4.3 Assessment of the ICESCR and the CESCR

The ICESCR guarantees everyone a right to social security as well as a number of other rights that support the realisation of this right. The right to equal enjoyment of the Covenant rights by men and women and the guarantee against discrimination mean that the right to social security has a close relationship to gender equality. The CESCR has provided an important evolving interpretation of the right to social security taking gender issues into account. General Comment 19, which provides necessary detail on the meaning of the right, must be read together with General Comments 16 and 20 to ensure that substantive equality is built into efforts to realise the right to social security. The CESCR is attentive to the various dimensions of substantive equality but this is not always evenly expressed or well developed. More detailed guidance to states on how to ensure that social security systems and programmes are formulated and implemented to address gender inequalities in diverse societies is required. The continued attachment to the ILO's traditional work-related formulation of social security is problematic from a gender perspective and in terms of its applicability to developing countries. The CESCR is, however, increasingly responsive to the social security challenges in these countries and the gender complexities that underlie them. More guidance could be offered by developing a statement on women's right to social security that includes specific recommendations on issues such as welfare conditionality, participation of women in social security programmes, and new approaches to issues of work and care in the context of social security.

The chapter now considers the work of the ILO and the Special Rapporteur on extreme poverty and human rights as they relate to gender and the right to social security.

3.5 The International Labour Organisation

3.5.1 Background

The ILO has pursued its mandate to address social security issues from its establishment in 1919. Early standard-setting was largely influenced by the concept of social insurance in what has been described by the ILO's Committee of Experts on the Application of Conventions and Recommendations (CEACR) as first-generation standards.[235] In 1944 it reaffirmed its social security mandate in the *Declaration of Philadelphia*, recognising that social security must be available to all who need it. This new, universal approach was followed in two key recommendations: *Income Security Recommendation*, 1944 (No. 67) and *Medical Care Recommendation*, 1944 (No. 69). These second-generation standards entailed the development of consolidated standards within a co-ordinated social security system, leading to the *Social Security (Minimum Standards) Convention*, 1952, (No. 102) which remains the point of reference for social security standards today.[236] From the 1960s through to the late 1980s a third generation of standards consolidated what had occurred before and both raised levels of protection

235 CEACR, 'Social security and the rule of law – General Survey concerning social security instruments in light of the 2008 Declaration on Social Justice for a Fair Globalization' (ILC.100/111/1B, International Labour Office, 2011), at 8.

236 Ibid., at 10.

and broadened social security to include new benefits and services.[237] The key Conventions from this period that remain up-to-date include:[238]

- *Equality of Treatment (Social Security) Convention*, 1962 (No. 118);
- *Employment Injury Benefits Convention*, 1964 (No. 121);
- *Invalidity, Old-Age and Survivors' Benefits Convention*, 1967 (No. 128);
- *Medical Care and Sickness Benefits Convention*, 1969 (No. 130);
- *Maintenance of Social Security Rights Convention*, 1982 (No. 157);
- *Employment Promotion and Protection against Unemployment Convention*, 1988 (No. 168); and
- *Maternity Protection Convention*, 2000 (No. 183).

The CEACR has noted that the standards produced in this period 'remained forever the product of the industrial society at its best, but adopted at the time when such notions as sustainable development, governance and globalization – key to understanding the present world – did not exist'.[239] It also stressed the changing context of the global labour market with increased flexibility, precariousness and migration.[240] As noted above, the ILO standards have been criticised for their gendered assumptions since the ideal worker around which they are modelled is male without significant family or care obligations.[241]

The 1990s saw little advancement of social security standards during a decade of structural adjustment in developing countries and a retreat from welfare in the developed world. During the 2000s the ILO reaffirmed the importance of social security as a human right as expressed by the International Labour Conference (ILC) in 2001[242] and again in 2008 where the ILO *Declaration on Social Justice for a Fair Globalization* emphasised the need for social protection and for a basic income for all in need.[243] In a 2010 report the ILO defined social security in accordance with the CESCR's General Comment 19, but added a fourth component for which social protection was needed – 'general poverty and social exclusion'.[244] This is a significant shift in moving from the work-related definition in ILO Convention 102 to a broader definition of need which is endorsed by reference to the *Declaration of Philadelphia*'s concept of a basic income for 'all in need' together with medical care.[245]

237 Ibid., at 11.

238 ILO (2011a), 'Social security for social justice and a fair globalization' (VI, International Labour Office, 2011), at 13.

239 Ibid., at 13.

240 Ibid. And see Lamarche, above n 184.

241 Lamarche, above n 185.

242 ILC, 89th Session, 2001, discussed in ILO (2011a), above n 238, at 12.

243 ILC, 97th Session, 2008.

244 ILO, 'World Social Security Report 2010/11: Providing Coverage in Times of Crisis and Beyond' (2010), at 13.

245 Ibid., at 14.

The CEACR has noted that the new ILO mandate, as expressed in the 2008 Declaration:[246]

> (H)as largely outgrown the standards with which it has to be implemented. … This is particularly evident as regards the objective of extending social security coverage to all, beyond the formal economy to the masses of population living in abject poverty and insecurity, which is placed at the heart of the ILO's mandate and mission.[247]

It was this analysis, coupled with the urgency generated by the global financial crisis of 2008, that led the ILO, in partnership with the UN, to work towards the establishment of a Recommendation on social protection floors.[248] This was a significant development for the ILO in bringing issues of social assistance more centrally into the ambit of social security. The Recommendation is now discussed and assessed from a gender rights perspective.

3.5.2 The Social Protection Floor Recommendation (R202)

The *Recommendation concerning National Floors of Social Protection*, 2012 (No. 202) (hereafter 'R202') provides guidance to Members to establish and maintain social protection floors (SPFs) which are 'nationally defined sets of basic social security guarantees which secure protection aimed at preventing or alleviating poverty, vulnerability and social exclusion'.[249] States are encouraged to extend this basic floor to all while also increasing the levels of coverage of the ILO's pre-existing social security standards. At a minimum, SPFs should provide the following four features:[250]

- (a) access to a nationally defined set of goods and services, constituting essential health care, including maternity care, that meets the criteria of availability, accessibility, acceptability and quality;
- (b) basic income security for children, at least at a nationally defined minimum level, providing access to nutrition, education, care and any other necessary goods and services;
- (c) basic income security, at least at a nationally defined minimum level, for

246 CEACR, above n 235, at 13.

247 Also note the statement by Juan Somavia, the ILO Director-General, on the adoption of the *Domestic Workers Convention*, 2011 (No. 189): 'We are moving the standards system of the ILO into the informal economy for the first time and this is a breakthrough of great significance.' Press release of 16 June 2011, www.ilo.org/ilc/ILCSessions/100thSession/media-centre/press-releases/WCMS_157891/lang--en/index.htm. Social security rights for domestic workers are covered in Article 14 of this Convention.

248 See ILO (2011c), 'Social protection floor for a fair and inclusive globalization: Report of the Social Protection Floor Advisory Group chaired by Michelle Bachelet' (International Labour Office, 2011).

249 *Recommendation concerning National Floors of Social Protection*, 2012 (No. 202) (hereafter 'R202'), at Article 2.

250 Ibid., at Article 5.

persons in active age who are unable to earn sufficient income, in particular in cases of sickness, unemployment, maternity and disability; and

(d) basic income security, at least at a nationally defined minimum level, for older persons.

R202 states that at the very least these features should be provided to 'residents' and children.[251]

While it is obviously important for states to provide all of the listed features, the repeated use of the term 'basic' is concerning given that the international law requires a 'full' rather than a basic right to social security, even if this must be progressively realised. The pragmatism underlying the Recommendation may be diluting the fundamental content of the right to social security. In addition, the prioritising of children (over, for example, adults with disabilities) and residents (over migrant workers) creates a hierarchy of vulnerability and deservedness that does not seem justified in human rights terms.

The Preamble to R202 notes that the right to social security is a human right. While the language of rights is important here, the Recommendation has been criticised for being 'an instrument essentially based on social policies and not on a legal rights-based approach'.[252] R202 sits alongside human rights instruments which more effectively reflect the inalienable right to social security. As a Recommendation it will not be enforceable on the same basis as a Convention. In addition, R202 makes the SPF the 'floor' and ILO *Social Security (Minimum Standards) Convention*, 1952, (No. 102) effectively becomes the 'ceiling' – thus, the previous minimum standards have been lowered.[253] This does not, however, address the lack of adequate ILO social security standards for informal workers.[254]

The SPF Recommendation makes reference to gender equality in the Preamble and lists non-discrimination and gender equality as principles Members should apply in giving effect to R202.[255] Significantly, maternity care is listed as a necessary service and free prenatal and postnatal medical care is recommended.[256] R202 also calls on members to include gender as an indicator in data collection.[257] The rest of the Recommendation is, however, largely devoid of gender content.[258] The simple introduction of social protection programmes does not guarantee gender equality. Without measures specifically designed to address men and women's unequal roles

251 Ibid., at Article 6.

252 Marius Olivier, 'International Labour and Social Security Standards: A Developing Country Critique' (2013) 29(1) *The International Journal of Comparative Labour Law and Industrial Relations* 21, at 34.

253 Ibid.

254 Ibid., at 35.

255 For an ILO discussion of the positive features of R202 from a gender perspective, see Lou Tessier et al., 'Social Protection Floors and Gender Equality: A brief overview' (ILO, 2013), at 23–5.

256 R202 at Article 8(a).

257 At Article 21.

258 See Lucie Lamarche, 'Unpacking the ILO's Social Protection Floor Recommendation from a Women's Rights Perspective' in Beth Goldblatt and Lucie Lamarche (eds), *Women's Rights to Social Security and Social Protection* (Hart, 2014) 65.

in care and women's disadvantage within the labour market, social security will simply reflect existing inequalities without changing their structural basis.

The inclusion of care in relation to basic income security for children raises important issues. It is positive that the care of children is acknowledged as a need that must be provided for by the State. It is less positive that carers, generally women, are not named as requiring support for undertaking these care functions, and that men are not encouraged to share this role.[259] An NGO coalition representing 30 NGOs, that made submissions to the International Labour Conference prior to its adoption of the SPF, encouraged the Conference to add the following words to paragraph 5(c) of the Recommendation that lists reasons for lack of sufficient earnings: 'and responsibility for the care of those unable to care for themselves'.[260] R202, as with other ILO instruments, fails to recognise women engaged in unpaid care and subsistence work as workers – instead, women are treated as dependents and members of vulnerable groups.[261] The Working Group on the issue of discrimination against women in law and in practice (a Human Rights Council special mandate holder) has supported the call by UN-Women for 'States to guarantee quality and accessible childcare as a social protection floor'. The Working Group has also called for the synchronisation of school hours and holidays with working hours.[262]

Basic incomes also contain their own complexities with regard to women's access and control of such income. Their formulation and design should take into account feminist work in this area.[263] The reference in R202 to 'persons in active age who are unable to earn sufficient income'[264] retains notions of paid work and the (male) worker as the model citizen – that is, it elevates the inability to work or earn over the issue of need. While basic pensions will assist poor women, they will not address the underlying inequalities that lead to most women being poorer on 'retirement' than men. It has been argued that the failure to link social protection to addressing job creation and the right to livelihoods for women is a gap in R202.[265]

259 See criticism of the South African Child Support Grant for failing to provide for carers' needs in Chapter 4 below.

260 Autonomous Recommendation on the Social Protection Floor (Joint statement by a group of NGOs), www.icsw.org/images/docs/UN/2012/2012-05-21-NGO-SPF-statement_FINAL_version_21May2012.pdf.

261 Priti Darooka, *Webinar on Women's Rights to Social Security and Social Protection*, www.cdp-hrc.uottawa.ca/?p=4575.

262 Working Group on the issue of discrimination against women in law and in practice, '*Thematic Report (eliminating discrimination against women in economic and social life with a focus on economic crisis)*: Annotated Version (Human Rights Council (26th session), 2014) A/HRC/26/39, at para 98.

263 See papers from panels on Gender and Care I: Should Feminists Embrace Basic Income? at BIEN World Congress on Basic Income-Dublin, Ireland, 2008, www.cori.ie/Justice/Basic_Income/541-bien-world-congress-on-basic-income-; also see Carole Pateman, 'Democratizing Citizenship: Some Advantages of a Basic Income' (2004) 32(1) *Politics and Society* 89.

264 R202 at Article 5(c).

265 Darooka, above n 261.

3.5.3 Assessment of the ILO

The ILO standards, despite their limitations, have value in providing detailed guidance to Members on their obligations with regard to social security, making them 'unique among international instruments on economic and social rights'.[266] The CEACR, in comparing the ILO standards with the CESCR's approach to the right to social security, has noted that the ILO standards view social security not as 'an individual right but rather as a social institution regulated by its own legislative framework ... The interaction between the international social security law and the human rights law provided the engine for the progressive development of social security worldwide, substantiating human rights by the minimum standards of protection.'[267] Nußberger argues, however, that while the new 'soft human rights oriented approach' provides flexibility given the different stages of development between countries, it can also be seen as a 'step back' because it lacks detailed obligations and controls.[268] The CEACR has observed that while the CESCR is moving 'toward the state social responsibility approach pursued by the ILO, the ILO is moving towards the human rights approach' of the UN Committee.[269] Fenwick notes that while social and economic rights require progressive realisation, ILO standards are based on the idea of 'minimum universal standards'.[270] This pragmatic approach acknowledges diversity of economic development across countries and creates flexibility such as through allowing states to comply with only certain parts of a Convention.[271] Both bodies continue to play important and complementary roles in interpreting the right to social security, monitoring compliance and producing recommendations and standards relating to the right.

The ILO's increasing focus on social security and its role in promoting social protection floors is potentially important in efforts to address global poverty. If realised, such floors would improve the lives of millions of people globally, including disadvantaged women. However, more sophisticated and enforceable interventions are needed from the ILO to address underlying gender inequalities in social structures and economic systems in pursuit of its social security mandate.

266 Colin Fenwick, 'The International Labour Organisation: An Integrated Approach to Economic and Social Rights' in Malcolm Langford (ed.), *Social Rights Jurisprudence: Emerging Trends in International and Comparative Law* (Cambridge University Press, 2008) 591, at 608.

267 Above n 235, at 67.

268 Angelika Nußberger, 'Evaluating the ILO's Approach to Standard-Setting and Monitoring in the Field of Social Security' in Eibe Reidel (ed.), *Social Security as a Human Right* (Springer, 2007) 103, at 111.

269 Above n 235, at 67.

270 Above n 266, at 594.

271 Ibid.

3.6 The UN Special Rapporteur on extreme poverty and human rights

The chapter now considers the work of the UN Special Rapporteur on extreme poverty and human rights (until 2011 titled the independent expert on the question of human rights and extreme poverty) who reports to the UN Human Rights Council and the UN General Assembly. It focuses on the reports produced by Magdalena Sepúlveda Carmona, the immediate past holder of this mandate (from 2008 to June 2014). Sepúlveda also co-authored a report on 'The Human Rights Approach to Social Protection' in a different capacity, as a synthesis of five of her official reports.[272] Although this is not a report to the UN, it will also be referred to in this brief consideration of Sepúlveda's work as it is a valuable summary of her official work and it offers useful discussion related to the right to social security and gender.

3.6.1 Gender and social protection in the work of the Special Rapporteur

The Special Rapporteur emphasised issues of gender in relation to poverty and human rights throughout her mandate period. Her work focused strongly on issues of social protection. She authored reports on cash transfer programmes,[273] social protection in the context of the global financial crisis,[274] non-contributory pensions,[275] social protection in achieving the Millennium Development Goals (MDGs),[276] and recovery from global economic crisis.[277] She also prepared guiding principles on extreme poverty and human rights that relate to issues of gender and social protection.[278] Her reports from country visits have also emphasised social protection. Her later reports considered key issues of concern to women in

272 Magdalena Sepúlveda and Carly Nyst, *The Human Rights Approach to Social Protection* (Ministry for Foreign Affairs Finland, 2012).

273 'Report of the independent expert on the question of human rights and extreme poverty, Magdalena Sepúlveda Carmona' (2009) HRC 11th Session, A/HRC/11/9.

274 'Report on the question of human rights and extreme poverty submitted by Magdalena Sepúlveda Carmona, independent expert on the question of human rights and extreme poverty' (2009) GA 64th Session, A/64/279.

275 'Report of the independent expert on the question of human rights and extreme poverty, Magdalena Sepúlveda Carmona' (2010) HRC 14th Session, A/HRC/14/31.

276 'Report on the question of human rights and extreme poverty submitted by Magdalena Sepúlveda Carmona, independent expert on the question of human rights and extreme poverty' (2010) GA 65th Session, A/65/259.

277 'Report of the Independent Expert on the question of human rights and extreme poverty, Magdalena Sepúlveda Carmona' (2011) HRC 17th Session, A/HRC/17/34.

278 'Final draft of the guiding principles on extreme poverty and human rights, submitted by the Special Rapporteur on extreme poverty and human rights, Magdalena Sepúlveda Carmona' (2012) HRC 21st Session, A/HRC/21/39.

the context of social protection: access to justice,[279] participation[280] and unpaid care work.[281]

The Special Rapporteur called on states to ensure that social protection programmes are 'designed, implemented and monitored' based on the different experiences of men and women.[282] She raised a number of issues that should be considered in ensuring gender-sensitive design of such programmes including:[283]

- Women's life-cycle risks and obstacles to accessing work, including their care responsibilities, must be taken into account;
- Gender-sensitive eligibility criteria must be developed to address issues such as lack of identification documents;
- Community targeted programmes must be designed to prevent women from being excluded by men in those communities;
- Household targeting can also reinforce inequalities within households and must be approached with this in mind. Delivery of benefits to women may also lead to violence against them in the household;
- Social protection programmes such as public works must remove obstacles to women's participation such as childcare and domestic responsibilities;
- Such programmes must always provide equal pay for men and women;
- Conditional cash transfer programmes that place the responsibility for fulfilling conditions on women 'may perpetuate gender stereotypes, limit women's ability to work and further undermine their well-being'. They may also limit their ability to seek work, obtain health care or enjoy leisure time and may expose them to violence in the home and abuse by officials;
- Programme design must consider its potential impact on gender divisions of labour in the household (for example, where mothers are removed from households to become involved in government programmes leaving girl children with household responsibilities that remove them from school);
- Public participation in proposed or actual social protection programmes must facilitate women's participation to prevent violence, abuse and sexual harassment and to ensure that women's voices are heard.

The Special Rapporteur also noted that gender-sensitive social services must accompany social protection programmes.[284] For example, women may fail to meet conditionalities of social transfer programmes such as ensuring their children attend school, where schools are far away and their daughters face rape on

279 'Report of the Special Rapporteur on extreme poverty and human rights' (2012) GA 67th Session, A/67/278.

280 'Report of the Special Rapporteur on extreme poverty and human rights, Magdalena Sepúlveda Carmona' (2013) HRC 23rd Session, A/HRC/23/36.

281 'Report of the Special Rapporteur on extreme poverty and human rights' (2013) GA 68th Session, A/68/293.

282 Above n 272, at 32.

283 A/65/259, above n 276, at paras 56–66.

284 Ibid., at para 65–6.

their way to school or where there are no separate sanitation facilities for them at school. 'Women rely on social services more than men owing to their reproductive and caregiving roles. Thus, if social services remain indifferent to the specific needs and vulnerabilities of women, and if economic barriers such as service fees for health and education remain in place, the potential benefits of social protection will be undermined'.[285]

It is evident from these recommendations that the Special Rapporteur showed an awareness of the complex challenges of conditional cash transfer programmes, public works programmes and other social protection initiatives that involve women but do not always take proper account of their needs and interests. She provided policy guidance within a human rights framework that could assist states to reform or redevelop their social assistance systems and programmes.

The Special Rapporteur emphasised the impact of care responsibilities on women's poverty and the role that poorly designed social protection programmes can have in exacerbating women's economic and social burdens.[286] She urged states to see care as a social and collective responsibility and to develop ways of redistributing care between men and women; from households to the State; and through the redistribution of time and resources to poorer households.[287] With regard to the right to social security, she recommended that unpaid care must inform the design of social insurance and social assistance programmes.[288]

The Special Rapporteur's report on unpaid care is a path-breaking document in the human rights field in building a rights framework within which states can address this often invisible but hugely significant burden on women. The Working Group on the issue of discrimination against women in law and in practice has taken some of these ideas further in recommending a social protection floor for care and in calling for the recognition, reduction and redistribution of unpaid care work as a 'fully-fledged economic and social right'.[289]

The Special Rapporteur also stressed the issue of women's participation in social protection programmes, arguing that participation is a human rights principle.[290] She urged states to take account of gender power relations when designing, implementing and monitoring participatory processes. Participation must take account of care responsibilities without reinforcing 'patterns of discrimination and negative stereotyping'.[291]

Overall, the Special Rapporteur said that:[292]

285 Ibid., at para 66.
286 Ibid., at paras 53–5.
287 A/68/293, above n 281, at 92.
288 Ibid., at 48–53.
289 Above n 262, at paras 90–8.
290 A/HRC/23/36, above n 280. See also the Working Group on the issue of discrimination against women in law and in practice, '*Report of the Working Group on the issue of discrimination against women in law and in practice (political representation and participation)*' (Human Rights Council (23rd Session), 2013), A/HRC/23/50.
291 A/HRC/23/36, at para 42.
292 A/65/259, above n 276, at para 79.

> social protection systems should actively promote gender equality and empower women. Policymakers must design, implement, monitor and evaluate social protection initiatives through a gender lens. Programmes should address asymmetries of power and structural inequalities, and enhance the realization of women's rights. They must take into account the multiple forms of discrimination that women experience, and ensure that women's specific needs are addressed throughout their lives: during adolescence, adulthood and old age.

3.6.2 Assessment of the Special Rapporteur

In adopting a gendered approach to the right to social security, the Special Rapporteur has demonstrated a strong awareness of the various dimensions of substantive equality. Her suggestions cover many recognition and redistribution issues such as the recommendation that social protection programmes are accompanied by the removal of legal restrictions on property ownership, access to credit, and full legal capacity.[293] She has also called for measures to end violence against women, within a rights framework. She has given strong emphasis to women's participation in all aspects of social protection programmes and points to transformative approaches that are needed to address issues of care.

The Special Rapporteur has elaborated, in some detail, clear direction for states in meeting their obligations with regard to the right to social security, taking account of gender issues and the principle of gender equality. She has also provided concrete guidance for policy development by states following this human rights approach to social protection. The work of the Special Rapporteur effectively addresses some of the gaps highlighted in the work of the other three bodies considered in this chapter (the CEDAW Committee, the CESCR and the ILO). While the Special Rapporteur's reports have a purely advisory status, they are likely to have some influence on the treaty committees and the UN human rights system as a whole, and may also affect the actions of states parties and other agencies.

3.7 Conclusion

This chapter has outlined the history and major sources of international human rights law on the right to social security. With the aim of undertaking a gendered analysis of this body of law, it has focused on four key sources: CEDAW and the work of the CEDAW Committee; ICESCR and the work of the CESCR; the ILO; and the UN Special Rapporteur on extreme poverty and human rights.

The chapter shows how social security was primarily the preserve of the ILO until the last decade. Prior to that, the ILO played a central role in defining international standards for social security. However, these standards have had most impact in the formal economy and in industrialised countries. The importance

293 Ibid., at para 87.

of social security in addressing poverty has only recently emerged as an urgent human rights issue requiring specific guidance to states. This led to the drafting of CESCR's General Comment 19 in 2007 which now stands as the most authoritative articulation of the right to social security in the human rights treaty body system. The General Comment is a detailed and positive contribution to the body of interpretation of human rights laws. There are, however, a number of limitations with its approach to gender, unpaid work, care and the breadwinner model of the worker as the social security recipient. The CEDAW Committee's approach to the right is, as expected, more focused on gender and more nuanced in its appreciation of the diversity of needs amongst different groups of women than the CESCR. However, it also fails to address adequately issues of care and unpaid work as they relate to the right to social security. Both Committees are alive to the changing and increasingly precarious nature of work, migration and globalisation, economic crisis and poverty and the associated gender dimensions. The ILO, too, has responded to this new context and, most recently, has produced Recommendation 202 on Social Protection Floors, framed within a human rights approach. The Recommendation is an important response to global poverty and insecurity but is insufficiently gendered and remains tied to a narrow conception of work and a limited understanding of care. The UN Special Rapporteur on extreme poverty and human rights has consistently emphasised the gender issues facing women in poverty and the need for sophisticated and principled responses within a human rights framework.

This survey and analysis of the international law on the right to social security from a gender perspective forms the backdrop for the three country studies that follow. The understanding of the strengths and weaknesses of the international legal framework, considered in light of the conceptual framework of this book, informs the analysis of the social security issues in each country. Each country study includes a short survey of the domestic legal framework as well as the international treaties to which that country has bound itself. In one of the country studies, Australia, compliance with international law on the right to social security arises as a prominent issue. In the other two country studies, India and South Africa, the existence of constitutional human rights models that refer to a right to social security means that recourse to international law has been less important. Nevertheless, the international law on this right has undoubtedly influenced the domestic laws of both countries and serves as a standard against which to test and analyse domestic interpretations of the right.

4 South African country study

4.1 Introduction

South Africa, with a population of 51 million, is an upper-middle-income developing country with very high levels of inequality of income and wealth.[1] South Africa's relatively extensive social assistance programme is a critical but inadequate poverty alleviation mechanism. This chapter tests elements of this programme against the conceptual approach and the principles for a substantively equal, gendered right to social security developed in this book. In so doing, it illustrates the value of assessing social security systems for their consistency with human rights, particularly the right to social security, developed from a gender perspective. Such an analysis draws out the inadequacies of a particular system and enables the formulation of recommendations for improvement that advance substantive gender equality.

The chapter begins by briefly setting out the history and nature of South Africa's social security system (in 4.2). It then examines this system from a gender perspective (in 4.3). Thereafter it considers the human rights framework in South Africa with a focus on the right to social security and the right to equality within the South African Constitution (in 4.4). The chapter then focuses on a selected example, a major social assistance payment, the Child Support Grant, and assesses it from a gender perspective, considering whether it meets the requirements of a substantively equal, gendered right to social security (in 4.5). It explores the recent inclusion of conditions into this previously unconditional grant (in 4.6). In doing so, it evaluates the concept of conditionality in social assistance programmes from a feminist and human rights perspective. In identifying the limitations of the Child Support Grant and the broader package of social assistance, the chapter concludes (in 4.7) with a consideration of what might be required to more fully realise the right to social security from a gender perspective in South Africa.

1 According to the World Bank GINI Index, http://data.worldbank.org/indicator/SI.POV.GINI.

4.2 South Africa's social security system

South Africa was a Dutch and British colony until 1910 when white settlers were given control of the unified country. English welfare policy strongly influenced the emerging social assistance laws[2] which were a response to growing poverty amongst whites following industrialisation and amongst Africans due to coerced labour migration.[3] A national old age pension was introduced for whites in 1928 and subsequently extended to other race groups. Maintenance grants to sole parent families were introduced in 1937 and some (urban) African children were allowed access to these.[4] Parent allowances, child grants and grants for people with disabilities were also introduced. However, the introduction of Apartheid after the National Party came to power in 1948 saw the increasing racialisation of the welfare system. Pension levels were much lower for Africans, means-tests were more stringent and welfare administration was separated according to race groups.[5] In 1994 when democracy was finally achieved in South Africa, the new government faced the challenge of deracialising the welfare system and reforming it to meet the policy objectives of what was termed 'developmental social welfare'.[6] That process led to a significant expansion of social assistance from 3 million beneficiaries in 1995 to 16 million beneficiaries in 2013.[7] This has been a contested process involving tension over neo-liberal economic efforts to control social spending and the need to address widespread poverty.[8]

The social security system contains a small social insurance component and a large social assistance programme. The main payments are the Older Persons Grant (OPG), the Disability Grant (DG) and the Child Support Grant (CSG), with other grants for foster carers, carers of children with disabilities, and veterans. The bulk of the grants are CSGs, which reach more than 11 million beneficiaries, while the OPG reaches 2.8 million beneficiaries and the DG reaches 1.1 million beneficiaries.[9] The OPG and the DG are provided in the

2 Leila Patel, 'Race, Inequality and Social Welfare: South Africa's Imperial Legacy' in James Midgley and David Pichaud (eds), *Colonialism and Welfare: Social Policy and the British Imperial Legacy* (Edward Elgar, 2011) 71.

3 Note that the accepted terms used to describe the various 'race' groups in South Africa are 'white, coloured, Asian and African'. The African group accounts for almost 80 per cent of the population: International Social Security Association, 'Social security coverage extension in the BRICS: A comparative study on the extension of coverage in Brazil, the Russian Federation, India, China and South Africa' (International Social Security Association, 2013).

4 Patel, above n 2, at 75.

5 Shireen Hassim, 'Gender Equality and Developmental Social Welfare in South Africa' in Shahra Razavi and Shireen Hassim (eds), *Gender and Social Policy in a Global Context: Uncovering the Gendered Structure of 'The Social'* (Palgrave and UNRISD, 2006) 109, at 111.

6 Ibid., at 114.

7 South African Social Security Agency, 'Fact sheet: Issue no 2 of 2013 – 28 February 2013: A statistical summary of social grants in South Africa' (SASSA, 2013).

8 Beth Goldblatt and Solange Rosa, 'Social Security Rights – Campaigns and Courts' in Malcolm Langford et al. (eds), *Socio-Economic Rights in South Africa: Symbols or Substance?* (Cambridge University Press, 2014) 253.

9 South African Social Security Agency, above n 7.

monthly amount of R1270 (approximately US $120) while the CSG is R300 (approximately US $30) per month. The grants are targeted at the poor through means-testing. The OPG is provided to people aged 60 years and older, with people 75 and older receiving a slightly higher amount. The DG requires medical testing to qualify. The CSG is provided to the primary caregiver of children under the age of 18.

The social assistance programme has a significant impact on poverty alleviation, nutritional status and access to health, education and employment.[10] Despite these benefits, the system is residualist, 'reacting only to the worst effects of market or family failures and providing assistance to social groups seen as "deserving"'.[11] There is no assistance for the millions of working-age poorly paid workers, informal sector workers, the under-employed and the unemployed. Structural unemployment is extensive in South Africa with government figures indicating the rate of unemployment is 23.9 per cent,[12] affecting approximately 4.5 million people.[13] Most employment is in the formal sector with a smaller informal and agricultural sector and a domestic workforce employed in private households.

Contributory social insurance provides those in formal employment with limited unemployment, maternity, sickness, adoption and survivor's benefits for a short period of time.[14] There is tax support for employees to privately fund voluntary health and retirement insurance but these typically benefit those who are better off.[15] The public health system is poorly funded and inadequate while the private health system is beyond the reach of the vast majority of South Africans, including most employed workers.

10 Debbie Budlender and Francie Lund, 'South Africa: a legacy of family disruption' (2011) 42(4) *Development and Change* 925, at 940–2.

11 Hassim, above n 5, at 126.

12 Statistics South Africa, 'Quarterly Labour Force Survey: Quarter 4 (October to December), 2012' (2013), www.statssa.gov.za/publications/P0211/P02114thQuarter2012.pdf, at v.

13 Statistics South Africa, ibid., at xiv. If a broader definition of unemployment including discouraged jobseekers is used, this figure would be 36.6 per cent: Avinash Govindjee and Ockert Dupper, 'Constitutional perspectives on unemployment security and a right to work in South Africa' (2011) 23 *Stellenbosch Law Review* 775, at 775.

14 Department of Social Development South Africa, *An Overview of South Africa's Social Security System*, Department of Social Development, at 8. See arguments for the extension of unemployment insurance: Ockert Dupper, Marius Olivier and Avinash Govindjee, 'Extending coverage of the unemployment insurance-system in South Africa' (2010) 21 *Stellenbosch Law Review* 438; Avinash Govinjdee, Marius Olivier and Ockert Dupper, 'Activation in the context of the unemployment insurance system in South Africa' (2011) 22 *Stellenbosch Law Review* 205; Marius Olivier, Ockert Dupper and Avinash Govindjee, 'Redesigning the South African unemployment insurance fund: selected key policy and legal perspectives' (2011) 22 *Stellenbosch Law Review* 396; Govindjee and Dupper, ibid.

15 Department of Social Development South Africa, ibid., at 9–10.

4.3 Gender in the South African social security system

Women in South Africa earn less than men, have fewer employment opportunities and are poorer than men.[16] Women dominate in domestic work but have a smaller share of the other types of work in the South African economy. They have a relatively low labour force participation rate of 47 per cent, and the participation gap between women and men is 14 per cent.[17] Women provide most of the care-giving functions in a society which has been deeply affected by Apartheid and its legacy of internal labour migration and consequent family breakdown.[18] A minority of children live in the same household as their fathers (35 per cent), while a slightly larger percentage live only with their mothers (40 per cent). Almost a quarter live without either parent (23 per cent), usually cared for by other female relatives, mostly grandmothers.[19] The HIV/AIDS epidemic has also had a major impact on family and community with 6.4 million people infected in 2012.[20] Women are infected at a higher rate than men.[21] Gender-based violence is a severe problem in South Africa[22] as is safety more generally. Race and culture intersect with gender and class to contribute to the burdens that the majority of South African women and girls face through the different stages of their lives.

Despite increased labour force participation,[23] women have less access to formal employment and their access to the social insurance system is accordingly more limited. However, the inclusion of domestic workers in the social security system since 2003 has been a positive step for women workers who make up the majority of this group. Informal sector work, subsistence work and unpaid work in family enterprises and the home, also dominated by women, are not recognised in the social insurance system. The social assistance system is the primary vehicle for poverty alleviation with the bulk of the grants reaching women recipients.[24] Women make up the overwhelming majority of recipients of the

16 Debbie Budlender, 'Women and poverty' (2005) 64 *Agenda* 30.

17 OECD, 'Closing the Gender Gap: Act Now – South Africa' (OECD Publishing, 2012), www.oecd.org/southafrica/Closing%20the%20Gender%20Gap%20-%20South%20Africa%20EN.pdf.

18 Budlender and Lund, above n 10. The migrant labour system saw men, and later women, move to urban areas to work, leaving older people and children behind. The legacy of this remains in South Africa today, putting strain on families and adding to the care burdens of women (both mothers and grandmothers or other female relatives).

19 Ibid., at 929.

20 L.C. Simbayi et al., 'South African National HIV Prevalence, Incidence and Behaviour Survey, 2012' (Human Sciences Research Council 2014).

21 Ibid.

22 Michelle Faul, '3 women killed each day in South Africa, world's worst gender violence', *The Star*, 8 March 2013, www.thestar.com/news/world/2013/03/08/3_women_killed_each_day_in_south_africa_worlds_worst_gender_violence.html.

23 There has been an increase of 38 per cent in female labour force participation since the mid-90s: OECD, above n 17.

24 Beth Goldblatt, 'The Right to Social Security – Addressing Women's Poverty and Disadvantage' in Beth Goldblatt and Kirsty McLean (eds), *Women's Social and Economic Rights: Developments in South Africa* (Juta, 2011) 34, at 35.

CSG and are usually the mothers of the children.[25] The OPG also reaches more women than men because of women's longer mortality and because the grant was historically provided to women at an earlier age than men, although this has since changed.[26] The huge increase in the reach of the social assistance system since the change to democracy in 1994 has been positive for women in their support of their households.[27] However, it is also limited because grants can only be accessed by women below pension age through their children and the grant size is very small.[28] Means-testing of grants creates some access difficulties for women who are required to provide evidence that may be difficult to obtain. Further access barriers relate to poverty, illiteracy, hostile officials, lack of identification documents, disempowerment, care responsibilities and safety concerns.[29] The disproportionate care burden carried by women in South Africa for children, the elderly, people with disabilities and illnesses is not adequately addressed through the social security system or through other forms of social provision. Childcare provided by the State and the private sector is very limited in addressing the 'care crisis' caused by AIDS and family fragmentation.[30]

4.4 South Africa's human rights framework and the right to social security

The end of Apartheid in 1994 saw the introduction of a new constitution and a far-reaching bill of rights which contains justiciable social and economic rights.[31] The guarantee in section 27(1)(b) of the Constitution provides that 'Everyone has the right to have access to social security, including, if they are unable to support themselves and their dependents, appropriate social assistance'.[32] The section requires the State to 'take reasonable legislative and other measures, within its available resources, to achieve the progressive realisation' of the right.[33] The Constitution contains a strong equality right that includes the grounds of

25 Leila Patel and Tessa Hochfeld, 'It buys food but does it change gender relations? Child Support Grants in Soweto, South Africa' (2011) 19(2) *Gender and Development* 229, at 231.

26 Budlender and Lund, above n 10, at 940.

27 Patel and Hochfeld, above n 25.

28 The CSG amount is not linked to increases in inflation and is not set according to a clear assessment of need: Ockert Dupper et al., 'The case for increased reform of South African family and maternity benefits' (2000) 4(1) *Law, Democracy and Development* 27, at 35.

29 Beth Goldblatt, 'Gender and social assistance in the first decade of democracy: a case study of South Africa's Child Support Grant' (2005) 32(2) *Politikon* 239; Beth Goldblatt, 'Gender, rights and the disability grant in South Africa' (2009) 26(3) *Development Southern Africa* 369.

30 For a discussion of the crisis in care, see Lisa Dancaster, *State and Employer Involvement in Work-Care Integration in South Africa* (PhD Thesis, University of Sydney, 2012), at 34–40.

31 *Constitution of the Republic of South Africa Act* 108 of 1996. For an overview on South Africa's social and economic rights, see Sandra Liebenberg, *Socio-Economic Rights Adjudication Under a Transformative Constitution* (Juta, 2010); David Bilchitz, *Poverty and Fundamental Rights: The Justification and Enforcement of Socio-Economic Rights* (Oxford University Press, 2007).

32 *Constitution of the Republic of South Africa Act* 108 of 1996, s 27(1)(b).

33 Ibid., at s 27(2).

both sex and gender in the listed grounds of discrimination.[34] Non-sexism is one of the founding values of the Constitution.[35] The Preamble to the Constitution lists one of the goals of the Constitution as being 'to improve the quality of life of all citizens and free the potential of each person'.[36] Equality and social and economic rights are linked in a constitutional project aimed at addressing both material and status-based disadvantage.[37] In addition to the right to social security, the Constitution also guarantees other social and economic rights including a right to housing, health care, food, water and education.

At the international level, South Africa is a party to CEDAW and a number of other treaties and has signed but only recently indicated its intention to ratify ICESCR.[38] The CEDAW Committee considered South Africa's periodic reports in 2011 but did not refer to any social security issues, other than maternity leave with pay.[39] This does not mean that South African women's social security rights are fully accommodated – as discussed above, there are many gaps that need to be addressed. At the regional level, South Africa is party to the *African Charter on Human and Peoples' Rights*, the *African Charter on the Rights and Welfare of the Child*, and the *Protocol to the African Charter on Human and Peoples' Rights on the Rights of Women in Africa*, the last of which has strong gender-related social security provisions.[40] At the sub-regional level South Africa is part of the Southern African Development Community (SADC) which has a *Charter of Fundamental Social Rights* (2003), a *Code on Social Security* (2007)[41] and a *Gender Protocol* (2008).[42] South Africa has ratified a number of ILO

34 Ibid., at s 9. There is a well-developed equality jurisprudence containing strong statements about women's substantive equality rights: Catherine Albertyn and Beth Goldblatt, 'Equality' in Stuart Woolman et al. (eds), *Constitutional Law of South Africa* (Juta 2nd edn, 2007) 58; Catherine Albertyn, 'Gendered transformation in South African jurisprudence: poor women and the constitutional court' (2011) 3 *Stellenbosch Law Review* 591.

35 *Constitution of the Republic of South Africa Act* 108 of 1996, s 1(b).

36 Ibid., Preamble.

37 Sandra Liebenberg and Beth Goldblatt, 'The interrelationship between equality and socio-economic rights in South Africa's transformative constitution' (2007) 23 *South African Journal on Human Rights* 335.

38 Marius Olivier, *Social Security: Framework*, The Law of South Africa (LexisNexis, 2nd edn, 2012), para 118. Section 231 of the *Constitution of the Republic of South Africa Act* 108 of 1996 deals with international agreements.

39 It recommended that South Africa ensure 'that all mothers receive leave with pay' and that it 'provide effective sanctions and remedies for violation of laws on maternity leave', CO South Africa CEDAW/C/ZAF/CO/4 (CEDAW, 2011), at para 34.

40 *African Charter on Human and Peoples' Rights* (1981) OAU Doc CAB/LEG/67/3, entered into force 1986; the *African Charter on the Rights and Welfare of the Child* (1990) OAU Doc CAB/LEG/24.9/49, entered into force 1999; the *Protocol to the African Charter on Human and Peoples' Rights on the Rights of Women in Africa* (2000) OAU CAB/LEG/66.6, entered into force 2005. The *Protocol to the African Charter on Human and Peoples' Rights on the Rights of Women in Africa* includes the following provision in Article 13(f): 'establish a system of protection and social insurance for women working in the informal sector and sensitise them to adhere to it'.

41 Discussed in Olivier, above n 38, at para 116.

42 Discussed in Kitty Malherbe and Lorenzo Wakefield, 'The effect of women's care-giving role on their social security rights' (2009) 2009 *Law, Democracy and Development* 47, at 62.

conventions[43] but none of the major social security conventions. Women's rights advocates in South Africa have focused, in large part, on the strong constitutional rights framework rather than international human rights in advocating for social security reforms.

Despite initial enthusiasm about the potential of social and economic rights litigation in South Africa, and some important successes, this avenue has proven disappointing in achieving far-reaching legal change. South Africa's Constitutional Court has resisted allowing direct and broad claims to social provision and has taken a restrained approach to reviewing the reasonableness of government policies.[44] Thus far, constitutional litigation to force government to extend the reach of social security has been based on the relationship between the right to social security and the right to equality.[45] In the *Khosa* case the Court found that permanent residents could not be excluded from social assistance grants since the right applied to 'everyone'.[46] The Court said that:[47]

> Sharing responsibility for the problems and consequences of poverty equally as a community represents the extent to which wealthier members of the community view the minimal well-being of the poor as connected with their personal well-being and the well-being of the community as a whole. In other words, decisions about the allocation of public benefits represent the extent to which poor people are treated as equal members of society.

There have also been a number of high court cases using the right to administrative justice to challenge poor social grant administration.[48]

Gender issues relating to the right to social security were raised in litigation around the Older Persons Grant (previously the Old Age Pension). At the time, the grant was provided to women at the age of 60 and to men at the age of 65, a legacy dating back to the 1930s. A group of men challenged the constitutionality of

43 For the list of ratifications see: www.ilo.org/dyn/normlex/en/f?p=NORMLEXPUB:11200:0::NO::P11200_COUNTRY_ID:102888.

44 Sandra Liebenberg, 'The Judicial Enforcement of Social Security Rights in South Africa: Enhancing Accountability for the Basic Needs of the Poor' in Eibe Reidel (ed.), *Social Security as a Human Right: Drafting a General Comment on Article 9 ICESCR – Some Challenges* (Springer, 2007) 69.

45 In the Constitutional Court cases of *Mashava v President of the RSA and Others* 2004 (12) BCLR 1243 (CC) and *Khosa v Minister of Social Development; Mahlaule v Minister of Social Development (Khosa)* 2004 (6) BCLR 569 (CC).

46 Discussed in Liebenberg and Goldblatt, above n 37. Despite the progressive judgment in this case, the extension of grants to permanent residents left refugees and other legal and illegal migrants outside of the social security system. For discussion of this aspect, see Lucy Williams, 'Issues and challenges in addressing poverty and legal rights: a comparative United States/South Africa analysis' (2005) 21 *South African Journal on Human Rights* 436. There have, however, been some positive developments in this area in recent years. See Olivier, above n 38, at paras 92–4.

47 Above n 45, para 74.

48 Liebenberg, above n 44; Nick de Villiers, 'Procedural fairness and reasonable administrative action within the social assistance system: implications of some settled class actions' (2006) 22 *South African Journal on Human Rights* 405.

the legislation on the basis of the rights to equality and social security.[49] Women's interests were represented by an *amicus curiae* who argued that the Court should avoid equalising down (that is, giving women the grants at age 65) as had occurred in similar European litigation. Before judgment was given, the government amended the legislation to allow for the phased inclusion of men aged 60–64.[50]

Litigation was also used in a challenge to the age range (0–13) of the Child Support Grant to ensure that it reached all children under the age of 18. Again, the government introduced the requested reforms before judgment was given and phased in the changes.[51] While this was primarily a challenge on the basis of children's right to social security, the equality rights of the parents, who are overwhelmingly women, were also integral to the argument.

4.5 The Child Support Grant – meeting women's social security rights?

This section uses the example of the Child Support Grant (CSG), an internationally applauded social assistance benefit, to examine whether a substantively equal, gendered right to social security is being realised in South Africa. The section contains a description of the grant; the background of the grant; the issues relating to the implementation and administration of the grant; a discussion of the concern that the grant is for children, not parents; a consideration of the negative discourse that has surrounded the grant; and an evaluation of the grant.

4.5.1 Description of the CSG

The CSG is a post-democracy social assistance grant that reaches more than 11 million children below the age of 18. It is overwhelmingly paid to women, mainly the mothers of the children for whom it is provided.[52] Despite its small monetary size, it has a critical impact in addressing the food needs of poor children and has some role in increasing school attendance.[53] It may also have broader impacts such as enabling mothers to look for paid employment.[54] Grants, often pooled, are used to support entire households rather than just the child for whom the grant is provided. The CSG is means-tested and generally well targeted, successfully reaching the poorest children in South Africa,[55] although a fraction of the

49 *Roberts and Others v Minister of Social Development and Others* (unreported decision of the Transvaal Provincial Division, (2010) Case Number 32838/05).

50 The case and the changes are discussed in Goldblatt, above n 24, at 51–4. Also see Malherbe and Wakefield, above n 42.

51 See Goldblatt and Rosa, above n 8, at 258–61.

52 Leila Patel and Tessa Hochfeld, 'The Gender Dynamics and Impact of the Child Support Grant in Doornkop, Soweto' (Centre for Development in Africa, University of Johannesburg, 2012), at 3.

53 Francie Lund, 'A step in the wrong direction: linking the South African Child Support Grant to school attendance' (2011) 19(1) *Journal of Poverty and Social Justice* 5.

54 Patel and Hochfeld, above n 25, at 230.

55 Ibid.

very poorest are not reached[56] because they cannot provide the documentation required or due to misunderstandings of the means-test.[57] Because the CSG is collected by such a large number of poor women, it offers a valuable example to evaluate using the gender approach and principles for a substantively equal, gendered right to social security developed in this book.

4.5.2 Background to the CSG

The CSG developed from the work of the Lund Committee for Child and Family Support which was established soon after the first democratic government began considering reforms to the welfare system.[58] It replaced the State Maintenance Grant which was a two-part payment for sole parents (initially only for women but later also for men) and their children. The application of racial criteria limited its scope to certain groups. Had it been extended to all those eligible following the removal of such criteria, it would have been unaffordable. Hence, the Committee chose a simpler, smaller benefit to be paid to the primary caregiver of the child. Targeting the primary caregiver was an important innovation in the context of family dislocation and diversity, allowing people other than biological parents to collect the payment on the principle that the benefit should 'follow the child'. The government first provided the grant to children from birth to age seven but later extended this, following significant pressure from welfare groups, to all children under 18.[59]

4.5.3 Issues in implementation and administration of the CSG

There were many early implementation issues and some problems still remain. Some of these had a gender dimension such as the unofficial requirement (for the purpose of means-testing, observed at certain offices) that women had to obtain proof that they had unsuccessfully sought private maintenance from the fathers of their children.[60] This requirement forced women to negotiate a very cumbersome court system that often resulted in them giving up in despair. They were also sometimes asked to obtain a statement from the father saying that he was unable to support his child. This put women into dangerous situations by requiring contact with former partners who may have been abusive. It also brought the

56 Francie Lund et al., 'Is there a rationale for conditional cash transfers for children in South Africa?' (2009) 70 *Transformation* 70, at 81.

57 Beth Goldblatt, Solange Rosa and Katharine Hall, 'Implementation of the Child Support Grant: a study of four provinces and recommendations for improved service delivery' (Centre for Applied Legal Studies, University of the Witwatersrand and the Children's Institute, University of Cape Town, 2006); DSD, SASSA and UNICEF, 'The South African Child Support Grant Impact Assessment: evidence from a survey of children, adolescents and their households' (UNICEF South Africa, 2012), at 29–30.

58 See Francie Lund, *Changing Social Policy: The Child Support Grant in South Africa* (HSRC Press, 2008) for an insider account of the Committee.

59 Goldblatt and Rosa, above n 8.

60 Goldblatt (2005), above n 29, at 249.

potential grant payments to the attention of fathers who sometimes demanded 'their share' from mothers.[61]

There have been local and regional variations in implementation. Different provinces and local offices had different requirements and different outcomes for some of the CSG applicants. In one province, the child had to be brought to the office to prove she or he was actually in the physical custody of the person applying. This was not required by the regulations and complicated the process for applicants who were required to wait for many hours with small babies and children.[62] In another province, applicants had to provide documentation (such as clinic cards and letters of residence) that were not required by the regulations, meaning that the most vulnerable groups such as farm workers, often not in receipt of these documents, were unsuccessful in their attempts to access the CSG.[63] Individual bias by officials was also observed. For example, an official who was interviewed admitted assisting older rather than younger women to access certain documents because 'young women waste the CSG and do not need it anyway'.[64]

These implementation problems are contrary to the principles for a substantively equal, gendered right to social security proposed in Chapter 2. The seventh Principle of full and equal access to social security by women has not been adequately met in the instances described above where women recipients of the CSG encountered obstacles to accessing the grant and were exposed to harm, bias and poor treatment. They experienced inequality in terms of the dimensions of recognition (certain women faced stigma and were exposed to conflict with former partners); redistribution (costly requirements such as numerous visits to obtain documents not required in the regulations); transformation (no efforts to involve fathers, provide childcare or acknowledge the positive caring work of the caregivers); participation (no consultation or engagement with affected applicants and beneficiaries about easier ways of applying for and collecting grants). The sixth Principle of gender-equal social security design was also not fully applied because of the failure to take account of the circumstances and needs of women applicants and beneficiaries of the grant.

Additionally, the administration of the CSG means that while it is designed to reach children from birth, it can take new mothers some time to apply for and receive it.[65] Moreover, pregnant women do not benefit from the grant before the birth. Both of these issues mean that the nutritional benefits of the CSG are not reaching foetuses and new babies at a critical point in their development. Some authors have recommended a pregnancy grant and other services to support pregnant mothers[66] and suggested a campaign to distribute CSG applications

61 Ibid., at 249.
62 Ibid., at 248.
63 Ibid., at 248.
64 Ibid., at 248.
65 DSD, SASSA and UNICEF, above n 57, at 30.
66 Alex van den Heever et al., 'Investigating the Potential Impact of State Support for Poor and

at birth.[67] While the arguments for such support may have some dangers if the focus is on women as mere reproductive receptacles and physical vehicles for the improved nutrition of their children, reforms to support and empower pregnant mothers would be a valuable contribution to their social security rights. Such support could be seen as an acknowledgment of women's unpaid reproductive functions and a recognition that the costs of pregnancy and childbirth should be borne by society and not just by the mothers themselves, in accordance with the first of the Principles for a substantively equal, gendered right to social security.

4.5.4 Lack of a grant for parents

A key feminist concern with the CSG is that it replaced the State Maintenance Grant and removed the parent component of the former grant. This loss was a 'major blow to the struggle for the recognition of women's unpaid caring work in society' since women were clearly expected to undertake caring work without state support for themselves, even when facing severe poverty.[68] Mothers became conduits for assistance to children with their own citizenship entitlements to social security subsumed in their children's rights.[69] This is because 'women mediate social assistance and deliver it on behalf of the State. They claim it, collect it and are then expected to turn it into food, shelter, clothing, education, health and other aspects of a child's maintenance through their own labours.'[70]

Sylvia Chant[71] discusses the difficulty of addressing female poverty through anti-poverty programmes. She argues that such programmes are often aimed at addressing women's *condition* rather than their *position* of disadvantage. Giving women money does not always translate into greater power, enhanced opportunities or increased leisure time. In fact, women are often used in development processes as a 'conduit of policy' to achieve development goals rather than to address unequal gender relations. These interventions may reinforce rather than alter traditional responsibilities for care and household reproduction.

The removal of the parent component of the State Maintenance Grant can be seen as a retrogressive measure[72] in unlawfully removing a right to social security

Vulnerable Pregnant Women in South Africa: An Options Assessment: Summary Report' (Centre for Health Policy, School of Public Health, University of the Witwatersrand, 2012).

67 DSD, SASSA and UNICEF, above n 57, at 30.

68 Goldblatt (2005), above n 29, at 241.

69 Ibid. The concept of women as a policy conduit is developed by Maxine Molyneux, 'Mothers at the service of the new poverty agenda: *Progresa/Oportunidades*, Mexico's conditional transfer programme' (2006) 40(4) *Social Policy and Administration* 425.

70 Goldblatt (2005), above n 29, at 242.

71 Sylvia Chant, 'The "Feminisation of Poverty" and the "Feminisation" of anti-poverty programmes: room for revision?' (2008) 44(2) *Journal of Development Studies* 165

72 The prohibition of retrogressive measures in relation to the right to social security is considered by the Committee for Economic Social and Cultural Rights in '*General Comment No 19: The Right to Social Security (Art. 9)*' (2008) 39th Session 2007, E/C.12/GC/19, at para 42. This is discussed in Chapter 3 above at 3.4.2.2 and specifically in footnotes 201 and 203 and the corresponding text.

held by certain parents and guardians – the group of sole women (which later included men) who were eligible for the grant. The failure to provide for the indigent carers of poor children is also a potential violation of the social security guarantee in South Africa's Bill of Rights which promises everyone a right to have access to social security 'including, if they are unable to support themselves and their dependants, appropriate social assistance'.[73] While the CSG provides for the dependent children of people who are unable to support them, it does not provide for those adults who are unable to support themselves. The millions of women who qualify for the CSG fall into this category as adults living in poverty without the means to support themselves. Consequently, it can be argued that the first Principle for a substantively equal, gendered right to social security put forward in this book, the requirement for the recognition and support of care work, is unmet. The fifth Principle, requiring social security for all who need it, is also not satisfied, and the sixth Principle, the design of social security systems to promote gender equality, has not been met either since the grant assists the children but not the mothers who care for them. Finally, the seventh Principle, requiring full and equal access is not satisfied since children are provided with access to social security while women (or men) who are in desperate need of poverty relief are not. Applying the four-dimensional equality approach makes it clear that women suffer discrimination through the removal of the State Maintenance Grant and the failure to create a grant to support their care responsibilities because they are financially disadvantaged (redistribution) and lack acknowledgment of their important social functions (recognition); because social assistance policy change has not challenged or shifted the burden of care work on women (transformation); and because the views of women on this issue have been excluded in the design of the CSG (participation).[74]

Francie Lund, the head of the Committee that recommended the CSG, has acknowledged that with the removal of a mothers' grant, 'race and poverty trumped gender' but that the 'design of the CSG around the "primary caregiver" was very clearly a gendered strategy in favour of women'.[75] Certainly, a more flexible approach to care-giving has been to the advantage of some of the female relatives who have been able to receive the grant without a direct biological link to the child. In addition, the notion of the primary caregiver has discursive importance in showing that the care of children is based on a relationship determined by function rather than by biology or gender; it was progressive, therefore, in moving away from formal gender presumptions around the care of children. However, as Patel and Hochfeld point out, the CSG has become 'feminised' because of strong social attitudes towards care as women's responsibility.[76] The problem of social security design remains – children are supported but not their

73 *Constitution of the Republic of South Africa Act* 108 of 1996, Section 27(1)(b).

74 It should however be noted that there was some consultation around the reshaping of the post-Apartheid welfare system through the Lund Committee (Lund, above n 58, at 20–35) and, later, active opposition around the proposed legislation (Hassim, above n 5, at 117–20).

75 Lund, above n 58, at 115–16.

76 Patel and Hochfeld, above n 25, at 231.

carers – as does the message that this sends about the role of (mainly) women in providing this unremunerated labour for society.

4.5.5 *Negative discourse around the CSG*

The introduction of the CSG, paid predominantly to young women, has given rise to an accompanying negative discourse about grant abuse. Recipients have been accused of falling pregnant to access the grant and of misusing the grants for their own benefit rather than in support of their children.[77] Mothers are also accused of leaving children with grandmothers and not giving them the grant money. This discourse is common to many countries where welfare mothers have been labelled as 'undeserving'.[78] Social security can be viewed as providing recognition and support for those performing care functions in society (the first of the book's principles); however, this is not widely accepted in the public domain. Indeed, the negative attitudes to the women recipients of the CSG reflect a lack of understanding of the costs and responsibilities involved in the care of babies and children. Such attitudes highlight the need to deepen and disseminate the understanding of social security as a right rather than a benefit, and as a right that young women (not just elderly pensioners or people with disabilities) are entitled to claim.

Government-commissioned research has refuted many of the claims about abuse of the CSG.[79] The grant provided to carers of children with severe disabilities has also been the subject of recent discussion with the allegation that women deliberately abuse alcohol while pregnant in order to bear children with Foetal Alcohol Syndrome.[80] This grant is paid at a higher amount than the CSG, providing the perceived incentive. Again, this type of unfounded speculation reinforces stereotypes about young women as being irresponsible and criminal. A recent study of CSG recipients found that many saw the grant as positive in alleviating poverty but also believed it led to perverse incentives and abuse, and worried about grants being withdrawn.[81] This indicates that negative perceptions are persistent despite the lack of evidence of abuse and that despite the strong rights framework in South Africa there is insecurity about the continued existence

77 Beth Goldblatt, 'Teen pregancy and abuse of the Child Support Grant: addressing the myths and stereotypes' (2003) 17(56) *Agenda: Empowering Women for Gender Equity* 79.

78 Nancy Fraser and Linda Gordon, 'A genealogy of dependency: tracing a keyword of the U.S. welfare state' (1994) 19(2) *Signs* 309; Lucy Williams, 'Race, rat bites and unfit mothers: how media discourse informs welfare legislation debate' (1994) 22(4) *Fordham Urban Law Journal* 1159.

79 Mark Steele, 'Report on Incentive Structures of Social Assistance Grants in South Africa' (Kesho Consulting and Business Solutions and Department of Social Development, South Africa, 2006); Monde Makiwane and Eric Udjo, 'Is the Child Support Grant associated with an increase in teenage fertility in South Africa? Evidence from National Surveys and Administrative Data' (Human Sciences Research Council, 2006).

80 Rebecca Davis, 'Sky really is the limit: the lowdown on Alex Crawford's reporting' (2013) *Daily Maverick*, www.dailymaverick.co.za/article/2013-01-24-sky-really-is-the-limit-the-lowdown-on-alex-crawfords-reporting#.UW4ngqJmh8E.

81 Patel and Hochfeld, above n 52.

of some forms of social assistance for poor women. Building a gendered rights culture around social security remains a challenge for South Africa.

4.5.6 Evaluation of the CSG

The CSG was not aimed at women's poverty – it was expressly directed at addressing children facing poverty (half of whom are girls). Consequently, it is difficult to evaluate and critique it in terms of the goals of addressing women's poverty or improving gender inequalities other than identifying the policy gap. The CSG can, however, be evaluated as an example of a social assistance programme that enables caregivers (usually women) to assist in achieving a policy goal of improving the life chances of South African children. Such an evaluation would consider whether women have been advantaged or disadvantaged by being given this role and the possible unintended impacts of the grant on gender relations. Applying the framework and principles for a substantively equal, gendered right to social security developed in this book, the following are some of the issues that can and should be considered in this type of evaluation of the CSG.

In terms of the first Principle, recognition and support of unpaid care, an evaluation should consider whether the CSG reinforces the role of women as the major source of unpaid reproduction and care in the society. In relation to the third and fourth Principles concerning work in the informal and formal sector, there should be a consideration of whether the grant has had any impact on the difficulties women face in accessing paid work and income. The seventh Principle, full and equal access to social security, requires consideration of whether there remain barriers to accessing the grant that impact negatively on women recipients. In relation to Principle 6, requiring the design of social security programmes to promote gender equality, it would be useful to evaluate whether the CSG could have been designed differently to address or transform unequal gender relations. Within this, the dimensions of substantive equality can be considered by asking: whether the CSG alters women's power and status in the home and in communities (recognition); whether it leads to men feeling less responsible for the provision of support for their children (redistribution); whether it has any impact on the extent to which men take responsibility for the care of their children (transformation); whether the grant fuels resentment from men, leading to conflict and violence in families (recognition); whether the grant has any positive or negative intergenerational impacts in households, particularly in relation to the status of young mothers (recognition); and whether the CSG enables or limits women's capacity to participate more fully as active citizens (participation).

Many of these questions cannot be answered without empirical evidence. Aside from implementation studies that considered the question of access to the grant,[82] there has only been one study of CSG recipients that considers some of these gendered questions. Patel and Hochfeld conducted a household survey in a poor urban area near Johannesburg, focusing on empowerment, decision-making

82 Goldblatt (2005), above n 29; Goldblatt, Rosa and Hall, above n 57.

and care responsibility.[83] They found that most respondents (women grant holders), since receiving the grant, felt more secure financially, more able to care for their families, and more positive and empowered.[84] However, the research also found some evidence that the CSG may be 'crowding' out financial support by fathers.[85] Moreover, the study found that women were continuing to perform the vast majority of care and domestic work in their households and that most held traditional views about gender roles in the home. Almost a quarter of respondents acknowledged the existence of domestic violence in their relationships with partners.[86] The authors of the study urged a better understanding 'of the impact of the CSG on care as a public good that contributes to economic and social development and that extends beyond the individual beneficiary'. They concluded that while 'social protection policies may contribute to transforming gender relations; … on their own, they are limited, and need to work in concert with other public policies, such as reform of the maintenance system and policies and programmes that reduce the burden of care on women and that promote more equitable social relations'.[87]

Clearly further research is required to develop a deeper understanding of the gendered impact of the CSG from a social security rights perspective. It seems likely, however, that the grant has simply mapped itself onto the existing topography of unequal gender relations in South Africa and that the consequences of the provision of the grant are largely neutral. Some advantages (such as improved feelings of empowerment) and disadvantages (such as possible withdrawal of financial support by some fathers) may be the unintended by-products of the grant.

4.6 The introduction of conditionality into the CSG

The above evaluation of the CSG from a gender rights perspective is altered to some extent by a new development which changes the nature of the grant. One of the notable features of the CSG in its original form is that it was an unconditional cash transfer.[88] In 2009 the South African government attached a condition to the grant requiring caregivers to regularly demonstrate that their children are attending school. This change has been met with surprise and condemnation in welfare circles and raises concerns about the burden that such a measure will place on women in receipt of the grant.

83 Patel and Hochfeld, above n 25; Patel and Hochfeld, above n 52.

84 Patel and Hochfeld, above n 25, at 236.

85 Ibid.

86 Ibid., at 237.

87 Ibid., at 238. Also see Fredman's discussion of Patel and Hochfeld's report and her evaluation of the CSG as an unconditional cash transfer: Sandra Fredman, 'Engendering Social Welfare Rights' in Beth Goldblatt and Lucie Lamarche (eds), *Women's Rights to Social Security and Social Protection* (Hart, 2014) 19, at 37–9.

88 A one-off immunisation requirement was initially required but this was dropped: DSD, SASSA and UNICEF, above n 57, at 2.

Before exploring these changes and their implications for women receiving the CSG it is necessary to discuss what is meant by 'conditions' or 'conditionality' in relation to social assistance and some of the views about the appropriateness of such conditions from a gender perspective and from other critical perspectives.

4.6.1 Debates around conditionality

Conditional Cash Transfers (CCTs) require 'behavioural compliance' on the part of grant recipients, usually in relation to ensuring children reach services such as schools and clinics. These measures, originating in the USA in the 1980s in relation to children, have become increasingly popular in developing countries.[89] The policy logic behind these measures is that cash payments on their own will not address intergenerational deprivation that causes poverty. Instead, conditions will direct people to services that are necessary for their development out of poverty.[90] Barrientos notes that to some extent, all social assistance programmes contain conditions.[91] Simply registering for a benefit may be difficult for many people due to access issues, lack of information and documentation problems. Targeted rather than universal social assistance programmes may require means-testing or other proof of eligibility. However, Lund et al. label such administrative requirements as access barriers rather than conditions.[92] They also identify regulatory requirements – for example, that the payments must be used in support of the child – as 'normative injunctions'. They suggest that 'true conditionalities' require ongoing behaviours such as ensuring school attendance, although one-off conditions may also exist in some programmes (such as immunisation of the child at a certain age). In many CCT programmes the focus is on mothers – as the favoured recipients of cash who will ensure it is properly spent and as the people most likely to comply with the conditions. In some schemes women are required to attend classes, meetings and undertake community work.

There are a number of critiques of CCTs, both practical and normative. Many evaluations of CCTs have found positive impacts both in poverty reduction and health and education utilisation. Critics note, however, that studies fail to differentiate between the impact of the cash and the conditions that generate certain behaviour changes in achieving these successes.[93] Gender-based critiques point to the demands that such programmes make on women's limited time, sometimes restricting their income-producing activities.[94] CCTs aimed at improving girls' attendance in schools might come at the cost of harm to girls who, for example, may not attend school for fear of exposure to sexual violence on their way to

89 Lund et al., above n 56, at 72.

90 Armando Barrientos, 'Conditions in Antipoverty Programmes' (2011) 19(1) *Journal of Poverty and Social Justice* 15, at 17–18.

91 Ibid., at 16–17.

92 Lund et al., above n 56, at 73–4.

93 Barrientos, above n 90, at 19.

94 Molyneux, above n 69.

or at school.[95] A further concern is that conditions will not be effective where there are 'supply-side' problems with services such as lack of schools and clinics[96] and that the costs of administering conditions could be better spent on creating much needed services.[97] The provision of increased and improved basic services alongside cash transfers, including the need for 'gender sensitive social services … and sexual and reproductive health care'[98] is critical.

Standing provides an ethical argument against conditionality.[99] He suggests that the roots of behavioural policies are in libertarian paternalism aimed at addressing deficiencies of individual character rather than structural causes of poverty and underdevelopment. His critique of conditionality relates to the full range of conditions discussed above including means-testing. He argues that controls imposed on some people and not on others violate the autonomy of poor people and questions their capacity for rational choice. They are also discriminatory since they require the poor to meet conditions not required of the rich. They may also create hierarchies of deservedness amongst the poor. A focus on directing people towards services does not address the structural reasons for the lack of service take-up. CCTs represent rights as charity and facilitate the removal of rights without due process since it is difficult to properly monitor compliance without arbitrariness or bias. This encourages corruption.

Molyneux raises gender-related concerns about the values that certain CCTs impose. In her case study of the *Oportunidades* CCT in Mexico she found that by premising the programme 'on normatively ascribed maternal responsibilities' the transfers effectively become conditional on 'good motherhood'.[100] Men were not included or encouraged to share responsibility with women for the betterment of their families. 'The social relations of reproduction therefore remain unproblematized, and the work performed easily naturalized.'[101]

The critiques of conditionality lead some authors to suggest that cash transfers should not only be unconditional (in the sense of 'true conditionalities' as defined by Lund et al.) but should also be universal (involving the removal of means-testing).[102]

From a human rights perspective, conditionalities appear problematic, but this issue has not been fully canvassed or resolved at the treaty body level. The CESCR General Comment 19 on the right to social security does not make specific mention of CCTs although the Committee has criticised welfare conditionality as

95 Magdalena Sepúlveda and Carly Nyst, *The Human Rights Approach to Social Protection* (Ministry for Foreign Affairs Finland, 2012), at 50.

96 Lund, et al., above n 56, at 77.

97 Sepúlveda and Nyst, above note 95, at 50.

98 Ibid., at 51.

99 Guy Standing, 'Behavioural conditionality: why the nudges must be stopped – an opinion piece' (2011) 19(1) *Journal of Poverty and Social Justice* 27.

100 Molyneux, above n 69, at 59. The Mexican CCT involves a stipend on condition that mothers take children to clinics, ensure they attend school, attend workshops on health and contribute a number of hours of community work such as cleaning public facilities.

101 Ibid.

102 Standing, above n 99, at 36; Lund, et al., above n 56, in relation to the CSG.

having a punitive effect on marginalized women[103] and encouraged Brazil to make one of its social assistance programmes universal.[104] General Comment 19 lists accessibility as an element of the right and as part of this examines eligibility. The Committee notes that:

> Qualifying conditions for benefits must be reasonable, proportionate and transparent. The withdrawal, reduction or suspension of benefits should be circumscribed, based on grounds that are reasonable, subject to due process, and provided for in national law.[105]

While this seems to relate to initial inclusion in a particular scheme, it may also refer to ongoing eligibility. Additionally, it is unclear what would make a CCT reasonable and proportionate and how this would be determined. This appears to be a gap in the General Comment where insufficient direction was provided for the evaluation of CCTs from the perspective of rights compliance.

Sepúlveda and Nyst, in discussing conditionality from a human rights perspective, echo Standing's points about the loss of individual autonomy and the assumption that poor people are not capable of making rational choices.[106] They view conditions as depriving people of their freedom to determine what is best for themselves and their families. They also note that states have an international obligation to immediately provide for the essential levels of the basic needs of their people. 'The enjoyment of these rights by all individuals is not conditional on the performance of certain actions or the meeting of requirements. Rather, these are inherent rights which are essential to the realisation of human dignity.'[107] Conditionalities might also impact on democratic solutions by communities (such as parental involvement in school management) if officials are given too much authority. Non-compliance with conditions must not result in exclusion of beneficiaries from programmes aimed at meeting their basic rights – on the contrary, this should alert officials to the need to assist those people to access services. Where conditions exist, these should operate as incentives rather than exclusionary or punitive measures. 'From a human rights perspective, these beneficiaries *must not be excluded* from their entitlements because the State has failed to improve the provision of public services or take an appropriate gender approach in designing the programme.'[108] They recommend that 'protections must be put in place to ensure that conditionalities do not create an unnecessary burden on women, expose them to abuse, or perpetuate traditional gender stereotypes within recipient households'.[109]

103 CO Australia E/C.12/AUS/CO/4 (42nd Session, CEDAW, 2009), para 20.
104 CO Brazil E/C.12/BRA/CO/2 (42nd Session, CEDAW, 2009), para 20(d).
105 CESCR, above n 72, at para 24.
106 Sepúlveda and Nyst, above n 95, at 49.
107 Ibid.
108 Ibid., at 53.
109 Ibid.

Sepúlveda and Nyst use a human rights perspective to conclude that CCTs have dangers in terms of autonomy, freedom, dignity and democracy. While cognisant of gender discrimination and stereotyping, they do not specifically consider equality rights violations that might arise in relation to conditional programmes. Fredman has analysed CCTs using her four-dimensional equality approach.[110] She finds that CCTs fail to ensure gender equality in terms of distribution, recognition, transformation and participation and that unconditional cash transfers are more likely to result in substantive equality. She concludes that 'real substantive equality is most likely to be achieved, not through making women bear the burden of breaking the inter-generational cycle of poverty but through universal, free access to good quality State schools, health clinics and other essential services'.[111]

In addition to using a substantive equality approach to evaluate conditional social security, the principles developed in this book can assist in such an evaluation.[112] The first Principle, requiring the recognition of reproductive and unpaid care work for the purpose of social security, and the second Principle, requiring the recognition of women's other unpaid work, are relevant to this issue. CCTs that require women to provide caring work and other work such as ensuring school and clinic attendance, and attending courses, without meeting their own rights to social security, are likely to contravene these principles. CCTs are also contrary to the fifth Principle that social security must be provided to all based on need, unrelated to work status, since this principle denotes an entitlement. A genuine right to social security must be unfettered. Lastly, the sixth and seventh Principles requiring that gender equality be incorporated into the design of, and access to, social security are unlikely to permit the imposition of conditions within social security programmes that target women or mothers who carry additional responsibilities and burdens. Where women are required to perform functions that the society as a whole should be responsible for, they should be remunerated and provided with accompanying social security benefits. However, to be transformative, social protection programmes should involve men alongside women in meeting these responsibilities.

4.6.2 New conditions attached to the CSG

The introduction of conditions into the CSG, which was previously an unconditional grant, is curious. The South African government may have been accommodating international agencies such as the World Bank that are very much in favour of CCTs.[113] Lund suggests that this might arise from a conservative shift at the macroeconomic and social policy levels away from a redistributive and

110 Fredman, above n 87.

111 Ibid., at 39.

112 See Chapter 5 for an application of the principles to an evaluation of the conditions imposed on social assistance in the Australian context.

113 Ariel Fiszbein et al., 'Conditional Cash Transfers: Reducing Present and Future Poverty' (World Bank, 2009).

inclusionary approach.[114] There is clearly a contest in the South African government between those who approach social assistance as rights-based and developmental and those who view it as dependency-producing.[115] Conditional grants may support the agenda of those with the latter ideological stance.

When the regulations to introduce the conditions were first published in 2009, they required primary caregivers to provide proof of the child's school attendance every six months; a failure to do so would result in the suspension of the CSG until the condition was complied with.[116] Welfare and human rights groups opposed the regulations. The government amended them and removed the suspension of the grant for failure to provide proof of attendance but retained the requirement for primary caregivers to report every six months. The amendment also placed a reporting requirement on school heads of department to inform the welfare department of the child's lack of enrolment or attendance. Once notified, the department must assign a social worker to investigate and report to the department. The department must then take steps to ensure enrolment and attendance by the child.[117] The regulations apply to all children in receipt of the CSG between the ages of 7 and 18, failing to differentiate children over 15 who are not required to attend school. This could result in the discriminatory outcome of compelling children on the CSG to attend school between the ages of 15 and 18 while those not on the grant would have a choice whether to remain in school or not.

Commentators have pointed to the irrationality of these conditions given the already high level of school enrolment (97 per cent)[118] which had improved under the previously unconditional CSG. They also note that the regulations imply that parents are responsible for the failure of children to attend school rather than allowing for or considering other reasons for non-attendance. Such reasons include lack of access to schools for reasons of affordability, disability/illness, because schools are full, and physical access issues such as distance and transport.[119] Moreover, the conditions create a harsh and unnecessary burden on school administrators who are already overloaded with the collection of fees and school maintenance resulting from the erosion of the post-democracy promise of free schooling.[120] Although the shift from the 'hard' conditions of the draft regulations requiring suspension of the CSG to the 'soft' condition of the final regulation requiring a social worker to investigate is an improvement, it sets up

114 Lund, above n 53, at 12.

115 Goldblatt and Rosa, above n 8.

116 Department of Social Development, 'Social Assistance Act, 2004: Amendment: Regulations relating to the application for and payment of social assistance and the requirements or conditions in respect of eligibility for social assistance' (G 32747, RG 9192, GoN 1116), 27 November 2009.

117 Department of Social Development, 'Social Assistance Act, 2004: Amendment: Regulations relating to the application for and payment of social assistance and the requirements or conditions in respect of eligibility for social assistance' (G 32747, RG 9192, GoN 1116), 31 December 2009.

118 Katharine Hall, 'The Child Support Grant: are conditions appropriate? Children count brief' (Children's Institute, University of Cape Town, 2011).

119 Ibid.

120 Lund, above n 53, at 11.

a highly impractical process. There are not enough social workers to undertake such investigations or provide support to the children concerned.[121]

Hall suggests that the regulations may not be constitutionally valid as they may violate children's rights to social security.[122] Lund et al. argue that conditionalities are 'inconsistent with the (essentially) social democratic social policy regime set out in the Constitution'. Placing conditions on social security assumes that parents are responsible for school non-attendance rather than focusing on the structural causes of poverty, the promised removal of which are 'implicit in the Constitution'.[123]

From the perspective of a substantively equal, gendered right to social security, the new conditions on the CSG are problematic. Although the enforcement burden of the conditions is placed on schools, reporting burdens are still placed on primary caregivers (mainly mothers who are the CSG recipients). As with other CCTs, there is a disregard of the first of the principles set out in this book, the recognition and support of care. Carers, usually women, are burdened with additional responsibilities rather than receiving support from government for their existing responsibilities. In terms of the second Principle, that social security should support other unpaid work, the conditions similarly add to rather than ease women's loads. The design and access elements of the new condition (Principles 6 and 7) do not enhance gender equality. On the contrary, they make the grant less accessible for recipients by adding duties that undermine the idea of rights-based entitlements. The conditions also challenge full and equal access to the right to social security as set out in South Africa's Constitution and in international law.

The application of the substantive equality dimensions of recognition, redistribution, transformation and participation also highlights the problematic nature of the new conditions. The conditions lead to potential stigmatisation of primary caregivers who fail to meet the reporting requirements and are blamed by officials for a failure that may have arisen from a range of possible difficult circumstances (recognition). Requiring carers to take school reports to departmental offices twice a year is very onerous for people who live a long distance from such offices or face difficulties such as disabilities, lack of childcare and lack of money for transport (redistribution). The requirement to ensure participation is absent as primary caregivers were not involved in the decision to add this condition to the CSG. Primary caregivers might have contributed important insights into the problems with education enrolment and attendance, had they been consulted. The measures fail to enhance their participation in society – on the contrary, they impinge on recipients' time. The measures are not transformative of gender relations – instead, they create difficulties for disadvantaged women who are already assuming the major responsibilities for childcare and household reproduction.

121 Ibid., at 12.
122 Hall, above n 118.
123 Lund et al., above n 56, at 86.

4.7 Conclusion – addressing the gaps

The approach and principles for a substantively equal, gendered right to social security, advanced in this book, can contribute to the interpretation of South Africa's right to social security. As demonstrated in this chapter, together they provide a means of evaluating existing realisation of the right to social security. They also offer guidance for the reform and redevelopment of South Africa's social security programme to address gendered poverty and fulfil the rights to social security and equality.

South Africa's social security system has a relatively large social assistance component that is critical to poverty alleviation efforts. As discussed in this chapter, the Child Support Grant is an important feature of this system. While it provides some of the food needs of children in poor households, it has had a limited impact on the poverty and inequality faced by millions of South African women. The major gap in the system is the lack of provision of state support, in line with the Constitution's promise, of social assistance to working-age people (aged 18–59). Women's disadvantaged status in relation to accessing the workforce means that the group excluded from employment and social assistance is disproportionately female. A large number of these women are, however, working – they are performing the necessary but unremunerated care and household labour of South African society. The principles for a substantively equal, gendered right to social security, applied to the South African example, demonstrate that the Child Support Grant and the social security system as a whole are failing to meet the human rights of women and to advance gender equality in South Africa.

There have been a number of proposals, both from within and outside of government, to address the social assistance gap. Progressives within government have examined ways of incrementally extending the social assistance net to disadvantaged groups. For example, a chronic illness benefit has been considered to assist people with HIV and other diseases who are not eligible for the disability grant but who need support to access medical care, shelter and nutritious food.[124] The major non-governmental demand has been for a Basic Income Grant (BIG) – the provision of a relatively small universal grant for all South Africans with a possible tax claw-back for those who do not need it. This recommendation emerged from the 2002 report of a government appointed Committee of Inquiry into a Comprehensive System of Social Security for South Africa (known as the Taylor Committee). The Committee recommended wide-ranging reforms to the social security system, including the introduction of a BIG to ensure universal coverage for all South Africans.[125] These recommendations have, in the main, not been followed due to the dominance of an economically conservative faction

124 Goldblatt and Rosa, above n 8, at 264–6.

125 Taylor Committee, 'Transforming the Present – Protecting the Future: Consolidated Report of the Committee of Inquiry into a Comprehensive System of Social Security for South Africa' (Department of Social Development, 2002).

within the ruling party that has seen social assistance as the preserve of the aged, children and the disabled while being dependency-producing for able-bodied, working-age people, despite the obvious unemployment crisis.[126] There is a failure to acknowledge, through the social assistance system, the particular vulnerabilities faced by women in poverty.

The argument that a BIG can be developmental if incomes are pooled in households has been approached somewhat cautiously from a feminist perspective.[127] There is a question of whether lack of trust between men and women in households might prevent such pooling, or if it does occur, whether women will have any control over decision making around expenditure choices. The extent of violence against women, prevalent in South Africa, might be worsened by conflict over grant funds. On the other hand, rural households, many of which are women-only households, might benefit from breaking their reliance on remittances, and might be able to use the BIG income developmentally.[128]

Responding to poverty and gender inequality through South Africa's social security system requires new and creative thinking. The expansive rights framework in South Africa provides a backdrop against which to engage in democratic deliberation over policy options for gender transformative social security. These policy solutions, informed by agreed values, would shape the evolving meaning of rights. This is the process suggested by Jennifer Nedelsky in her consideration of the gendered division of household labour as an issue of constitutional rights.[129] She recognises, as many feminists have previously, that this division of labour has a severe impact on women's enjoyment of their rights. Rather than exploring solutions that accommodate women's care and household responsibilities, she argues that transformative solutions that encourage men to participate in care, while concurrently restructuring institutions and altering attitudes, are essential for real change. She argues for a deliberative project that goes beyond law and courts, reaching people in all areas of society. This approach, a form of a feminist constitutionalism, 'brings together rights, values, and participation in norm creation to give a sense of urgency about finding ways to reflect on what our core values really are and to hold ourselves and our institutions to account'.[130] It is hard to envisage this occurring in a developed context, and even harder to envisage in the South African context where gender relations are shaped by poverty, violence, a history of brutalisation and injustice, AIDS and many other challenges. Nevertheless, such a deliberative process must be attempted, alongside

126 Goldblatt and Rosa, above n 8, at 266–8.

127 Hassim, above n 5, at 123–6.

128 The developmental use of grant income arises where grants are used, not just for survival purposes, but to advance the position of the grant holder and/or their household – for example, by using the income for food production, job seeking, retraining or for entrepreneurial purposes.

129 Jennifer Nedelsky, 'The Gendered Division of Household Labor: An Issue of Constitutional Rights' in Beverley Baines, Daphne Barak-Erez and Tsvi Kahana (eds), *Feminist Constitutionalism: Global Perspectives* (Cambridge University Press, 2012) 15.

130 Ibid., at 47.

other strategies, to expand and reinterpret the right to social security from a gender perspective in South Africa. This can contribute to the development of the right so that it becomes a gender-responsive vehicle for fundamental social change rather than a gender-neutral instrument that simply reinforces existing inequalities.

5 Australian country study

5.1 Introduction

Australia, with a population of 23 million, is an advanced industrialised country with a strong economy and a wealthy population.[1] Despite this, poverty affects a sizeable portion of the population, particularly women.[2] Assessed in terms of the conceptual approach of the book, including the principles for a substantively equal, gendered right to social security, elements of the Australian social security system are found to be inadequate and unfair. This chapter briefly outlines the history and nature of the Australian social security system (in 5.2). It then discusses the gender dimensions of the development of the social security system and the context of gendered poverty and inequality under the current system (in 5.3). Thereafter, it considers Australia's human rights framework and the capacity for the realisation of the right to social security in the Australian context (in 5.4).

The chapter goes on to examine two recent policy developments that highlight the relationship between gender, social security and human rights: cuts to Parenting Payments (a social assistance benefit) for sole parents, most of whom are women (in 5.5); and the introduction of income management (measures to control the spending of social assistance benefits) with harsh effects on Indigenous people, particularly women (in 5.6). Analysis of these examples using the gender rights framework of the book identifies human rights violations by Australia including lack of access to and inadequacy of social security, as well as discrimination in the design of social security policies and laws. The analysis demonstrates that the exclusion of gender in the application of a human rights analysis of legal and policy measures may leave out critical issues that impact particularly on women. The chapter concludes by arguing that the application of a substantively equal, gendered right to social security enables a reconsideration

1 Peter Whiteford, 'Poverty in a time of prosperity' (2012) 21(2) *Human Rights Defender* 7, citing a 2011 Credit Suisse Global Wealth Report estimating that Australia has the 'highest median household wealth in the world', at 7.

2 Between 12.8 per cent and 20.9 per cent of Australians live below the poverty line depending on the measure used. Women are more likely to be poor than men while sole parent families (usually women) are significantly overrepresented amongst the poor: Australian Council of Social Service, 'Poverty in Australia' (Australian Council of Social Service, 2012).

of the design of welfare measures to promote better outcomes for women and gender equality in Australia (in 5.7). In so doing, it contributes to the overall argument of the book by demonstrating the utility of the redeveloped right as a tool to evaluate and challenge law and policy and as a mechanism to guide the reformulation of such law and policy to advance gender equality.

5.2 Australia's social security system

Australian social security takes the form of social assistance rather than social insurance as found in many European countries. The payments are funded through the tax system and paid at a flat rate on the basis of means-testing of targeted groups.[3] The major grants are the aged pension, disability pension, parenting payments and unemployment payments (this last known as the 'Newstart' allowance). Approximately 4.9 million people (about 20 per cent of the population) receive income support.[4] Esping-Andersen, famous for his welfare state typology, has placed Australia's welfare system within the 'liberal' or residual welfare state regime-type. He sees this regime as restrictive of social rights with stratification of the poor on welfare below others within the market.[5] This characterisation has been challenged by writers who argue that the welfare system is supported by high wage rates through wage fixing and home ownership.[6] They argue that despite lower levels of social spending and lower taxes relative to other OECD countries, Australia is very effective in reaching the poorest people,[7] including through its system of universal health insurance. However, those arguments must be considered in light of indications that in recent years, unemployment payments have fallen significantly in relation to wages and other pensions. This group of welfare recipients is falling deeper into poverty as are larger numbers of sole parents who are being moved onto Newstart.[8] Inadequate rental assistance, the high cost of housing and limited availability of housing also put strain on the poor. Middle-class long-term security has been reduced by fluctuations in financial markets, which have impacted on the retirement-saving system of superannuation and created uncertainty on property prices.[9]

3 Philip Mendes, *Australia's Welfare Wars Revisited: The Players, the Politics and the Ideologies* (UNSW Press, 2008), at 15.
4 As at June 2010: Australian Bureau of Statistics, 'Year Book Australia 2012' (2012), www.abs.gov.au/ausstats/abs@.nsf/Lookup/by%20Subject/1301.0~2012~Main%20Features~Income%20and%20community%20support~194.
5 Gøsta Esping-Andersen, *The Three Worlds of Welfare Capitalism* (Polity Press, 1990), at 167–8.
6 Peter Saunders and Chris Deeming, 'The impact of the crisis on Australian social security policy in historical perspective' (2011) 45(4) *Social Policy and Administration* 371, at 376.
7 Peter Whiteford, 'How Fair is Australia's Welfare State?' (2011) *Inside Story*, http://inside.org.au/how-fair-is-australia%E2%80%99s-welfare-state.
8 Whiteford (2012), above n 1, at 8.
9 Saunders and Deeming, above n 6, at 376. The superannuation system has been described by Saunders and Deeming as an 'attempt to forge a new bond between the wage and social security systems in a modernized (mixed economy) wage earners' welfare state' despite its having been introduced to constrain wage demands rather than to improve the retirement system (at 382).

The Coalition government under John Howard (1996–2007) adopted the ideology and policies of the United States' (US) workfare approach in linking unemployment (and other) benefits to job-seeking and work-for-the-dole and the introduction of a more punitive system including monitoring and harsh penalties for fraud and violation of welfare rules.[10] Conservative welfare reform shifted public perceptions away from notions of welfare as a social right of citizenship to a conditional entitlement based on mutual obligation.[11] There was also a shift from the sovereignty of the welfare consumer to state supervision and the removal of choice – 'a denial of the equality of selfhood as the price of welfare assistance'.[12] Under the Labor government (2007–2013) many of these neoliberal policy features and the accompanying ideology remained, with low unemployment and parenting payments seen by government as incentives to find work. The Coalition government (elected in September 2013) is likely to further entrench this approach, having already signalled its intention, in the 2014 and 2015 budgets, to (amongst other things) cut youth unemployment benefits, parenting payments and family tax benefits.

5.3 Gender in the Australian social security system

Australia's welfare system began with a focus on wage fixing and the protection of the family through the male wage-earner, alongside income support for those in need such as the aged. The assumption was that if men were paid adequately they could provide for their families.[13] In 1907 the *Harvester* judgment set a minimum wage as the amount required for a male worker, his wife and three children to live in 'frugal comfort'.[14] The model of a male breadwinner with a wife at home has been eroded over the past century. Approximately two-thirds of couple families have two working parents. However, women in such couples are likely to work part-time and earn half the income of men,[15] while performing the major care functions. This 'modified-breadwinner model reinforces gender inequality, casting women as the primary carers and men as the primary earners'.[16] Two-thirds of women participate in the labour market (compared with more than three-quarters

10 Mendes, above n 3, at 33–4; Lesley Chenoweth, 'Redefining welfare: Australian social policy and practice' (2008) 2(1) *Asian Social Work and Policy Review* 53. Also see Terry Carney, 'Neoliberal welfare reform and "rights" compliance' (2006) 12(1) *Australian Journal of Human Rights* 223. For a discussion of Australia's 'breach penalty regime' as a violation of human rights, see Tamara Walsh, 'Breaching the right to social security' (2003) 12(1) *Griffith Law Review* 43.

11 Sheila Shaver, 'Australian welfare reform: from citizenship to supervision' (2002) 36(4) *Social Policy and Administration* 331. Also see Terry Carney, *Social Security Law and Policy* (The Federation Press, 2006).

12 Shaver, ibid., at 342.

13 Chenoweth, above n 10, at 54.

14 Mary Leahy, 'Women and Work in Australia' (2011) *Australian Policy Online*, http://apo.org.au/sites/default/files/Women_and_work_in_Australia_APO_guide_Mary_Leahy_0.pdf.

15 Ibid., at 2.

16 Ibid., at 2; Sara Charlesworth, 'Law's Response to the Reconciliation of Work and Care: the Australian Case' in Grace James and Nicole Busby (eds), *Families, Care-giving and Paid Work: Challenging Labour Law in the 21st Century* (Edward Elgar, 2011) 86, at 86.

of men) but almost half of them are in part-time work (as opposed to 16.5 per cent of men).[17] These workers face income and job insecurity as well as limited access to the benefits usually attached to work.[18] Women also face job segregation and a persistent gender pay gap of 17.1 per cent.[19] As a result of lower pay and interruptions during women's working lives, on retirement, men have 1.7 times the amount of superannuation as women.[20] Moreover, women perform a significant majority of unpaid reproductive and care work in Australia.[21] The employment rate of mothers with young children is lower than in many OECD countries.[22] It is in this context that women make up a higher portion of the poor than men in Australia[23] and are in greater need of income support. Sole parents, overwhelmingly women, face significant financial hardship.[24]

Australian social security policy has played a major role in creating and reinforcing gender inequalities in work and care.[25] During the 1940s a range of social security transfers were provided to address the needs of children and spouses.[26] Some of the transfers such as widow's pensions where there were different pension ages for men and women were overtly gendered. From the 1970s onwards, feminists, in alliance with the trade union movement and various Labor governments, removed most of the formal inequality from the Australian social security system. Various child support and childcare policies were introduced to bring women into the labour force and to support families. However, the Howard years (1993–2006) resulted in some inconsistent policies that encouraged women both to earn wages and to be primarily responsible for domestic and caring roles in the home.[27] The Howard government refused to introduce paid maternity leave but instead introduced the 'Baby Bonus' – a one off, means-tested payment to new mothers whether they were in the paid workforce or not. The ideology behind this measure was to encourage women to have children

17 Australian Human Rights Commission, 'Investing in Care: Recognising and Valuing Those who Care, Volume 1 (Research Report)' (Australian Human Rights Commission, 2013), at 5; Also see Marian Baird et al., 'Women, Work and the Global Economic Downturn' (2011), www.fahcsia.gov.au/our-responsibilities/women/publications-articles/general/women-work-and-the-global-economic-downturn?HTML#fn_13.

18 Charlesworth, above n 16, at 89.

19 Workplace Gender Equality Agency, 'Gender Pay Gap Statistics' (2014), www.wgea.gov.au/sites/default/files/2014-03-04-Gender_Pay_Gap_factsheet_website.pdf.

20 Patricia Easteal, *Women and the Law in Australia* (LexisNexis Butterworths, 2010), at 6.

21 Ibid., at 3–4.

22 Jennifer Baxter, 'Timing of mothers' return to work after childbearing: variations by job characteristics and leave use' (Australian Institute of Family Studies, 2008), at 1.

23 ACOSS, above n 2, at 14–15.

24 Almost half of all children living in poverty are in sole parent families: ACOSS, ibid., at 19.

25 Bettina Cass, 'Citizenship, work, and welfare: the dilemma for Australian women' (1994) *Social Politics* 106.

26 Helen Hodgson and Rebecca Boden, 'Not-so-distant cousins: family benefits in the United Kingdom and Australia' (2008) 61(3) *International Social Security Review* 29, at 30.

27 Deborah Brennan, 'Babies, budgets, and birthrates: work/family policy in Australia 1996–2006' (2007) 14(1) *Social Politics: International Studies in Gender, State and Society* 31.

and to stay at home to care for them. Brennan suggests that Howard's deep conservatism included a 'commitment to full-time mothering'.[28]

Two further policies were introduced during the Howard years: family tax benefits that effectively encouraged women to become primary carers rather than joint earners and carers;[29] and, a policy requiring poor parents receiving parenting payments to seek or engage in certain hours of paid work in order to retain benefits.[30] Brennan notes the class divide entailed in Howard's two policies: the 'choice' to remain out of work for mothers in income-earning families; as opposed to the compulsion to work for those families (usually containing sole mothers) relying on social assistance.[31] Childcare benefits to pay for approved childcare, like family tax benefits, have been criticised for failing to provide strong incentives to encourage women into full-time work.[32]

In January 2011, under the Labor government (2007–2013) Paid Parental Leave was finally introduced in Australia. Until this occurred, Australia and the US were the only industrialized countries not to have paid maternity leave. In fact, on ratification of CEDAW, Australia entered a reservation to Article 11(2) which deals with maternity benefits stating 'it is not at present in a position … to introduce maternity leave with pay or comparable social benefits throughout Australia'.[33] Prior to the introduction of Paid Parental Leave, there was only a right to unpaid parental leave. Some employers provided paid leave but this was not legislatively mandated. Parental leave is paid under the Paid Parental Leave scheme at the minimum wage for a period of 18 weeks. However, superannuation payments by the employer do not continue during the period of paid parental leave, so parents, usually women, lose out on retirement savings over this period. From January 2013 two weeks of 'Dad and Partner Pay' were also introduced at the minimum wage, to be taken at any time during the child's first year. 'Dad and Partner Pay' cannot be transferred to the birth mother. While this is an important development in recognising the need for men to be involved in childcare, it is for a short period of time at a low rate and, on its own, is unlikely to significantly shift the gender division of labour around childcare responsibility. The Coalition government has promised childcare reform but has also flagged future limitations to what parents can claim from employers and the government under the current

28 Ibid., at 37. The Baby Bonus was discontinued by the Coalition government with effect from March 2014.

29 Ibid., at 38–9.

30 Ibid. Also see Natasha Cortis and Gabrielle Meagher, 'Women, work and welfare in the activation state: an agenda for Australian research' (2009) 35(4) *Australian Bulletin of Labour* 629.

31 Ibid.

32 Terry Carney, 'Women and Social Security/Transfer Payments Law' in Patricia Easteal (ed.), *Women and the Law in Australia* (LexisNexis Butterworths, 2010) 424, at 430.

33 The absence of maternity pay was also arguably inconsistent with Article 10 of the ICESCR which states that 'working mothers should be accorded paid leave or leave with adequate social security benefits'. The Committee on Economic, Social and Cultural Rights (CESCR) '*General Comment No 19: The Right to Social Security (Art. 9)*' (2008) 39th Session 2007, E/C.12/GC/19, at para 32, states the right requires adequate maternity leave for women, paternity leave for men, and parental leave for both men and women.

parental leave scheme following an earlier debate about whether a better scheme was needed.[34]

In brief, the major income and tax benefit support for parents in Australia currently includes the following:[35] Parenting Payment (to support low income families with the costs of care for children, single or partnered); Family Tax Benefit A (to assist with the costs of raising children); Family Tax Benefit B (to provide additional support for sole parents and families with a carer not working); Child Care Benefit (to pay the costs of childcare in approved care); Child Care Rebate (to provide additional childcare costs, not means-tested); and, Paid Parental Leave.

Certain features of the current social security system have been criticised for continuing to assume women's dependency and failing to treat them as independent citizens. The total household income is used in means- and asset-testing for social security benefits. It is also used for certain family taxes that amount to an alternative form of social security (against the stated policy of treating the individual as the unit of assessment for income tax).[36] This changes the tax distribution within the partnership as the lower income earner (usually the woman) pays higher tax even though the couple as a whole pays lower tax. Consequently, 'a large number of women are bearing an unfair share of the tax burden'.[37] Family Tax Benefits are income support payments that are often channelled through the tax system to the male breadwinner which raises issues of women's capacity to control intra-household spending. However, there have been reforms to allow primary carers (usually mothers) to claim the Family Tax Benefit as a fortnightly direct payment (most applicants use this method). Commentators have argued that naming it as a tax benefit (by the Howard government) is misleading as it is usually 'delivered through the welfare system'.[38]

Within the social security system, being part of a couple affects the amount of most income support payments. The partnered rate for each person in the couple is less than the single rate, and being part of a couple also affects the type of Parenting Payment (single and partnered).[39] Sole parents risk losing higher benefits if they enter into a new relationship.[40] The focus on couples is gendered

34 This earlier debate arose in response to then Prime Minister Tony Abbott who promised a higher level of payment, even for wealthy women. For discussion of this debate, see, for example: Eva Cox, 'Let's acknowledge Abbott's parental leave plan is better' (2013) *Crickey*, www.crikey.com.au/2013/05/08/cox-lets-acknowledge-abbotts-parental-leave-plan-is-better; Adele Horin, 'To the labour ward in a Roller', *Sydney Morning Herald* 10 March 2012, www.smh.com.au/federal-politics/political-opinion/to-the-labour-ward-in-a-roller-20120309-1upmo.html.

35 Australian Human Rights Commission, 'Investing in Care: Recognising and Valuing Those who Care, Volume 2 (Technical papers)' (2013), at 72–5. There are further forms of income and tax assistance for carers of people with disabilities.

36 Miranda Stewart, 'Women and Tax' in Patricia Easteal (ed.), *Women and the Law in Australia* (LexisNexis Butterworths, 2010) 441, at 446.

37 Ibid., at 447.

38 Hodgson and Boden, above n 26, at 41–2.

39 Carney, above n 32, at 433.

40 Ibid., at 435.

in terms of 'assumptions of dependency of women on male providers'.[41] Women will continue to lose payments or face reductions on the basis of the assumption that if they are partnered they are sharing income.[42] However, there is evidence that this assumption is mistaken and that a wide variety of financial arrangements exist including where partners do not share all or any of each other's costs.[43]

Carney notes that while Australia's social security system is formally equal, it does not play a sufficient role in addressing the systemic disadvantages faced by women within Australian society.[44] Recent proposals to improve women's retirement savings by recognising the impact of care on their working lives have been advanced by the Australian Human Rights Commission within a broader set of recommendations to more effectively structure the role of care in the society, but it remains to be seen whether these will be adopted.[45]

5.4 Australia's human rights framework and the right to social security

Australia is a party to the ICCPR and ICESCR as well as to many of the major human rights conventions including CEDAW. Australia has also ratified seven of the eight major ILO conventions and a number of governance and technical conventions.[46] It has not, however, ratified ILO *Social Security (Minimum Standards) Convention*, 1952, (No. 102). While it attempts to fulfil its international human rights obligations through certain domestic mechanisms including anti-discrimination legislation,[47] human rights commissions and more recently parliamentary oversight mechanisms, it does not have general human rights legislation (at the federal level) or a bill of rights.[48] Australia has been widely criticised

41 Ibid., at 434.

42 Ibid., at 435.

43 Stewart, above n 36, at 448.

44 (2010), above n 32, at 439.

45 Australian Human Rights Commission, above n 17.

46 The seven major conventions include: *Forced Labour Convention*, 1930 (No. 29), ratified on 2 January 1932; *Freedom of Association and Protection of the Right to Organise Convention*, 1948 (No. 87), ratified on 28 February 1973; *Right to Organise and Collective Bargaining Convention*, 1949 (No. 98), ratified on 28 February 1973; *Equal Remuneration Convention*, 1951 (No. 100), ratified on 10 December 1974; *Abolition of Forced Labour Convention*, 1957 (No. 105), ratified on 7 June 1960; *Discrimination (Employment and Occupation) Convention*, 1958 (No. 111), ratified on 15 June 1973; *Worst Forms of Child Labour Convention*, 1999 (No. 182), ratified on 19 December 2006.

47 Social security legislation is broadly exempted from anti-discrimination legislation. See Carney (2006), above n 10, at 231.

48 For a discussion of the history of attempts to put in place a bill of rights in Australia, see Andrew Byrnes, Hilary Charlesworth and Gabrielle McKinnon, *Bills of Rights in Australia: History, Politics and Law* (UNSW Press, 2009). In 2009, following a government-initiated national human rights consultation, the Brennan Committee tasked with the responsibility for making recommendations to government recommended the introduction of federal human rights legislation. See National Human Rights Consultation Committee, 'National Human Rights Consultation' (Commonwealth of Australia, 2009). This recommendation was not followed. Note that there is human rights legislation in some of the Australian states and territories. The parliamentary mechanisms to meet

for this gap and encouraged to improve its human rights protections.[49] Human rights, as found in government discourse and public consciousness, is generally understood to include civil and political rights rather than social and economic rights.[50] There is a very limited understanding across Australian society of social security as a human right, including the gender dimensions of this right.[51]

Treaty bodies, in particular the CESCR, and various UN special rapporteurs have commented on and made recommendations regarding Australia's social security system. In 2009 the CESCR recommended measures to address the gender wage gap and the level of unemployment affecting Indigenous people, asylum-seekers, migrants and people with disabilities.[52] The committee made the following recommendation concerning Australia's social security system[53]:

> The Committee recommends that the State party take additional measures, legislative or otherwise, to ensure universal coverage of the social security system so as to include asylum-seekers, newly arrived immigrants and indigenous peoples. The Committee also recommends that social security benefits, including unemployment benefits, old age pensions and youth allowance enable recipients to enjoy an adequate standard of living. The Committee strongly recommends that the State party review conditionalities such as 'mutual obligations' in the welfare to work programme and the 'quarantining' of welfare payments under the Northern Territory Intervention that may have a punitive effect on disadvantaged and marginalized families, women and children. The Committee further recommends that the State party consider ratifying ILO Convention No. 102 (1952) concerning Minimum Standards of Social Security.

Australia's human rights obligations will be considered in more detail below in the discussion of Parenting Payment cuts (in 5.5) and Income Management (in 5.6).

49 See the Conclusions and Recommendations of the Universal Periodic Review of Australia: Human Rights Council, *Report of the Working Group on the Universal Periodic Review (Australia)*, 24 March 2011, A/HRC/17/10, para 86.22. For criticism of the lack of women's rights protections, see Henrietta Zeffert, 'Identifying the Invisible: Women's Human Rights and Substantive Gender Equality in Australia' in Paula Gerber and Melissa Castan (eds), *Contemporary Perspectives on Human Rights Law in Australia* (Thomson Reuters, 2013) 223.

50 This general understanding was confirmed in the recommendations of the Brennan Committee report: National Human Rights Consultation, above n 48, at 365, but see contrary views from those consulted during the inquiry, at 78–82. For a discussion of the failure to include social and economic rights in the human rights legislation recommended by the Brennan Committee, see Andrew Byrnes, 'Second-class rights yet again? Economic, social and cultural rights in the report of the National Human Rights Consultation' (2010) 33(1) *UNSW Law Journal* 193. Also see Andrew Byrnes, 'The Protection and Enjoyment of Economic, Social and Cultural Rights' in Paula Gerber and Melissa Castan (eds), *Contemporary Perspectives on Human Rights Law in Australia* (Thomson Reuters, 2013) 125.

51 The language of rights is used by certain NGOs operating within the social security system such as the National Welfare Rights Network but Carney says that 'human rights precepts have acquired little purchase in Australia as a basis for adoption of constructions of the substantive law which would be more favourable to the interests of social security clients' ((2006), above n 10, at 238).

52 Concluding Observations, CESCR, 12 June 2009, E/C.12/AUS/CO/4, at paras 17–18.

53 Ibid., at para 20.

This recommendation related to the Committee's concern that Australia's social security benefits were not adequate as an 'effective income support system'.[54] The Committee also expressed concern at the rate of poverty in Australia, especially amongst disadvantaged and marginalised groups.[55]

The CEDAW Committee, in its 2010 Concluding Observations on the combined sixth and seventh reports of Australia, focused specifically on the limits of the newly introduced Paid Parental Leave Scheme and issues of care. It said the following:[56]

> The Committee calls on the State party to ensure that the statutory independent review of the Paid Parental Leave Act gives due consideration both to an increase in compensation and to the provision of superannuation on paid leave in order to protect better women's financial security and to encourage equal participation of both parents in child care. The Committee urges the State party to develop a comprehensive child care policy to include out of school hours and vacation care and to increase the supply of affordable and quality child care.

Additional strong criticism against Australia has come from the UN Special Rapporteur on the situation of human rights and fundamental freedoms of Indigenous people, James Anaya. In his 2010 report, Anaya found that, in particular, aspects of the Northern Territory Emergency Response (NTER or 'the Intervention') violated Australia's human rights obligations and were racially discriminatory.[57] This included the introduction of income management of social security payments.[58] In 2012 the UN Special Rapporteur on extreme poverty and human rights and the Working Group on the issue of discrimination against women in law and in practice wrote to the Australian government to ask it to respond to claims that the cuts to Parenting Payments were a violation of human rights.[59]

The issues of income management and cuts to Parenting Payments as (gendered) violations of human rights, specifically the right to social security, are now discussed in more detail.

5.5 Parenting Payments cuts

5.5.1 History of Parenting Payment

As discussed above, historically Australia supported wives/widows and single mothers on the basis that these were needy recipients without male breadwinners

54 Ibid.

55 At para 24.

56 Concluding Observations CEDAW, 12–30 July 2010, CEDAW/C/AUS/CO/7, at para 39.

57 Anaya, J., Special Rapporteur on the Situation of Human Rights and Fundamental Freedoms of Indigenous People, *Situation of Indigenous People in Australia*, 4 March 2010, A/HRC/15/37/Add.4, appendix B, para 37.

58 Ibid. See 5.6 below for a more detailed discussion of income management.

59 This is discussed in greater detail in 5.5.6 below.

on whom they could depend. In 1973 the Commonwealth Supporting Mothers Benefit was introduced for single mothers (who were not on widows' pensions) as an unconditional entitlement. From 2002 compulsory interviews were introduced as was a minimal activity requirement (six hours of work or study per week) for parents of older children. A major shift occurred in 2006 when parents with school-aged children were brought under the job-search requirements applied to the unemployed.[60] Sole parents are now defined by their employment status rather than their caring status and are moved onto Newstart when their children start school.[61] Newstart is paid at a lower rate and with 'tighter income and activity tests and a more punitive compliance regime'.[62] This policy change was seen as a 'significant' shift 'in the structure of the Australian welfare state' from a 'male-breadwinner' to an 'adult worker family model'.[63] For new claimants after 1 July 2006 job-search requirements and the Newstart rate apply for sole parents with children over the age of six. The rules mean that parents must be in paid work for a minimum of 15 hours a week or job-seeking for 15–25 hours per week. Jobseekers may also be required to participate in activities aimed at improving their chances of work.[64] Those who had already made claims before this date received Parenting Payments for children born prior to 1 July 2011 and still under the age of 16,[65] and were expected to meet participation requirements once their youngest child turned seven.[66] This latter group is known as 'grandfathered' or 'saved' beneficiaries.

5.5.2 *The 2012 cuts*

In 2012 the Labor government took a decision to remove the benefits previously provided to the 'grandfathered' group of parents with effect from 1 January 2013 and to transfer them onto Newstart, at a lower rate of pay.[67] Not all the 'grandfathered' group of parents are eligible for Newstart as the income threshold is lower.[68] The government described this as a measure to introduce consistency

60 Teresa Grahame and Greg Marston, 'Welfare-to-work policies and the experience of employed single mothers on income support in Australia: where are the benefits?' (2012) 65(1) *Australian Social Work* 73, at 74.

61 Cortis and Meagher, above n 30, at 632.

62 Ibid.

63 Ibid., at 631.

64 There were some minor changes made in 2009 to include study and volunteering (Grahame and Marston, above n 60, at 74).

65 This age was changed to 12 or 13 for applicable groups in May 2012.

66 Maree O'Halloran (ed.), *The Independent Social Security Handbook* (Welfare Rights Centre, 7th edn, 2012), at 300.

67 Eligibility for all Parenting Payments (including the grandfathered group) ceases when the youngest child turns six (partnered) or eight (single). Participation requirements for grandfathered parents commences when the youngest child turns six instead of the previous seven (*Social Security Legislation Amendment (Fair Incentives to Work Bill* 2012 (Cth): Explanatory Memorandum, at 9).

68 It was estimated that almost a third (30 per cent) of Parenting Payment recipients would not be eligible for Newstart and with a lower income-free threshold they would thus face earlier reductions in payments than they had previously experienced: Parliamentary Joint Committee on Human Rights, 'Examination of legislation in accordance with the *Human Rights (Parliamenary*

between groups of parents in receipt of Parenting Payments and a measure to encourage parents of school-age children to 're-engage with the workforce and provide strong working role models for their children'.[69] It was clearly also a cost-saving measure estimated to reduce spending by $728 million over four years.[70]

5.5.3 *Initial response to cuts*

Welfare advocates said the cuts affected more than 100,000 sole parents with income reductions of more than $100 per week.[71] They noted that 95 per cent of Parenting Payment (Single) recipients were female in August 2011 (304,589 women).[72] An analysis of government data showed that despite government rhetoric about getting parents back to work, 60 per cent of the affected group were already in work.[73] Testimony from sole mothers showed that they would have to give up studying, move inter-state or cancel their children's participation in certain activities following the cuts. Many talked about the hardships relating to inadequate family support, the need to escape violence, children with special needs, and the lack of childcare and its impact on their job situations and how reduced income would compound these difficulties.[74] The implications of moving sole mothers, an already vulnerable and disadvantaged group,[75] onto Newstart, a benefit criticised by the government's own tax review as inadequate,[76] appeared harsh, unfair and even counter-productive.[77] It was arguably a breach of a promise made by the government to support this cohort of parents who were relying on the higher income for a longer period of time.

Scrutiny) Act 2011 – Social Security Legislation Amendment (Fair Incentives to Work) Act 2012: Final Report' (Commonwealth of Australia, 2013) ('Final Report'), at 5.

69 Ibid.

70 Patricia Karvelas, 'Single-mother cuts to hit hardest in PM's seat', *The Weekend Australian* 22–23 September 2012.

71 Around 63,000 people were affected by the change on the commencement date of the legislation, 1 January 2013. Eventually, the changes will affect 147,000 grandfathered recipients (Parliamentary Joint Committee on Human Rights, above n 68, at 4).

72 Based on government figures (Australian Council of Social Service, 'Inquiry by the Parliamentary Joint Committee on Human Rights into the *Social Security Legislation Amendment (Fair Incentives to Work) Bill* 2012 (Supplementary Submissions)' (ACOSS, 2012), www.aph.gov.au/Parliamentary_Business/Committees/Joint/Human_Rights/Committee_Inquiries/socialsecurity/qon/~/media/Committees/Senate/committee/humanrights_ctte/activity/social_security/qon/acoss_250612.ashx, at 9.

73 Maree O'Halloran, 'Working Single Parents Kicked', *The Australian* 6 March 2013.

74 Verbatim testimony provided by the National Council for Single Mothers and their Children, ACOSS (2012), above n 72, at 11–12.

75 Peter Saunders and Melissa Wong, 'Promoting Inclusion and Combating Deprivation: Recent Changes in Social Disadvantage in Australia' (Social Policy Research Centre, University of New South Wales, 2012), at 54.

76 *Australia's Future Tax System: Final Report* (Commonwealth of Australia, 2010), at Chapter 9.1.

77 Eva Cox, 'What the Government Wants to Ignore About Sole Parents and Jobseeking' (2013) *The Conversation*, http://theconversation.edu.au/what-the-government-wants-to-ignore-about-sole-parents-and-jobseeking-11582.

5.5.4 *The human rights response*

The cut to sole mothers' benefits, even by a Labor government, was not entirely surprising in the context of international austerity measures following the global financial crisis that began in 2008. Australia was looking for ways to bring the budget out of deficit and grandfathered sole parents were one possible revenue source. What was significant, however, was the new role for human rights in efforts by those opposing the measure. Welfare and human rights advocates challenged the Bill introducing the changes by calling for an inquiry into the proposed legislation by the Parliamentary Joint Committee on Human Rights. The Committee is a body set up under the *Human Rights (Parliamentary Scrutiny) Act* 2011.[78] The Act was introduced following a national human rights consultation in 2008 that called for human rights legislation along the lines of similar legislation in the United Kingdom.[79] This was rejected, but the recommendation for the establishment of a new Parliamentary Committee to carry out human rights scrutiny of new legislation was adopted. In addition, new Bills would be accompanied by statements of compatibility with international human rights.[80] The Parliamentary Joint Committee on Human Rights was consequently established with the mandate to examine and inquire into Bills, Acts and legislative instruments in terms of Australia's international human rights obligations.

The Parenting Payment cuts were the subject of the first inquiry by the Committee and thus an important test of Australia's minimalist new human rights framework. On 15 June 2012 the Australian Council of Social Service (ACOSS), together with 14 other individuals representing welfare and human rights organisations across Australia,[81] requested an inquiry by the Parliamentary Committee into the *Social Security Legislation Amendment (Fair Incentives to Work) Bill* 2012 which contained the cuts. The letter of request[82] described the proposed removal of Parenting Payments to the grandfathered recipients as a human rights violation. It argued that the Bill violated rights under the ICESCR and CEDAW as it impinged on the social security rights of sole parents, most of whom are women. It also argued that the measure violated the principle of non-retrogression by removing an existing benefit and was contrary to the require-

78 *Human Rights (Parliamentary Scrutiny) Act* 2011, No. 186 of 2011 (Cth).

79 National Human Rights Consultation, above n 48.

80 See George Williams and Lisa Burton, 'Australia's exclusive parliamentary model of rights protection' (2013) 34(1) *Statute Law Review* 58.

81 The author was a signatory of the letter in her capacity as Visiting Fellow, Australian Human Rights Centre, University of New South Wales. She also provided oral evidence at the inquiry and contributed to the supplementary written submissions provided to the Committee following the inquiry.

82 Letter from the Australian Council of Social Service (ACOSS) and others to Mr Harry Jenkins MP, Committee Chair, Parliamentary Joint Committee on Human Rights, 'Request for Inquiry by the Parliamentary Joint Committee on Human Rights into the *Social Security Legislation Amendment (Fair Incentives to Work) Bill* 2012' (15 June 2012), www.aph.gov.au/Parliamentary_Business/Committees/Joint/Human_Rights/Committee_Activity/socialsecurity/correspondence/~/media/Committees/Senate/committee/humanrights_ctte/activity/social_security/correspondence/letter_inquiry_joint_committee_human_rights.ashx.

ment of progressive realisation of rights. The letter stated that the Minister's statement of compatibility which accompanied the Bill[83] was manifestly inadequate and called for a public inquiry by the Committee.

The Committee agreed to hold an inquiry and invited oral evidence by the government and the letters' authors on 21 June 2012.[84] It also allowed further written submissions after the hearing. It produced an interim report in September 2012 recommending that the Bill be deferred until the outcome of a Senate Committee into the adequacy of Newstart,[85] since it said that if Newstart did not provide an adequate standard of living for beneficiaries, then the proposed Bill would 'risk being incompatible with the obligation in article 9 of ICESCR to ensure minimum essential levels of social security'.[86] Despite this recommendation, the Bill was passed by both Houses of Parliament on 9 October 2012. The Senate inquiry into Newstart found that the payment did not provide for an acceptable standard of living for anyone but the short-term unemployed.[87] The Parliamentary Joint Committee on Human Rights produced a final report in March 2013.[88]

5.5.5 Discussion of report of Parliamentary Joint Committee on Human Rights

The reports of the Parliamentary Joint Committee on Human Rights demonstrate a real engagement with the meaning of the right to social security and the right to non-discrimination. The Committee also carefully considered issues of justification in relation to limitations of rights under ICESCR as well as issues of non-retrogression. It developed a framework for analysis looking at the legitimate objective of the measure, the rational connection between the measure and the objective, and whether the measure is proportionate to the objective.[89] Its final report raised concerns that the cuts to Parenting Payments would create additional financial stress for sole parent families without improving

83 Department of Education, Employment and Workplace Relations, 'Statement of Compatibility with Human Rights Prepared in accordance with Part 3 of the *Human Rights (Parliamentary Scrutiny) Act* 2011', *Social Security Legislation Amendment (Fair Incentives to Work) Bill* 2012, Explanatory Memorandum, at 15–17.

84 Parliamentary Joint Committee on Human Rights, 'Examination of legislation in accordance with the *Human Rights (Parliamentary Scrutiny) Act* 2011: Interim Report – *Social Security Legislation Amendment (Fair Incentives to Work) Bill* 2012 Fourth Report of 2012', (Canberra, Commonwealth of Australia, 2012), ('Interim Report'), at 6.

85 An inquiry by the Senate Education, Employment and Workplace Relations References Committee which was due to report by 29 November 2012. For this committee's report, see Senate Education, Employment and Workplace Relations References Committee, 'The adequacy of the allowance payment system for jobseekers and others, the appropriateness of the allowance payment system as a support into work and the impact of the changing nature of the labour market' (Commonwealth of Australia, 2012).

86 Parliamentary Joint Committee on Human Rights, Interim Report, above n 84, at 19.

87 Senate Education, Employment and Workplace Relations References Committee, above n 85, at Chapter 3.6.6.

88 Above n 68.

89 Parliamentary Joint Committee on Human Rights, Interim Report, above n 84, at 14–15.

their employment prospects.[90] It also questioned the unwillingness of the government to establish an official poverty measure.[91] It found that the government had failed to adequately incorporate its human rights obligations in developing the new laws. In particular, the government had failed to consult properly or consider alternative measures; it failed to explore the likely impact of the measures on the human rights of affected people; and it had not put in place impact assessment mechanisms.[92] On this latter point, the Committee proposed a review after 12 months to consider the impact of the legislation and whether reasonable adjustments would be required. Overall, it found that the government had not demonstrated that the right to social security of affected individuals was being met. It was thus unable to conclude that the 'measures are compatible with human rights'.[93] The Committee's report is a welcome first consideration by the Australian Parliament of social security measures in terms of Australia's international human rights obligations.

5.5.6 Involvement of UN Special Rapporteur

The ACOSS network that had initiated the inquiry, anticipating that Parliament would ignore the Committee's interim recommendations and pass the Bill, wrote to the United Nations Special Rapporteur on extreme poverty and human rights on 5 October 2012. The letter called on the Special Rapporteur to send an 'urgent appeal' to the government to delay the Bill pending the Senate Newstart inquiry.[94] The UN Special Rapporteur together with the Chair-Rapporteur of the UN Working Group on the issue of discrimination against women in law and in practice wrote to the Australian government on 19 October 2012.[95] In this letter they stated they did not want to prejudge the issue but wished to draw the government's attention to the applicable human rights norms and standards. These included, among others, Article 9 of ICESCR and CESCR General Comment 19 on the right to social security and its adequacy. They also emphasised the right to non-discrimination and the specific rights of children and women. The authors set out the ICESCR and CESCR requirements regarding limitations of rights and non-retrogression. Finally, they asked for the Australian government's co-operation and observations on a set of questions to inform their report to the UN Human Rights Council. The questions included the following:

90 Parliamentary Joint Committee on Human Rights, Final Report, above n 68, at 28.

91 Ibid., at 28.

92 Ibid., at 29.

93 Ibid., at 30.

94 ACOSS, 'Urgent appeal to the United Nations Special Rapporteur on Extreme Poverty and Human Rights on the proposed introduction of the *Social Security Legislation Amendment (Fair Incentives to Work) Bill* 2012 in Australia', (5 October 2012), on file with the author.

95 Letter from Maria Magdalena Sepúlveda Carmona, Special Rapporteur on Extreme Poverty and Human Rights, and Kamala Chandrakirana, Chair of the Working Group on the Issue of Discrimination Against Women in Law and Practice (19 October 2012), Reference: UA Poverty (1998-11) AUS 2/2012, https://spdb.ohchr.org/hrdb/22nd/public_-_UA_Australie_19.10.12_(2.2012).pdf.

1. Is the above information pertaining to the content of the Act accurate?
2. What measures have been put into place to ensure that individuals and families affected by the Act enjoy their rights to social security and to an adequate standard of living without discrimination of any kind?
3. Were alternative measures carefully considered? If so, please provide details of this examination.
4. Was an impact assessment conducted with regard to the impact of the Act on the level of enjoyment of the right to an adequate standard of living by the individuals and families affected by the Act?
5. Was an impact assessment carried out with regard to the impact of the Act on children's rights and interests?
6. Where those affected by the measures in any way consulted? If so, please provide details.
7. What measures have been put in place to ensure that the implementation of the Act would not indirectly discriminate against women?
8. What monitoring mechanisms have been put in place to assess the implementation of the Act and its impact on the rights of those affected? What processes or mechanisms for redress will be included?
9. The Statement of Compatibility with Human Rights stated that, to the extent that the Act may have any adverse impact on human rights, that impact is reasonable and for legitimate reasons. Please give details of how this conclusion was reached.

The questions are significant because they emphasise consultation with affected groups, principles of non-discrimination and impact assessment to inform the test of reasonableness of the chosen policy/law. The Special Rapporteur's letter appears to have had some influence on the approach taken by the Parliamentary Joint Committee on Human Rights in its final report, particularly with reference to the issues of consultation, impact assessment and monitoring. At the time of writing (30 June 2014) the government had not publicly responded to the Special Rapporteur's letter. The legislation took effect on 1 January 2013. It is evident that the UN appointed bodies' request to the government was ignored.

Despite Australia's stated commitment to international human rights, there is a growing 'disconnect' in its implementation of these rights in practice. Human rights commentator Phil Lynch notes that 'in the relatively small number of cases where Australia is found to have breached international law, we are increasingly refusing to play by the rules'.[96] He lists a number of instances where Australia has refused to implement decisions of UN human rights treaty bodies in recent years.[97] Nevertheless, the efforts to bring human rights arguments into the debate around welfare reform are important in the Australian context and offered welfare

96 Phil Lynch, 'Human rights movement needs better and bolder leaders' (2012) *The Drum*, www.abc.net.au/unleashed/4416618.html.

97 Phil Lynch, 'Australia's duplicitous approach to United Nations treaty bodies is undermining human rights and the rule of law' (2012) *The Drum*, www.abc.net.au/news/2012-08-13/lynch-human-rights/4190968.

rights advocates an additional set of strategic tools and a discourse for framing the Parenting Payment issue.

5.5.7 *Discussion*

The legislative changes have had a harsh impact on thousands of families.[98] They violate the right to social security of affected sole parents by providing insufficient resources for an adequate standard of living and a dignified life. They are also unreasonably retrogressive by removing existing benefits from a group that had expected to continue receiving them.

The removal of Parenting Payments does not accord with the principles for a substantively equal, gendered right to social security advanced in this book. In particular, the removal of the payments shows disregard for Principle 1 relating to the recognition of care work; Principle 5 relating to social security as an entitlement regardless of the person's relationship to work; Principle 6 relating to the design of social security to promote gender equality and to the adequacy of social security; and Principle 7 regarding full and equal access to social security.

The cuts are indirectly discriminatory against women as they are the group overwhelmingly affected. The failure to consider the context in which the cuts would operate reflects a lack of acknowledgment of the gendered realities faced by this group of parents. Their access to the labour market is shaped by their unremunerated childcare work and the impact that sole responsibility for children has on their life circumstances. By expecting these mothers to seek work, retrain or work and look after children without the necessary supports to do so and on very limited incomes effectively marginalises them even further. It fails to provide recognition of sole mothers' care responsibilities in assuming that they are equally placed with dual parent families and people without children to find paid employment or to manage and balance work and childcare. In fact, almost 60 per cent of the parents affected by the new law were already working and the removal of some of their social assistance made it considerably more difficult for them to balance their work and domestic commitments.[99] The removal of Parenting Payments illustrates the government's lack of understanding of the challenges of caring alone for school-aged children who need care in school holidays, when they are ill and before and after school hours, while also balancing these demands against employer expectations that are not always sensitive to these realities.[100] The caring work that these women provide is thus not valued as socially necessary and beneficial labour. Failure to take account of this context leads to violations of their rights to social security.

98 Rachel Kleinman, 'A single-minded struggle to get by', *Sydney Morning Herald* 23 August 2013, www.smh.com.au/federal-politics/federal-election-2013/a-singleminded-struggle-to-get-by-20130822-2se9f.html.

99 O'Halloran, above n 73.

100 Eva Cox and Terry Priest, 'Welfare to Work: At What Cost to Parenting?' (2008), http://pandora.nla.gov.au/pan/95161/20090223-1020/www.women.nsw.gov.au/PDF/Welfare_to_Work_At_what_cost_to_parenting.pdf.

A substantive equality approach to the cuts, using the dimensions of recognition, redistribution, participation and transformation further highlights gender rights violations. On the level of recognition there is a failure to acknowledge sole parents' care responsibilities and the challenges they face as well as the contributions they make, while burdening them with conditions and stigma. With regard to redistribution, parents are further impoverished rather than being provided with greater resources to place them on a more equal footing with others in society. In relation to participation, there is a failure to involve sole parents in formulating approaches to address their specific circumstances, while imposing new conditions on them contrary to past promises. Further, with respect to transformation there is a failure to develop policies that consider ways of changing the conditions that lead to a significant group of vulnerable sole mothers being unable to compete in the labour market, care for themselves and their children, and contribute fully to society. Transformative responses that assist sole mothers are likely to be linked to broader social policies that address gendered divisions of labour and inadequate provision of care.[101]

Using the principles for a substantively equal, gendered right to social security to examine Australia's response to this issue highlights its failure to meet its human rights obligations towards this group of sole parents. Rather than progressively realising the rights of this disadvantaged group, their existing provision has been diminished.

This discussion of Parenting Payment cuts illustrates that a human rights approach provided opponents of the social assistance cuts with a legal and normative framework within which to critique and challenge the measure as a violation of the right to social security. The addition of a gender equality analysis made it evident that women were the primary target of this violation. Thus, to fully interrogate the government's policy requires a substantive gender equality approach to the right to social security, combined with a contextual and evidence-based appreciation of the position of the group of women that are the subject of the measure.

5.6 Income management

The second example of a policy with profound implications for the right to social security, examined in terms of the gender perspective of this book, is the introduction of income management – the 'quarantining' of social assistance payments, mainly affecting Indigenous people, the majority of whom are women.

5.6.1 Background

In June 2007 the Howard government introduced the Northern Territory Emergency Response (NTER, also known as 'the Intervention') in response to

101 Cortis and Meagher, above n 30, at 643, point to comparative research by Lambert that links higher labour market participation and income by working mothers to supportive policies such as childcare and paid leave. Australia does not do well in this regard in comparison with other rich democracies.

shocking reports of child abuse and violence against women in Aboriginal communities in the Northern Territory.[102] The most significant report was prepared by the Northern Territory Board of Inquiry into the Protection of Aboriginal Children from Sexual Abuse entitled 'Little Children are Sacred' and called for a wide range of measures and services along with extensive consultation with the communities affected.[103] The government used the rhetoric of crisis to speedily introduce a raft of measures without any consultation with local communities. Measures included bans on alcohol and pornography, reforms to the justice system and employment projects, compulsory acquisition of Aboriginal land and, significantly, the introduction of compulsory income management.[104] A portion of income support (arising from various social assistance payments) is withheld and placed in a managed account which can be accessed only for use on certain items of expenditure with a 'basics card' that can only be used at approved stores.[105]

The rationale behind income management was 'the belief that undesirable behaviour can be modified by the regulation of personal income'.[106] Quarantined income was to be used for goods needed for the care of children. Women were also to be protected from 'humbugging' whereby they are forced, sometimes violently, to share their income support payments with relatives.

The *Racial Discrimination Act* 1975 was suspended so that the measures could be applied only to Indigenous residents of listed communities.[107] This action drew strong criticism from domestic human rights groups and international human rights bodies.[108] When Labor came to power late in 2007, it continued supporting the NTER. It eventually reinstated the *Racial Discrimination Act* in 2010 when it extended the NTER measures to non-Indigenous members of the Northern Territory.[109] In June 2012 the government enacted the 'Stronger

102 Australia is made up of states and territories with the federal government having certain additional powers in relation to territories. The Northern Territory, while sparsely populated, has a disproportionately large Indigenous population compared with other states and territories.

103 Northern Territory Board of Inquiry into the Protection of Aboriginal Children from Sexual Abuse, 'Ampe Akelyernemane Meke Mekarle: "Little Children are Sacred"' (Northern Territory Government, 2007), www.inquirysaac.nt.gov.au/pdf/bipacsa_final_report.pdf. Discussed in Nicole Watson, 'The northern territory emergency response – has it really improved the lives of aboriginal women and children?' (2011) 35 *Australian Feminist Law Journal* 147, at 148–9.

104 Philip Mendes, 'Compulsory income management: a critical examination of the emergence of conditional welfare in Australia' (2012) *Australian Social Work* 1, at 4; Watson, ibid., at 149–50 and 161–3.

105 O'Halloran, above n 66, at 108. Income management applies to certain categories of people such as 'long-term welfare recipients' or 'disengaged youth' and can also be required for people identified as vulnerable. In addition to compulsory income management, there is provision for voluntary income management. Fifty per cent or more of a recipient's payment is managed.

106 Watson, above n 103, at 150.

107 In terms of s132(1) and (2) of the *Northern Territory Emergency Response Act 2007* (Cth) and ss 4(1), (2) and (4) and 6(2) and (3) of the *Social Security and Other Legislation Amendment (Welfare Payment Reform) Act 2007* (Cth).

108 Such as the Australian Human Rights Commission and the UN Special Rapporteur on the situation of human rights and fundamental freedoms of Indigenous people, James Anaya, above n 57.

109 *Social Security and Other Legislation Amendment (Welfare Reform and Reinstatement of Racial*

Futures' legislation which extended income management for a trial period of five years to five areas outside of the Northern Territory.[110] The additional areas contain high numbers of culturally and linguistically diverse communities of recent migrants and refugees.[111] It also extended the School Enrolment and Attendance through Welfare Reform Measure (SEAM), designed to suspend or cancel income support where a parent or guardian fails to ensure school enrolment and attendance by children, to further sites in the Northern Territory.[112]

5.6.2 *Response to the measures*

The NTER and Stronger Futures met with angry criticism from many quarters. A general complaint was the lack of consultation. This was problematic in the top-down way in which the Howard government introduced the legislation but even subsequent consultation efforts by the Labor government were the subject of scathing condemnation.[113] The National Congress of Australia's First Peoples said that the consultations were flawed and did not involve sufficient opportunity for Indigenous people to develop their own solutions to the problems in accordance with international human rights.[114] The Intervention has been divisive in the Indigenous community both within and beyond the Northern Territory.[115] Despite the government's claim that the Stronger Futures legislation promotes rather than violates human rights,[116] the Parliamentary Joint Committee on Human Rights found that the government had been unable to demonstrate that the measures were not racially discriminatory or in violation of the right to social security, privacy and family of the affected groups.[117]

Discrimination Act) Act 2010 (Cth). The Act allowed the continued use of 'special measures' to address issues such as alcohol-related harm.

110 *Stronger Futures in the Northern Territory Act 2012* (Cth). It was further extended in June 2013.

111 Australian Human Rights Commission, '*Stronger Futures in the Northern Territory Bill* 2011 and two related Bills: Australian Human Rights Commission – Submission to the Senate Community Affairs Legislation Committee' (2012), at 29.

112 *Social Security Legislation Amendment Act 2012* (Cth).

113 Emma Partridge, Sarah Maddison and Alistair Nicholson, 'Human rights imperatives and the failings of the Stronger Futures consultation process' (2013) 18(2) *Australian Journal of Human Rights* 21.

114 National Congress of Australia's First Peoples, 'Statement to the Parliamentary Joint Committee on Human Rights on the Parliamentary Scrutiny of Human Rights as applied to the *Stronger Futures in the Northern Territory Bills* (2011)' (2012), at 6.

115 See Watson, above n 103, for a discussion of some of the different views between Aboriginal women on the Intervention. Also see Mendes, above n 104, at 8–9 on some of the reasons for the different perspectives.

116 Jenny Macklin, 'Assessment of Policy Objectives with Human Rights – *Stronger Futures in the Northern Territory Bill* 2012; *Stronger Futures in the Northern Territory (Consequential and Transitional Provisions) Bill* 2011' (Attached to letter to the Parliamentary Joint Committee on Human Rights, 27 June 2012), www.aph.gov.au/Parliamentary_Business/Committees/Joint/Human_Rights/Committee_Activity/strongerfutures/background/~/media/Committees/Senate/committee/humanrights_ctte/activity/stronger_futures/correspondence/mfcsia_chair_280612.ashx.

117 Parliamentary Joint Committee on Human Rights, 'Examination of legislation in accordance with

Additionally, particularly relating to the income management provisions, Cox has argued that the Intervention has been used to mask a significant policy change from welfare entitlement to control, using the NTER as a 'pilot' for further roll-out to the broader non-Indigenous population and particularly to those marginalised individuals and groups who are regarded as dysfunctional.[118] In a similar vein, Mendes suggests that compulsory income management reflects a shift from structural to individualistic explanations of social disadvantage and is a continuation of the increasing conditions being imposed on social security recipients.[119] There is also a strong argument about the failure of the government to support its assertion that the measures are beneficial with adequate evidence.[120] Moreover, the situation facing children and others who were meant to be assisted by the Intervention has worsened.[121]

5.6.3 Gender analysis

The gender impact of the measures has not always been evident in the wide-ranging public debate on the Intervention. In pure numerical terms the income management provisions affect women disproportionately since almost two-thirds (61 per cent) of income-managed people in October 2011 were women.[122] It is generally women who do the shopping for families. A study of women's experience of income management showed a majority felt demeaned by having to use the basics card and most had not felt any safer since its introduction.[123] Many interviewees found the basics card confusing. It also limited their shopping choices, preventing them from making purchases at smaller non-approved stores or, for example, from buying medicine from a pharmacy that was closer but did not take the card. Interviewees expressed feelings of shame at being identified as basics cardholders and as a result of the stereotyped assumption that they could not manage their finances responsibly on their own.

Family violence (often highly gendered) is one of the triggers for the categorisation of a person requiring income management. The Australian Law Reform Commission examined the link between family violence and income management and found that compulsory income management can be dangerous and

the *Human Rights (Parliamentary Scrutiny) Act* 2011: *Stronger Futures in the Northern Territory Act* 2012 and related legislation' (June 2013), at para 1.223.

118 Eva Cox, 'Evidence-free policy making? The case of income management' (2011) (12) *Journal of Indigenous Policy* 1. As noted above, this has occurred with the inclusion of five communities outside of the Northern Territory under the 2012 legislation.

119 Above n 104.

120 Cox, above n 118.

121 Cox, ibid., at 85, says this is evidenced by government's own statistics.

122 J. Rob Bray et al., 'Evaluating New Income Management in the Northern Territory: First Evaluation Report' (Social Policy Research Centre, 2012), at 57–8.

123 Equality Rights Alliance, 'Women's Experience of Income Management in the Northern Territory' (Equality Rights Alliance, 2011).

inappropriate in the context of family violence.[124] It recommended that it not be used in such cases. Ironically, the prevention of family violence is one of the stated objectives for the introduction of income management. The Commission noted that people experiencing family violence are often denied agency and control over themselves and their households, and suggested that government measures that further remove control are likely to be harmful in deepening the sense of disempowerment of such people.[125]

Watson has argued for the need to locate an understanding of the Intervention within the historical context of control over Aboriginal women coupled with their invisibility as holders of rights.[126] Protectionist legislation was historically used to control Aboriginal women's sexuality, relationships and families. As wards of protectors, Aboriginal women had to surrender their wages which were administered on their behalf, a practice which continued late into the twentieth century.[127] Similarly, welfare payments were controlled or recipients were subject to surveillance until their trustworthiness was established.[128]

5.6.4 Discussion: gender rights analysis

The women's rights dimensions of income management have largely been missing from human rights objections to the measures.[129] Yet the measures, in impacting harshly on Indigenous women, constitute indirect discrimination on the basis of race and gender. This results in both multiple and intersectional forms of discrimination for the group of women involved. Because of their race and their gender, women in the income-managed communities face daily indignities and a loss of autonomy. Their vulnerability as a marginalised group in Australia is intensified. While violations of the right to social security have been identified in human rights objections to the Intervention, as have issues of race discrimination, there has been a failure to consider the specific gender dimensions of the right to social security in relation to women who are the subjects of the laws. This omission reinforces the value of a framework that builds a gender analysis into the right to social security.

Attention to the context in which the measures have been administered, based on evidence of the impact they are having on women in the Northern Territory, exposes the forms of discrimination and the complex nature of the rights violations being suffered. Women's care responsibilities and unpaid work in household reproduction contribute to their disproportionate representation as welfare recipients. Indigenous women face discrimination in their access to the right to

124 Australian Law Reform Commission, 'Family Violence and Commonwealth Laws – Improving Legal Frameworks: Final Report' (2011), at 247–83.

125 Ibid., at 260.

126 Watson, above n 103, at 156–8.

127 Ibid., at 157.

128 Ibid., at 158.

129 Though note the mention of possible sex discrimination by the Parliamentary Joint Committee on Human Rights, above n 117, at para 1.217.

social security, which serves to heighten their already considerable disadvantage. The approach followed in this book, including the principles for a substantively equal, gendered right to social security, assists in revealing the infringements of the rights of women in the Northern Territory. Evaluated against these principles, the violations of women's right to social security become apparent in the context of income management in the Northern Territory and the further locations where it is being introduced. The NTER measures fail in relation to the first Principle on the recognition of and support for care work; the fifth Principle concerning the provision of social security to all who need it regardless of their relationship to work; the sixth Principle relating to the design of social security systems that promote equality; and the seventh Principle of full and equal access by women to social security.

Applying the four dimensions of substantive equality used in this book – recognition, redistribution, participation and transformation – to income management is revealing. Women who are subject to the income management provisions face 'misrecognition'[130] in the way in which they are targeted, demeaned and stigmatized by the laws. From a distributive point of view they are prevented from making choices about expenditure, sometimes leading to financial disadvantage.[131] In terms of participation, they have been inadequately consulted and have not shaped the measures introduced to address the difficulties they face – instead, they feel imposed upon, confused by the changes and disempowered.[132] Rather than seeking transformative means of empowering Indigenous communities to find ways of tackling violence against women and children, income management has reinforced an historical pattern of colonial paternalism and control, particularly over women. Controlling social assistance payments unreasonably coupled with discrimination violates the right to social security of people in the Northern Territory, with disproportionate and distinct impacts on women. The extension of these measures to other vulnerable communities such as recent migrants and refugees, where women face additional forms of intersectional discrimination on the basis of nationality and migrant status, race, ethnicity, religion, language and culture, along with gender, is problematic.

The introduction of compulsory income management introduces greater conditionality and control within the Australian social security system. The shift from social security as a right to a requirement that a person must prove that they are deserving is a troubling trend.[133] Greater conditionality is accompanied

130 The term used by Nancy Fraser, *Scales of Justice: Reimagining Political Space in a Globalizing World* (Polity Press, 2008), at 16. See Equality Rights Alliance, above n 123, at 29–32.

131 Equality Rights Alliance, ibid., at 21–5.

132 Ibid., at 17 and 39.

133 The SEAM laws, within the NTER and the Stronger Futures package, are an example of conditionality in reverse. In many social protection programmes internationally, such as conditional cash transfer programmes, social assistance is provided after women have met certain conditions such as ensuring school attendance or vaccination of children. Under SEAM they risk losing existing social security benefits if they fail to ensure school enrolment and attendance. This is similar to measures introduced into South Africa's Child Support Grant (see Chapter 4). This, like income

by increased monitoring and punitive controls that undermine the right to social security.[134] Such an approach affects rights of access to social security. Imposing conditions that control expenditure of social assistance payments raises further human rights concerns regarding autonomy, dignity and privacy.

Income management imposes hardships on women recipients of social security who are carrying the care burdens of society, in poverty, and who should be entitled to welfare support, without limitations, despite their lack of paid work. This support should be fully accessible without harsh, discriminatory and inappropriate conditions attached to it, within a social security system that is designed to improve the position of women rather than one which stigmatises and burdens them. Instead, the measures hinder women's access to the right to social security and, rather than promoting gender equality, reinforce women's disproportionate household responsibilities while imposing unfair new requirements.

5.7 Conclusion

The use of a gender analysis within a human rights approach promotes an understanding of the specific violations of the right to social security that affect certain groups of disadvantaged women in Australia. The conceptual approach and the principles for a substantively equal, gendered right to social security developed in this book contribute to this understanding of the Australian situation. This understanding can be used to address violations and deficiencies in the social security system to ensure that disadvantaged groups of women are substantively included and that the system advances rather than impedes the realisation of gender equality in the society. This deeper understanding of the right to social security from a gender perspective is needed to inform improvements to social security in Australia.

The Australian social security system, while sufficient in part, does not adequately meet the needs of a significant section of the poor. This failing has important gender dimensions as women comprise the majority of the poor, of those providing care in the society and an overwhelming majority of sole parents. Social security, previously approached as an entitlement, is increasingly dependent on the fulfilment of conditions, many of which are difficult for women with care responsibilities to comply with. Sole mothers are being transferred onto social assistance that does not provide an adequate standard of living. The Northern Territory measures added a race discrimination dimension to social security and are having a harsh impact on Indigenous women, as well as on other vulnerable groups who have subsequently been included under these measures.

management, is a problematic approach to social protection from a human rights perspective. See the discussion of conditionality and human rights in Chapter 4. Also see Sandra Fredman, 'Engendering Social Welfare Rights' in Beth Goldblatt and Lucie Lamarche (eds), *Women's Rights to Social Security and Social Protection* (Hart, 2014) 19; and Magdalena Sepúlveda and Carly Nyst, *The Human Rights Approach to Social Protection* (Ministry for Foreign Affairs Finland, 2012), at 48–53.

134 Walsh, above n 10.

Both measures relate, in part, to the structuring role of care in the gendered division of labour and its adverse impact on women across the life course in Australia. They also highlight the failure of government to address this structural inequality. On the contrary, the current policies reinforce the marginalisation of the most disadvantaged groups of women and leave existing divisions intact.

Tested against the gender approach of the book including the principles for a substantively equal, gendered right to social security, Australia performs poorly in relation to the two examples selected and discussed in this chapter. Parenting Payment cuts are forcing a large group of women and their children into poverty in the guise of efforts to encourage their further employment. Many mothers are already in work and will struggle to balance further work and care without adequate social provision of affordable childcare, and to find appropriate work in the current employment context. Poor sole mothers are facing violations of their rights to social security since the current measures are retrogressive, inadequate, and substantively unequal and fail to address principles of the inclusion of care and unpaid work. Similarly, Indigenous and other marginalised women have encountered violations of their rights to social security with the introduction of income management. Their full and equal access to social security has been circumscribed as a result of their race and historic disadvantage, their physical location as well as their gender location, which is in turn related to their caring responsibilities in society. Application of the principles advanced in this book relating to recognition of care and unpaid work, and access to and design of social security expose policy inadequacies. The stigma and shame that accompanies these measures results in indirect, intersectional race and gender discrimination in violation of the equality and social security rights of the affected women.

The lack of comprehensive human rights laws within the domestic context means that options to challenge these deficiencies using human rights are limited. Despite the utilisation of international mechanisms by advocates, these clearly have minimal persuasive power in the Australian setting. Nevertheless, there appears to be a new, albeit small, space for engagement around human rights with the establishment of the Parliamentary Joint Committee on Human Rights, even if its recommendations were ignored by Parliament in the cases discussed in this chapter. The recent advocacy around both the Parenting Payment Cuts and the Northern Territory laws has introduced some human rights discourse on social security into public debate. The gender dimensions of this debate have, however, been more limited.

6 Indian country study

6.1 Introduction

India is a lower-middle-income economy with a population of 1.2 billion.[1] The vast majority (77 per cent) of India's people are poor, consuming the equivalent of US$2 a day or less.[2] Recent developments in the expansion of social protection are notable, but the challenges of addressing poverty and disadvantage in India remain massive. This chapter examines the provision of social security in India from a gender rights perspective. It analyses the extent to which India's social security system is assisting women and girls to overcome grinding poverty and inequality. It finds that social security and social protection are developing rapidly but that, on examination of two key programmes, there are important respects in which such programmes fail to align with the principles for a substantively equal, gendered right to social security. Analysis of some of the positive and negative features of these two programmes may assist in the project to realise a gendered right to social security in India.

The chapter begins with an outline of the Indian social security system (at 6.2). It then discusses the gender dimensions of poverty in India and the need for social security that responds effectively to these conditions (at 6.3). A description then follows of the human rights framework that operates in India as it relates to the right to social security (at 6.4). Having provided this background discussion, the chapter uses the conceptual framework developed in the book (including the principles for a substantively equal, gendered social security right) to analyse the government's National Social Assistance Programme (at 6.5) and also an acclaimed social protection scheme, the *Mahatma Gandhi National Rural Employment*

1 Government of India, Census of India, www.censusindia.gov.in/Census_Data_2001/National_Summary/National_Summary_DataPage.aspx. India is set to overtake China as the most populous country by 2030.

2 P.S. Vijay Shankar and Mihir Shah, 'Rethinking Reforms: A New Vision for the Social Sector in India' in R. Nagaraj (ed.), *Growth, Inequality and Social Development in India: Is Inclusive Growth Possible?* (Palgrave Macmillan and UNRISD, 2012) 135, at 135. Note that there is vast regional diversity in India, with significant differences in social indicators across the 28 states and seven union territories. Shankar and Shah, ibid., describe this as a 'regionally concentrated pattern of human deprivation', at 139.

Guarantee Act (known as NREGA) (at 6.6). The conclusion considers, from the gender perspective developed in this book, some of the issues and challenges facing India as it endeavours to expand social security provision (at 6.7).

6.2 India's social security system

Following independence in 1948, India introduced social security for formal sector workers (described in India as the 'organised sector') including public sector workers.[3] After a crisis in agriculture in the 1970s, anti-poverty programmes were introduced that continued into the 1980s.[4] These included programmes to subsidise credit and create assets as well as to provide public distribution of food. These policies had an impact on poverty but also had some coverage and implementation problems. The 1990s saw cuts to social protection budgets following economic reforms.[5] Political pressure forced some programmes to be reinstated. Since the early 2000s, campaigns for rights to food, work and information have challenged government to introduce policy reforms.[6] The last decade has seen the introduction of legislation framed in terms of social rights and a growing number of social protection programmes.[7]

Although such programmes are having a beneficial impact on the reduction of poverty, the challenges facing India are extensive. While the country has experienced rapid economic growth in recent decades, which has resulted in major urbanisation, more than half of the labour force remains in the agricultural sector.[8] Agricultural workers earn low wages, resulting in 'significant working poverty in rural areas'.[9] Despite high growth, the rate of employment has declined relative to growth,[10] particularly in rural areas, and poverty and inequality are increasing. Almost half of children below the age of three are underweight and more than three-quarters (79 per cent) are anaemic.[11] Sen and Rajasekhar comment that the massive 'scale of need' in India together with the deprivations in all

3 Gita Sen and D. Rajasekhar, 'Social Protection Policies, Experiences and Challenges' in R. Nagaraj (ed.), *Growth, Inequality and Social Development in India: Is Inclusive Growth Possible?* (Palgrave Macmillan and UNRISD, 2012) 91, at 99.

4 Ibid., at 94.

5 Ibid.

6 Ibid., at 94–5.

7 Jayna Kothari, 'A social rights model for social security: learnings from India' (2014) 1 *Verfassung und Recht in Ubersee* 5; Deepta Chopra, 'The Indian Case: Towards a Rights-Based Welfare State?' in Gabriele Koehler and Deepta Chopra (eds), *Development and Welfare Policy in South Asia* (Routledge, 2014) 85.

8 Sukti Dasgupta and Ratna M. Sudarshan, 'Issues in labour market inequality and women's participation in India's National Rural Employment Guarantee Programme' (International Labour Organisation, 2011), at 1.

9 Ibid.

10 T.S. Papola and Alakh N. Sharma, 'Labour and Employment in a Fast Growing Country: Issues of Employment and Inclusiveness' in Alexandre Barbosa and Maria Cristina Cacciamali (eds), *The 'Dynamic South', Economic Development and Inclusive Growth: The Challenges Ahead* (IDRC, CEBRAP and ABET, 2013) 89, at 100.

11 Shankar and Shah, above n 2, at 136.

areas of social provision (education, health, housing, etc.) as well as income poverty mean that cash transfers cannot be a 'panacea'.[12] In the context of a largely informal sector (described in India as the 'unorganised sector'), social assistance alongside broader social provision within a rights-based and socially transformative approach is necessary.[13] The potential of this approach is put at risk by the lack of support from the 'politically powerful middle classes', real issues of financial capacity given the small tax base arising from the small formal sector, as well as the serious problems with implementation and corruption that blight India.[14] The change of government from the Congress-led Coalition that introduced social rights-based legislation to the more free market-oriented Bharatiya Janata Party (BJP) under Narendra Modi in May 2014 may result in a shift from the expansion of social protection programmes in India.

6.2.1 *The formal sector*

Formal social security covers approximately 8 per cent[15] of the workforce (the organised sector) through legislation that provides for employee provident fund schemes, workmen's compensation, health insurance, maternity benefits and a gratuity payment when a worker's employment ends.[16] Some of these laws require joint contributions from workers and employers (with additional expenditure by government in some cases), while others only require contributions from employers. Employers are increasingly looking for ways of replacing permanent employees with temporary or casual contract workers who continue to work beside permanent staff in the same enterprises but without the additional benefits.[17]

6.2.2 *The unorganised sector, the unemployed and others facing poverty*

The majority of workers who make up the unorganised sector that accounts for 92 per cent of the labour force are classified as poor.[18] These workers have no access to social security and generally face precarious and for many, 'inhuman' working conditions, whether as casual or regular wageworkers.[19] They are described as the '"unfree" – bound by grinding poverty, exploitation, discrimination and constant flux'.[20] These workers generally have no assurance of a minimum wage.

12 Sen and Rajasekhar, above n 3, at 95.
13 Ibid., at 96.
14 Ibid., at 96–7.
15 Papola and Sharma, above n 10, at 100.
16 The gratuity payment is provided on retirement, resignation, superannuation and death. For details of these benefits, see Sen and Rajasekhar, above n 3, at 98–102.
17 Ibid., at 102; Papola and Sharma, above n 10, at 100.
18 Sen and Rajasekhar, above n 3, at 104.
19 Sen and Rajasekhar, citing the National Commission for Enterprises in the Unorganised Sector (NCEUS), ibid., at 105–6.
20 Paromita Goswami, 'A critique of the Unorganised Workers' Social Security Act' (2009) XLIV(11) (March 14, 2009) *Economic and Political Weekly* 17, at 17.

The National Commission for Enterprises in the Unorganised Sector (NCEUS) was set up in 2004 to investigate the conditions of informal sector workers and report to government. It made recommendations for legislation including contributory life insurance, old age pensions and health insurance for all unorganised workers. The *Unorganised Workers Social Security Bill*, 2007 was strongly opposed by state governments, which would have had to carry the costs of schemes where there were no identifiable employers (a common situation). The Bill was revised to exclude workers above the poverty line (a line set by the State), leaving the majority of workers without protection.[21] The number of people living below this poverty line is approximately 300 million or one-quarter of the population.[22] *The Unorganised Workers Social Security Act* (UWSSA) was introduced in December 2008, in a 'watered down' form of the original Bill.[23] The Act simply listed some of the social assistance and insurance schemes that were already in existence[24] and brought them under its cover but did not require the creation of any new schemes or any minimum level of social security for every worker.[25] The legislation was seen by some as an 'act of political expediency' just before an election, and was severely criticised.[26] The Act was silent in relation to a minimum wage or the regulation of decent working conditions, without which unorganised workers are denied basic security and rights.[27]

Social insurance

Two of the newer social security schemes (referred to in UWSSA) introduced to assist the working poor in the unorganised sector and other poor households that fall below the poverty line are the Rashtriya Swasthya Bima Yojana and the Janashree Bhima Yojana.

21 Tina Dutta and Parthapratim Pal, 'Politics Overpowering Welfare: Unorganised Workers' Social Security Act 2008' (2012) XLVII(7) *Economic and Political Weekly* 26.

22 Anil Swarup and Nishant Jain, 'Rashtriya Swasthya Bima Yojana' in UNDP (ed.), *Sharing Innovative Experiences: Successful Social Protection Floor Experiences* (UNDP, 2011) vol 18, 259, at 261. The government sets the poverty line based on a rural household survey conducted by the states.

23 Sen and Rajasekhar, above n 3, at 124.

24 These schemes include the Indira Gandhi National Old Age Pension Scheme; National Family Benefit Scheme; Janani Suraksha Yohana; Handloom Weavers' Comprehensive Welfare Scheme; Handicraft Artisans Comprehensive Welfare Scheme; Pension to Master Craft Persons; National Scheme for Welfare of Fishermen and Training and Extension; Janshree Bima Yojana; Aam Admi Bima Yojana; Rashtriya Swasthya Bima Yojana.

25 Goswami, above n 20, at 17.

26 J. Breman and K.P Kannan, 'Unto the Last? An Introduction' in J. Breman and K.P. Kannan (eds), *The Long Road to Social Security* (Hivos, 2012) 7, at 12. Also see: Letter from 'Social Security Now', a campaign group calling for amendment to the Act, dated 29 July 2009, www.socialsecuritynow.org/SSNOW%20WEBSITE/Memorandum-Final_Rawat.pdf. Also see J. John, 'Towards a People's Movement for a Universal Social Security', paper for the National Convention on Social Security for Unorganised Workers on 8–10 January 2010 www.socialsecuritynow.org/Campaign_documents/john_sir's_article-English.pdf; and Miracle Aasra, http://miracleaasra.com/?page_id=25.

27 Goswami, above n 20, at 18.

The Rashtriya Swasthya Bima Yojana (RSBY) is a health insurance scheme launched in 2008 to provide access to public or private health care (up to a defined sum) for people below the poverty line. It uses smart card fingerprint technology to overcome illiteracy issues and requires a minimal co-payment to ensure 'buy-in'. The government subsidises medical treatment by paying insurers who pay the hospitals for services used, without payment required from the individual patients. The programme is currently reaching 110 million people (almost 10 per cent of the population).[28]

The Janashree Bhima Yojana (JBY) was introduced in 2000 for people aged 18–60 in households below the poverty line and belonging to certain occupation groups.[29] It provides death and disability insurance as well as school scholarships and requires annual contributions from participants that are matched by government.[30] Like some of the other measures for the poor, the JBY has been criticised for applying only to people below the poverty line, a measure that leaves out a vast section of those facing poverty measured on a less restrictive scale.[31]

Social assistance

Limited social assistance is provided to the poorest of the elderly, people with disabilities, widows and families who have lost a breadwinner at the national and state level. The National Social Assistance Programme (NSAP), introduced in 1995, has the following components:[32]

1. The Indira Gandhi National Old Age Pension Scheme for aged people living below the poverty line;
2. The Indira Gandhi National Widow Pension Scheme;
3. The Indira Gandhi National Disability Pension Scheme;
4. The National Family Benefits Scheme, providing one-off payments for families who have lost a breadwinner;
5. Annapurna (food security for the destitute not falling under the Age Pension).

The National Maternity Benefit Scheme (NMBS), administered separately by the Ministry of Health since 2001, provides a lump-sum payment to pregnant women over 18 in poor households for the first two live births. In 2005 this scheme was modified and renamed the Janani Suraksha Yojana (JSY) or 'Safe Pregnancy Scheme'. The scheme is described as the largest conditional

28 Victoria Fan, 'The Early Success of India's Health Insurance for the Poor, RSBY' (2013), www.cgdev.org/sites/default/files/early-success-indias-health-insurance.pdf, at 1.

29 Department of Financial Services, Ministry of Finance, Government of India, 'Government sponsored Socially Oriented Insurance Schemes: Janashree Bima Yojana', http://financialservices.gov.in/insurance/gssois/jby.asp.

30 Sen and Rajasekhar, above n 3, at 119–21.

31 Ibid., at 120.

32 Note that these schemes are created by executive action rather than legislation.

cash transfer programme in the world and is proving successful in increasing institutional deliveries and reducing neonatal mortality; however, its impact on maternal mortality is not yet known.[33]

Despite recent improvements in coverage and increases in grant size, these schemes reach a small proportion of the total population in need; the amounts of benefits are very small and are 'inadequate to address the problem of acute poverty and vulnerability'.[34] A task force established to consider proposals for a comprehensive national social assistance programme has recommended that the amounts, the coverage and the delivery of grants should be improved with the gradual universalisation of all schemes.[35]

In addition to central government schemes, there are a variety of state programmes offering social assistance and social insurance, including, in some cases, for informal sector workers, but the quantity, quality and access to the schemes varies significantly across states.[36] The plethora of benefits within states and the lack of information about the schemes make it extremely difficult to know what is available to citizens, both on paper and on the ground.[37]

Social protection

Other forms of social protection including the provision of food through the Public Distribution System, school meals and nutrition for pregnant women are provided by the national and state governments. Recently, parliament passed the *National Food Security Act* 2013 which guarantees defined amounts of grain to poor households, pregnant and lactating women and children.[38] There are also programmes to organise women into self-help groups and to provide subsidies and credit (such as the Swarna Jayanti Gram Swarozgar Yojna (SGSY) programme). The most celebrated recent scheme, established under the *Mahatma Gandhi National Rural Employment Guarantee Act* (known as NREGA) of 2005, is a public works programme that began operating in 2006 and provides 100 days of work per year paid at the minimum-wage rate to rural households engaged in unskilled manual work. The NREGA is seen as India's first legislative expression of the 'right to employment'[39] but also contains a social security

33 Stephen S. Lim et al., 'India's Janani Suraksha Yojana, a conditional cash transfer programme to increase births in health facilities: an impact evaluation' (2010) 375(9730) *The Lancet* 2009. See below at 6.5.4 for a discussion of the conditionality of this programme.

34 Sen and Rajasekhar, above n 3, at 118.

35 Report of the Task Force 'Proposal for Comprehensive National Social Assistance Programme,' Ministry for Rural Development, March 2013, http://rural.nic.in/sites/downloads/latest/Report_Task_Force_Comprehensive_NSAP.pdf. This is discussed further below in 6.5.

36 For a gender analysis in the wealthier state of Kerala, see Shoba Arun and T.G. Arun, 'Gender issues in social security policy of developing countries: lessons from the Kerala experience' (2001) 54(4/2001) *International Social Security Review* 93.

37 Guy Standing et al., *Social Income and Insecurity: A Study in Gujarat* (Routledge, 2010), at 117.

38 The background to the Act and its provisions are discussed in Kothari, above n 7, at 16–18. This is discussed further in 6.4 below.

39 Dasgupta and Sudarshan, above n 8, at 3.

component since applicants who are not provided with work must be provided with an unemployment benefit. The categorisation of this programme as a social security measure within the context of the right to social security will be considered below (in 6.6). The gender rights issues raised by its design and implementation will also be considered. NREGA does not cover the urban poor.

India's social security system, while containing some very positive features and significant recent advances, is clearly inadequate in addressing the needs of all those living in poverty. Sen and Rajasekhar suggest that major improvements could be achieved with better financing, design and implementation, greater attention to the multidimensionality of deprivation in India, and by embracing a rights-based approach.[40] The gender dimensions of poverty and the response of the Indian social security system to this are now considered.

6.3 Gender, poverty and the need for social security in India

6.3.1 The nature of women's poverty and disadvantage

Providing the right to social security for women in India is a critical need in response to their particular vulnerability and poverty. Although there have been some improvements in gender development indicators such as maternal health and illiteracy over the past decade, Indian women continue to face severe inequality and poverty as well as a growing exposure to gender-based violence.[41] A notable feature of India's social context is the central role of caste and religion which intersect with gender and other categories of discrimination to generate multiple and compounded forms of disadvantage for women.[42] This is illustrated in a strong cultural preference for sons and the privileging of boys over girls in access to food and education.[43] Women's identity is constructed around their roles as providers of reproductive and care work as well as household labour. Even where women are engaged in work outside of the home, this is generally regarded as secondary to their primary responsibilities in the home.[44] These attitudes also affect women's ownership and control of land.[45] Divorced, separated, deserted and widowed women are particularly vulnerable groups facing stigma

40 Sen and Rajasekhar, above n 3, at 125–9.

41 UNDP India Factsheet: Gender and Social Exclusion Indicators, www.in.undp.org/content/dam/india/docs/india_factsheet_gender_n_social_exclusion_indicators.pdf.

42 For a discussion of the colonial history of caste and its role in contemporary anti-discrimination policy, see N. Jayaram, 'Caste, Corporate Disabilities and Compensatory Discrimination in India: Colonial Legacy and Post-Colonial Paradox' in James Midgley and David Pichaud (eds), *Colonialism and Welfare: Social Policy and the British Imperial Legacy* (Edward Elgar, 2011) 85.

43 Elizabeth Hill, *Worker Identity, Agency and Economic Development: Women's Empowerment in the Indian Informal Economy* (Routledge, 2010), at 62.

44 Ibid.

45 Nisha Srivastava and Ravi Srivastava, 'Women, work, and employment outcomes in rural India' (2010) XLV(28) *Economic and Political Weekly* 49, at 53–4.

and poverty.[46] Similarly, women's citizenship is limited by 'restrictions on personal mobility and visibility outside the home' which affects their access to work and other areas of life.[47]

6.3.2 *Women's employment profile*

The rate of female workforce participation has declined in India[48] – from 37 per cent in 2004–2005 to 29 per cent in 2009–2010.[49] Less than a third of Indian women have paid employment, and the bulk of this work is in agriculture, the poorest paid sector, where women have a growing share.[50] Even with this greater share, the unemployment rate of rural women is increasing.[51] Since women provide a 'flexible labour force in agriculture – as own account workers, casual agricultural labour or unpaid family workers',[52] their work is often insecure. The most marginalised groups of women, women in scheduled tribes and castes, have the highest rates of workforce participation amongst women because 'extreme poverty leaves them with little choice but to work and because they do not face social taboos that disapprove of work'.[53] Muslim women have the lowest workforce participation rates because of religious norms that keep women in the home.[54] The lack of childcare facilities keeps women with young children out of the paid workforce.[55] Unequal division of household labour between men and women is a major barrier to women's workforce participation. Women spend approximately 34 hours per week on unpaid household work and care.[56] Their higher burden of total work leads to 'less time for rest, sleep, and recreation' with resulting poorer health for women.[57]

This workforce profile indicates that most women are not located within the paid workforce. Of those that are, the majority are involved in poorly paid informal sector work with very limited access to occupational social security. Within the informal sector there is a significant gender gap in income.[58] Maternity and

46 Meena Gopal, 'Gender, ageing and social security' (2006) 41(42) *Economic and Political Weekly* 4477, at 4479.

47 Ibid.

48 UNDP India Factsheet: Economic and Human Development Indicators, www.in.undp.org/content/dam/india/docs/india_factsheet_economic_n_hdi.pdf.

49 ILO 'World of Work 2013: Snapshot of India' (2013), www.ilo.org/wcmsp5/groups/public/---dgreports/---dcomm/documents/briefingnote/wcms_214477.pdf.

50 Dasgupta and Sudarshan, above n 8, at 4–5.

51 Ibid., at 6.

52 Ibid.

53 Srivastava and Srivastava, above n 45, at 50.

54 Ibid.

55 Ibid., at 58.

56 Indira Hirway and Sunny Jose, 'Understanding women's work using time-use statistics: the case of India' (2011) 17(4) *Feminist Economics* 67, at 85.

57 Ibid., at 86.

58 Shalini Sinha, 'Social Security for Women Workers in the Informal Economy: SEWA's Social Security Programme' in Eibe Reidel (ed.), *Social Security as a Human Right: Drafting a General Comment on Article 9 ICESCR – Some Challenges* (Springer, 2007) 117, at 118.

childcare benefits are entirely inadequate for Indian women. Women's unpaid, and often even their paid work, is invisible.[59]

6.3.3 Inadequate social security

The majority of Indian women lack access to the resources needed for adequate livelihoods, decent work and social security. Strong responses are needed to address cultural and religious attitudes that prevent women from engaging in paid employment and burden them with the majority of household and reproductive labour. Government efforts to provide social security must not increase the burdens that Indian women already face in the home and in the workplace. The different needs of elderly women, girls, tribal and dalit (lower caste) women, women with disabilities, Muslim women, women who are immigrants and internal migrants, widows and single women require specific attention within the social security system. In addition, certain occupational groups that are women-dominated such as domestic workers, sex workers and home-based workers also require targeted policies.

As discussed above, small sums of social assistance are available for certain groups (the aged, widows and people with disabilities) within the poorest section of the population. This leaves millions of poor women without any form of social assistance, along with limited access to social insurance and social protection. Even where there are social security entitlements, there are significant access barriers to these, many of which relate to gender, such as illiteracy, lack of access to information, safety concerns and intra-household control of income.[60]

A more detailed discussion of two specific social security schemes, analysed in terms of the conceptual framework and principles for a substantively equal, gendered right to social security developed in this book, follows below (at 6.5 and 6.6).

6.3.4 Private/collective social security

A positive response to women's poverty and lack of state services is private or collective social insurance. The Self Employed Women's Association (SEWA) is the best-known example of this. SEWA, in existence since 1972, is a national registered trade union for self-employed women workers.[61] It has 1.2 million members.[62] SEWA's goal for its members is full employment including 'work and income security, food security and social security – at least health care, child care, insurance and shelter'.[63] The organisation offers advice and training, runs a co-operative bank and an insurance scheme, and provides some childcare, health care and housing services. SEWA views social security as integrally linked to eco-

59 Priti Darooka, 'Social Security: A Woman's Human Right' (PWESCR, 2008) 1, at 6.

60 Ibid., at 10.

61 Renana Jhabvala, Sapna Desai and Jignasa Dave, 'Empowering Women in an Insecure World: Joining SEWA Makes a Difference' (2010); Hill, above n 43; Sinha, above n 58.

62 Jhabvala et al., ibid., at 1.

63 Sinha, above n 58, at 122.

nomic security. Thus, it attempts to strengthen workers' capacity to overcome constraints and improve their access to markets while supporting them through social security to remain, or become more, productive.[64] SEWA has called for state-provided childcare as well as for implementation of the *Unorganised Workers Social Security Act* in collaboration with organisations working with the poor.[65] While SEWA is a valuable example of the impact of worker agency in addressing the inadequate conditions of Indian women working in the informal sector,[66] it makes only a small contribution to the overall social security needs of Indian women. Further, it is the State, rather than NGOs, that has the primary obligation to fulfil its citizens' rights, including to social security.

The chapter now examines the right to social security within India's human rights framework.

6.4 India's human rights framework and the right to social security

6.4.1 International treaties

India is a party to the major international human rights treaties including the *International Covenant on Economic, Social and Cultural Rights* and the *Convention on the Elimination of All Forms of Discrimination against Women* (CEDAW). It has ratified four of the eight fundamental conventions of the International Labour Organisation (ILO)[67] (but not the *Social Security (Minimum Standards) Convention*, 1952, (No. 102)). The CEDAW Committee's most recent recommendations to India in 2007 included the speedy enactment of the *Unorganised Workers Social Security Bill* (which has since occurred, as discussed above), the closing of the wage gap between men and women and a comprehensive response to women's poverty in urban areas.[68] The Committee on Economic, Social and Cultural Rights (CESCR), in 2008, called on India to ratify ILO Convention No 102 and to extend coverage to the informal sector and the large sections of the population not covered by social security. It also called for comprehensive anti-discrimination legislation to cover a range of areas including social security.[69] In the 2012 universal periodic review, India was encouraged to ratify various ILO and UN conventions including the *Optional Protocol to CEDAW*.[70]

64 Ibid., at 122–3.

65 Jhabvala et al., above n 61, at 51–2.

66 See Hill, above n 43.

67 *Forced Labour Convention*, 1930 (No. 29), ratified on 2 January 1932; *Equal Remuneration Convention*, 1951 (No. 100), ratified on 10 December 1974; *Abolition of Forced Labour Convention*, 1957 (No. 105), ratified on 7 June 1960; *Discrimination (Employment and Occupation) Convention*, 1958 (No. 111), ratified on 15 June 1973.

68 CEDAW/C/IND/CO/3 (2007), at para 45.

69 CESCR E/C.12/IND/CO/5 (2008), at paras 64 and 52.

70 Human Rights Council (2012) *Report of the Working Group on the Universal Periodic Review – India* A/HRC/21/10, at paras 138.1, 138.10 and 138.19.

6.4.2 *Constitutional rights*

India has strong civil and political rights protections in its Constitution.[71] It also contains directive principles that must inform governance and law-making relating to certain social and economic rights. These are set out in Part IV of the Constitution (Articles 36 to 51) and include Articles 41, 42, 43 and 47, which directly relate to the State's role in the provision of social security.[72] Article 41 says:

> The State shall, within the limits of its economic capacity and development, make effective provision for securing the right to work, to education and to public assistance in cases of unemployment, old age, sickness and disablement, and in other cases of undeserved want.

Articles 42 and 43 direct the State to secure just working conditions including a living wage, while Article 47 requires the State to raise the standard of living of its people and to ensure the improvement of public health. Other provisions of the Constitution include strong and judicially enforceable equality rights (Articles 14–17) including prohibitions of discrimination on the basis of sex.[73]

6.4.3 *The courts*

The courts have developed a body of enforceable social rights through interpretation of the constitutional rights in light of the directive principles and international law.[74] Indian courts are empowered to incorporate international human rights treaties directly into domestic law.[75] There is extensive commentary on the prominent role of the courts and of public interest litigation in India in challenging the State to realise rights.[76] There is also a body of writing on public interest

71 *The Constitution of India* (as on 1 December 2011) (2011), Government of India, Ministry of Law and Justice.

72 For a discussion of these, see J.P. Yadav (ed.), *Human Rights and Social Security* (Institute for Sustainable Development, 2004), at 431.

73 See Kamala Sankaran, 'Special provisions and access to socio-economic rights: women and the Indian constitution' (2007) 23(2) *South African Journal on Human Rights* 277; Martha Nussbaum, 'India, Sex Equality and Constitutional Law' in Beverley Baines and Ruth Rubio-Marin (eds), *The Gender of Constitutional Jurisprudence* (Cambridge University Press, 2005) 174.

74 For an examination of the nature and limitations of Indian social rights, see Madhav Khosla, 'Making social rights conditional: lessons from India' (2010) 8(4) *International Journal of Constitutional Law* 739; Sankaran, ibid.

75 Colin Gonsalves, 'Reflections on the Indian Experience' in John Squires, Malcolm Langford and Bret Thiele (eds), *The Road to a Remedy: Current Issues in the Litigation of Economic, Social and Cultural Rights* (UNSW Press, 2005) 177, at 177.

76 For a selection of writings, see Christine M. Forster and Vedna Jivan, 'Public interest litigation and human rights implementation: the Indian and Australian experience' (2008) 3(1) *Asian Journal of Comparative Law* 1; Varun Gauri, 'Fundamental rights and public interest litigation in India: overreaching or underachieving?' (2010) 1(1) *Indian Journal of Law and Economics* 71; Sandra Fredman, *Human Rights Transformed: Positive Rights and Positive Duties* (Oxford University Press, 2008), at Chapter 5; and Gonsalves, above n 75.

litigation and women's rights.[77] It has, however, been observed that the progressive constitutional framework stands in stark contrast to the reality of women's lived experience in India.[78]

The Supreme Court of India has held in a number of cases that the right to social security is an indirect right relating to the right to life in article 21 of the Constitution.[79] In a leading case, *L.I.C. of India v. Consumer Education and Research Centre*, concerning the permissibility of restrictive conditions in life insurance policies to insure only certain classes of salaried employees, the Court held that 'the basic framework of the Constitution is to provide a decent standard of living to working people and especially provides security from cradle to grave'.[80] The Court referred to international human rights law as well as to the renowned case of *Olga Tellis v Bombay Municipal Corporation*[81] brought by slum dwellers in Mumbai facing eviction. In this case the Supreme Court held that the right to life includes the right to livelihood and that the right to social security and protection are integral to the right to life.[82] The Court also noted that insurance, which it said was a social security measure, had to be consistent with socio-economic justice as required by the Constitution.[83]

The 'Right to Food' case, *PUCL v. Union of India and Others*, first brought by the People's Union for Civil Liberties in 2001, has become the basis for ongoing supervisory litigation in the Supreme Court on a range of poverty-related issues including social assistance programmes.[84] The supervisory jurisdiction allows for interim orders by the Supreme Court on a range of issues related to implementation of schemes to realise the right to food. Relevant Court orders are referred to below in this chapter.

77 For example, Avani Mehta Sood, 'Gender justice through public interest litigation: case studies from India' (2008) 41 *Vanderbilt Journal of Transnational Law* 833; Sankaran, above n 73; Catharine A. MacKinnon, *Are Women Human? And Other International Dialogues* (Harvard University Press, 2006) at Chapter 13.

78 Martha Nussbaum, *Women and Human Development: The Capabilities Approach* (Cambridge University Press, 2000), at 24–30.

79 Discussed in ILO (2011b), 'Social Security and the Rule of Law: General Survey Concerning Social Security Instruments in Light of the 2008 Declaration on Social Justice for a Fair Globalization' (2011), at 118. Also see Kothari, above n 7, at 10–13.

80 *L.I.C. of India & ANR v. Consumer Education and Research Centre and ORS etc.* 1995 AIR 1811 1995 SCC (5) 482, at 7.

81 1985 Supp (2) SCR 51.

82 *L.I.C. of India & ANR v. Consumer Education and Research Centre and ORS etc*, above n 80, at 8.

83 Ibid., at 9.

84 *PUCL v. Union of India & Others* WP (Civil) No. 196/2001, 23 July 2001, unreported. Also see Anup Kumar Srivastava and Manisha Tiwary, *Right to Food* (Human Rights Law Network, 4th edn, 2009), at 16–18; Fredman, above n 76, at 130–1. For more information on the case see the PUCL website at www.righttofoodindia.org/case/case.html and the list of Supreme Court orders at www.righttofoodindia.org/orders/interimorders.html.

6.4.4 *Rights-based legislation*

Over the past decade the legislature has played an active role in introducing rights-based legislation in response to pressure from civil society and the electorate as a whole. This has included a *Right to Information Act* 2005, a *Forest Rights Act* 2006, a *Right to Education Act* 2009 which followed a constitutional amendment (2002), and the NREGA (2005) which is seen as providing a right to work (in rural areas).

The most recent addition to the list of rights-based legislation is the *National Food Security Act* 2013, which guarantees the provision of food to certain groups. The Act followed a prominent right to food campaign which itself derived from the Right to Food case.[85] The Act does not specifically include a right to food but it does use terms such as 'entitlement', 'live a life with dignity' and 'progressively realise' that point to some acknowledgement of the rights underscoring this legislation. The Act, which restricts the provision of food to 75 per cent of the rural population and 50 per cent of the urban population, has been criticised for its limited reach. However, it supports existing programmes such as the Midday Meal Scheme for children and provides for the distribution of a defined quantity of food to a large number of poor households. An earlier version of the Bill to that eventually enacted contained reference to social security pensions but these were removed by government on the basis that it was unaffordable. The Act continues to include a cash transfer for pregnant and lactating women which is described as a maternity benefit.[86] This is additional to a free daily meal during pregnancy and for six months after the birth.[87] The Act also provides for cash allowances in the event that entitled persons do not receive their meals or grains.[88]

Chapter V of the Act contains provisions for progressively reforming the public distribution system including by providing cash transfers if these are needed to ensure food grain entitlements to certain groups.[89] Schedule III of the Act refers to provisions for advancing food security. These provisions include access to water and sanitation; health care; nutritional, health and education support to adolescent girls; and adequate pensions for senior citizens, persons with disability and single women.[90] All these elements suggest that there is some overlap between the rights realised in the Act – rights to food and to social security, alongside other social rights including health, water and sanitation. There is also a commitment to empower women in the Act with a requirement that the eldest

85 Reetika Khera, 'Democratic Politics and Legal Rights: Employment Guarantee and Food Security in India' (2–3 August 2013), paper presented at the Second Azim Premji University International Conference on Law, Governance and Development – Right to Welfare: Education, Food and Work, on file with the author.

86 *The National Food Security Act* 2013, at s 4(b).

87 Ibid., at s 4(a).

88 Ibid., at s 8.

89 Ibid., at 12(2)(h).

90 Ibid., at Schedule III, s 3.

adult woman in an eligible household be deemed the household head for the purpose of the issue of ration cards.[91]

6.4.5 Conclusion

The combination of constitutional rights, progressive courts and rights-based legislation offers an enabling context for the realisation of social and economic rights in India, including social security rights. The focus on women's equality is also an encouraging feature of the legal and human rights framework. Nevertheless, rights protections do not always lead to actual realisation of rights because of problems with implementation including corruption, uneven delivery across states, and barriers facing the poor such as difficulties in meeting identity requirements in proving their entitlements.

6.5 National Social Assistance Programme (NSAP)

The chapter now discusses the NSAP, a major social assistance programme, and evaluates its compliance with the right to social security from a gender perspective as developed in this book.

6.5.1 Dimensions of the NSAP

The NSAP was introduced in 1995 with the aim of providing a national minimum standard of social assistance additional to further provision by states. Implementation of the scheme occurs through each state's social welfare department but payments are funded by the central government.[92] As outlined in 6.2 above, under the NSAP payments are made to the eligible elderly, widows and people with disabilities. There are also one-off payments of Rs 20,000 (US$ 332) to families who have lost a 'primary breadwinner'.[93] The primary breadwinner can be a man or woman between the ages of 18 and 59. The old age pension is the sum of Rs 200 (US$ 3.32) per month paid to people of 60 and over who are below the poverty line.[94] People of 80 years and over are entitled to Rs 500 (US$ 8.31) per month.[95] Widows (aged 40–79) and people with 'severe and multiple disabilities' (aged 18–79) who are below the poverty line are also entitled to monthly sums of Rs 300 (US $5).[96] The Annapurna scheme provides 10kg of food grain per month to senior citizens who, although eligible for the old age

91 Ibid., at s 13(1).

92 NSAP Division Ministry of Rural Development, *FAQs*, http://nsap.nic.in/nsap/FAQ_ON_NSAP_NEW.pdf.

93 Ministry of Rural Development, 'Annual Report 2012–13' (Ministry of Rural Development, Government of India, 2012), http://rural.nic.in/sites/downloads/annual-report/MoRD English_AR2012_13.pdf, at 78.

94 Ibid., at 77.

95 Ibid.

96 Ibid.

pension, are not in receipt of the pension.[97] The programme applies in rural and urban areas.

In December 2012 the old age pension had 22.3 million beneficiaries, the widows pension reached 4.2 million women, the disability pension reached 800,000 people, as did the Annapurna scheme, and the family benefit for the loss of a breadwinner reached almost 300,000 people.[98]

The social assistance programme accounts for a small percentage of the total social safety net spending in India (4 per cent based on 2008–2009 figures),[99] which is about 2 per cent of GDP.[100] Half of the safety net budget goes to subsidised food and a third to public works.[101] This relatively small investment in pensions appears to be increasing as the Indian government recognises the benefits of cash transfers to address poverty.[102] This is because the food distribution programmes (and some of the other social programmes) have experienced significant leakage and inefficiency. Cash transfers, like NREGA payments, are more easily protected through computerisation and payment into bank and post office accounts. Social assistance coverage is increasing but still has a long way to go to reach all those in need.[103] Awareness-raising and removal of access barriers (including corruption) and waiting periods are some of the measures that need to be taken to achieve greater reach of the programme. Bribes to obtain grants and to receive payments are common.[104]

6.5.2 Recommendations for reform

A task force appointed in November 2012 by the Ministry for Rural Development (the Ministry responsible for the NSAP) proposed an increase in the amount of the old age and widows pensions from Rs 200 to Rs 300 per month.[105] It also recommended extending the widows pension to other categories of single women who face the 'same kind of discrimination as widows especially stigmatization leading to social exclusion and imposition of restrictions on socio-economic development'.[106] Such categories include single, divorced, separated and abandoned women. It proposed reducing the age of eligibility of the widows pension from 40 to 18 for all categories except 'single never married' women. Women whose husbands are 'missing'/disappeared (described as 'half widows') should be able to claim the pension after three years rather than seven. It called

97 Ibid.

98 Ibid., at 76–9.

99 Puja Dutta, Stephen Howes and Rinku Murgai, 'Small but effective: India's targeted unconditional cash transfers' (2010) XLV(52) *Economic and Political Weekly* 63, at 63.

100 Ibid.

101 Ibid.

102 See Sony Pellissery and Armando Barrientos, 'Expansion of social assistance: does politics matter?' (2013) XLVIII(9) *Economic and Political Weekly* 47.

103 Dutta et al., above n 99, at 65.

104 Ibid., at 65 and 67, based on a study of two states.

105 Report of the Task Force, above n 35, at 7.

106 Ibid., at 7.

for removal of the age restrictions on the disability pension and a reduction in the severity of the disability/activity limitation for eligibility, with double the amount going to the most severely disabled.

The task force noted that despite the availability of the National Family Benefit Scheme to male or female breadwinners, in practice the grant is only provided on the death of a male family member. They recommended that any adult household member's death, including that of a woman who was a 'homemaker', should attract the grant given the contribution by all such adults to the livelihood of poor households.[107]

The task force also recommended indexation of pension amounts to inflation and the expansion of coverage of the programme to all households eligible for benefits under the *National Food Security Act* by 2017. This would mean coverage of 75 per cent of the rural population and 50 per cent of the urban population. The task force also suggested a range of measures to improve implementation of the programme and to avoid corruption and wastage including central administration of the scheme rather than by the states.

Two members of the task force provided minority reports in their recommendations to the Minister. These reports both questioned the proposed increase from Rs 200 per month to Rs 300 per month as not based on rationality or social equity. They showed that on the basis of various measures (minimum wages and poverty lines) the pension amount should be between Rs 1000 and Rs 2000 per month and the National Family Benefit Scheme should also be higher. They also recommended that eligibility based on the Below Poverty Line measure be abandoned and that government move towards universal coverage.[108]

One of the task force members, Dr Mihir Shah, commented to the media that the Task Force Committee had made 'basic and minimal recommendations, keeping in view the support for these changes from the Cabinet as a whole'.[109] It seems, however, that even these modest suggestions were too demanding for the previous government and that the new BJP government is even less likely to pursue them. Although the task force recommendations have not been followed by the government (as at June 2014), they offer a valuable itemisation of some of the limitations of India's NSAP.

6.5.3 *Legislation and the courts*

The unconditional cash transfer schemes under the NSAP and the conditional cash transfer under the Janani Suraksha Yojana (JSY) for pregnant women are listed within the *Unorganised Workers Social Security Act* (UWSSA) of 2008. There is no distinct legislative framework for these social assistance programmes other than

107 Ibid., at 8.

108 Ibid., at 37.

109 Staff Reporter, 'Govt. duty-bound to raise old-age pension', *The Hindu*, 18 January 2014 www.thehindu.com/todays-paper/tp-national/govt-dutybound-to-raise-oldage-pension/article5588657.ece.

their listing within the UWSSA – they are simply government policy implemented following executive decision. A more comprehensive legislative framework, ideally that creates legislative rights similar to the NREGA and the *National Food Security Act*, would benefit the development of social security law in India.

As discussed above, the Right to Food case included supervisory orders on issues of social assistance.[110] These included orders relating to the improved implementation of the National Old Age Pension Scheme involving earlier payment and a larger financial allocation by the Central Government and the states.[111] The Supreme Court has also considered the National Maternity Benefit Scheme (NMBS) and the government's attempt to remove this benefit and replace it with the JSY scheme. Unlike the other social assistance schemes, the JSY is a conditional cash transfer requiring institutional delivery for receipt of the payment with certain poorly performing states receiving greater support.[112] The Supreme Court required the government to retain the benefits of the NMBS and ensure its improved implementation.[113] This was based on the evidence that the NMBS provided cash assistance to pregnant women while the JSY was designed to promote institutional delivery. Since the two policies served different purposes, the Court required that both policies be offered.[114] It ordered that cash assistance be provided 8–12 weeks prior to delivery regardless of the age of the mother and for any number of children. This contradicted the wording of the new scheme that provided payment to women aged 19 and over and only for the first two births. Following discussions between the Commissioner appointed by the Supreme Court and government officials, the government decided to remove the condition on the benefit under the JSY for those mothers who chose non-institutional delivery in certain 'low performing states'.[115]

6.5.4 *Evaluation*

An examination of India's social assistance programme in terms of the principles for a substantively equal, gendered right to social security developed in this book highlights a number of issues that are now discussed.

Reach and quantity of NSAP

The programme is positive in offering some support to the elderly, people with disabilities and families who have lost a breadwinner as these groups are likely to have limited access to income-earning opportunities. The fifth Principle,

110 *PUCL* case, above n 84; Srivastava and Tiwary, above n 84.

111 Srivastava and Tiwary, above n 84, at 16–18.

112 Chandrakant Lahariya, 'Cash incentives for institutional delivery: linking with antenatal and post natal care may ensure "continuum of care" in India' (2009) 34(1) *Indian Journal of Community Medicine* 15.

113 *PUCL* case, above n 84; Srivastava and Tiwary, above n 84, at 109–14.

114 Srivastava and Tiwary, above n 84, at 17.

115 Ibid., at 110.

provision of social security for those in need, unlinked to work, is acknowledged through the NSAP. Since women are disproportionately represented within the poor, this is a critical response to their difficult circumstances. However, the payment amounts are extremely small and raise doubts about the compliance of the NSAP with the CESCR's General Comment 19 requirement that social security be adequate.[116] Obviously, any evaluation must be cognisant of the financial capacity of the Indian State to provide higher sums to a huge number of people.

The widows pension

The inclusion of widows as a category deserving support raises interesting questions under the sixth Principle, the design of social security systems that promote gender equality. The widows pension is an important recognition of the stigma facing widows in India and the economic consequences of widowhood.[117] However, as the government task force noted, this grant currently excludes many other types of single women who face similar stigma and poverty due to the lack of a male partner.[118] If the function of the system is to address vulnerability, then the existence or lack of a marriage, and death rather than abandonment by the male partner, are not appropriate factors to take into account in determining eligibility. It is also possible that men who lose female partners may suffer from loss of income or household labour and should also be considered for this benefit. Gender inequalities in India are created through the cultural construction of widowhood and require special measures to address this pervasive disadvantage. However, without undermining the need for such measures and without attempting to equalise out of context, it may also be necessary to address the needs of indigent men who have lost a partner. The recognition that men may depend on women's income or unpaid labour, whether in or outside of the household, acknowledges the value of women's different types of work for the purposes of social security (Principles 1 to 4).

Loss of breadwinner

The National Family Benefit Scheme is formally gender-neutral as it provides one-off support to families that have lost a breadwinner of any gender. It has been noted, however, that in practice the benefit is generally paid only on the loss of a male household member who was the primary breadwinner. This is a contrary to Principle 7 relating to full and equal access to social security. While men rather than women are more likely to face access barriers, there may be girls and

116 CESCR '*General Comment No 19: The Right to Social Security (Art. 9)*' (2008) 39th Session 2007, E/C.12/GC/, at para 22.

117 For a discussion of the situation of widows in India, see Robert T. Jensen, 'Caste, Culture, and the Status and Well-Being of Widows in India' in David A. Wise (ed.), *Analyses in the Economics of Aging* (University of Chicago Press, 2005) 357.

118 The report refers to 'single women and divorced/abandoned/separated women', Report of the Task Force, above n 35, at 7.

other women within a household who lose out when the benefit is not paid. The task force proposal to extend this scheme to cover the loss of any householder, regardless of whether their contribution was the largest in terms of income, is a valuable recommendation. This recognises that the loss of any adult member of a household who has been contributing in some way (whether through their labour or their income) results in hardship for a household and that support is therefore required. The acknowledgement that unpaid household labour should be compensable would reflect a significant shift in traditional approaches to social security. As with the widows pension this would provide recognition of the value of women's different types of work (Principles 1 to 4).

Disability benefit

The disability benefit reaches a very small number of people and has very restrictive eligibility criteria. As with other pensions, the recommendation that this be extended in terms of reach and amount is positive. Women with disabilities face intersecting and multiple forms of discrimination. Greater access to social security (Principle 7), even where people are unable to work (Principle 5), would assist this particularly vulnerable group.

Conditionality of JSY

A positive feature of the Indian system is that the social assistance programme is largely unconditional. As noted in the discussion of conditionality in the chapters on South Africa (Chapter 4) and Australia (Chapter 5), conditional benefits often place burdens on poor women and undermine their human rights. However, the JSY, a maternity scheme, placed the condition of institutional delivery on women wishing to receive a cash grant. The lack of facilities, transport, ignorance of the programme and choice to deliver at home are reasons why women fail to reach clinics. As recognised by government following discussions with the Commissioner appointed by the Supreme Court, benefits for women who deliver at home should also be available (in certain states).[119] Alongside social assistance measures, efforts to improve quality and access to health facilities are a crucial part of the overall provision of social protection for Indian women. This is in accord with Principles 6 and 7 regarding gender-equal design of and access to social security. From the four-dimensional substantive equality perspective, denying maternity benefits to any women who may not be able to fulfil the condition of institutional delivery has negative impacts on their access to adequate social assistance (redistribution), violates their dignity (recognition), fails to address the structural circumstances that prevent them from delivering in clinics (transformation), and fails to gauge their reasons for low institutional attendance and address their lack inclusion in society (participation).

119 Srivastava and Tiwary, above n 84, at 17.

Gaps in coverage

There is no social assistance benefit for a range of categories of people living in poverty including children, children with disabilities, unemployed adults, under-employed adults, adults unable to work due to sickness or injury and women unable to work due to maternity (other than the JSY). These categories correspond to the ILO and CESCR's listed contingencies and risks that must be covered in order to realise the right to social security.[120] Even for those who are able to work but cannot produce an adequate livelihood for themselves, the lack of social assistance is a severe hardship and a violation of their right to social security. Working-age women, overrepresented among the working poor in India, urgently require social assistance measures to make up the shortfall from their meagre incomes (in terms of Principles 2 to 4). Similarly, unemployed women who are not elderly, widowed or disabled cannot currently expect any social assistance benefits. This gap in provision is contrary to Principle 5 which requires provision of social security on the basis of need, not relationship to work.

It could be argued that other social policies meet the needs of these groups. NREGA, discussed below, provides up to 100 days a year of work to every rural household. While this is making a significant impact on the income of many by reaching millions of poor households, the gaps in coverage must be acknowledged. Urban households are excluded and there is only provision for 100 work days of each year. The remaining 265 days are not accommodated. While the midday meal scheme, a very important anti-poverty measure, provides a daily cooked meal for every child in India, it does not address the other needs of poor children.[121] As noted, there is a persistent problem of stunting and nutritional deficiency in Indian children.[122] The *National Food Security Act* 2013 contributes to but does not absolve the Indian government of its obligations to realise the full social security entitlements of its people. Since women and girls make up the majority of the poor and face multidimensional disadvantage, a comprehensive social security system is particularly important for meeting their needs.

Research needed

Lastly, there is limited research on India's social assistance programme[123] and even less on the gender and rights dimensions of the programme. Further study would be important to consider the impact of the pensions on individuals and households in receipt. An understanding of intra-household expenditure on pensions and how this relates to dynamics within households (based on gender, age and other factors) would be informative. It would also be useful to study access to the programme to

120 Set out in ILO, *Social Security (Minimum Standards) Convention*, 1952, (No. 102); and CESCR General Comment 19, above n 116, at paras 12–21.

121 For a discussion of the scheme, see Reetika Khera, 'Mid-day meals in primary schools: achievements and challenges' (2006) 41(46) *Economic and Political Weekly* 4742.

122 Above n 11.

123 Dutta et al., above n 99, at 64.

ascertain who is being left out and why; and whether women are equally able to access the benefits. Exploring the relationship between access to pensions and other social programmes such as NREGA could reveal the extent to which individuals can access multiple social programmes. Multiple access is not allowed in central or state social assistance schemes which may mean that multiple disadvantage is not recognised, leading to the possible perpetuation of multiple inequality.[124]

6.6 The Mahatma Ghandi National Rural Employment Guarantee Act (NREGA)

The chapter now examines the history, features and implementation of NREGA. It discusses the nature of NREGA in terms of the right to work and the right to social security. It then outlines some of the positive and negative assessments of the scheme. Lastly, it evaluates NREGA in terms of the principles for a substantively equal, gendered right to social security developed in this book.

6.6.1 History

NREGA was a response both to drought in some Indian states in the early 2000s and to a campaign for public works programmes. The latter programmes already had a presence in some states and existed as emergency relief in others.[125] A national employment guarantee appeared in the election manifesto of the Congress Party in 2004, with most people believing that the party would not win the election.[126] The party did win and came to power as part of the United Progressive Alliance in May 2004 which identified the employment guarantee as a policy priority.[127] The Act was passed in August 2005 and came into operation in February 2006.

6.6.2 The Act[128]

The Act entitles every rural household whose adult members volunteer to undertake unskilled manual work at least 100 days work per year at the statutory minimum wage (where possible within 5 kilometres from the village in which the household members reside). If an applicant is not provided with work within 15 days, he/she must be provided with an unemployment allowance by the state government.[129] This allowance cannot be less than a quarter of the wage rate for

124 As suggested by Jayna Kothari, Centre for Law and Policy Research, Bangalore, India (personal communication with author, 28 February 2014).

125 Khera, above n 85, at 9.

126 Jean Drèze, 'Employment Guarantee and the Right to Work' in Reetika Khera (ed.), *The Battle for Employment Guarantee* (Oxford University Press, 2011) 3, at 6.

127 Drèze, ibid., at 6.

128 The *National Rural Employment Guarantee Act* 42 of 2005.

129 This acts as an incentive to states to ensure that there is work for applicants. The central government pays the wages: Reetika Khera (ed.), *The Battle for Employment Guarantee* (Oxford University Press, 2011), at 124.

the first 30 days and a half of the wage rate for the remaining period. A third of workdays are reserved for women. The Act provides that, where there are five or more children under the age of six accompanying women workers, one of the women workers will be given the task of looking after these children instead of her other work.[130] The Act requires that safe drinking water and shade must be provided on site although there is no mention of any other provision of facilities for these children. The Act assumes, problematically, that it is women who will bring children to the worksite and women who will be tasked to look after such children. However, more positively, the Act requires the involvement of women in the management of the scheme. (The Act also builds in similar representation of scheduled castes and tribes).

6.6.3 *Implementation*

NREGA was initially rolled out to 200 'backward' districts but reached all rural districts by 2008.[131] In the financial year of 2012–2013 NREGA reached almost 50 million households with women accounting for 51 per cent of all days worked under the scheme.[132] The average number of person days of employment provided to each household is approximately 46.[133] In line with the Act's requirements, NREGA has involved a minimum of 60 per cent expenditure on wages and the remaining amount has gone to capital expenditure. The scheme does not permit the use of external contractors. The wages, which correspond to the minimum wages in the various states, are paid into bank or post office accounts. These measures have been crucial in limiting corruption and waste in the scheme. The roll-out of what has been hailed as the world's largest public works programme has had important benefits for rural India. It has played a role in arresting the trend of urban migration and has cushioned the shock of the 2008 financial crisis.[134] It has also resulted in valuable infrastructure development that is helping rural communities with important environmental benefits. There have, however, been implementation problems including the lack of timely payment of wages with almost a quarter of all payments delayed by more than 30 days.[135]

6.6.4 *Right to work and social security*

NREGA is seen as a limited 'step towards legal enforcement of the right to work' in India.[136] It is also significant that it is a legislated scheme representing a

130 S 28 of Schedule II of the *National Rural Employment Guarantee* Act 42 of 2005.

131 Dasgupta and Sudarshan, above n 8, at 3.

132 Government figures obtained from the Ministry of Rural Development, India at http://164.100.129.6/netnrega/dash_brd.aspx?fin_year=2012-2013.

133 Ibid.

134 Amita Sharma, 'The Mahatma Gandhi National Rural Employment Guarantee Act' (UNDP, 2011), at 272.

135 Government figures obtained from the Ministry of Rural Development, above n 132.

136 Drèze, above n 126, at 4.

shift from discretionary government programmes towards a legal entitlement to employment. It is clearly, first and foremost, a public works programme. It is also, however, relevant to the right to social security since it contains a strong social security component in the form of a guaranteed unemployment allowance when work is not provided within 15 days. The focus on work creation, together with a built-in right to unemployment benefits, is a positive feature of the scheme that links the right to work with the right to social security.

Additional social security benefits are linked to NREGA. The operational guidelines of the Act note that workers are covered under the Janashree Bima Yojana scheme which provides life coverage and disability benefits.[137] The health insurance scheme, the Rashtriya Swasthya Bima Yojana, has also been extended to workers who have worked more than 15 days in the previous year.[138] Officials are required to make workers aware of these social insurance schemes. The guidelines also allow states to offer to offset social insurance contributions against wages and to provide matching grants. The guidelines provide for hospitalisation in the event of occupational injury and an ex gratia payment for death or disablement caused while working, although amounts for these are not specified.[139] The inclusion of social insurance entitlements within NREGA may provide workers with their first experience of having social security rights linked to work. Drèze points out that the existence of the unemployment insurance component in NREGA might encourage rural workers in the private sector to demand social security rights.[140]

The Guidelines to the Act describe NREGA as 'social protection for the most vulnerable people living in rural India by providing employment opportunities' and also note the additional goal of women's empowerment.[141] Khera describes NREGA as 'an opportunity to provide social security, create assests in rural areas, enhance women's economic independence, and revitalise institutions of local government'.[142] The reference to social security may mean a broader notion of social protection or livelihood security, but is nevertheless an important dimension of the identified benefits of NREGA. The objective of NREGA (along with other public works schemes elsewhere in the world) is described as creating 'a form of social security by providing a basic income through labour intensive employment, while contributing to public assets'.[143] The multiple purposes and benefits of NREGA indicate that this enormous social programme contributes to the realisation of more than one distinct social right. The right to work, the right to livelihood, the right to social security and the right to development, alongside

137 Minister of Rural Development, 'Mahatma Gandhi National Rural Employment Guarantee Act, 2005: Operational Guidelines' (Department of Rural Development, Government of India, 2013), at 76.

138 Ibid.

139 Ibid., at 2.1.1 (xi).

140 Drèze, above n 126, at 5.

141 Above n 137, at 3.

142 Khera, above n 85, at 4.

143 Dasgupta and Sudarshan, above n 8, at 3.

women's rights, Indigenous rights and environmental rights, are some of the rights implicated in this scheme. Thus, for the purpose of this study, NREGA is important as a broad social protection measure but also, more narrowly, for its social security component.

6.6.5 *Positive features*

The promotion of vulnerable groups, particularly women, through NREGA is a significant feature of the scheme. It empowers rural women by giving them access to employment outside of the home and their own income, often for the first time. Similarly, for women who are not provided with work but who are paid through the unemployment allowance, this may be a rare opportunity to access income in their own right. In addition, women are paid at the same rate as men, unusual for many women in India.[144] Women are paid into their own bank or post office accounts (which is mandatory unless there is an official exemption of this requirement), also a beneficial new experience for many rural women. Since payment is at a higher rate than in the private sector this may push up women's wages in the agricultural sector as a whole and reduce the gender wage gap.[145]

The guidelines for the implementation of the Act recognise the vulnerability and particular needs of 'women in special circumstances' (widowed women, deserted women and destitute women).[146] This is critically important in the Indian context where single women often face discrimination and stigma. The guidelines recommend that the administering body identify such women and ensure they are provided with 100 days of work.[147] They also make special provision for pregnant women and lactating mothers (eight months before delivery and ten months after) recommending work requiring less effort and that is closer to their homes.[148] The needs of other vulnerable groups including the elderly, people with disabilities, people who are internally displaced, nomadic tribes and particularly vulnerable tribal groups are also addressed in the guidelines.[149] The need to provide childcare, recognised in the Act, is an important acknowledgement of women's care burden and that this can be a barrier to participation in work. Employment under NREGA is often less dangerous, exploitative or harsh than the working conditions in the private sector.[150] As government work with defined conditions of service and other 'checks and balances', it is regarded as 'safer' than the private sector in terms of harassment of women workers. NREGA work is seen as beneficial since it is close to home and better paid, and is seen as more 'socially acceptable'.[151] Fixed

144 Reetika Khera and Nandini Nayak, 'Women Workers and Perceptions of the NREGA' in Reetika Khera (ed.), *The Battle for Employment Guarantee* (Oxford University Press, 2011) 81.
145 Dasgupta and Sudarshan, above n 8, at 14–15.
146 Guidelines, above n 137, at 9.6.
147 Ibid., at 9.6.
148 Ibid., at 9.6.1.
149 Ibid., at paras 9.2–9.9.
150 Khera and Nayak, above n 144, at 86.
151 Ibid., at 87.

hours, unusual in private employment, mean that women can combine paid work and housework. The fact that the government is the employer breaks down some of the caste-based restrictions that apply to other employers.[152]

Khera and Nayak's study of women NREGA workers found many social and economic benefits including the prevention of hunger, the ability to buy medicine and to avoid migration.[153] Women gained some control of their lives through the capacity to determine expenditure of household income. There were also benefits for widows and other single women both materially and in terms of the enhancement of their dignity.

Generally, the design of NREGA is positive since it is universal in relation to rural people and entails self-selection rather than targeting. This is valuable in preventing exclusion of marginal groups and individuals who are sometimes unable to provide the necessary documentation to satisfy means-tests in targeted social protection programmes.

6.6.6 Problematic features

The term 'household' is defined in the Act as 'members of a family related to each other by blood, marriage or adoption and normally residing together and sharing meals or holding a common ration card'.[154] This definition is discriminatory in that it excludes same-sex partners as well as non-marital domestic partners of the opposite sex. This may prejudice women where the male partner registers the household and the woman is not recognised as a valid household member. It also precludes people who simply live together as friends or 'house mates' for the purpose of sharing resources. The definition reflects a traditional approach to relationships focusing on form rather than function. While non-marital households may be highly unusual in rural India due to cultural factors, the Act should not reinforce the dominance of a single form of family.

More significantly, the use of 'household' as the unit of entitlement in the Act has serious consequences for women. Khera and Nayak suggest that NREGA could involve greater participation by women if it was available as an entitlement to individuals rather than households as this would 'assure women 100 days of work in their own right, without having to negotiate within the household'.[155] Prominent economist, Jean Drèze has noted that: 'The word household had no place in an entitlement-based law. Job cards should be given separately in the name of men and women.'[156] The choice of the household as the unit of entitlement does create the potential for unfairness. First, because a household with

152 Ibid., at 88.

153 Ibid., at 91.

154 S 2(f) of NREGA.

155 Above n 144, at 103.

156 'Women to have more say in job scheme', *Deccan Herald* (Lucknow), 4 December 2012, www.deccanherald.com/content/296432/women-have-more-say-job.html; also see UN Women, http://asiapacific.unwomen.org/en/news-and-events/stories/2012/12/jairam-ramesh-commits-to-making-mgnrega-more-women-friendly.

one member has the same entitlement to work as a household with 20 members. Second, because intra-household inequalities may shape access to work and to the income generated by this work. Obviously, extending the provision to all adults rather than households would bring in a greater number of potential claimants and would be more costly for government. It would, however, advance gender equality more effectively to provide an individual guarantee of work, even if for less than 100 days, with the aim of progressively increasing this number over time.

A number of suggestions have been made to improve women's participation in NREGA. The creation of individual bank accounts for women, increased numbers of women officials on the scheme, and greater participation of women in scheme management would improve the position of women within the programme.[157] Dasgupta and Sudarshan suggested that there should be separate job cards and bank accounts for each household member.[158] These suggestions were supported by the minister who was, until May 2014, responsible for the Act.[159]

In an early study on NREGA in one state, Narayan found that despite the major benefits of the scheme, 70 per cent of women workers were not provided with the childcare facilities promised in the Act.[160] Some of the mothers who brought their children to the worksite were sent away, harassed or had their wages cut. The women respondents who preferred to bring their children to work but were forced to leave them at home explained that the young children were sometimes left in the care of older children or on their own. This caused significant worry for the mothers. The majority of women who left their young children (aged 0–3) at home said they would prefer to bring them to a crèche at work. Lack of childcare was identified by the women workers as a barrier to work on some occasions. Narayan suggested that more detailed guidelines be created for the implementation of the childcare provisions under the Act. Despite this suggestion, these details do not appear in the 2013 version of the guidelines to the Act.[161] It appears that inadequate attention is being paid to this central feature of the scheme, with the likelihood that this is impacting negatively on women workers and their children as well as on women who would like to work but cannot do so due to the lack of childcare.

While NREGA work is generally less demanding and dangerous than some of the private sector work undertaken by women, Dasgupta and Sudarshan suggest that had the programme included 'other kinds of social service work where working conditions for women are more conducive' women's participation may have been higher.[162]

A final and major gap in the policy framework is that it provides a work guarantee to rural but not urban people. This excludes the huge numbers of urban

157 Khera and Nayak, above n 144, at 103.

158 Above n 8, at 4.

159 UN Women, above n 156.

160 Sudha Narayan, 'Employment guarantee, women's work and childcare' (2008) 43(9) (1–7 March 2008) *Economic and Political Weekly* 10.

161 Guidelines, above n 137.

162 Above n 8, at 19.

poor and unemployed who are not provided with similar opportunities to their rural counterparts. For women in urban areas who encounter gendered barriers in accessing decent work at equal wages, a state-provided scheme that guarantees employment with social security entitlements is likely to have significant value in addressing poverty.

6.6.7 *Evaluation of NREGA*

NREGA is rightly celebrated as an innovative and effective social protection programme for India's rural poor. The scheme will now be assessed against the principles for a substantively equal, gendered right to social security developed in this book. This assessment recognises that NREGA is a mixed social policy measure that combines public works with social security elements in a broad social protection policy framed, to some extent, around rights. The inclusion of an unemployment benefit in the absence of the provision of work builds in entitlements that India's rural poor have never previously enjoyed. Similarly, the provision of compensation to workers who receive their wages late promotes the idea of workers' rights.

NREGA does not address the first Principle that household reproductive labour and care work be recognised. The scheme offers work without reducing women's existing domestic burden. The inclusion of childcare in the Act is an acknowledgment that women workers may have care responsibilities; however, childcare facilities are not available in many instances. The Act assumes that it is women alone who bear care responsibilities and it is women workers who must provide the on-site care. This fails to challenge gender divisions of labour – in fact, it reinforces them. An alternative approach could require men to participate in providing the childcare, possibly in equal numbers to the women.

NREGA does assist in meeting the second Principle, which is the recognition of women's unpaid work that occurs in subsistence production and family industries. Rural women in India are often not acknowledged by their husbands, communities or themselves as workers despite their double workloads in production and reproduction. The employment scheme has changed this in many cases by providing women with their own jobs, with wages and bank accounts in some cases as well as with social security entitlements. This is a potentially important outcome in terms of empowering women to regard themselves as workers and as entitled citizens.

Similarly, NREGA contributes to the third Principle, the recognition that women's work in the informal sector requires accompanying social security rights. By providing an example to rural employers, NREGA may encourage such employers to extend social security benefits to women workers and lead women workers to demand these.

The fourth Principle that women's work in the formal sector is equally valued and attracts equal and sufficient social security is to some extent addressed by NREGA. The inclusion of unemployment benefits, minimum wages, fairer working hours and some provision for childcare facilities creates a formal framework for rural labour that is new for many women in India. In addition, the social insurance schemes that are being paired with NREGA are a positive development, as is the promise of medical treatment in the event of injury. There are, however, social security components that are missing from NREGA such as payment in the event of contingencies such as illness or maternity. The commitment to equal pay for men and women under the scheme sends a powerful message to the society that employment under the State scheme will not reinforce existing unfair cultural or economic practices that entrench hierarchies and inequalities. This may have a tangible economic impact in altering the wages women can command within the rural employment market. Providing childcare goes some way to addressing barriers women face in equal access to formal work but unless this provision is adequate, women will still struggle to access work and balance it with their care responsibilities. A more transformative scheme could have given men some of the childcare work in NREGA.

The fifth Principle, that social security is provided to all who need it, regardless of their relationship to work, is to some extent addressed through the scheme. The focus on the household as the point of access to the scheme seems to imply that the benefits of the scheme are designed to reach all household members, whether they are capable of working or not. This implicitly assumes that those who can work will use their NREGA income to support the rest of the household. The positive impact of NREGA in addressing extreme poverty in rural India is evidence that the income is reaching household members. However, there may not be consistent sharing and pooling of incomes in all households. Unequal gender relations may have an impact on expenditure of NREGA money as might other intra-household dynamics such as intergenerational conflict and family conflict.

The scheme's guidelines reflect an effort to accommodate people with disabilities in NREGA. However, there will be people who are not capable of doing any form of work due to their disabilities who will be excluded. People with disabilities may also be excluded as a result of uneven implementation of the guidelines. While social assistance grants reach some poor elderly, widows, and people with disabilities, this is not comprehensive or adequate and there are gaps in provision of support to many in need. Individual rights to social security mean that every member of society in need of State support, whether capable of working or not, should have access to social security. NREGA, together with the NSAP, does not adequately fulfil this right.

The sixth Principle is that the design of the social security system should promote gender equality. NREGA is well designed in that it promotes women's work and women's equality through the provision of work at equal pay in rural areas where women were traditionally exploited or not given recognition as workers, and by guaranteeing a third of workdays to women. By providing some positive working conditions and social security measures, NREGA brings women into a formal employment environment with guaranteed social security entitlements. The failure to provide for individual rights rather than household rights is, however, a weakness. This prevents women in some households from accessing work, income and social security payments due to unequal gender relations in the household.

Lastly, the seventh Principle is that women have full and equal access to social security. As noted, the provision of work in rural areas with accompanying social security is a major advance for many Indian women. The location of projects close to home is also critical in ensuring women's access to the scheme, as is the provision of childcare, should this be adequately implemented. Again, however, the registration of the household rather than the individual may limit access by some women to the scheme, where they are unable to negotiate within households for their own entitlement to work and to receive income. These contextual factors should be carefully considered by the implementers of NREGA to ensure that women are not being excluded from work and/or social security to which they are entitled due to discrimination within the scheme or within families and communities where such women are located. The lack of adequate consultation around the design of the scheme, particularly with women, may be a reason for some of the deficiencies. The scheme would benefit from ongoing and careful evaluation based on gender equality and other human rights including the right to social security. Such evaluation should be accompanied by mechanisms to ensure the participation of the beneficiaries of the scheme in proposals for its reform and improvement. These mechanisms should ensure the full and equal participation of women in all their diversity.

6.7 Conclusion

This chapter has demonstrated the utility of the conceptual approach and principles for a substantively equal, gendered right to social security developed in this book and applied to the Indian country study. The analysis leads to a deeper understanding of the strengths and weaknesses of the social protection programme in India. This understanding can be used to inform improvements to this programme and contribute more broadly to the advancement of gender equality.

The Indian social security system has witnessed significant expansion and development over the past decade. The historical provision of social insurance to the small percentage of formal sector workers left the majority of Indian workers without social security protections. However, recent health, disability and life insurance schemes provide some support to informal sector workers and recognition of their long-neglected needs.

For the large numbers of unemployed or underemployed workers in rural India, NREGA has provided a limited right to work with some rights to social security – a new experience for millions of people. More than half of NREGA places are now occupied by women workers in excess of the reservation of a third of NREGA work for women. This is giving millions of women their first opportunity to earn an income and their first access to social security rights. It is uncertain, however, whether all women who wish to access NREGA work are able to. The scheme is a source of income for a limited period of time in each year, leaving households without support for the rest of the year. In addition, the urban poor do not have similar opportunities.

The social assistance programme is aimed at providing for those who cannot support themselves – the elderly, people with disabilities and widows. These benefits are critical for many Indian women facing poverty and disadvantage. This programme has historically reached a limited number of the potential beneficiaries in need with payments of very small sums of money. There appears to be a growing effort to expand the reach of these grants to greater proportions of the poor. This is important but insufficient to address the spectrum of need and the multidimensional nature of disadvantage. Cash transfers alone will not be enough without greater access to food, livelihoods, health care, education and housing.

The development of rights-creating legislation that gives meaning to the positive Indian constitutional rights framework in the areas of work, education and food suggests a favourable climate for future social security legislation that entrenches and extends existing social assistance programmes. This could provide an opportunity for a push for more comprehensive coverage. Framing social security as a right might also provide a greater role for legal challenge, including equality-based challenges aimed at addressing the rights of those groups excluded from the system. This could assist women facing multiple forms of discrimination of all ages and circumstances. Given India's size and global importance, a more gender-equal, entitlement-based social security system would provide an enormously positive example to other countries of the world.

The use of the book's approach and principles for a substantively equal, gendered right to social security in evaluating social security provision in India highlights a positive trend towards greater coverage of the poor. Efforts to address the needs of women, whether they are widows, pregnant women or the rural poor, are encouraging. However, not all of these measures have been adequately designed to challenge existing gender inequalities in Indian society. The evaluation also points to the significant gaps in provision of social security to urban women, women of working age who are unpaid, unemployed or underemployed, and girls and women who face poverty and complex disadvantage. Using the principles for a substantively equal, gendered right to social security to craft new approaches that build gender equality into expanded social security provision would have a profound impact on some of the most vulnerable women in India.

This chapter is the last of the three country studies of the book. The next chapter, the conclusion, draws out the major themes of the book and its contribution to the development of the right to social security to advance women's rights and gender equality.

7 Conclusion

7.1 Introduction

The purpose of this book, as set out in the introductory chapter, has been to develop the interpretation of the right to social security from a gender perspective. A gender perspective interrogates traditional assumptions about rights holders, demands a careful examination of the context in which rights operate, and requires a reorientation of rights to take account of the circumstances and needs of men and women, and the goal of transformed gender relations in society.[1] Social and economic rights have a special importance for women given the close link between poverty and gender-related disadvantage, exclusion and marginalisation.[2] The book has focused on the right to social security, a central social and economic right aimed at ensuring the redistribution of wealth in society so as to address need and promote equality and dignity. Social security generally takes the form of social insurance that is contribution-based, social assistance to mitigate difficult circumstances, and universal programmes.[3] A gender-neutral application of the right to social security will not address the complex inequalities that leave women, in general, poorer than men.[4] A right to social security that is developed from a gender perspective serves a dual purpose: first, it provides a normative basis against which to test the current provision of the right to social security as it affects men and women. Second, it provides a principled framework for ensuring improved design and implementation of social security policies and programmes that advance gender equality.

This concluding chapter will discuss the arguments and findings of the book as follows: first, it will restate the major features of the theoretical approach to the development of the right from a gender perspective and the principles for a substantively equal, gendered right to social security and explore the policy

1 Discussed in Chapter 2 at 2.2.

2 'Montreal principles on women's economic, social and cultural rights' (2004) 26 *Human Rights Quarterly* 760; Gwen Brodsky and Shelagh Day, 'Denial of the means of susbistence as an equality violation' (2005) 2005 *Acta Juridica* 149.

3 Discussed in Chapter 1 at 1.2.2.

4 Magdalena Sepúlveda and Carly Nyst, *The Human Rights Approach to Social Protection* (Ministry for Foreign Affairs Finland, 2012), at 32.

implications flowing from these (in 7.2). Second, it will summarise the main findings of the survey and analysis of the international law, highlighting the gaps in the interpretation of the right to social security from a gender perspective (in 7.3). Third, it will compare and analyse the three country studies thematically to distil lessons from the application of the theoretical framework to these different contexts (in 7.4). Lastly, it will discuss the value of the arguments and findings of this book to scholarship and to broader efforts to advance women's rights (in 7.5).

7.2 Theoretical approach and principles: policy implications

The book has used a gender perspective, drawn from feminist and feminist legal theory. This perspective views gender as socially constructed, arising from material and ideological/cultural institutions that result in the disadvantage, oppression and marginalisation of women. The gender perspective acknowledges that 'women' are themselves differentiated by other social constructions such as race, class, ethnicity and disability. Gender constructions of male and female, and masculinity and femininity, also have negative impacts on male identity and experience through assigned roles. Systemic and transformative approaches are necessary to redefine gender roles in society. The book has applied this gender perspective to the critical examination of the right to social security, reformulating it to reflect women's experiences so as to contribute to the elimination of gender inequality and the transformation of gender relations in society.

The right to social security, as it is set out in international law and interpreted by treaty bodies, is closely related to the concept of 'work' and the protection of workers and their families when paid work is absent. As noted by feminist scholars, the assumed subject of social security rights has traditionally been the male breadwinner (employed in formal, full-time work).[5] The changing global context of work has resulted in growing numbers of women in the workforce but much of this work is informal, low paid and insecure,[6] without attendant social security benefits. Even with such changes, paid work is still the exception for the majority of the world's women.[7] The right to social security must reflect the reality of women's experiences in two respects: first, it must recognise that the many forms of labour that women do is work. This includes reproductive work (paid and unpaid), unpaid work in subsistence and family enterprises, and paid informal

5 Linda Luckhaus, 'Equal treatment, social protection and income security for women' (2000) 139(2) *International Labour Review* 149; Lucie Lamarche, 'Le *Pacte international relatif aux droits économiques, sociaux et culturels*, les femmes et le droit à la sécurité sociale: des considérations et des propositions pour un droit "universel" à la sécurité sociale' (2002) 14(1) *Canadian Journal of Women and the Law* 53.

6 Shahra Razavi et al., 'Gendered Impacts of Globalization – Employment and Social Protection' (UNRISD, 2012).

7 World Bank, 'World Development Report 2013: Jobs' (2012), at 6.

and formal work. Second, it must acknowledge that social security is not always linked to work but is an entitlement that should be available to all who need it.

Globalisation has led to rapid changes in the international labour market with growing numbers of women migrating to work within and between countries.[8] This requires the right to social security to operate at the transnational level. Nancy Fraser's writing on justice at the global 'scale'[9] provides a helpful conceptual lens to look outside of the 'Westphalian' frame to ensure that the right to social security is fully realised. The work of Susan Williams, drawing on Fraser's concept of scale to argue for justice at the sub-national level,[10] is also valuable for ensuring the greater reach of the right to social security.

The book, having explored the issues of work and scale in relation to the content and reach of the right to social security, has considered the relationship between the right to social security and equality. Equality, a central feminist value and right, has a prominent role in ensuring that the right to social security addresses gender discrimination and facilitates a gender-equal society. Understood substantively, equality requires the removal of underlying inequalities that generate disadvantage. Substantive equality, understood transformatively, requires the fundamental restructuring of society to address gender inequality. Sandra Fredman's multidimensional concept of substantive equality is used in this book.[11] It has four aims: breaking the cycle of disadvantage (the redistribution dimension); promoting dignity by redressing stigma, stereotyping, humiliation and violence (the recognition dimension); the accommodation of difference for structural change (the transformation dimension); and full participation in society (the participation dimension). The right to social security, developed from a gender perspective here, entails a commitment to substantive equality containing these four dimensions.

The theoretical framework of the book emphasises the multiple and intersecting forms of discrimination that different groups of women encounter and urges close attention to diversity, vulnerability and the complexity of discrimination in developing the right to social security from a gender perspective. It also notes the interrelationship between the right to social security and other rights such as the right to livelihood, the right to work and the right to health.

The four-dimensional substantive equality approach, together with the reconceived content of the right to social security (relating to concepts of work and scale), has been used to develop a set of principles for the interpretation of the right to social security from a gender perspective. Essential elements of the right

8 Naila Kabeer, *Mainstreaming Gender in Social Protection for the Informal Economy* (Commonwealth Secretariat, 2008), 43–6.

9 Nancy Fraser, *Scales of Justice: Reimagining Political Space in a Globalizing World* (Polity Press, 2008).

10 Susan H. Williams, 'Customary Law, Constitutional Law, and Women's Equality' in Kim Rubenstein and Katherine Young (eds), *The Public Law of Gender: From the Local to the Global* (Cambridge University Press, 2016) forthcoming.

11 Sandra Fredman, *Discrimination Law* (Oxford University Press, 2nd edn, 2011).

to social security (availability, adequacy and accessibility)[12] have also been incorporated into the principles. The principles for a substantively equal, gendered right to social security are, in summary, the following:

1. Women's household reproductive labour and care work is recognised and supported for the purpose of social security and care is understood as a responsibility of the whole society.
2. The other unpaid work that women do in subsistence production and family industries is recognised and supported for the purpose of social security.
3. Women's work in the informal sector in the many forms this takes entails accompanying social security rights.
4. Women's work within formal employment is valued and attracts sufficient and equal social security.
5. Social security is provided to all men and women who need it, regardless of their relationship to work.
6. The design of social security systems promotes gender equality.
7. Women have full and equal access to social security.

The conceptual framework and principles inform the analysis of the international law and the three country studies in this book. They provide a tool for evaluation and a guide for the development of social security law and policy in national and transnational settings. The framework and principles have potentially profound implications for social policy and decisions regarding the distribution of resources in society on a just basis. Some of these implications are now considered.

The conceptual approach and principles for a substantively equal, gendered right to social security provide a broad framework for the reformulation of social security policies and programmes. The policy considerations flowing from this principled approach are complex and will necessarily result in significant variation depending on the country contexts in which they are applied. This principled approach does not mandate a particular form of social security system. There are many different models that choose between or combine social insurance, social assistance and universal benefits that could comply with these principles. As has been seen in the country studies discussed in this book, historical developments, economic circumstances and political variables are just some of the factors that shape the social security systems in different countries. Improving such systems in line with the proposed rights framework will require careful attention to the demands of each context and the views of different stakeholders in those societies (this is a central feature of Principle 6). Important considerations of distributive justice will necessarily arise in weighing up the financing of social security schemes through tax, individual and employee contributions. The issues will differ greatly in developed countries with high levels of formal employment and established

12 As set out in CESCR '*General Comment No 19: The Right to Social Security (Art. 9)*' (2008) 39th Session 2007, E/C.12/GC/19, at para 10–27.

social security institutions from those in developing countries with small formal economies, a limited tax base and little welfare infrastructure.

This section, without wishing to prescribe a particular form for a country's social security system, considers some of the practical and policy implications and applications of the principles of this book. In teasing these out it leaves a number of questions unanswered or open for future consideration and study.

7.2.1 Unemployment: implications of Principle 5

The right to social security is a universal right and hence should be available to all who need it. If this premise is accepted, there is likely to be broad agreement concerning those elements of the right that are not tied to work such as access to affordable health care or support for children and adults who are unable to work. The issue becomes thornier in relation to working-age people who, while capable of working, are not engaged in paid work. Principle 5 requires that 'social security is provided to all men and women who need it, regardless of their relationship to work'. Where work is available and appropriate and people have the opportunities (enabled by social support for child- and other care) to engage in this work, then society should not be expected to fund those who choose not to work. But where decent work is not available or is insufficient to provide an adequate livelihood, then society has a responsibility to assist its members to the fullest extent possible. This will require that those in employment and employers and other owners of capital, will, through their taxes, support those who are not employed. (This does not preclude the operation of social insurance schemes that provide employer and employee contributions to support working people). This idea of shared responsibility for the welfare of all society's members underpins universal human rights.[13] Where this principle requires translation into policy choice is in relation to more specific questions such as the size of income support payments relative to wage rates, costs and standards of living in society; whether such support should be dependent on monitored work-seeking; whether people should be required to undertake work allocated to them by the state in exchange for welfare; and whether welfare should be conditional on certain behaviours or actions of those claiming it. These and other questions are the practical challenges that inform many societies' responses to the problem of unemployment, a growing global concern. Some of these critical questions about how to align social policy with human rights and their gendered implications have been considered in the country studies above[14] but others are beyond the scope of this particular study.

13 See Chapter 3, at 3.2.

14 For example, the issue of welfare conditionality is considered in Chapter 4 and in section 7.4.6 below.

7.2.2 Reproductive and care work v other unpaid work: implications of Principles 1 and 2

The principles relating to women's reproductive and care work (Principle 1) and women's other unpaid work such as in subsistence labour and family enterprises (Principle 2) may require different policy responses. Ensuring that women in family enterprises are able to enjoy the same social security rights that paid workers have, such as maternity leave, sickness and retirement benefits, may require greater regulation and public education to ensure compliance. Public and private funding may be marshalled to meet these costs. Reproductive and care work could require different responses such as the provision of services to shift responsibility for certain care work from individuals to the society and to incentivise care of children by fathers through the provision of leave. Such policies may encourage changed behaviours or require them through mandatory measures. There are a wide range of existing policy models in Scandinavia and elsewhere and other proposals that have not yet been tested in the social policy field to achieve this objective. The principles developed in this book do not lead of necessity to a particular system of socialised care and regulation of unpaid work. A variety of models entailing different financial, policy and regulatory solutions appropriate to each country context could lead to the same principled outcome of a significant shift away from gender-based inequalities in work and care.

7.2.3 Reproduction: implications of Principles 1, 2, 3, 4 and 5

Working women who are pregnant and give birth require both social security rights – for example, to address their lost income during maternity – and labour rights – for example, to be allowed to return to work after a period of leave. The social security rights related to reproduction should be available to women in the formal labour market (Principles 1 and 4) as well as in the informal labour market (Principles 1 and 3) whether this is met through social insurance schemes or provided by the State. Women engaged in unpaid work (Principle 2) should have similar entitlements, as should women who do not work (Principle 5). But this may take a different form from those in the paid labour market. Women who are not receiving pay will not be directly out of pocket when they give birth but they will still be prevented, due to their maternity, from undertaking the unpaid functions of subsistence labour and care work that they normally perform. They require support to address this gap. Social security, whether in the form of services, provision of food or social assistance should be available to support women who are performing the social function of reproducing society. This might entail individual provision or social responses in the form of collective services. Using social security and social services to meet this need avoids imposing additional obligations on other people, usually family members, often women, who step in to assist the woman giving birth and caring for an infant. Once again, different countries may choose different policy formulations but attention to the principle of addressing the various consequences of reproduction through social security should create a more substantively equal society.

7.2.4 *The State's role in the provision of care: implications of Principle 1*

The provision of social security for those undertaking caring functions (Principle 1) is a complex issue that throws up a range of policy problems. One of these arises where caring work prevents people from engaging in paid labour. Here, it is appropriate for a society to either provide care services to free up the time of such people or remunerate them for this work. This entails a policy choice that raises a set of questions: thus, if a society provides comprehensive care services but refuses to remunerate a worker's time taken off work to provide care, does this undermine that worker's choice to perform caring functions? Is choice of this sort a valid public policy consideration and are there human rights and ethical implications? These questions raises issues for debate that concern gender construction, the objectives of social policy, the value of individual agency and how care is understood. The principles developed in this book do not prescribe a particular policy response to these questions. In deliberating on and answering these questions, each society should acknowledge that the views of those receiving and providing care are central to resolving such debates.

A further issue relates to the provision of care for children and other family members outside of working hours. Here, working and non-working carers have the same care obligations and needs for these particular care responsibilities. This raises questions about whether society has an obligation to support such caring activities (whether through the provision of benefits or services) or whether this remains a private responsibility. Treating such care as 'private' serves to reinforce existing gender inequalities in the provision of care. Even if a society chooses to leave such care within the family, it has a role to play in challenging the gender divisions in the performance of such care. In addition, different family configurations (such as dual earner, one earner–one carer, non-earning couples and single carers (whether earning or not)) may require different policy responses depending on the way care is provided in the society and the forms of family that the market and social policy have promoted or neglected.

The broad principle that social security requires attention to and support for unpaid care work can be given concrete form in a variety of ways. Different societies approach this in different ways depending on a wide range of factors. It is of central importance to ensure that policy responses are gender-conscious rather than gender-neutral so as to avoid solutions that reinforce a gender-unequal status quo. The conceptual framework and principles outlined above provide broad guidance to countries in reshaping social security responses to care that promote gender equality. Detailed policy solutions remain the task and responsibility of states and their citizens, with the participation of those most affected by the need for far-reaching reform being of central importance. Transnational co-operation is also necessary to ensure that such solutions have application beyond national boundaries.

7.3 International law

The past decade has seen unprecedented interest by a range of United Nations (UN) human rights bodies in the reinterpretation of the right to social security to match contemporary conditions. The rise in social protection programmes in (primarily) middle-income developing countries has led to attempts to link development strategies to human rights principles. The book has undertaken a survey of these recent interpretations of the right to social security by three of the key UN bodies with mandates relating to the right: the Committee on Economic, Social and Cultural Rights (CESCR), the International Labour Organisation (ILO) and the Special Rapporteur on extreme poverty and human rights. The work of the Committee on the Elimination of Discrimination against Women (the CEDAW Committee) was also examined because of its special role in relation to gender discrimination and the right to social security. The survey and analysis of this law from a gender perspective using the theoretical approach of the book and the principles for a substantively equal, gendered right to social security has identified significant positive developments as well as certain key gaps.

The work of the ILO since 2000 has shifted from a narrow focus on social security standards for workers, a minority of whom experience the benefits of formal employment in the context of globalisation, to an emphasis on social protection floors concurrent with the extension of social security coverage for previously unprotected workers.[15] This is an important advance that brings the ILO closer to other UN human rights bodies in addressing the issue of state responsibility for overcoming poverty. However, the social protection floor's minimalist approach might dilute the obligations arising from the right to social security. While gender equality is a principle underlying the ILO's Social Protection Floor Recommendation No. 202, detailed attention to gender issues is missing from the Recommendation.[16]

The work of the Special Rapporteur on extreme poverty and human rights, Magdalena Sepúlveda Carmona, between 2008 and 2014, has generated valuable insights and recommendations on the human rights approach to social protection.[17] Her work has involved careful consideration of gender equality in developing this approach. This has included a report on the issue of unpaid care,[18] a ground-breaking consideration of the recognition of women's care work, including within the design of social security and social protection programmes. Read together with the work of the UN treaty body committees dealing with the right to social security, the reports of the Special Rapporteur elaborate and advance the

15 ILO, *Recommendation concerning National Floors of Social Protection*, 2012 (R 202).

16 Also see Lucie Lamarche, 'Unpacking the ILO's Social Protection Floor Recommendation from a Women's Rights Perspective' in Beth Goldblatt and Lucie Lamarche (eds), *Women's Rights to Social Security and Social Protection* (Hart, 2014) 65.

17 For a summary, see Sepúlveda and Nyst, above n 4.

18 A/68/293.

normative content of the right, while also providing in-depth policy guidance to states and other agencies involved in development and human rights.

The CESCR's General Comment 19 on the right to social security in the *International Covenant on Economic, Social and Cultural Rights*, adopted in 2007, provides a detailed elaboration of the content of the right to social security and the obligations of states parties. It offers the fullest articulation of the right within international law and is thus a central document for the purpose of this book. The definition of social security within the General Comment links the protection of the right to circumstances that follow a lack of 'work-related income'.[19] The focus on the lack of work in the definition leads to a failure to include 'general poverty and social exclusion' as a condition triggering the operation of the right (an omission the ILO has recently addressed in its own definition). As argued in Chapter 3, this deficiency in the definition operates harshly on the world's women, the majority of whom have no ties to the workforce. While the General Comment makes important statements on gender equality in relation to the right to social security, it fails to note the issue of unpaid work including care work, which is deeply gendered, as well as other issues that affect women's access to social security such as violence. While additional CESCR General Comments dealing with non-discrimination[20] and the equal rights of men and women[21] address some of the deficiencies of General Comment 19, a clearer articulation of the right to social security from a gender perspective by the CESCR, possibly together with the CEDAW Committee, would provide valuable guidance.

The CEDAW Committee has played a positive role in expanding the interpretation of the right to social security beyond the limited text of the Convention, which considers social security only in relation to formal work (Article 11) and rural women (Article 14). The Committee has recognised in its Concluding Observations, General Recommendations and other statements the many forms of work, formal and informal, paid and unpaid, that women perform. It has also been attentive to the circumstances of different groups of women, such as migrants, older women and women with disabilities, in relation to their specific needs regarding the right to social security. The Committee has emphasised the need for social security to address poverty in both developed and developing countries, particularly in the context of the recent financial crisis. A strong understanding of substantive equality has allowed the Committee to appreciate the structural conditions that underlie unequal access to social security. A greater focus on women's unpaid household work and care and their social security entitlements arising from this socially necessary work would, however, strengthen

19 Above n 12, at para 2. It also refers to the lack of affordable health care and insufficient family support.

20 CESCR '*General Comment No 20: Non-discrimination in economic, social and cultural rights (art. 2, para. 2, of the International Covenant on Economic, Social and Cultural Rights)*' (2009) 42nd Session 2009, E/C 12/GC/20.

21 CESCR '*General Comment No 16: Article 3: the equal right of men and women to the enjoyment of all economic, social and cultural rights*' (2005) 34th Session 2005, E/C 12/2005/4.

the views of the Committee coupled with a clearer elaboration of the features of social assistance necessary to address women's poverty.

The important progress of the past decade in bringing the right to social security to prominence as a central human right should be built on in the future through efforts to ensure that gender issues are more fully integrated and that gender equality-enhancing mechanisms are built into the human rights framework. Greater attention should also be given to ensuring that cognisance of transnational migration and migration within countries, a growing feature of the global economy that affects women's rights in multiple ways, leads to improved rights and standards. Aggarwal and Jivan suggest that the CEDAW Committee prepare General Recommendations on some of the economic and social rights including women's equal rights to social security (particularly in relation to poverty and development). They also suggest a General Recommendation on the right to adequate livelihood which could draw on a range of rights including the right to social security.[22] A related suggestion would be for a joint General Comment/Recommendation by the two committees responsible for CEDAW and ICESCR on the right to social security, identifying and highlighting the gender issues involved in the right to social security. This would provide important guidance to states parties in the development and improvement of their social security provision.

The survey of international law has found that there has been significant progress in the interpretation and elaboration of the right to social security by UN human rights bodies but that further development of the right from a gender perspective would enhance the potential of the right to advance gender equality. The discussion of international law has provided the international human rights backdrop against which to examine the right to social security from a gender perspective in the three country studies that follow it.

7.4 Thematic analysis of country studies

The book has examined three differently situated countries to assess the utility of the gender perspective, including the approach and principles for a substantively equal, gendered right to social security developed in Chapter 2, in evaluating the realisation of the right to social security. Within each country study, particular features of the social security system were chosen for examination. In South Africa, a middle-income developing country, the Child Support Grant and recent attempts to impose conditions on this grant were considered.[23] In Australia, a wealthy developed country, the cuts to the payments of sole parents and the introduction of income management to Indigenous communities were

22 Alison Aggarwal and Vedna Jivan, 'Consideration of Women's Equality to Economic Social and Cultural Rights by the CEDAW Committee' (International Women's Action Rights Watch – Asia Pacific, 2010), at 20.

23 Chapter 4.

analysed.[24] In India, a lower-middle-income developing country facing enormous poverty challenges, the social assistance programme and the rural employment scheme were explored.[25] While comparison of these diverse contexts should be approached with care, there is value in a thematic analysis of the findings of the three chapters. Such an approach points to some of the strengths of the social security programmes in these countries, common and different problems facing these nations, and issues that may have universal relevance to the advancement of the right to social security equally for men and women. The themes mirror, in the main, the broad conceptual issues raised in Chapter 2 and include the following: the importance of a gender perspective; the value of a rights framework; understanding women's work and care; four-dimensional substantive equality; intersectionality; conditional social security; social security at different levels; and social security in relation to other rights.

7.4.1 The importance of a gender perspective

All three country studies demonstrate that the use of a gender perspective in considering the rights-compliance of social security programmes illustrates the positive features of such programmes as well as their failures to address the needs of women. These failures are sometimes overlooked or ignored by programme designers.[26] In Australia, the introduction of income management in the Northern Territory was criticised for its racially discriminatory impact but the gender discrimination that income management imposed on Indigenous women, the major recipients of social security payments, was largely ignored. The application of a gender perspective also highlighted how claims of retrogressive violations of the social security rights of sole parents, whose payments were cut by the Australian government, entrenched inequalities faced by a group almost entirely constituted by women.

In South Africa, the Child Support Grant (CSG), aimed at reaching poor children but collected predominantly by women, is a critical poverty-alleviation social assistance benefit. Analysis of the grant from a gender rights perspective illustrates, however, that mothers and other female carers are expected to collect this grant and use it for the maintenance of their children in the absence of an adequate response to their own poverty and their own rights to social security.

In India, the National Social Assistance Programme similarly fails to support women of working age unless they are widowed, disabled or in a family that has lost a breadwinner. The *National Rural Employment Guarantee Act* (NREGA) addresses this gap by providing public works with a third of places reserved for women. A gender perspective identifies the valuable features of this programme such as the inclusion of women in rural areas in formal employment with accompanying social security entitlements. However, it also highlights the weaknesses

24 Chapter 5.
25 Chapter 6.
26 And even by commentators and human rights advocates.

of the Act which guarantees work to households rather than individuals to the disadvantage of women householders; the lack of detail and implementation of the childcare provisions of the Act; and the gap in coverage through the exclusion of the urban poor, many of whom are unemployed or poorly paid women.

The gender-based approach and principles for the right to social security require a careful consideration of the context of gender inequality in each country and close scrutiny of social security laws and programmes and their impact on women and men. The approach and principles also inform alternative proposals for social security design that are rights-based and have the potential to advance gender equality. Thus, the right to social security, informed by the gender perspective proposed in this book, can lead to more equitable, appropriate and comprehensive social security provision.

7.4.2 The value of a rights framework

The three country studies showcase a spectrum of constitutional rights models. In South Africa, the right to social security is a justiciable right in the Constitutional Bill of Rights. In India, social security, while not a right, forms part of the directive principles in the Constitution that guide law-making and governance. Both countries have strong equality rights. Australia has neither a bill of rights nor human rights legislation guaranteeing the right to social security, and its equality laws do not apply to social security legislation. These differences affect the way social security laws are designed, implemented and challenged.

In Australia, public outcry against both parenting payment cuts and income management was framed in terms of international human rights. The laws were found to fall short of such rights by a parliamentary committee. Despite this, and despite condemnation from UN human rights bodies, the laws were enacted. A right to social security and stronger equality rights written into Australian law would have strengthened efforts to challenge these measures.

In India, the move from executive-initiated social assistance programmes to rights-based social legislation (including NREGA) has been hailed by commentators as a significant advance.[27] This rights-based legislation is having a positive influence on social security and social protection law and policy, even if problems with design and implementation remain. The 'Right to Food' case which houses the Supreme Court's orders on a broad range of anti-poverty measures has also had a powerful impact on aspects of social security and social protection.[28]

The South African constitutional guarantee of the right to social security and the litigation that has sought to enforce it has had a notable impact on

27 Jayna Kothari, 'A social rights model for social security: learnings from India' (2014) 1 *Verfassung und Recht in Ubersee* 5; Deepta Chopra, 'The Indian Case: Towards a Rights-Based Welfare State?' in Gabriele Koehler and Deepta Chopra (eds), *Development and Welfare Policy in South Asia* (Routledge, 2014) 85.

28 *PUCL v. Union of India & Others* WP (Civil) No. 196/2001, 23 July 2001, unreported; Anup Kumar Srivastava and Manisha Tiwary, *Right to Food* (Human Rights Law Network, 4th edn, 2009).

the government with regard to the social assistance programme.[29] Litigation to extend the Child Support Grant to older children and the old age pension to certain men influenced government to approve such changes.[30]

The country studies indicate that strong domestic rights protections, including a right to social security and a right to equality, are likely to be valuable in efforts to realise the international right to social security, developed from a gender perspective. While stronger rights protections are important, an improved rights framework at the international level may have value for countries without such guarantees where governments or citizens look to international law to inform reform efforts. Rights frameworks, such as the one developed here, can be used to monitor and evaluate existing social security provision, and can be used in lobbying, advocacy and litigation to secure change.

However, as discussed above,[31] human rights are not always effective in achieving change. Some commentators suggest that feminist efforts within the human rights system have little impact on gender inequalities and harms, and may in fact contribute to their maintenance.[32] Despite half a century of human rights and decades of women's rights, women still remain poorer and more disadvantaged than men, and face violence and discrimination.[33]

This requires responses both within the human rights system and framework and outside of it through various feminist engagements (in alliance with other groups) at the national and international level.[34] Transnational efforts are becoming increasingly important to highlight the impact of global economic and political processes on women's poverty.

7.4.3 Understanding women's work and care

The three countries and the examples selected within each of them focus on social assistance and, in the case of NREGA, social protection. The social insurance programmes in each of these countries are limited and none of them has universal social security (with the exception of Australia's health care system). The social assistance programmes in all three countries can be criticised for the

29 Beth Goldblatt and Solange Rosa, 'Social Security Rights – Campaigns and Courts' in Malcolm Langford et al. (eds), *Socio-Economic Rights in South Africa: Symbols or Substance?* (Cambridge University Press, 2014) 253.

30 Ibid, at 258–61.

31 In Chapter 1, at 1.4.

32 Ratna Kapur, 'The tragedy of victimisation rhetoric: resurrecting the "native" subject in international/postcolonial feminist legal politics' (2002) 15 *Harvard Human Rights Law Journal* 1; Diane Otto, 'Disconcerting "Masculinities": Reinventing the Gendered Subject(s) of International Human Rights Law' in Doris Buss and Ambreena Manji (eds), *International Law: Modern Feminist Approaches* (Hart, 2005) 105.

33 Dianne Otto, 'Women's Rights' in Daniel Moeckli, Sangeeta Shah and Sandesh Sivakumaran (eds), *International Human Rights Law* (Oxford University Press, 2010) 345, at 346.

34 A more detailed version of these points is canvassed in Sandra Fredman and Beth Goldblatt, *Gender Equality and Human Rights*, UN Women Discussion Paper No. 4 for *Progress of the World's Women 2015–2016* (UN Women, 2015) 1–65, at 40–1.

failure to fully acknowledge and accommodate the circumstances of women in relation to work and care as required by a substantively equal, gendered right to social security.

In South Africa, structural unemployment, affecting women particular severely, means that women without income require social security to meet their survival needs. Social assistance is available for the elderly, people with disabilities and children. Working-age adults under the age of 60, however, do not have access to such assistance. The CSG is collected primarily by women; however, the care provided by such women is not compensated by society and their own poverty is not addressed through the social security system. The CSG is innovative in targeting 'primary care givers' rather than mothers, based on a functional understanding that care in South Africa is often provided by people other than parents. This progressive approach to the design of the grant has not, however, altered the underlying reality that the overwhelming majority of CSG recipients are women. Contrary to the requirements of a substantively equal, gendered right to social security, this social assistance measure has not played any role in addressing the gender division of care in South African society. The grant that preceded the CSG, although racially discriminatory in its application, contained both carer and child components, hence acknowledging the financial needs of carers. Even where costs challenges are significant in the development of social assistance programmes in poor countries, policy approaches should attempt to build gender rights considerations into their formulations.

The NREGA programme in India provides an interesting example of an effort to address the issue of care by requiring childcare support within the public works projects it generates. The problem, however, is that the legislation assumes that women should perform these caring functions,[35] thus reinforcing gender stereotypes around care and failing to promote transformative solutions such as involving men in care work. Like South Africa, social assistance is targeted at the elderly and people with disabilities. Those who are able to work but without income (the majority of whom are women), are left outside of the protection of the right to social security. India's response to this gap, the rural public works programme of NREGA, while commendable, still fails to address the needs of the urban poor.

The 2012 cuts to the payments of sole parents by Australia's government were based on the view that such parents (usually women) should return to work when their children begin school. This assumes that sole parents are able to combine work and care for their children in a context where childcare can be costly or limited and where access to work opportunities may be constrained by previous years spent caring for children. Thus, the government not only fails to acknowledge the difficult circumstances facing sole mothers, but also locates the problem in the women themselves, rather than accepting, as a gendered right to social security demands, that the problem is one to be addressed by the society as a whole.

35 S 28 of Schedule II of the *National Rural Employment Guarantee Act* 42 of 2005.

Even where countries attempt to improve provision of social security and meet their human rights obligations in this regard, the absence of a gender perspective that exposes women's relationship to work and care results in laws and policies that fail to fully realise the right equally for men and women.

7.4.4 Four-dimensional substantive equality

Achieving substantive equality, understood in terms of its four-dimensional aims, in relation to the full realisation of the right to social security requires greater effort by each of the countries studied. An analysis of the three countries using these four dimensions reveals some positive features but also limitations in each of their social security programmes.

The importance of the *distributive dimension* of substantive equality is illustrated through the NREGA scheme in India which attempts to address the disadvantage experienced by the rural poor, with women amongst the most vulnerable. The provision of an income and social security benefits to rural women who have limited access to employment is a significant achievement. In contrast, the removal of benefits to sole parents in Australia undermines the rights of this disadvantaged group to substantive equality. The government's argument that the measure was aimed at consistency between the 'grandfathered' group historically allowed to retain the higher benefit and the newer group of sole parents on lower benefits is a perversion of the idea of substantive equality since it 'levels down' benefits, creating equal disadvantage for both groups. A substantively equal distributive measure would have improved the position of the newer group or at the very least retained the historical promise to the older group. Instead, the government chose retrogression over progressive realisation, couched as an equalising measure. Similarly, the removal of the parent component of the State Maintenance Grant in South Africa, while arguably fiscally necessary in the creation of the deracialised CSG, was retrogressive in removing a distributive benefit to disadvantaged carers.

The *recognition dimension* is absent from the income management measures in the Northern Territory in Australia. The stigma and discomfort suffered by the (majority women) recipients of social assistance benefits under such measures is a violation of their right to substantively equal social security. Having to use the 'basics card' and stand in separate lines at stores affects their dignity and sense of worth. The NREGA scheme in India, on the other hand, provides women with the benefits and status attached to formal work that they may never have experienced before. This provides recognition of their dignity and equal rights to work and social security. The poor administration of the Child Support Grant in South Africa has resulted in women grant applicants and beneficiaries being exposed to violence and abuse by former partners and officials. Improved design and implementation of social security programmes can be critical to the recognition dimension of substantive equality.

The reservation of one-third of the places in NREGA for women is an attempt to address the poverty and low workforce participation rate of women in rural

India. Acknowledging that women have less access to work than men, the government has approached this inequality by structurally altering the composition of the rural labour force employed in public works programmes. This measure contributes towards the substantive equality aim of ***transformation***. The use of a quota ensures that a defined portion of the income from NREGA reaches women. While this goes some way to addressing the transformative dimension of substantive equality, reserving a larger number of places for women or providing such places to individuals rather than households might have had a greater impact on gender equality. Similarly, while acknowledgment of the need for childcare in NREGA is a significant achievement of this legislation, a fully ***transformative*** response would have included male workers in the care of children. In Australia income management was introduced by government as a special measure to address violence against Indigenous women and children. While special measures form part of the transformative dimension of substantive equality, this particular policy was not aimed at the achievement of substantive equality. Indeed, instead of assisting women it has imposed additional burdens on them. A transformative response to this problem would have improved the social security rights of women in these communities so as to give them greater economic independence alongside other measures to address abuse.

South Africa's CSG provides money for children in poverty with the expectation that carers (mainly women) will spend the money to feed and support these children. Women are thus expected to perform care services for society but are neither remunerated nor supported. Their capacity to participate fully in society is limited by this care work. The ***dimension of participation*** is also absent. Carers were not consulted before recent reforms to the CSG to include conditions relating to school attendance. Similarly, sole parents were not consulted about payment cuts in Australia, and their ability to participate as equal citizens was further hindered by these cuts. Greater consultation with women could lead to improvements in all of the social security programmes examined in this study. This might result in policies that empower women and promote their greater participation in the workplace and the community.

This analysis reveals the complex nature of inequality and the need for sophisticated responses to ensure that social security contributes to multi-dimensional gender equality. Policies that fail to address any of the four-dimensional aims of redistribution, recognition, transformation and participation will not be substantively equal in the transformative understanding of this concept.

7.4.5 ***Intersectionality***

Substantive equality requires close attention to multiple and intersecting forms of discrimination. Social security measures are often designed to benefit certain groups identified as needing support. However, failure to understand the differences within groups or the special needs of certain groups will lead to inadequate social security policies. The case studies reveal a variety of instances where groups of women face additional forms of discrimination because of their membership of other disadvantaged groups and where social security policies have added to this disadvantage or have failed to find ways to overcome it.

Indigenous women in Australia's Northern Territory had income management measures imposed upon them because of their membership of the Indigenous community. As women, they are most likely to be the adults in the community receiving welfare income and having to deal with the consequences of its management. Poverty leads such women to rely on social assistance and it is their gender and their race that has contributed to their poverty. The combination of race/Indigenous status together with gender and poverty lead to compound inequalities that make this one of the most vulnerable groups in Australia. Rather than supporting this group, the policy of income management has heightened their disadvantage and increased their burdens.[36]

India's NREGA provides income or unemployment payments to rural people because of the particular poverty challenges facing rural communities trying to survive off the land. In addition, the programme acknowledges the need to support women in these communities by reserving one-third of the places in the public works projects for them. While this addresses rural women's vulnerability and disadvantage, it fails to support urban women who also face poverty. The Act, in assisting rural women alone, privileges one form of vulnerability over another. Without diminishing the challenges facing India in designing affordable and appropriate social protection, this issue deserves further consideration if the right to social security is to be equally realised. An intersectional approach encourages a deeper examination of groups such as women with disabilities, single women or lower-caste and tribal women within NREGA. By exposing some of the layers of inequality and their complex interaction in Indian society, it provokes questions about the social, political and economic structures that entrench such divides.

Carers of children in South Africa who receive the CSG are generally the young mothers of such children. They are also likely to be black because of historical patterns of racial discrimination that linked poverty to race. Young, black and poor women with caring responsibilities are a severely disadvantaged group. They lack access to opportunities to earn an income and because of their caring responsibilities, are further constrained in their capacity to work outside of the home. The lack of social assistance to support this group heightens their disadvantage and violates their rights to social security and equality. While sole parents in Australia may not experience the same level of poverty or some of the additional difficulties, such as membership of a historically disadvantaged racial group (aside from Indigenous women), there are common features of the intersectional discrimination faced by both groups – poor women with the responsibilities of caring for children alone. They are generally unemployed or underemployed and low-paid.

A substantively equal, gendered right to social security provides a framework for the development of law and policy that takes account of the diversity of women's experiences and addresses intersecting forms of discrimination. Close attention to

36 Equality Rights Alliance, 'Women's Experience of Income Management in the Northern Territory' (Equality Rights Alliance, 2011).

the history and social context in any country (and within and between countries) is needed to unpack the specific forms of intersectional discrimination that arise and require redress. An intersectional approach also requires that evaluations of social security schemes ask the correct questions and collect the correct data to uncover who is assisted and who is left out so as to ensure that the needs of the most marginal are not overlooked.

7.4.6 Conditional social security

The debate about whether social assistance should be conditional on recipients meeting certain obligations is occurring within the development field. The human rights considerations are also a feature of this debate which considers whether entitlements should be subject to conditions that require certain behavioural compliance before a social security benefit is provided.[37] It is an important issue in relation to a gendered right to social security since conditional cash transfer programmes often target mothers who are required to ensure their children's attendance at school and clinics. A substantively equal, gendered right to social security does not permit conditions that require women to provide care and related services in exchange for payments to which they should be unconditionally entitled. Conditional cash transfer programmes additionally reinforce existing societal expectations that women will fulfil these functions without challenging such assumptions. In each of the country examples, conditionality has been employed in some of the social assistance programmes.

In South Africa, the government has introduced conditions into the previously unconditional CSG. These are both unnecessary and problematic and threaten to burden the grant recipients with responsibilities additional to their unremunerated care work. The conditions may be in violation of the right to social security and the right to equality in South Africa's Bill of Rights and they are contrary to the principles for a substantively equal, gendered right to social security.

The motivation behind income management measures in Australia's Northern Territory is closely related to the ideology that underlies welfare conditionality. Social assistance benefits are removed from the control of recipients and shifted to the control of the State. This loss of entitlement to social assistance as a right without attendant constraints mirrors the loss of rights experienced by recipients of conditional cash transfers (CCTs) who receive benefits only in exchange for behavioural compliance. Income management, like CCTs, imposes stigma and burdens on already vulnerable women.[38]

In India, conditionality has also entered the previously unconditional social assistance system in the Janani Suraksha Yojana (JSY). This payment for pregnant women has been made conditional on institutional delivery. The intervention of the Commissioner appointed by the Supreme Court did, however, result in

37 This debate is discussed in Chapter 4 at 4.6.
38 Discussed in Chapter 5 at 5.6.

modifications to the scheme to provide the benefits for women choosing non-institutional delivery in certain states.[39]

In all three countries, conditionality has been met with opposition because it is viewed as an intrusion on the rights of the (primarily) women recipients of the payments. Engaging with conditionality from a social security rights perspective that takes account of gender is important in challenging attempts to limit and control women's behaviours, choices and access to social security.

7.4.7 *Social security at different levels*

The right to social security must be available and accessible to all who need it transnationally and within countries. As discussed, Nancy Fraser's consideration of justice at the global 'scale' and Susan Williams' adaptation of this to the sub-national 'scale' apply to a gendered right to social security. While the particular social security programmes in the three countries studied here do not relate to intra- or transnational labour migration, issues relating to the realisation of the right to social security at different levels within a country do arise.

In India, the provision of public works and accompanying social security rights through NREGA for rural people but not urban dwellers reveals rights disparities within the Indian State. The lens of 'scale' provides a framework to observe and challenge the justice of this distinction.

In Australia, the imposition of income management on some members of the society (Indigenous people in the Northern Territory and, later, to people in certain designated disadvantaged areas) rather than to all Australians also highlights the need for justice equally across the society. Seen from the perspective of an equal entitlement to the right to social security, the government's intervention becomes a violation of justice and a discriminatory breach of rights.

7.4.8 *Social security and other rights*

The right to social security is closely linked to other human rights, as evidenced by the examples in the three country studies. The cuts to parenting payments in Australia are a violation of the equality and social security rights of women as well as those of the children in their care. The income management measures reduce the rights of Indigenous peoples and demonstrate the intersection of race discrimination with gender discrimination. They also diminish the rights to dignity and autonomy of the people affected.

The right to work and the right to social security alongside the right to equality are firmly united in India's NREGA. NREGA is a very significant development for the rural poor in India, many of whom have never been paid a minimum wage nor had any entitlement to social security. For women in these areas, this is likely to be even more unusual. NREGA demonstrates the need for a package of rights for women facing poverty. Social security alone will not address this poverty

39 Discussed in Chapter 6 at 6.5.3.

without the realisation of accompanying rights to work, health, education, housing and others.

In South Africa, litigation to extend the CSG has been based on arguments for the equal rights of different age groups of children to benefit from this payment. Similarly, the equality rights of women responsible for the care of different age groups of children have been raised. Additional rights under South Africa's Constitution including rights to food and nutrition, social services, basic education, dignity and life were included in the legal challenge.[40]

The rights of migrant workers, the rights to work and livelihood, and other social and economic rights such as health, education, housing, water and basic services all link to the right to social security, developed from a gender perspective.

7.5 Value of the 'gender-developed' right to social security

The examination of international law and the thematic analysis of the country studies points to the utility of a gender rights-based analysis of social security provision. The development of the right to social security from a gender perspective in this book contributes to a project by feminist human rights scholars and activists to give gender content to human rights and, more specifically, to social and economic rights.[41] It also contributes to scholarship on equality as a foundational principle of justice and as a right by considering its application to the gendered development of the right to social security.

The approach taken in this book may inform the development of other human rights from a gender perspective. In particular, the conceptualisation of work developed here in relation to the right to social security may inform feminist interpretations of the right to work and the right to a livelihood. The emphasis on 'scale' may encourage a greater focus on the transnational and sub-national issues relevant to the gendered development of other rights.

The ideas and findings of this book can assist those working on a number of issues including the following: the further development of the gender content of the ILO's Social Protection Floor Recommendation;[42] the rights of women migrant workers; the obligations of business including multi-national corporations regarding the social security rights of women workers; and the gender dimensions of the Maastricht Principles on Extraterritorial Obligations of States in the area of Economic, Social and Cultural Rights (2012).[43]

A rights-based approach to development and social policy ensures that universally agreed principles and laws are central to such disciplines. The principles for a substantively equal, gendered right to social security may prove useful to scholars and practitioners working in these fields.

40 Goldblatt and Rosa, above n 29, at 260.

41 As articulated, for example, in the 'Montreal Principles', above n 2.

42 Above n 15.

43 Olivier De Schutter et al., 'Commentary to the Maastricht Principles on Extraterritorial Obligations of States in the Area of Economic, Social and Cultural Rights' (2012) 34 *Human Rights Quarterly* 1084.

The approach developed in this book may assist lawyers and women's rights advocates within a range of countries to challenge social security programmes, resist retrogressive measures and propose more equitable approaches to social security. It may also help to link domestic engagement with social security rights to the body of international human rights law and commentary.

Within international law, the ideas developed here can assist the various UN bodies dealing with the right to social security. As proposed above, a joint General Comment should be developed on the equal rights of men and women to social security by the CEDAW Committee and the CESCR, perhaps with input from the Special Rapporteur on extreme poverty and human rights, the ILO and the Committee on Migrant Workers,[44] as well as other relevant bodies. This would provide the detailed guidance needed by states parties to realise the rights of men and women to social security on an equal basis.

The findings of this book identify areas for future research on the right to social security from a gender perspective. The recognition of care and unpaid household labour requires further elaboration in relation to the right to social security and in relation to other human rights.[45] Specific consideration of how to quantify and value care work and how to develop a flexible rights framework that can accommodate different societies' policy choices on how to address the provision of care is important. Further research on what is needed to give effect (legally and politically) to a gendered right to social security would take the findings of this book forward into the policy terrain. Some of the philosophical, political and economic debates about the extent of the State's responsibility for the welfare of its people (and what this means for human rights)[46] could include an engagement with the ideas developed here for a (gendered) right to social security. It might also be useful to engage critically with the limits of a right to social security (as with other rights) and to develop alternative routes for achieving a society free of poverty and inequality.

44 The UN treaty body responsible for monitoring the implementation of the *International Convention on the Protection of the Rights of All Migrant Workers and Members of Their Families* (ICMW) (adopted 18 December 1990, entered into force 1 July 2003) 2220 UNTS 3.

45 This has been considered by the UN Special Rapporteur on extreme poverty and human rights in a report on unpaid care work, above n 18, and by the Working Group on the issue of discrimination against women in law and in practice, '*Thematic Report (eliminating discrimination against women in economic and social life with a focus on economic crisis)*' (Human Rights Council (26th session), 2014), at 18–19, but further engagement with this issue would be valuable.

46 See, for example, the work of Thomas Pogge and Amartya Sen: Thomas Pogge (ed.), *Freedom from Poverty as a Human Right: Who Owes What to the Very Poor?* (Oxford University Press, 2007); Thomas Pogge, 'Are we violating the human rights of the world's poor?' (2011) 14(2) *Yale Human Rights and Development Law Journal* 1; Amartya Sen, 'Elements of a theory of human rights' (2004) 32(4) *Philosophy and Public Affairs* 315; Amartya Sen, 'Human rights and capabilities' (2005) 6(2) *Journal of Human Development* 151.

7.6 Conclusion

This chapter has restated the major arguments, theoretical foundations and findings of the book. It has demonstrated the utility of the conceptual framework and principles for a substantively equal, gendered right to social security developed in this book in analysing international law on the right to social security; and considering the right to social security from a gender perspective in three countries. The issues emerging from the three country studies have been analysed thematically to reach conclusions about the importance of a substantively equal, gendered right to social security. The book has demonstrated that the redevelopment of the right to social security from a gender perspective has utility in reshaping the way the right is understood; in assisting with the critique and evaluation of social security programmes; and in the reframing and design of new social security programmes that advance gender equality and address gendered poverty.

Bibliography

Books

Ackerly, Brooke and Jacqui True, *Doing Feminist Research in Political and Social Science* (Palgrave Macmillan, 2010)

Albertyn, Catherine and Elsje Bonthuys, *Gender, Law and Justice* (Juta, 2007)

Barrett, Michelle, *Women's Oppression Today: Problems in Marxist Feminist Analysis* (Verso, 1981)

Barrientos, Armando, *Social Assistance in Developing Countries* (Cambridge University Press, 2013)

Bilchitz, David, *Poverty and Fundamental Rights: The Justification and Enforcement of Socio-Economic Rights* (Oxford University Press, 2007)

Butler, Judith, *Gender Trouble: Feminism and the Subversion of Identity* (Routledge, 1990)

Byrnes, Andrew, Hilary Charlesworth and Gabrielle McKinnon, *Bills of Rights in Australia: History, Politics and Law* (UNSW Press, 2009)

Carney, Terry, *Social Security Law and Policy* (Federation Press, 2006)

Charlesworth, Hilary and Christine Chinkin, *The Boundaries of International Law: A Feminist Analysis* (Manchester University Press, 2000)

Connell, Raewyn, *Gender in World Perspective* (Polity Press, 2nd edn, 2009)

Cook, Rebecca J. and Simone Cusack, *Gender Stereotyping: Transnational Legal Perspectives* (University of Pennsylvania Press, 2010)

Easteal, Patricia, *Women and the Law in Australia* (LexisNexis Butterworths, 2010)

Esping-Andersen, Gøsta, *The Three Worlds of Welfare Capitalism* (Polity Press, 1990)

Faraday, Fay, Margaret Denike and M. Kate Stephenson, *Making Equality Rights Real: Securing Substantive Equality Under the Charter* (Irwin Law, 2009)

Fineman, Martha Albertson, *The Illusion of Equality: The Rhetoric and Reality of Divorce Reform* (University of Chicago Press, 1991)

Fineman, Martha Albertson, *The Autonomy Myth: A Theory of Dependency* (New Press, 2004)

Fineman, Martha Albertson, *The Neutered Mother, the Sexual Family and Other Twentieth Century Tragedies* (Routledge, 1995)

Folbre, Nancy, *The Invisible Heart: Economics and Family Values* (New Press, 2001)

Fraser, Nancy, *Adding Insult to Injury: Nancy Fraser Debates Her Critics* (Verso, 2008)

Fraser, Nancy, *Scales of Justice: Reimagining Political Space in a Globalizing World* (Polity Press, 2008)

Fredman, Sandra, *Human Rights Transformed: Positive Rights and Positive Duties* (Oxford University Press, 2008)

Fredman, Sandra, *Discrimination Law* (Oxford University Press, 2nd edn, 2011)

Grabham, Emily, Davina Cooper, Jane Krishnadas and Didi Herman (eds), *Intersectionality and Beyond: Law, Power and the Politics of Location* (Routledge, 2009)

Graycar, Regina and Jenny Morgan, *The Hidden Gender of Law* (Federation Press, 2nd edn, 2002)

Heredero, Ana Gómez, *Social Security as a Human Right: The Protection Afforded by the European Convention on Human Rights* (Council of Europe Publishing, 2007)

Heredero, Ana Gómez, *Social Security: Protection at the International Level and Developments in Europe* (Council of Europe Publishing, 2009)

Hill, Elizabeth, *Worker Identity, Agency and Economic Development: Women's Empowerment in the Indian Informal Economy* (Routledge, 2010)

Holmes, Rebecca and Nicola Jones, *Gender and Social Protection in the Developing World* (Zed, 2013)

Jagger, Gill, *Judith Butler: Sexual Politics, Social Change and the Power of the Performative* (Routledge, 2008)

Kabeer, Naila, *Mainstreaming Gender in Social Protection for the Informal Economy* (Commonwealth Secretariat, 2008)

Liebenberg, Sandra, *Socio-Economic Rights Adjudication under a Transformative Constitution* (Juta, 2010)

Lister, Ruth et al., *Gendering Citizenship in Western Europe: New Challenges for Citizenship Research in a Cross-National Context* (Policy Press, 2007)

Lund, Francie, *Changing Social Policy: The Child Support Grant in South Africa* (HSRC Press, 2008)

MacKinnon, Catharine A., *Feminism Unmodified: Discourses on Life and Law* (Harvard University Press, 1987)

MacKinnon, Catharine A., *Are Women Human? And Other International Dialogues* (Harvard University Press, 2006)

Mendes, Philip, *Australia's Welfare Wars Revisited: The Players, the Politics and the Ideologies* (UNSW Press, 2008)

Midgley, James and David Pichaud, *Colonialism and Welfare: Social Policy and the British Imperial Legacy* (Edward Elgar, 2011)

Minow, Martha, *Making All the Difference* (Harvard University Press, 1990)

Morsink, Johannes, *The Universal Declaration of Human Rights: Origins, Drafting and Intent* (University of Pennsylvania Press, 1999)

Nedelsky, Jennifer, *Law's Relations: A Relational Theory of Self, Autonomy, and Law* (Oxford University Press, 2011)

Neville, Ann, *Human Rights and Social Policy* (Edward Elgar, 2010)

Nussbaum, Martha, *Frontiers of Justice: Disability, Nationality, Species Membership* (Harvard University Press, 2006)

Nussbaum, Martha, *Women and Human Development: The Capabilities Approach* (Cambridge University Press, 2000)

O'Donovan, Katherine, *Sexual Divisions in Law* (Weidenfeld and Nicolson, 1985)

Olivier, Marius, *The Law of South Africa 13 Part 2: Social Security: Framework* (LexisNexis, 2nd edn, 2012)

Paskalia, Vicki, *Free Movement, Social Security and Gender in the EU* (Hart Publishing, 2007)

Pennings, Frans, *European Social Security Law* (Intersentia, 5th edn, 2010)

Rhode, Deborah L., *Justice and Gender: Sex Discrimination and the Law* (Harvard University Press, 1989)

Saul, Ben, David Kinley and Jacqueline Mowbray, *The International Covenant on Economic, Social and Cultural Rights: Commentary, Cases and Materials* (Oxford University Press, 2014)

Sen, Amartya *Development as Freedom* (Oxford University Press, 1999)

Sepúlveda, Magdalena and Carly Nyst, *The Human Rights Approach to Social Protection* (Ministry for Foreign Affairs Finland, 2012)

Sohrab, Julia, *Sexing the Benefit: Women, Social Security, and Financial Independence in EC Sex Equality Law* (Dartmouth Publishing, 1996)

Srivastava, Anup Kumar and Manisha Tiwary, *Right to Food* (Human Rights Law Network, 4th edn, 2009)

Standing, Guy, *The Precariat: The New Dangerous Class* (Bloomsbury Academic, 2011)

Standing, Guy, Jeemol Unni, Renana Jhabvala and Uma Rani, *Social Income and Insecurity: A Study in Gujarat* (Routledge, 2010)

Steiner, Henry J. and Philip Alston, *International Human Rights in Context: Law, Politics, Morals* (Oxford University Press, 3rd edn, 2008)

van Ginneken, Wouter, *Sustaining European Social Security Systems in a Globalised Economy* (Council of Europe Publishing, 2011)

Walby, Sylvia, *Patriarchy at Work* (Polity Press, 1986)

Waring, Marilyn, *Counting For Nothing: What Men Value and What Women are Worth* (University of Toronto Press, 1999)

Waring, Marilyn, Anit N. Mukherjee, Elizabeth Reid and Meena Shivdas, *Anticipatory Social Protection: Claiming Dignity and Rights* (Commonwealth Secretariat, 2013)

Williams, Joan, *Unbending Gender: Why Family and Work Conflict and What to Do about It* (Oxford University Press, 2000)

Book chapters

Albertyn, Catherine and Beth Goldblatt, 'Equality' in Stuart Woolman and M. Bishop (eds), *Constitutional Law of South Africa* (Juta, 2nd edn, 2007) 58

Banda, Fareda, 'Article 14' in Marsha A. Freeman, Christine Chinkin and Beate Rudolf (eds), *The UN Convention on the Elimination of All Forms of Discrimination against Women: A Commentary* (Oxford University Press, 2012) 357

Barrientos, Armando, 'Social Protection for Poverty Reduction: Approaches, Effectiveness and Challenges' in Katja Bender, Markus Kaltenborn and Christian Pfleiderer (eds), *Social Protection in Developing Countries: Reforming Systems* (Routledge, 2013) 24

Breman, J. and K.P. Kannan, 'Unto the Last? An Introduction' in J. Breman and K.P. Kannan (eds), *The Long Road to Social Security* (Hivos, 2012) 7

Byrnes, Andrew, 'Article 1' in Marsha A. Freeman, Christine Chinkin and Beate Rudolf (eds), *The UN Convention on the Elimination of All Forms of Discrimination Against Women: A Commentary* (Oxford University Press, 2012) 51

Byrnes, Andrew, 'The Protection and Enjoyment of Economic, Social and Cultural Rights' in Paula Gerber and Melissa Castan (eds), *Contemporary Perspectives on Human Rights Law in Australia* (Thomson Reuters, 2013) 125

Carney, Terry, 'Women and Social Security/Transfer Payments Law' in Patricia Easteal (ed.), *Women and the Law in Australia* (LexisNexis Butterworths, 2010) 424

Charlesworth, Hilary, 'Talking to Ourselves? Feminist Scholarship in International Law' in Sari Kouvo and Zoe Pearson (eds), *Feminist Perspectives on Contemporary International Law: Between Resistance and Compliance?* (Hart, 2011) 17

Charlesworth, Sara, 'Law's Response to the Reconciliation of Work and Care: The

Australian Case' in Grace James and Nicole Busby (eds), *Families, Care-giving and Paid Work: Challenging Labour Law in the 21st Century* (Edward Elgar, 2011) 86

Chinkin, Christine, Shelley Wright and Hilary Charlesworth, 'Feminist Approaches to International Law: Reflections from Another Century' in Doris Buss and Ambreena Manji (eds), *International Law: Modern Feminist Approaches* (Hart, 2005) 17

Chopra, Deepta, 'The Indian Case: Towards a Rights-Based Welfare State?' in Gabriele Koehler and Deepta Chopra (eds), *Development and Welfare Policy in South Asia* (Routledge, 2014) 85

Clements, Luke and Alan Simmons, 'European Court of Human Rights – Sympathetic Unease' in Malcolm Langford (ed.), *Social Rights Jurisprudence: Emerging Trends in International and Comparative Law* (Cambridge University Press, 2008) 409

Conaghan, Joanne, 'Intersectionality and the Feminist Project in Law' in Emily Grabham, Davina Cooper, Jane Krishnadas and Didi Herman (eds), *Intersectionality and Beyond: Law, Power and the Politics of Location* (Routledge, 2009) 21

Conant, Lisa, 'Regional Legal Frameworks for Human Rights and Social Policy in Europe' in Ann Neville (ed.), *Human Rights and Social Policy: A Comparative Analysis of Values and Citizenship in OECD Countries* (Edward Elgar, 2010) 47

Davies, Margaret, 'Taking the Inside out – Sex and Gender in the Legal Subject' in Ngaire Naffine and Rosemary J. Owens (eds), *Sexing the Subject of Law* (Sweet and Maxwell, 1997) 25

Drèze, Jean, 'Employment Guarantee and the Right to Work' in Reetika Khera (ed.), *The Battle for Employment Guarantee* (Oxford University Press, 2011) 3

Elson, Diane 'Gender Justice, Human Rights, and Neo-Liberal Economic Policies' in Maxine Molyneux and Shahra Razavi (eds), *Gender Justice, Development, and Rights* (Oxford University Press, 2002) 78

Engle, Karen, 'International Human Rights and Feminisms: When Discourses Keep Meeting' in Doris Buss and Ambreena Manji (eds), *International Law: Modern Feminist Approaches* (Hart Publishing, 2005) 47

Farha, Leilani, 'Committee on the Elimination of Discrimination Against Women: Women Claiming Economic, Social and Cultural Rights – The CEDAW Potential' in Malcolm Langford (ed.), *Social Rights Jurisprudence: Emerging Trends in International and Comparative Law* (Cambridge University Press, 2008) 553

Fenwick, Colin, 'The International Labour Organisation: An Integrated Approach to Economic and Social Rights' in Malcolm Langford (ed.), *Social Rights Jurisprudence: Emerging Trends in International and Comparative Law* (Cambridge University Press, 2008) 591

Fraser, Nancy, 'Women, Welfare, and the Politics of Need Interpretation' in *Unruly Practices: Power, Discourse and Gender in Contemporary Social Theory* (Polity Press, 1989) 144

Fraser, Nancy, 'Equality, Difference and Democracy: Recent Feminist Debates in the United States' in Jodi Dean (ed.), *Feminism and the New Democracy* (Sage, 1997) 98

Fraser, Nancy 'Social Justice in the Age of Identity Politics' in Nancy Fraser and Axel Honneth (eds), *Redistribution or Recognition? A Political-Philosophical Exchange* (Verso, 2003) 7

Fredman, Sandra, 'Beyond the Dichotomy of Formal and Substantive Equality: Towards a New Definition of Equal Rights' in Ineke Boerefijn, Fons Coomans, Jenny E. Goldschmidt, Rikki Holtmaat and Ria Wolleswinkel (eds), *Temporary Special Measures: Accelerating de facto Equality of Women under Article 4(1) UN Convention on the Elimination of All Forms of Discrimination Against Women* (Intersentia, 2003) 111

Fredman, Sandra, 'Positive Rights and Duties: Addressing Intersectionality' in Dagmar Schiek and Victoria Chege (eds), *European Union Non-Discrimination Law: Comparative Perspectives on Multidimensional Equality Law* (2008, Routledge-Cavendish) 73

Fredman, Sandra, 'Engendering Social and Economic Rights' in Beth Goldblatt and Kirsty McLean (eds), *Women's Social and Economic Rights: Developments in South Africa* (Juta, 2011) 4

Fredman, Sandra, 'Engendering Social Welfare Rights' in Beth Goldblatt and Lucie Lamarche (eds), *Women's Rights to Social Security and Social Protection* (Hart, 2014) 19

Goldblatt, Beth, 'The Right to Social Security – Addressing Women's Poverty and Disadvantage' in Beth Goldblatt and Kirsty McLean (eds), *Women's Social and Economic Rights: Developments in South Africa* (Juta, 2011) 34

Goldblatt, Beth and Lucie Lamarche, 'Introduction: Interpreting and Advancing Women's Rights to Social Security and Social Protection' in Beth Goldblatt and Lucie Lamarche (eds), *Women's Rights to Social Security and Social Protection* (Hart, 2014) 1

Goldblatt, Beth and Solange Rosa, 'Social Security Rights – Campaigns and Courts' in Malcolm Langford, Ben Cousins, Jackie Dugard and Tshepo Madlingozi (eds), *Socio-Economic Rights in South Africa: symbols or substance?* (Cambridge University Press, 2014) 253

Gonsalves, Colin, 'Reflections on the Indian Experience' in John Squires, Malcolm Langford and Bret Thiele (eds), *The Road to a Remedy: Current Issues in the Litigation of Economic, Social and Cultural Rights* (UNSW Press, 2005) 177

Hassim, Shireen, 'Gender Equality and Developmental Social Welfare in South Africa' in Shahra Razavi and Shireen Hassim (eds), *Gender and Social Policy in a Global Context: Uncovering the Gendered Structure of 'the Social'* (Palgrave and UNRISD, 2006) 109

Hobson, Barbara, 'The Evolution of the Women-friendly State: Opportunities and Constraints in the Swedish Welfare State' in Shahra Razavi and Shireen Hassim (eds), *Gender and Social Policy in a Global Context: Uncovering the Gendered Structure of 'the Social'* (Palgrave Macmillan, 2006) 151

Holtmaat, Rikki, 'Article 5' in Marsha A Freeman, Christine Chinkin and Beate Rudolf (eds), *The UN Convention on the Elimination of All Forms of Discrimination Against Women: A Commentary* (Oxford University Press, 2012) 141

Jansen van Rensburg, Linda and Lucie Lamarche, 'The Right to Social Security and Assistance' in Danie Brand and Christof Heyns (eds), *Socio-Economic Rights in South Africa* (PULP, 2005) 209

Jayaram, N., 'Caste, Corporate Disabilities and Compensatory Discrimination in India: Colonial Legacy and Post-Colonial Paradox' in James Midgley and David Pichaud (eds), *Colonialism and Welfare: Social Policy and the British Imperial Legacy* (Edward Elgar, 2011) 85

Jensen, Robert T., 'Caste, Culture, and the Status and Well-Being of Widows in India' in David A. Wise (ed.), *Analyses in the Economics of Aging* (University of Chicago Press, 2005) 357

Khaliq, Urfan and Robin Churchill, 'The European Committee of Social Rights – Putting Flesh on the Bare Bones of the European Social Charter' in Malcolm Langford (ed.), *Social Rights Jurisprudence: Emerging Trends in International and Comparative Law* (Cambridge University Press, 2008) 428

Khera, Reetika and Nandini Nayak, 'Women Workers and Perceptions of the NREGA' in Reetika Khera (ed.), *The Battle for Employment Guarantee* (Oxford University Press, 2011) 81

Kulke, Ursula, Michael Cichon and Karuna Pal, 'Changing Tides: A Revival of a Rights-Based Approach to Social Security' in Jef Van Langendonck (ed.), *The Right to Social Security* (Intersentia, 2007) 13

Lacey, Nicola, 'Feminist Legal Theory and the Rights of Women' in Karen Knop (ed.), *Gender and Human Rights* (Oxford University Press, 2004) 13

Lamarche, Lucie, 'Unpacking the ILO's Social Protection Floor Recommendation from a Women's Rights Perspective' in Beth Goldblatt and Lucie Lamarche (eds), *Women's Rights to Social Security and Social Protection* (Hart, 2014) 65

Lamarche, Lucie, 'The Right to Social Security in the International Covenenant on Economic, Social and Culural Rights' in Audrey Chapman and Sage Russell (eds), *Core Obligations: Building a Framework for Economic, Social and Cultural Rights* (Intersentia, 2002) 87

Lamarche, Lucie, 'Social Protection is a Matter of Human Rights: Exploring the ICESCR Right to Social Security in the Context of Globalisation' in Koen De Feyter and Felipe Gomez Isa (eds), *Privatisation and Human Rights in the Age of Globalisation* (Intersentia, 2005) 129

Langford, Malcolm and Jeff A. King, 'Committee on Economic, Social and Cultural Rights: Past, Present and Future' in Malcolm Langford (ed.), *Social Rights Jurisprudence: Emerging Trends in International and Comparative Law* (Cambridge University Press, 2008) 447

Langford, Malcolm, 'The Right to Social Security and Implications for Law, Policy and Practice' in Eibe Reidel (ed.), *Social Security as a Human Right* (Springer, 2007) 29

Lessard, Hester, 'Participatory Inclusion and Women's Rights to Social Security' in Beth Goldblatt and Lucie Lamarche (eds), *Women's Rights to Social Security and Social Protection* (Hart, 2014) 41

Li, Mankui, 'Social Protection in China: Is There a Gender Equality Problem?' in Beth Goldblatt and Lucie Lamarche (eds), *Interpreting and Advancing Women's Rights to Social Security and Social Protection* (Hart, 2014) 89

Liebenberg, Sandra, 'The Judicial Enforcement of Social Security Rights in South Africa: Enhancing Accountability for the Basic Needs of the Poor' in Eibe Reidel (ed.), *Social Security as a Human Right: Drafting a General Comment on Article 9 ICESCR – Some Challenges* (Springer, 2007) 69

Mikkola, Matti, 'Common Denominators of European Social Security' in Jef van Langendonck (ed.), *The Right to Social Security* (Intersentia, 2007) 225

Naffine, Ngaire, 'Sexing the Subject (of Law)' in Margaret Thornton (ed.), *Public and Private: Feminist Legal Debates* (Oxford University Press, 1995) 18

Nedelsky, Jennifer, 'The Gendered Division of Household Labor: An Issue of Constitutional Rights' in Beverley Baines, Daphne Barak-Erez and Tsvi Kahana (eds), *Feminist Constitutionalism: Global Perspectives* (Cambridge University Press, 2012) 15

Nuβberger, Angelika, 'Evaluating the ILO's Approach to Standard-Setting and Monitoring in the Field of Social Security' in Eibe Reidel (ed.), *Social Security as a Human Right* (Springer, 2007) 103

Nussbaum, Martha, 'Women's Capabilities and Social Justice' in Maxine Molyneux and Shahra Razavi (eds), *Gender Justice, Development, and Rights* (Oxford University Press, 2002) 45

Nussbaum, Martha, 'India, Sex Equality and Constitutional Law' in Beverley Baines and Ruth Rubio-Marin (eds), *The Gender of Constitutional Jurisprudence* (Cambridge University Press, 2005) 174

Orloff, Ann, 'Should Feminists Aim for Gender Symmetry? Why a Dual-Earner/

Dual-Caregiver Society Is Not Every Feminist's Utopia' in Janet C. Gornick and Marcia K. Meyers (eds), *Gender Equality: Transforming Family Divisions of Labor* (Verso, 2009) 129

Otto, Dianne, 'Defending Women's Economic and Social Rights: Some Thoughts on Indivisibility and a New Standard of Equality' in Isfahan Merali and Valerie Oosterveld (eds), *Giving Meaning to Economic, Social and Cultural Rights* (University of Pennsylvania Press, 2001) 52

Otto, Dianne, 'Disconcerting "Masculinities": Reinventing the Gendered Subject(s) of International Human Rights Law' in Doris Buss and Ambreena Manji (eds), *International Law: Modern Feminist Approaches* (Hart, 2005) 105

Otto, Dianne, 'Women's Rights' in Daniel Moeckli, Sangeeta Shah and Sandesh Sivakumaran (eds), *International Human Rights Law* (Oxford University Press, 2010) 345

Otto, Dianne, 'International Human Rights Law: Towards Rethinking Sex/Gender Dualism' in Margaret Davies and Vanessa E. Munroe (eds), *The Ashgate Research Companion to Feminist Legal Theory* (Ashgate, 2013) 197

Otto, Dianne, 'Gendering the Right to Social Security in the Era of Crisis Governance: The Need for Transformative Strategies' in Beth Goldblatt and Lucie Lamarche (eds), *Women's Rights to Social Security and Social Protection* (Hart, 2014) 215

Papola, T.S. and Alakh N. Sharma, 'Labour and Employment in a Fast Growing Country: Issues of Employment and Inclusiveness' in Alexandre Barbosa and Maria Cristina Cacciamali (eds), *The "Dynamic South", Economic Development and Inclusive Growth: The Challenges Ahead* (IDRC, CEBRAP and ABET, 2013) 89

Patel, Leila, 'Race, Inequality and Social welfare: South Africa's Imperial Legacy' in James Midgley and David Pichaud (eds), *Colonialism and Welfare: Social Policy and the British Imperial Legacy* (Edward Elgar, 2011) 71

Pateman, Carole, 'The Patriarchal Welfare State' in Carole Pateman (ed.), *The Disorder of Women* (Polity Press, 1989) 179

Raday, Frances, 'Article 11' in Marsha A. Freeman, Christine Chinkin and Beate Rudolf (eds), *The UN Convention on the Elimination of All Forms of Discrimination Against Women: A Commentary* (Oxford University Press, 2012) 279

Reidel, Eibe, 'The Human Right to Social Security: Some Challenges' in Eibe Reidel (ed.), *Social Security as a Human Right* (Springer, 2007) 17

Reynaud, Emmanuel, 'The Right to Social Security – Current Challenges in International Perspective' in Eibe Reidel (ed.), *Social Security as a Human Right* (Springer, 2007) 1

Rudolf, Beate, 'Article 13' in Marsha A. Freeman, Christine Chinkin and Beate Rudolf (eds), *The UN Convention on the Elimination of All Forms of Discrimination Against Women: A Commentary* (Oxford University Press, 2012) 335

Scheinin, Martin, 'The Right to Social Security' in Asbjorn Eide, Catarina Krause and Allan Rosas (eds), *Economic, Social and Cultural Rights: A Textbook* (Martinus Nijhoff Publishers, Revised 2nd edn, 2001) 211

Scheinin, Martin, 'Human Rights Committee – Not Only a Committee on Civil and Political Rights' in Malcolm Langford (ed.), *Social Rights Jurisprudence* (Cambridge University Press, 2008) 540

Sen, Gita and D. Rajasekhar, 'Social Protection Policies, Experiences and Challenges' in R. Nagaraj (ed.), *Growth, Inequality and Social Development in India: Is Inclusive Growth Possible?* (Palgrave Macmillan and UNRISD, 2012) 91

Sinha, Shalini, 'Social Security for Women Workers in the Informal Economy: SEWA's Social Security Programme' in Eibe Reidel (ed.), *Social Security as a Human Right:*

Drafting a General Comment on Article 9 ICESCR – Some Challenges (Springer, 2007) 117

Smith, Belinda, 'What Would an Engendered Human Rights Approach to Social Security Mean for Sole Parents in Australia?' in Beth Goldblatt and Lucie Lamarche (eds), *Women's Rights to Social Security and Social Protection* (Hart, 2014) 191

Stewart, Miranda, 'Women and Tax' in Patricia Easteal (ed.), *Women and the Law in Australia* (LexisNexis Butterworths, 2010) 441

Tooze, Jennifer, 'The Rights to Social Security and Social Assistance: Towards an Analytical Framework' in Mashood A. Baderin and Robert McCorquodale (eds), *Economic, Social and Cultural Rights in Action* (Oxford University Press, 2007) 331

Townsend, Peter, 'Social Security and Human Rights' in Peter Townsend (ed.), *Building Decent Societies: Rethinking the Role of Social Security in Development* (Palgrave Macmillan, 2009) 29

Van Langendonck, Jef, 'The Meaning of the Right to Social Security' in Jef Van Langendonck (ed.), *The Right to Social Security* (Intersentia, 2007) 3

van Marle, Karin and Elsje Bonthuys, 'Feminist Theories and Concepts' in Elsje Bonthuys and Catherine Albertyn (eds), *Gender, Law and Justice* (Juta, 2007) 15

Vijay Shankar, P.S. and Mihir Shah, 'Rethinking Reforms: A New Vision for the Social Sector in India' in R. Nagaraj (ed.), *Growth, Inequality and Social Development in India: Is Inclusive Growth Possible?* (Palgrave Macmillan and UNRISD, 2012) 135

Watson, Philippa, 'European Court of Justice – Creative Responses in Uncharted Territory' in Malcolm Langford (ed.), *Social Rights Jurisprudence: Emerging Trends in International and Comparative Law* (Cambridge University Press, 2008) 453

Williams, Lucy A., 'Rethinking Social Protection Beyond Waged Work: A United States Perspective' in Beth Goldblatt and Lucie Lamarche (eds), *Women's Rights to Social Security and Social Protection* (Hart, 2014) 145

Williams, Susan H., 'Customary Law, Constitutional Law, and Women's Equality' in Kim Rubenstein and Katherine Young (eds), *The Public Law of Gender: From the Local to the Global* (Cambridge University Press, 2016) forthcoming.

Zeffert, Henrietta, 'Identifying the Invisible: Women's Human Rights and Substantive Gender Equality in Australia' in Paula Gerber and Melissa Castan (eds), *Contemporary Perspectives on Human Rights Law in Australia* (Thomson Reuters, 2013) 223

Edited books

Arellano Ortiz, Pablo, Marius Olivier and Gijsbert Vonk (eds), *Social Security and Migrant Workers: Selected Studies of Cross-Border Social Security Mechanisms* (Kluwer Law International, 2013)

Balakrishnan, Radhika and Diane Elson (eds), *Economic Policy and Human Rights: Holding Governments to Account* (Zed Books, 2011)

Boyd, Susan (ed.), *Challenging the Public/Private Divide: Feminism, Law, and Public Policy* (University of Toronto Press, 1997)

Ehrenreich, Barbara and Arlie Russell Hochschild (eds), *Global Woman: Nannies, Maids, and Sex Workers in the New Economy* (Metropolitan/Holt, 2002)

Goldblatt, Beth and Kirsty McLean (eds), *Women's Social and Economic Rights: Developments in South Africa* (Juta, 2011)

Goldblatt, Beth and Lucie Lamarche (eds), *Women's Rights to Social Security and Social Protection* (Hart, 2014)

Gordon, Linda (ed.), *Women, the State, and Welfare* (University of Wisconsin Press, 1990)

Khera, Reetika (ed.), *The Battle for Employment Guarantee* (Oxford University Press, 2011)

Kouvo, Sari and Zoe Pearson (eds), *Feminist Perspectives on Contemporary International Law: Between Resistance and Compliance?* (Hart, 2011)

O'Halloran, Maree (ed.), *The Independent Social Security Handbook* (Welfare Rights Centre, 7th edn, 2012)

Pennings, Frans (ed.), *Between Soft and Hard Law: The Impact of Social Security Standards on National Social Security Law*, Studies in Employment and Social Policy (Kluwer Law International, 2006)

Pogge, Thomas (ed.), *Freedom From Poverty as a Human Right: Who Owes What to the Very Poor?* (Oxford University Press, 2007)

Quinot, Geo and Sandra Liebenberg (eds), *Law and Poverty: Perspectives from South Africa and Beyond* (Juta, 2012)

Razavi, Shahra and Shireen Hassim (eds), *Gender and Social Policy in a Global Context: Uncovering the Gendered Structure of 'the Social'* (Palgrave Macmillan, 2006)

Reidel, Eibe (ed.), *Social Security as a Human Right: Drafting a General Comment on Article 9 ICESCR – Some Challenges* (Springer, 2007)

Sainsbury, Diane (ed.), *Gendering Welfare States* (Sage, 1994)

Spaventa, Eleanor and Michael Dougan (eds), *Social Welfare and EU Law* (Hart, 2005)

Townsend, Peter (ed.), *Building Decent Societies: Rethinking the Role of Social Security in Development* (Palgrave Macmillian, 2009)

Van Langendonck, Jef (ed.), *The Right to Social Security* (Intersentia, 2007)

Williams, Lucy (ed.), *International Poverty Law: An Emerging Discourse* (Zed Books, 2006)

Yadav, J.P. (ed.), *Human Rights and Social Security* (Institute for Sustainable Development, 2004)

Young, Margot, Susan B. Boyd, Gwen Brodsky and Shelagh Day (eds), *Poverty: Rights, Social Citizenship, and Legal Activism* (UBC Press, 2007)

Journal articles

Albertyn, Catherine and Beth Goldblatt, 'Facing the challenge of transformation: difficulties in the development of an indigenous jurisprudence of equality' (1998) 14 *South African Journal on Human Rights* 248

Albertyn, Catherine, 'Substantive equality and transformation in South Africa' (2007) 23(2) *South African Journal on Human Rights* 253

Albertyn, Catherine, Sandra Fredman and Judy Fudge, 'Special issue: substantive equality, social rights and women: a comparative perspective' (2007) 23(2) *South African Journal on Human Rights* 209

Albertyn, Catherine, 'Gendered transformation in South African jurisprudence: poor women and the constitutional court' (2011) 3 *Stellenbosch Law Review* 591

Arun, Shoba and T.G. Arun, 'Gender issues in social security policy of developing countries: lessons from the Kerala experience' (2001) 54(4/2001) *International Social Security Review* 93

Barrientos, Armando, 'Conditions in antipoverty programmes' (2011) 19(1) *Journal of Poverty and Social Justice* 15

Bradshaw, Sarah, 'From structural adjustment to social adjustment: a gendered analysis of conditional cash transfer programmes in Mexico and Nicaragua' (2008) 8(2) (August 1, 2008) *Global Social Policy* 188

Brennan, Deborah, 'Babies, budgets, and birthrates: work/family policy in Australia 1996–2006' (2007) 14(1) *Social Politics: International Studies in Gender, State and Society* 31

Brodsky, Gwen, 'Gosselin v. Quebec (Attorney General): autonomy with a vengeance' (2003) 15(1) *Canadian Journal of Women and the Law* 194

Brodsky, Gwen and Shelagh Day, 'Beyond the social and economic rights debate: substantive equality speaks to poverty' (2002) 14(1) *Canadian Journal of Women and the Law* 185

Brodsky, Gwen and Shelagh Day, 'Denial of the means of susbistence as an equality violation' (2005) 2005 *Acta Juridica* 149

Brodsky, Gwen, Rachel Cox, Shelagh Day and M. Kate Stephenson 'Gosselin v. Quebec (Attorney General)' (2006) 18 *Canadian Journal of Women and the Law* 189

Brown, Wendy, 'The most we can hope for ...: human rights and the politics of fatalism' (2004) 103 *South Atlantic Quarterly* 451

Budlender, Debbie, 'Women and poverty' (2005) 64 *Agenda* 30

Budlender, Debbie and Francie Lund, 'South Africa: a legacy of family disruption' (2011) 42(4) *Development and Change* 925

Butler, Judith, 'Performative acts and gender constitution: an essay in phenomenology and feminist theory' (1988) 40(4) *Theatre Journal* 519

Byrnes, Andrew, 'Second-class rights yet again? Economic, social and cultural rights in the report of the National Human Rights Consultation' (2010) 33(1) *UNSW Law Journal* 193

Carney, Terry, 'Neoliberal welfare reform and "rights" compliance' (2006) 12(1) *Australian Journal of Human Rights* 223

Cass, Bettina, 'Citizenship, work, and welfare: the dilemma for Australian women' (1994) *Social Politics* 106

Chant, Sylvia, 'Re-thinking the "Feminization of Poverty" in relation to aggregate gender indices' (2006) 7(2) *Journal of Human Development* 201

Chant, Sylvia, 'The "Feminisation of Poverty" and the "Feminisation" of anti-poverty programmes: room for revision?' (2008) 44(2) *Journal of Development Studies* 165

Charlesworth, Hilary, Christine Chinkin and Shelley Wright, 'Feminist approaches to international law' (1991) 85(4) *The American Journal of International Law* 613

Chenoweth, Lesley, 'Redefining welfare: Australian social policy and practice' (2008) 2(1) *Asian Social Work and Policy Review* 53

Conaghan, Joanne, 'Reassessing the feminist theoretical project in law' (2000) 27(3) *Journal of Law and Society* 351

Conaghan, Joanne, 'Gender and the idea of labour law' (2014) 4(1) *feminists@law* 1

Cornwall, Andrea and Maxine Molyneux, 'The politics of rights – dilemmas for feminist praxis: an introduction' (2006) 27(7) *Third World Quarterly* 1175

Cortis, Natasha and Gabrielle Meagher, 'Women, work and welfare in the activation state: an agenda for Australian research' (2009) 35(4) *Australian Bulletin of Labour* 629

Cox, Eva, 'Evidence-free policy making? The case of income management' (2011) 12 *Journal of Indigenous Policy* 1

Crenshaw, Kimberle, 'Demarginalizing the intersection of race and sex: a black feminist critique of antidiscrimination doctrine, feminist theory and antiracist politics' (1989) *University of Chicago Legal Forum* 139

Cullen, Holly, 'The collective complaints system of the European social charter: interpretative methods of the European Committee of Social Rights' (2009) 9(1) *Human Rights Law Review* 61

Davy, Ulrike, 'Social citizenship going international: changes in the reading of UN-sponsored economic and social rights' (2013) 22 *International Journal of Social Welfare* S15

De Schutter, Olivier et al., 'Commentary to the Maastricht principles on extraterritorial obligations of states in the area of economic, social and cultural rights' (2012) 34 *Human Rights Quarterly* 1084

de Villiers, Nick, 'Procedural fairness and reasonable administrative action within the social assistance system: implications of some settled class actions' (2006) 22 *South African Journal on Human Rights* 405

Dixon, Rosalind, 'Feminist disagreement (comparatively) recast' (2008) 31 *Harvard Journal of Law and Gender* 277

Doz Costa, Fernanda, 'Poverty and human rights: from rhetoric to legal obligations – a critical account of conceptual frameworks' (2008) Year 5(9) *SUR – International Journal on Human Rights* 81

Dupper, Ockert, Marius Olivier and Avinash Govindjee, 'Extending coverage of the unemployment insurance-system in South Africa' (2010) 21 *Stellenbosch Law Review* 438

Dupper, O., K. Malherbe, B. Shipman and E. Bolani, 'The case for increased reform of South African family and maternity benefits' (2000) 4(1) *Law, Democracy and Development* 27

Dutta, Tina and Parthapratim Pal, 'Politics overpowering welfare: Unorganised Workers' Social Security Act 2008' (2012) XLVII(7) *Economic and Political Weekly* 26

Dutta, Puja, Stephen Howes and Rinku Murgai, 'Small but effective: India's targeted unconditional cash transfers' (2010) XLV(52) *Economic and Political Weekly* 63

Elson, Diane and Jasmine Gideon, 'Organising for women's economic and social rights: how useful is the International Covenant on Economic, Social and Cultural Rights?' (2004) 8(1&2) *Journal of Interdisciplinary Gender Studies* 133

Fineman, Martha Albertson, 'The vulnerable subject and the responsive state' (2010) 60 *Emory Law Journal* 251

Fineman, Martha Albertson, 'Gender and law: feminist legal theory's role in the new legal realism' (2005) 2005 *Wisconsin Law Review* 405

Fineman, Martha Albertson, 'Contract and care' (2001) 76 *Chicago-Kent Law Review* 1403

Finley, Lucinda M., 'Breaking women's silence in law: the dilemma of the gendered nature of legal reasoning' (1989) 64 *Notre Dame Law Review* 886

Forster, Christine M. and Vedna Jivan, 'Public interest litigation and human rights implementation: the Indian and Australian experience' (2008) 3(1) *Asian Journal of Comparative Law* 1

Franke, Katherine M, 'The central mistake of sex discrimination law: the disaggregation of sex from gender' (1995) 144(1) *University of Pennsylvania Law Review* 1

Fraser, Nancy, 'After the family wage: gender equity and the welfare state' (1994) 22(4) *Political Theory* 591

Fraser, Nancy, 'Injustice at intersecting scales: on "social exclusion" and the "global poor"' (2010) 13(3) *European Journal of Social Theory* 363

Fraser, Nancy, 'Social exclusion, global poverty, and scales of (in)justice: rethinking law and poverty in a globalizing world' (2011) 3 *Stellenbosch Law Review* 452

Fraser, Nancy and Linda Gordon, 'A genealogy of dependency: tracing a keyword of the U.S. welfare state' (1994) 19(2) *Signs* 309

Fredman, Sandra, 'The potential and limits of an equal rights paradigm in addressing poverty' (2011) 3 *Stellenbosch Law Review* 566

Fudge, Judy, 'Global care chains, employment agencies and the conundrum of jurisdiction: decent work for domestic workers in Canada' (2011) 23 *Canadian Journal of Women and the Law* 235

Fudge, Judy, 'Precarious migrant status and precarious employment: the paradox of international rights for migrant workers' (2012) 34(1) *Comparative Labor Law and Policy Journal* 95

Gauri, Varun, 'Fundamental rights and public interest litigation in India: overreaching or underachieving?' (2010) 1(1) *Indian Journal of Law and Economics* 71

Gideon, Jasmine, 'Accessing economic and social rights under neoliberalism: gender and rights in Chile' (2006) 22(7) *Third World Quarterly* 1269

Goldblatt, Beth, 'Teen pregancy and abuse of the Child Support Grant: addressing the myths and stereotypes' (2003) 17(56) *Agenda: Empowering Women for Gender Equity* 79

Goldblatt, Beth, 'Gender and social assistance in the first decade of democracy: a case study of South Africa's Child Support Grant' (2005) 32(2) *Politikon* 239

Goldblatt, Beth, 'Gender, rights and the disability grant in South Africa' (2009) 26(3) *Development Southern Africa* 369

Goldblatt, Beth, 'Gender, poverty and the development of the right to social security' (2014) 10(4) *International Journal of Law in Context* 460

Goldblatt, Beth, 'Social security in South Africa – a gender and human rights analysis' (2014) 47(1) *Verfassung und Recht in Übersee VRÜ* 22

Goldblatt, Beth, 'Intersectionality in international anti-discrimination law – addressing poverty in its complexity' (2015) 21(1) *Australian Journal of Human Rights* 47

Golder, Ben, 'Beyond redemption? Problematizing the critique of human rights in contemporary international legal thought' (2014) 2(1) *London Review of International Law* 77

Gopal, Meena, 'Gender, ageing and social security' (2006) 41(42) *Economic and Political Weekly* 4477

Goswami, Paromita, 'A critique of the Unorganised Workers' Social Security Act' (2009) XLIV(11) (March 14, 2009) *Economic and Political Weekly* 17

Govindjee, Avinash and Ockert Dupper, 'Constitutional perspectives on unemployment security and a right to work in South Africa' (2011) 23 *Stellenbosch Law Review* 775

Govinjdee, Avinash, Marius Olivier and Ockert Dupper, 'Activation in the context of the unemployment insurance system in South Africa' (2011) 22 *Stellenbosch Law Review* 205

Grahame, Teresa and Greg Marston, 'Welfare-to-work policies and the experience of employed single mothers on income support in Australia: where are the benefits?' (2012) 65(1) *Australian Social Work* 73

Harris, Angela, 'Race and essentialism in feminist legal theory' (1989–1990) 42 *Stanford Law Review* 581

Hassim, Shireen, 'Global constraints on gender equality in care work' (2008) 36(3) *Politics and Society* 388

Hirway, Indira and Sunny Jose, 'Understanding women's work using time-use statistics: the case of India' (2011) 17(4) *Feminist Economics* 67

Hodgson, Helen and Rebecca Boden, 'Not-so-distant cousins: family benefits in the United Kingdom and Australia' (2008) 61(3) *International Social Security Review* 29

Kapur, Ratna, 'The tragedy of victimisation rhetoric: resurrecting the "native" subject in international/postcolonial feminist legal politics' (2002) 15 *Harvard Human Rights Law Journal* 1

Kasente, Deborah, 'Gender and social security reform in Africa' (2000) 53(3) *International Social Security Review* 27

Kennedy, David, 'The international human rights movement: part of the problem?' (2002) 15 *Harvard Human Rights Journal* 101

Khera, Reetika, 'Mid-day meals in primary schools: achievements and challenges' (2006) 41(46) *Economic and Political Weekly* 4742

Khosla, Madhav, 'Making social rights conditional: lessons from India' (2010) 8(4) *International Journal of Constitutional Law* 739

Klein, Marlee, 'Race, racism, and feminist legal theory' (1989) 12 *Harvard Women's Law Journal* 115

Kothari, Jayna, 'A social rights model for social security: learnings from India' (2014) 1 *Verfassung und Recht in Ubersee* 5

Kotiswaran, Prabha, 'Abject labors, informal markets: revisiting the law's (re)production boundary', (2014) 18(1) *Employee Rights and Employment Law Journal*, 353

Lacey, Nicola, 'Theories of justice and the welfare state' (1992) 1 *Social and Legal Studies* 323

Lahariya, Chandrakant, 'Cash incentives for institutional delivery: linking with antenatal and post natal care may ensure "continuum of care" in India' (2009) 34(1) *Indian Journal of Community Medicine* 15

Lamarche, Lucie, 'Le *Pacte international relatif aux droits économiques, sociaux et culturels*, les femmes et le droit à la sécurité sociale: des considérations et des propositions pour un droit "universel" à la sécurité sociale' (2002) 14(1) *Canadian Journal of Women and the Law* 53

Liebenberg, Sandra, 'Value of human dignity in interpreting socio-economic rights' (2005) 21(1) *South African Journal on Human Rights* 1

Liebenberg, Sandra and Beth Goldblatt, 'The interrelationship between equality and socio-economic rights in South Africa's transformative constitution' (2007) 23 *South African Journal on Human Rights* 335

Lim Stephen S., Lalit Dandona, Joseph A. Hoisington, Spencer L. James, Margaret C. Hogan and Emmanuela Gakidou, 'India's Janani Suraksha Yojana, a conditional cash transfer programme to increase births in health facilities: an impact evaluation' (2010) 375(9730) *The Lancet* 2009

'Limburg Principles on the implementation of the International Covenant on Economic, Social and Cultural Rights' (1987) 9 *Human Rights Quarterly* 122

Lister, Ruth, 'A Nordic nirvana? Gender, citizenship, and social justice in the Nordic welfare states' (2009) 16(2) (June 20, 2009) *Social Politics: International Studies in Gender, State and Society* 242

Luckhaus, Linda, 'Equal treatment, social protection and income security for women' (2000) 139(2) *International Labour Review* 149

Lund, Francie, 'A step in the wrong direction: linking the South African Child Support Grant to school attendance' (2011) 19(1) *Journal of Poverty and Social Justice* 5

Lund, Francie, Michael Noble, Helen Barnes and Gemma Wright, 'Is there a rationale for conditional cash transfers for children in South Africa?' (2009) 70 *Transformation* 70

'Maastricht guidelines on violations of economic, social and cultural rights' (1998) 20 *Human Rights Quarterly* 691

Malherbe, Kitty and Lorenzo Wakefield, 'The effect of women's care-giving role on their social security rights' (2009) 2009 *Law, Democracy and Development* 47

Mendes, Philip, 'Compulsory income management: a critical examination of the emergence of conditional welfare in Australia' (2012) *Australian Social Work* 1

Mishra, Ramesh, 'Social rights as human rights: globalizing social protection' (2005) 48(1) (January 1, 2005) *International Social Work* 9

Molyneux, Maxine, 'Mothers at the service of the new poverty agenda: *Progresa/ Oportunidades*, Mexico's conditional transfer programme' (2006) 40(4) *Social Policy and Administration* 425

'Montreal principles on women's economic, social and cultural rights' (2004) 26 *Human Rights Quarterly* 760

Narayan, Sudha, 'Employment guarantee, women's work and childcare' (2008) 43(9) (1–7 March 2008) *Economic and Political Weekly* 10

Nussbaum, Martha, 'Capabilities and human rights' (1997) 66(2) *Fordham Law Review* 273

Olivier, Marius, 'International labour and social security standards: a developing country critique' (2013) 29(1) *The International Journal of Comparative Labour Law and Industrial Relations* 21

Olivier, Marius, Ockert Dupper and Avinash Govindjee, 'Redesigning the South African unemployment insurance fund: selected key policy and legal perspectives' (2011) 22 *Stellenbosch Law Review* 396

Oloka-Onyango, J. and Sylvia Tamale, '"The personal is political", or why women's rights are indeed human rights: an African perspective on international feminism' (1995) 17 *Human Rights Quarterly* 691

Olsen, Frances, 'The family and the market: a study of ideology and legal reform' (1983) 96 *Harvard Law Review* 1497

Orloff, Ann, 'Gender and the social rights of citizenship: the comparative analysis of gender relations and welfare states' (1993) 58(3) *American Sociological Review* 303

Otto, Dianne, 'Gender comment: why does the UN Committee on Economic, Social and Cultural Rights need a general comment on women?' (2002) 14(1) *Canadian Journal of Women and the Law* 1

Partridge, Emma, Sarah Maddison and Alistair Nicholson, 'Human rights imperatives and the failings of the Stronger Futures consultation process' (2013) 18(2) *Australian Journal of Human Rights* 21

Patel, Leila and Tessa Hochfeld, 'It buys food but does it change gender relations? Child Support Grants in Soweto, South Africa' (2011) 19(2) *Gender and Development* 229

Pateman, Carole, 'Democratizing citizenship: some advantages of a basic income' (2004) 32(1) *Politics and Society* 89

Pellissery, Sony and Armando Barrientos, 'Expansion of social assistance: does politics matter?' (2013) XLVIII(9) *Economic and Political Weekly* 47

Pogge, Thomas, 'Are we violating the human rights of the world's poor?' (2011) 14(2) *Yale Human Rights and Development Law Journal* 1

Pruitt, Lisa, 'Gender, geography and rural justice' (2008) 23 *Berkeley Journal of Gender, Law and Justice* 338

Razavi, Shahra, 'Engendering social security and protection: challenges for making social security and protection gender equitable' (2011) *Dialogue on Globalization (Friedrich Ebert Stiftung)* 1

Razavi, Shahra, 'Rethinking care in a development context: an introduction' (2011) 42(4) *Development and Change* 873

Sankaran, Kamala, 'Special provisions and access to socio-economic rights: women and the Indian constitution' (2007) 23(2) *South African Journal on Human Rights* 277

Saunders, Peter and Chris Deeming, 'The impact of the crisis on Australian social security policy in historical perspective' (2011) 45(4) *Social Policy and Administration* 371

Sen, Amartya, 'Elements of a theory of human rights' (2004) 32(4) *Philosophy and Public Affairs* 315

Sen, Amartya, 'Human rights and capabilities' (2005) 6(2) *Journal of Human Development* 151

Shaver, Sheila, 'Australian welfare reform: from citizenship to supervision' (2002) 36(4) *Social Policy and Administration* 331

Smart, Carole, 'Shifting horizons: reflections on qualitative methods' (2009) 10(3) *Feminist Theory* 295

Sood, Avani Mehta, 'Gender justice through public interest litigation: case studies from India' (2008) 41 *Vanderbilt Journal of Transnational Law* 833

Srivastava, Nisha and Ravi Srivastava, 'Women, work, and employment outcomes in rural India' (2010) XLV(28) *Economic and Political Weekly* 49

Standing, Guy, 'Behavioural conditionality: why the nudges must be stopped – an opinion piece' (2011) 19(1) *Journal of Poverty and Social Justice* 27

Walsh, Tamara, 'Breaching the right to social security' (2003) 12(1) *Griffith Law Review* 43

Watson, Nicole, 'The northern territory emergency response – has it really improved the lives of aboriginal women and children?' (2011) 35 *Australian Feminist Law Journal* 147

West, Robin, 'Rights, capabilities and the good society' (2001) 69 *Fordham Law Review* 1901

Whiteford, Peter, 'Poverty in a time of prosperity' (2012) 21(2) *Human Rights Defender* 7

Williams, Christine L., Chandra Muller and Kristine Kilanski, 'Gendered organizations in the new economy' (2012) 26 *Gender and Society*, 549

Williams, George and Lisa Burton, 'Australia's exclusive parliamentary model of rights protection' (2013) 34(1) *Statute Law Review* 58

Williams, Lucy, 'Issues and challenges in addressing poverty and legal rights: a comparative United States/South Africa analysis' (2005) 21 *South African Journal on Human Rights* 436

Williams, Lucy, 'The legal construction of poverty: gender, "work" and the "social contract"' (2011) 2011(3) *Stelllenbosch Law Review* 463

Williams, Lucy, 'Race, rat bites and unfit mothers: how media discourse informs welfare legislation debate' (1994) 22(4) *Fordham Urban Law Journal* 1159

Electronic articles

Baird, M., S. Charlesworth, R. Cooper and A. Heron, 'Women, Work and the Global Economic Downturn' (2011) www.fahcsia.gov.au/our-responsibilities/women/publications-articles/general/women-work-and-the-global-economic-downturn?HTML#fn_13

Cox, Eva, 'Let's acknowledge Abbott's parental leave plan is better' (2013) *Crickey*, www.crikey.com.au/2013/05/08/cox-lets-acknowledge-abbotts-parental-leave-plan-is-better/

Cox, Eva, 'What the Government Wants to Ignore about Sole Parents and Jobseeking' (2013) *The Conversation*, http://theconversation.edu.au/what-the-government-wants-to-ignore-about-sole-parents-and-jobseeking-11582

Cox, Eva and Terry Priest, 'Welfare to Work: At What Cost to Parenting?' (2008), http://pandora.nla.gov.au/pan/95161/20090223-1020/www.women.nsw.gov.au/PDF/Welfare_to_Work_At_what_cost_to_parenting.pdf

De Schutter, Olivier and Magdalena Sepúlveda, 'Underwriting the Poor – A Global Fund for Social Protection' (2012), www.srfood.org/images/stories/pdf/other documents/20121009_gfsp_en.pdf

Fan, Victoria, 'The Early Success of India's Health Insurance for the Poor, RSBY' (2013), www.cgdev.org/sites/default/files/early-success-indias-health-insurance.pdf

Lamarche, Lucie, 'The Canadian Experience and CEDAW: Internationalisation by Default' (2011), http://ssrn.com/abstract=1855734

Leahy, Mary, 'Women and Work in Australia' (2011) *Australian Policy Online*, http://apo.org.au/sites/default/files/Women_and_work_in_Australia_APO_guide_Mary_Leahy_0.pdf

Lynch, Phil, 'Australia's Duplicitous Approach to United Nations Treaty Bodies is Undermining Human Rights and The Rule Of Law' (2012) *The Drum*, www.abc.net.au/news/2012-08-13/lynch-human-rights/4190968

Lynch, Phil, 'Human Rights Movement Needs Better and Bolder Leaders' (2012) *The Drum*, www.abc.net.au/unleashed/4416618.html

Sen, Gita, 'Engendering Social Security and Protection: The Case of Asia' (2011) *International Policy Analysis* 1, http://library.fes.de/pdf-files/iez/08436.pdf

Whiteford, Peter, 'How Fair is Australia's Welfare State?' (2011) *Inside Story*, http://inside.org.au/how-fair-is-australia%E2%80%99s-welfare-state

Newspaper articles

Davis, Rebecca, 'Sky really is the limit: the lowdown on Alex Crawford's reporting' (2013) *Daily Maverick*, www.dailymaverick.co.za/article/2013-01-24-sky-really-is-the-limit-the-lowdown-on-alex-crawfords-reporting#.UW4ngqJmh8E

Faul, Michelle, '3 women killed each day in South Africa, world's worst gender violence', *The Star* 8 March 2013, www.thestar.com/news/world/2013/03/08/3_women_killed_each_day_in_south_africa_worlds_worst_gender_violence.html

Horin, Adele, 'To the labour ward in a Roller', *Sydney Morning Herald* 10 March 2012, www.smh.com.au/federal-politics/political-opinion/to-the-labour-ward-in-a-roller-20120309-1upmo.html

Karvelas, Patricia 'Single-mother cuts to hit hardest in PM's seat', *The Weekend Australian* 22–23 September 2012

Kleinman, Rachel, 'A single-minded struggle to get by', *Sydney Morning Herald* 23 August 2013, www.smh.com.au/federal-politics/federal-election-2013/a-singleminded-struggle-to-get-by-20130822-2se9f.html

Molyneux, Maxine, 'Cash transfers do not address the underlying causes of women's poverty', 2012 <http://www.theguardian.com/global-development/poverty-matters/2012/mar/07/cash-transfers-not-addressing-women-poverty>

O'Halloran, Maree, 'Working Single Parents Kicked', *The Australian* 6 March 2013

Staff Reporter, 'Govt. duty-bound to raise old-age pension', *The Hindu*, 18 January 2014, www.thehindu.com/todays-paper/tp-national/govt-dutybound-to-raise-oldage-pension/article5588657.ece

'Women to have more say in job scheme', *Deccan Herald* (Lucknow), 4 December 2012, www.deccanherald.com/content/296432/women-have-more-say-job.html

Reports

Aggarwal, Alison and Vedna Jivan, 'Consideration of Women's Equality to Economic Social and Cultural Rights by the CEDAW Committee' (International Women's Action Rights Watch – Asia Pacific, 2010)

Alderman, Harold and Christina H. Paxson, 'Do the Poor Insure? A Synthesis of the Literature on Risk and Consumption in Developing Countries' (Policy Research Working Paper Series No 1008, World Bank, 1992)

Australian Council of Social Service, 'Poverty in Australia' (Australian Council of Social Service, 2012)

Australian Human Rights Commission, 'Stronger Futures in the Northern Territory Bill 2011 and two related Bills: Australian Human Rights Commission – Submission to the Senate Community Affairs Legislation Committee' (Australian Human Rights Commission, 2012)

Australian Human Rights Commission, 'Investing in Care: Recognising and Valuing Those Who Care, Volume 1 (Research Report)' (Australian Human Rights Commission, 2013)

Australian Human Rights Commission, 'Investing in Care: Recognising and Valuing Those Who Care, Volume 2 (Technical papers)' (Australian Human Rights Commission, 2013)

Australian Law Reform Commission, 'Family Violence and Commonwealth Laws – Improving Legal Frameworks: Final Report' (Australian Law Reform Commission, 2011)

Australian Council of Social Service, 'Inquiry by the Parliamentary Joint Committee on Human Rights into the Social Security Legislation Amendment (Fair Incentives to Work) Bill 2012 (Supplementary Submissions)' (ACOSS, 2012), www.aph.gov.au/Parliamentary_Business/Committees/Joint/Human_Rights/Committee_Inquiries/socialsecurity/qon/~/media/Committees/Senate/committee/humanrights_ctte/activity/social_security/qon/acoss_250612.ashx

Baxter, Jennifer, 'Timing of Mothers' Return to Work after Childbearing: Variations by Job Characteristics and Leave Use' (Australian Institute of Family Studies, 2008)

Bray, J. Rob, Matthew Gray, Kelly Hand and Ilan Katz, 'Evaluating New Income Management in the Northern Territory: First Evaluation Report' (Social Policy Research Centre, 2012)

Darooka, Priti, 'Social Security: A Woman's Human Right' (PWESCR, 2008) 1

Equality Rights Alliance, 'Women's Experience of Income Management in the Northern Territory' (Equality Rights Alliance, 2011)

Fiszbein, Ariel, Norbert R. Schady, Francisco H.G. Ferreira, Margaret Grosh, Nial Kelleher, Pedro Olinto and Emmanuel Skoufias, 'Conditional Cash Transfers: Reducing Present and Future Poverty' (World Bank, 2009)

Fredman, Sandra, 'Comparative Study of Anti-Discrimination and Equality Laws of the US, Canada, South Africa and India' (European Commission, 2012)

Fredman, Sandra and Beth Goldblatt, 'Gender Equality and Human Rights: UN Women Discussion Paper No. 4 for *Progress of the World's Women 2015–2016*' (UN Women, 2015)

Goldblatt, Beth, Solange Rosa and Katharine Hall, 'Implementation of the Child Support Grant: A Study of Four Provinces and Recommendations for Improved Service Delivery' (Centre for Applied Legal Studies, University of the Witwatersrand and the Children's Institute, University of Cape Town, 2006)

Hall, Katharine, 'The Child Support Grant: Are Conditions Appropriate? Children Count Brief' (Children's Institute, University of Cape Town, 2011)

International Social Security Association, 'Social Security Coverage Extension in the BRICS: A Comparative Study on the Extension of Coverage in Brazil, the Russian Federation, India, China and South Africa' (International Social Security Association, 2013)

Jhabvala, Renana, Sapna Desai and Jignasa Dave, 'Empowering Women in an Insecure World: Joining SEWA Makes a Difference' (SEWA, 2010)

Makiwane, Monde and Eric Udjo, 'Is the Child Support Grant Associated with an Increase in Teenage Fertility in South Africa? Evidence from National Surveys and Administrative Data' (Human Sciences Research Council, 2006)

McFerran, Ludo, 'Safe at Home, Safe at Work? National Domestic Violence and the Workplace Survey (2011)' (Australian Domestic and Family Violence Clearinghouse, 2011), www.adfvc.unsw.edu.au/PDF%20files/Domestic_violence_and_work_survey_report_2011.pdf

Mehta, Anupma, 'Women's Social Security and Protection in India: A Report. National Conference 6–7 May 2013, New Delhi' (Programme on Women's Economic, Social and Cultural Rights, 2013)

Minister of Rural Development, 'Mahatma Gandhi National Rural Employment Guarantee Act, 2005: Operational Guidelines' (Department of Rural Development, Government of India, 2013)

Ministry of Rural Development, 'Annual Report 2012–13' (Ministry of Rural Development, Government of India, 2012), http://rural.nic.in/sites/downloads/annual-report/MoRDEnglish_AR2012_13.pdf

Ministry of Rural Development, 'Report of the Task Force: Proposal for Comprehensive National Social Assistance Programme' (March 2013), http://rural.nic.in/sites/downloads/latest/Report_Task_Force_Comprehensive_NSAP.pdf

Molyneux, Maxine, 'Conditional Cash Transfers: A "Pathway to Women's Empowerment"?' (Institute of Development Studies, 2008)

National Congress of Australia's First Peoples, 'Statement to the Parliamentary Joint Committee on Human Rights on the Parliamentary Scrutiny of Human Rights as applied to the Stronger Futures in the Northern Territory Bills (2011)' (National Congress of Australia's First Peoples, 2012)

National Human Rights Consultation Committee, 'National Human Rights Consultation' (Commonwealth of Australia, 2009)

Northern Territory Board of Inquiry into the Protection of Aboriginal Children from Sexual Abuse, 'Ampe Akelyernemane Meke Mekarle: "Little Children are Sacred"' (Northern Territory Government, 2007), www.inquirysaac.nt.gov.au/pdf/bipacsa_final_report.pdf

OECD, 'Closing the Gender Gap: Act Now – South Africa' (OECD Publishing, 2012), www.oecd.org/southafrica/Closing%20the%20Gender%20Gap%20-%20South%20Africa%20EN.pdf

Patel, Leila and Tessa Hochfeld, 'The Gender Dynamics and Impact of the Child Support Grant in Doornkop, Soweto' (Centre for Development in Africa, University of Johannesburg, 2012)

Phillips, Barbara Y., 'Dignity and Human Rights: A Missing Dialogue?' (PWESCR, 2011)

Saunders, Peter and Melissa Wong, 'Promoting Inclusion and Combating Deprivation: Recent Changes in Social Disadvantage in Australia' (Social Policy Research Centre, University of New South Wales, 2012)

Sharma, Amita, 'The Mahatma Gandhi National Rural Employment Guarantee Act' (UNDP, 2011)

Simbayi, L.C., O. Shisana, T. Rehle, D. Onoya, S. Jooste, N. Zungu, D. Labadarios and K. Zuma, 'South African National HIV Prevalence, Incidence and Behaviour Survey, 2012' (Human Sciences Research Council, 2014)

South African Social Security Agency, 'Fact Sheet: Issue No 2 of 2013 – 28 February 2013: A Statistical Summary of Social Grants in South Africa' (SASSA, 2013)

Statistics South Africa, 'Quarterly Labour Force Survey: Quarter 4 (October to December), 2012' (2013), www.statssa.gov.za/publications/P0211/P02114thQuarter2012.pdf

Steele, Mark, 'Report on Incentive Structures of Social Assistance Grants in South Africa' (Kesho Consulting and Business Solutions and Department of Social Development, South Africa, 2006)

Taylor Committee, 'Transforming the Present – Protecting the Future: Consolidated Report of the Committee of Inquiry into a Comprehensive System of Social Security for South Africa' (Department of Social Development, 2002)

van den Heever, Alex et al., 'Investigating the Potential Impact of State Support for Poor and Vulnerable Pregnant Women in South Africa: An Options Assessment: Summary Report' (Centre for Health Policy, School of Public Health, University of the Witwatersrand, 2012)

World Bank, 'World Development Report 2012: Gender Equality and Development' (World Bank, 2011)

World Bank, 'World Development Report 2013: Jobs' (World Bank, 2012)

Theses

Dancaster, Lisa, *State and Employer Involvement in Work-Care Integration in South Africa* (PhD Thesis, University of Sydney, 2012)

Web pages

Australian Bureau of Statistics, 'Year Book Australia 2012' (2012), www.abs.gov.au/ausstats/abs@.nsf/Lookup/by%20Subject/1301.0~2012~Main%20Features~Income%20and%20community%20support~194

Australian Council of Social Service, 'Letter from the Australian Council of Social Service (ACOSS) and others to Mr Harry Jenkins MP, Committee Chair, Parliamentary Joint Committee on Human Rights, "Request for Inquiry by the Parliamentary Joint Committee on Human Rights into the Social Security Legislation Amendment (Fair Incentives to Work) Bill 2012"' (15 June 2012), www.aph.gov.au/Parliamentary_Business/Committees/Joint/Human_Rights/Committee_Activity/socialsecurity/correspondence/~/media/Committees/Senate/committee/humanrights_ctte/activity/social_security/correspondence/letter_inquiry_joint_committee_human_rights.ashx

Autonomous Recommendation on the Social Protection Floor (Joint statement by a group of NGOs), www.icsw.org/images/docs/UN/2012/2012-05-21-NGO-SPF-statement_FINAL_version_21May2012.pdf

BIEN World Congress on Basic Income-Dublin, Ireland, (2008), www.cori.ie/Justice/Basic_Income/541-bien-world-congress-on-basic-income-

Darooka, Priti, *Webinar on Women's Rights to Social Security and Social Protection*, www.cdp-hrc.uottawa.ca/?p=4575

Department of Financial Services, Ministry of Finance, Government of India 'Government sponsored Socially Oriented Insurance Schemes: Janashree Bima Yojana', http://financialservices.gov.in/insurance/gssois/jby.asp

Department of Social Development South Africa, *An Overview of South Africa's Social Security System*, Department of Social Development

Equality Now, *Global Sex Trafficking Fact Sheet*, www.equalitynow.org/node/1010

Government of India, 'Census of India', www.censusindia.gov.in/Census_Data_2001/National_Summary/National_Summary_DataPage.aspx

ILO, 'World of Work 2013: Snapshot of India' (2013), www.ilo.org/wcmsp5/groups/public/---dgreports/---dcomm/documents/briefingnote/wcms_214477.pdf

John, J., 'Towards a People's Movement for a Universal Social Security', paper for the National Convention on Social Security for Unorganised Workers on 8–10 January 2010, www.socialsecuritynow.org/Campaign_documents/john_sir's_article-English.pdf.

Miracle Aasra 'Unorganized Workers' Social Security', http://miracleaasra.com/?page_id=25

Lukas, Karin, *The Scope and Boundaries of an Effective Right to Social Security: The Experience of the European Committee of Social Rights* University of Ottawa, www.cdp-hrc.uottawa.ca/?p=4776

Lund, Francie, *The Informal Economy, Gender and the Right to Social Protection*, webinar presentation, University of Ottawa, www.cdp-hrc.uottawa.ca/?p=4776

Ministry of Rural Development, NSAP Division, *FAQs*, http://nsap.nic.in/nsap/FAQ_ON_NSAP_NEW.pdf

Ministry of Rural Development, 'Financial Year 2012–2013', http://164.100.129.6/netnrega/dash_brd.aspx?fin_year=2012-2013

Social Security Now, 'Letter' (29 July 2009), www.socialsecuritynow.org/SSNOW%20WEBSITE/Memorandum-Final_Rawat.pdf

Somavia, Juan 'Press release of 16 June 2011', www.ilo.org/ilc/ILCSessions/100th Session/media-centre/press-releases/WCMS_157891/lang--en/index.htm

UNDP India, 'Factsheet: Gender and Social Exclusion Indicators', www.in.undp.org/content/dam/india/docs/india_factsheet_gender_n_social_exclusion_indicators.pdf

UNDP India, 'Factsheet: Economic and Human Development Indicators', www.in.undp.org/content/dam/india/docs/india_factsheet_economic_n_hdi.pdf.

United Nations, 'Special Rapporteur on extreme poverty and human rights', www.ohchr.org/EN/ISSUES/POVERTY/Pages/SRExtremePovertyIndex.aspx

University of Ottawa, *International Initiative to Promote Women's rights to Social Security and Protection Webinars*, www.cdp-hrc.uottawa.ca/?p=4575

UN Women, http://asiapacific.unwomen.org/en/news-and-events/stories/2012/12/jairam-ramesh-commits-to-making-mgnrega-more-women-friendly

Workplace Gender Equality Agency, 'Gender Pay Gap Statistics' (2014), www.wgea.gov.au/sites/default/files/2014-03-04-Gender_Pay_Gap_factsheet_website.pdf

World Bank, 'Country and Lending Groups', http://data.worldbank.org/about/country-classifications

World Bank, 'GINI Index', http://data.worldbank.org/indicator/SI.POV.GINI

World Health Organisation, *Violence against Women: Intimate Partner and Sexual Violence against Women*, www.who.int/mediacentre/factsheets/fs239/en/

Other sources

Australian Council of Social Service, 'Urgent appeal to the United Nations Special Rapporteur on Extreme Poverty and Human Rights on the proposed introduction of the Social Security Legislation Amendment (Fair Incentives to Work) Bill 2012 in Australia', (5 October 2012), on file with the author.

Goldblatt, Beth 'Intersectionality in international anti-discrimination law – addressing poverty in its complexity' conference paper presented at FGV Direito SP, 12 November 2014, Sao Paulo, Brazil.

Khera, Reetika, 'Democratic Politics and Legal Rights: Employment Guarantee and Food Security in India' (2–3 August 2013), paper presented at the Second Azim Premji University International Conference on Law, Governance and Development – Right to Welfare: Education, Food and Work, on file with the author.

Legal sources

Treaties and other international instruments

Universal treaties

International Convention on the Elimination of All Forms of Racial Discrimination (adopted 21 December 1965, entered into force 4 January 1969) 660 UNTS 195

International Covenant on Economic, Social and Cultural Rights (adopted 16 December 1966, entered into force 23 March 1976) 993 UNTS 3

International Covenant on Civil and Political Rights (adopted 16 December 1966, entered into force 3 January 1976) 999 UNTS 171

Convention on the Elimination of All Forms of Discrimination Against Women (adopted 18 December 1979, entered into force 3 September 1981) 1249 UNTS 13

Convention on the Rights of the Child (adopted 20 November 1989, entered into force 2 September 1990) 1577 UNTS 3

Optional Protocol to CEDAW (adopted 6 October 1999, entered into force 22 December 2000) 2131 UNTS 83

International Convention on the Protection of the Rights of All Migrant Workers and Members of Their Families (adopted 18 December 1990, entered into force 1 July 2003) 2220 UNTS 3

Convention on the Rights of Persons with Disabilities (adopted 13 December 2006, entered into force 3 May 2008) UN Doc A/61/106

Optional Protocol to the International Covenant on Economic, Social and Cultural Rights (adopted 11 December 2009, entered into force 5 May 2013) 869 UNTS 34

ILO treaties

Forced Labour Convention, 1930, (No. 29)

Declaration Concerning the Aims and Purposes of the International Labour Organisation (Declaration of Philadelphia), 1944

Income Security Recommendation, 1944, (No. 67)

Medical Care Recommendation, 1944, (No. 69)

Freedom of Association and Protection of the Right to Organise Convention, 1948, (No. 87)

Migration for Employment Convention (Revised), 1949, (No. 97)

Right to Organise and Collective Bargaining Convention, 1949, (No. 98)
Equal Remuneration Convention, 1951, (No. 100)
Social Security (Minimum Standards) Convention, 1952, (No. 102)
Abolition of Forced Labour Convention, 1957, (No. 105)
Discrimination (Employment and Occupation) Convention, 1958, (No. 111)
Equality of Treatment (Social Security) Convention, 1962, (No. 118)
Employment Injury Benefits Convention, 1964, (No. 121)
Invalidity, Old-Age and Survivors' Benefits Convention, 1967, (No. 128)
Medical Care and Sickness Benefits Convention, 1969, (No. 130)
Migrant Workers (Supplementary Provisions) Convention, 1975, (No. 143)
Workers with Family Responsibilities Convention, 1981, (No. 156)
Maintenance of Social Security Rights Convention, 1982, (No. 157)
Employment Promotion and Protection against Unemployment Convention, 1988, (No. 168)
Home Work Convention, 1996, (No. 177)
Worst Forms of Child Labour Convention, 1999, (No. 182)
Maternity Protection Convention, 2000, (No. 183)
Declaration on Social Justice for a Fair Globalization, 2008 (adopted by the International Labour Conference at its 97th Session, 10 June 2008)
Domestic Workers Convention, 2011, (No. 189)
Recommendation concerning National Floors of Social Protection, 2012, (No. 202)

Regional treaties

EUROPE

The European Social Charter, adopted by the Council of Europe 1961 (CETS No. 35)
Revised European Social Charter, adopted by the Council of Europe 1996 (CETS No. 163)
The Charter of Fundamental Rights of the European Union 2000/C 364/01
European Code of Social Security (1964) (CETS No. 48)
European Social Security Protocol (2004) (CETS No. 48A)

AMERICA

The American Declaration of the Rights and Duties of Man (1948)
The Additional Protocol to the American Convention on Human Rights in the Area of Economic, Social And Cultural Rights ('Protocol of San Salvador') adopted at San Salvador, El Salvador, on 17 November, 1988, at the eighteenth regular session of the General Assembly

AFRICA

The African Charter on Human and People's Rights (1981) OAU Doc CAB/LEG/67/3, entered into force 1986
The African Charter on the Rights and Welfare of the Child, (1990) OAU Doc CAB/LEG/24.9/49, entered into force 1999
The Protocol to the African Charter on Human and Peoples' Rights on the Rights of Women in Africa (2000) OAU CAB/LEG/66.6, entered into force 2005

Southern African Development Community (SADC) *Charter of Fundamental Social Rights* (2003)
Southern African Development Community (SADC) *Code on Social Security* (2007)
Southern African Development Community (SADC) *Gender Protocol*

Treaty body reports

CEDAW CONCLUDING OBSERVATIONS

CO Angola CEDAW/C/AGO/CO/6 (CEDAW, 2013)
CO Australia E/C.12/AUS/CO/4 (42nd Session, CEDAW, 2009)
CO Australia CEDAW/C/AUS/CO/7 (CEDAW, 2010)
CO Austria CEDAW/C/AUT/CO/6 (CEDAW, 2007),
CO Austria CEDAW/C/AUT/CO/7-8 (CEDAW, 2013)
CO Bahamas CEDAW/C/BHS/CO/1-5 (CEDAW, 2012)
CO Belgium CEDAW/C/BEL/CO/6 (CEDAW, 2008)
CO Brazil E/C.12/BRA/CO/2 (42nd Session, CEDAW, 2009)
CO Bulgaria CEDAW/C/BLG/CO/4-7 (CEDAW, 2012)
CO Cambodia CEDAW/C/KHM/CO/3 (CEDAW, 2006)
CO Canada A/58/38(SUPP) (CEDAW, 2003)
CO Chile CEDAW/C/CHL/CO/5-6 (CEDAW, 2012)
CO China CEDAW/C/CHN/CO/6 (CEDAW, 2006)
CO France CEDAW/C/FRA/CO/6 (CEDAW, 2008)
CO Greece CEDAW/C/GRC/CO/7 (CEDAW, 2013)
CO India CEDAW/C/IND/CO/3 (2007)
CO Kuwait CEDAW/C/KWT/CO/3-4 (CEDAW, 2011)
CO Lebanon CEDAW/C/LBN/CO/3 (CEDAW, 2008)
CO Liechtenstein CEDAW/C/LIE/CO/4 (CEDAW, 2011)
CO Lesotho CEDAW/C/LSO/CO/1-4 (CEDAW, 2011)
CO Mozambique CEDAW/C/MOZ/CO/2 (CEDAW, 2007)
CO Netherlands CEDAW/C/NLD/CO/5 (CEDAW, 2010)
CO Pakistan CEDAW/C/PAK/CO/4 (CEDAW, 2013)
CO Peru A/57/38(SUPP); 27th Session (CEDAW, 2002)
CO Republic of Korea CEDAW/C/KOR/C/7 (CEDAW, 2011)
CO Romania A/55/38(SUPP) (CEDAW, 2000)
CO South Africa CEDAW/C/ZAF/CO/4 (CEDAW, 2011)
CO Surinam CEDAW/C/SUR/CO/3 (CEDAW, 2007)
CO Togo CEDAW/C/TGO/CO/6-7 (CEDAW, 2012)
CO Turkey CEDAW/C/TUR/CO/6 (CEDAW, 2010)
CO Uganda A/57/38(SUPP) 27th Session (CEDAW, 2002)
CO Uganda CEDAW/C/UGA/CO/7 (CEDAW, 2010)
CO United Kingdom CEDAW/C/UK/CO/6 (CEDAW, 2009)
CO United Kingdom CEDAW/C/GBR/CO/7 (CEDAW, 2013)
CO Vietnam CEDAW/C/VNM/CO/6 (CEDAW, 2007)

CEDAW GENERAL RECOMMENDATIONS

CEDAW, '*General Recommendation 16 on unpaid women workers in rural and urban family enterprises*' (1991) 10th session, HRI/GEN/1/Rev.9 (vol II)

CEDAW, '*General Recommendation 17 on measurement and quantification of the unremunerated domestic activities of women and their recognition in the GNP*' (1991) 10th session, HRI/GEN/1/Rev.9 (vol II)

CEDAW, '*General Recommendation 18 on women with disabilities*' (1991) 10th session, HRI/GEN/1/Rev.9 (vol II)

CEDAW, '*General recommendation No. 25, on article 4, paragraph 1, of the Convention on the Elimination of All Forms of Discrimination against Women, on temporary special measures*' (2004) 30th Session, UN Doc A/59/38, annex I

CEDAW, '*General Recommendation 26 on women migrant workers*' (2008) 42nd Session, CEDAW/C/2009/WP.1/R

CEDAW, '*General Recommendation 27 on older women*' (2010) 47th Session, CEDAW/C/GC/27

CEDAW, '*General Recommendation 28 on the core obligations of States parties under article 2 of CEDAW*' (2010) 47th Session, CEDAW/C/GC/28

CEDAW, '*General Recommendation 29 on the economic consequences of marriage, family relations and their dissolution*' (2013) 54th Session, CEDAW/C/GC/29

CEDAW, '*General Recommendation 30 on women in conflict prevention, conflict and post-conflict situations*' (2013) 56th Session, CEDAW/C/GC/30

CEDAW, '*General Statement of the Committee on the Elimination of Discrimination against Women on Rural Women*' (2011) 50th Session, E/CN.6/2012/CRP.1 (Annex v)

CESCR CONCLUDING OBSERVATIONS

CO Australia E/C.12/1/ADD.50 (CESCR, 2000)

CO Australia E/C.12/AUS/CO/4 (CESCR, 2009)

CO Chile E/C.12/1/ADD.105 (CESCR, 2004)

CO China E/C.12/1/ADD.107 (CESCR, 2005)

CO Cyprus E/C.12/CYP/CO/5 (CESCR, 2009)

CO Dominican Republic E/C.12/DOM/CO/3 (CESCR, 2010)

CO Ecuador E/C.12/ECU/CO/3 (CESCR, 2012)

CO France E/C.12/FRA/CO/3 (CESCR, 2008)

CO India CESCR E/C.12/IND/CO/5 (CESCR, 2008)

CO Japan E/C.12/JPN/CO/3 (CESCR, 2013)

CO Poland E/C.12/POL/CO/5 (CESCR, 2009)

CO Spain E/C.12/ESP/CO/5 (CESCR, 2012)

CO Sri Lanka, E/C.12/LKA/CO/2-4 (CESCR, 2010)

CO Turkey, E/C.12/TUR/CO/1 (CESCR, 2011)

CO United Kingdom E/C.12/GBR/CO/5 (CESCR, 2009)

CESCR GENERAL COMMENTS

CESCR, '*General Comment No. 5: Persons with Disabilities*' (1994) 11th Session 1994, E/1995/22

CESCR '*General Comment No. 6: The Economic, Social and Cultural Rights of Older Persons*' (1995) 30th Session 1995, E/1996/22

CESCR '*General Comment No 16: Article 3: the equal right of men and women to the enjoyment of all economic, social and cultural rights*' (2005) 34th Session 2005, E/C 12/2005/4

CESCR '*General Comment No 19: The Right to Social Security (Art. 9)*' (2008) 39th Session 2007, E/C.12/GC/19

CESCR '*General Comment No 20: Non-discrimination in economic, social and cultural rights (art. 2, para. 2, of the International Covenant on Economic, Social and Cultural Rights)*' (2009) 42nd Session 2009, E/C 12/GC/20

CESCR '*Guidelines on Treaty-Specific Documents to be Submitted by States Parties Under Articles 16 And 17 of the International Covenant on Economic, Social and Cultural Rights*' (2008), E/C.12/2008/2

Other United Nations documents

Anaya, J., Special Rapporteur on the Situation of Human Rights and Fundamental Freedoms of Indigenous People, *Situation of Indigenous People in Australia*, 4 March 2010, A/HRC/15/37/Add.4

DSD, SASSA and UNICEF, 'The South African Child Support Grant Impact Assessment: evidence from a survey of children, adolescents and their households.' (UNICEF South Africa, 2012)

Heintz, James and Francie Lund, 'Welfare Regimes and Social Policy: A Review of the Role of Labour and Employment' (UNRISD, 2012)

Human Rights Council, 'Conclusions and Recommendations of the Universal Periodic Review of Australia', *Report of the Working Group on the Universal Periodic Review (Australia)*, 24 March 2011, A/HRC/17/10

Human Rights Council 'Final draft of the guiding principles on extreme poverty and human rights, submitted by the Special Rapporteur on extreme poverty and human rights, Magdalena Sepúlveda Carmona' (2012) HRC 21st Session, A/HRC/21/39

Human Rights Council, *Report of the Working Group on the Universal Periodic Review – India* (2012) A/HRC/21/10

Letter from Maria Magdalena Sepúlveda Carmona, Special Rapporteur on Extreme Poverty and Human Rights and Kamala Chandrakirana, Chair of the Working Group on the Issue of Discrimination Against Women in Law and Practice (19 October 2012), Reference: UA Poverty (1998-11) AUS 2/2012, https://spdb.ohchr.org/hrdb/22nd/public_-_UA_Australie_19.10.12_(2.2012).pdf

'Limburg Principles on the Implementation of the International Covenant on Economic, Social and Cultural Rights' (1987), E/CN.4/1987/17

'Maastricht Guidelines on Violations of Economic, Social and Cultural Rights' (1998), E/C.12/2000/13

Ortiz, Isabel and Matthew Cummins (eds), *A Recovery for All Rethinking Socio-Economic Policies for Children and Poor Households* (UNICEF, 2012)

Pillay, A.G. (Chairperson of CESCR), 'Letter dated 16 May 2012 addressed by the Chairperson of the Committee on Economic, Social and Cultural Rights to States parties to the International Covenant on Economic, Social and Cultural Rights' (4 June 2012) http://tbinternet.ohchr.org/_layouts/treatybodyexternal/TBSearch.aspx?Lang=en&TreatyID=9&DocTypeID=68

Razavi, Shahra, '*World Development Report 2012: Gender Equality and Development.* An Opportunity Both Welcome and Missed (An Extended Commentary)' (United Nations Research Institute for Social Development (UNRISD), 2011)

Razavi, Shahra et al., 'Gendered Impacts of Globalization – Employment and Social Protection' (UNRISD, 2012)

'Report of the independent expert on the question of human rights and extreme poverty, Magdalena Sepúlveda Carmona' (2009) HRC 11th Session, A/HRC/11/9

'Report on the question of human rights and extreme poverty submitted by Magdalena Sepúlveda Carmona, independent expert on the question of human rights and extreme poverty' (2009) GA 64th Session, A/64/279

'Report of the independent expert on the question of human rights and extreme poverty, Magdalena Sepúlveda Carmona' (2010) HRC 14th Session, A/HRC/14/31

'Report on the question of human rights and extreme poverty submitted by Magdalena Sepúlveda Carmona, independent expert on the question of human rights and extreme poverty' (2010) GA 65th Session, A/65/259

'Report of the Independent Expert on the question of human rights and extreme poverty, Magdalena Sepúlveda Carmona' (2011) HRC 17th Session, A/HRC/17/34

'Report of the Special Rapporteur on extreme poverty and human rights' (2012) GA 67th Session, A/67/278

'Report of the Special Rapporteur on extreme poverty and human rights, Magdalena Sepúlveda Carmona' (2013) HRC 23rd Session, A/HRC/23/36

'Report of the Special Rapporteur on extreme poverty and human rights' (2013) GA 68th Session, A/68/293

Swarup, Anil and Nishant Jain, 'Rashtriya Swasthya Bima Yojana' in UNDP (ed.), *Sharing Innovative Experiences: Successful social protection floor experiences* (UNDP, 2011) vol 18, 259

UNDP, 'Sharing Innovative Experiences: Successful Social Protection Floor Experiences' (UNDP, 2011)

Universal Declaration of Human Rights, GA Res 217A (III), UN Doc A/810 (1948)

UNRISD, 'Combating Poverty and Inequality: Structural Change, Social Policy and Politics' (2010)

UN Women, 'Realizing Women's Rights to Land and Other Productive Resources' (2013)

Vienna Declaration and Programme of Action (1993) adopted by the World Conference on Human Rights, 25 June 1993, A/CONF.157/23

Wiliams, Fiona, 'Claiming and Framing in the Making of Care Policies: The Recognition and Redistribution of Care' (United Nations Research Institute for Social Development, 2010)

Working Group on the issue of discrimination against women in law and in practice, Background Paper for 2014 Report to the Human Rights Council by Professor Frances Raday, 'Gender Pension Gap' (2013), www.ohchr.org/EN/Issues/Women/WGWomen/Pages/ESL.aspx

Working Group on the issue of discrimination against women in law and in practice, *Report of the Working Group on the issue of discrimination against women in law and in practice (political representation and participation)* (Human Rights Council (23rd Session), 2013) A/HRC/23/50

Working Group on the issue of discrimination against women in law and in practice, *Thematic Report (eliminating discrimination against women in economic and social life with a focus on economic crisis)*: Annotated Version (Human Rights Council (26th session), 2014) A/HRC/26/39

ILO documents

Barrientos, Armando and Miguel Niño-Zarazúa, 'Effects of non-contributory social transfers in developing countries. A compendium' (International Labour Office Social Security Department, 2010)

CEACR, 'Social security and the rule of law – General Survey concerning social security instruments in light of the 2008 Declaration on Social Justice for a Fair Globalization' (ILC.100/111/1B, International Labour Office, 2011)

Dasgupta, Sukti and Ratna M. Sudarshan, 'Issues in labour market inequality and women's participation in India's National Rural Employment Guarantee Programme' (International Labour Organisation, 2011)

ILO, 'Social security for social justice and a fair globalization' (VI, International Labour Office, 2011a)

ILO, 'Social Security and the Rule of Law: General Survey concerning social security instruments in light of the 2008 Declaration on Social Justice for a Fair Globalization' (2011b)

ILO, 'Social protection floor for a fair and inclusive globalization: Report of the Social Protection Floor Advisory Group chaired by Michelle Bachelet' (International Labour Office, 2011c)

International Labour Office, 'World Social Security Report 2010/11: Providing coverage in times of crisis and beyond' (ILO, 2010)

International Labour Office, 'World Social Protection Report 2014/15: Building economic recovery, inclusive development and social justice' (ILO, 2014)

Sabates-Wheeler, Rachel and Naila Kabeer, 'Gender equality and the extension of social protection' (16, ILO, 2003)

Tessier, Lou et al., 'Social Protection Floors and Gender Equality: A brief overview' (ILO, 2013)

Domestic legislation

India

The Constitution of India (as on 1st December 2011)

Right to Information Act 2005

Mahatma Gandhi National Rural Employment Guarantee Act 2005

Forest Rights Act 2006

The Unorganised Workers Social Security Bill 2007

The Unorganised Workers Social Security Act 2008

Right to Education Act 2009

Minister of Rural Development, '*Mahatma Gandhi National Rural Employment Guarantee Act*, 2005: Operational Guidelines' (Department of Rural Development, Government of India, 2013)

The National Food Security Act 2013

USA

Social Security Act 1934

South Africa

Constitution of the Republic of South Africa Act 1996
Department of Social Development, '*Social Assistance Act*, 2004: Amendment: Regulations relating to the application for and payment of social assistance and the requirements or conditions in respect of eligibility for social assistance' (G 32747, RG 9192, GoN 1116), 27 November 2009
Department of Social Development, '*Social Assistance Act*, 2004: Amendment: Regulations relating to the application for and payment of social assistance and the requirements or conditions in respect of eligibility for social assistance' (G 32747, RG 9192, GoN 1116), 31 December 2009

Canada

Charter of Rights and Freedoms, Part 2 of the *Constitution Act* 1982

Australia

Racial Discrimination Act 1975 (Cth)
Northern Territory Emergency Response Act 2007 (Cth)
Social Security and Other Legislation Amendment (Welfare Payment Reform) Act 2007 (Cth)
Social Security and Other Legislation Amendment (Welfare Reform and Reinstatement of Racial Discrimination Act) Act 2010 (Cth)
Human Rights (Parliamentary Scrutiny) Act 2011 (Cth)
Social Security Legislation Amendment (Fair Incentives to Work) Bill 2012 (Cth)
Stronger Futures in the Northern Territory Act 2012 (Cth)
Social Security Legislation Amendment Act 2012 (Cth)

Australia: Other

Australia's Future Tax System: Final Report (Commonwealth of Australia, 2010)
Parliamentary Joint Committee on Human Rights, 'Examination of legislation in accordance with the *Human Rights (Parliamenary Scrutiny) Act 2011 – Social Security Legislation Amendment (Fair Incentives to Work) Act 2011:* Final Report' (Commonwealth of Australia, 2013)
Parliamentary Joint Committee on Human Rights, 'Examination of legislation in accordance with the *Human Rights (Parliamentary Scrutiny) Act 2011* Interim Report – *Social Security Legislation Amendment (Fair Incentives to Work) Bill 2012 Fourth Report of 2012*, (Canberra, Commonwealth of Australia, 2012)
Social Security Legislation Amendment (Fair Incentives to Work) Bill 2012 (Cth): Explanatory Memorandum
Macklin, Jenny, 'Assessment of Policy Objectives with Human Rights – *Stronger Futures in the Northern Territory Bill 2012; Stronger Futures in the Northern Territory (Consequential and Transitional Provisions) Bill* 2011' (Attached to letter to the Parliamentary Joint Committee on Human Rights, 27 June 2012), <www.aph.gov.au/Parliamentary_Business/Committees/Joint/Human_Rights/Committee_Activity/strongerfutures/background/~/media/Committees/Senate/committee/humanrights_ctte/activity/stronger_futures/correspondence/mfcsia_chair_280612.ashx

Case law

International

HUMAN RIGHTS COMMITTEE

Broeks v the Netherlands (Communication No.172/1984), Views of 9 April 1987
Pauger v Austria (Communication No. 716/1996), Views of 30 April 1999
Vos v The Netherlands Communication No. 786/1997), Views of 26 July 1999
Zwaan-de Vries v the Netherlands (Communication No. 182/1984), Views of 9 April 1987

CEDAW COMMITTEE

B.-J. v. Germany 1/2003 (2004) CEDAW/31st Session, Excerpt from A/59/38 Annex VIII
Dung Thi Thuy Nguyen v The Netherlands, Communication 3/2004 (2006) CEDAW/C/36/D/3/2004
Elisabeth de Blok et al. v The Netherlands, Communication 36/2012 (2014) CEDAW/C/57/D/36/2012

National

SOUTH AFRICA

Mashava v President of the RSA and Others 2004 (12) BCLR 1243 (CC)
Khosa v Minister of Social Development; Mahlaule v Minister of Social Development (Khosa) 2004 (6) BCLR 569 (CC)
Roberts and Others v Minister of Social Development and Others (unreported decision of the Transvaal Provincial Division, Case Number 32838/05)

INDIA

L.I.C. of India & ANR v. Consumer Education and Research Centre and ORS etc. 1995 AIR 1811 1995 SCC (5) 482
Olga Tellis v Bombay Municipal Corporation 1985 Supp (2) SCR 51
PUCL v. Union of India and Others WP (Civil) No. 196/2001, 23 July 2001, unreported

AUSTRALIA

Ex parte H.V. McKay, 2 Commonwealth Arbitration R.1 (1907) ('The Harvester case')

Index

For Product Safety Concerns and Information please contact our EU
representative GPSR@taylorandfrancis.com
Taylor & Francis Verlag GmbH, Kaufingerstraße 24, 80331 München, Germany

www.ingramcontent.com/pod-product-compliance
Ingram Content Group UK Ltd.
Pitfield, Milton Keynes, MK11 3LW, UK
UKHW022133190926
475702UK00013B/1794
9780815354598